OUR POWER IS THAT OF
THE WORKING PEOPLE

FIDEL CASTRO SPEECHES VOL. II

OUR POWER IS THAT OF THE WORKING PEOPLE

BUILDING SOCIALISM IN CUBA

PATHFINDER PRESS
New York

Edited by Michael Taber
Copyright © 1983 by Pathfinder Press

Library of Congress Catalog Card Number 81-80717
ISBN 0-87348-624-2 cloth/ 0-87348-650-1 paper
Manufactured in the United States of America
First edition 1983

Pathfinder Press
410 West Street
New York, N.Y. 10014

Contents

Fidel Castro

Fidel Castro Ruz was born into a wealthy farming family in 1926 in Oriente Province, in the eastern part of Cuba. He got involved in politics as a student at the University of Havana, where he joined one of the student action groups, the Unión Insurreccional Revolucionaria — Revolutionary Insurrectional Union — in 1946. He was a founding member of the Partido del Pueblo Cubano — Cuban People's Party (the Ortodoxos) — in 1947, and became a leader of its left wing. That same year he was part of an aborted armed expedition that had planned to go to the Dominican Republic to overthrow the dictatorship of Rafael Trujillo. Attending a student conference in Bogotá, Colombia, in 1948, he participated in the *Bogotazo*, a massive upsurge that broke out while he was there.

After graduating from law school, Castro ran for representative on the Ortodoxo ticket in the 1952 elections, but these never took place because of a coup d'etat by Fulgencio Batista. Castro then began to map out plans for an insurrection. On July 26, 1953, he led an attack on the Moncada army barracks in Santiago de Cuba which was crushed. After being arrested and miraculously surviving an attempt to summarily execute him, he was tried and sentenced to fifteen years' imprisonment. Castro's defense speech, "History Will Absolve Me," later became the program of the July 26 Movement. After being released in 1955 as a result of a mass public pressure campaign, he went to Mexico, where he began to organize what was to become the Rebel Army. Sailing on the yacht *Granma* with eighty-one other guerrillas including Che Guevara, Camilo Cienfuegos, Juan Almeida, and his brother Raúl, Castro landed in Oriente Province on December 2, 1956, where, from the Sierra Maestra mountains, he led the revolutionary war to victory. With Batista's flight on January 1, 1959, the war came to an end, and Castro arrived triumphantly in Havana on January 8. He served as prime minister of the revolutionary government from February 1959 until December 1976, when he became president of the Council of State and the Council of Ministers. He has been first secretary of the Communist Party of Cuba since its founding in 1965.

Introduction

Since the triumph of its revolution in 1959 Cuba has been a center of international attention. Hundreds of millions of people around the world look to it as an example — a symbol of social and economic progress in a world plagued by economic inequality, social injustice, and political oppression. Here in the United States, on the other hand, the government and mass media paint a different picture. They portray Cuba as a one-man totalitarian dictatorship, an economic failure, and a "Soviet pawn."

What is the reality?

Prior to its revolution Cuba was virtually a colony of the United States. U.S. corporations owned 90 percent of Cuba's mineral wealth and cattle ranches, 80 percent of its public utilities, 50 percent of its railroads, and 40 percent of its sugar production. Three-quarters of Cuba's foreign trade was with the United States. The capital city of Havana was a center of gambling and prostitution, catering to U.S. businessmen, military personnel, and tourists. Cuba's successive dictatorships were completely subservient to the wishes of Washington. And Cuba was under the U.S. government's military tutelage. For many years U.S. troops occupied the island; even today the U.S. maintains a naval base at Guantánamo, against the wishes of Cuba.

The consequences of this situation for the Cuban people were staggering. One-third of the working-age population was unemployed, a quarter of the people were illiterate, and hundreds of thousands suffered from malnutrition and curable diseases, especially in the countryside. Almost half the children did not attend school, tens of thousands were forced into lives of prostitution or begging, and the several million Blacks faced racist discrimination everywhere. Those seeking to effect progressive social and political changes encountered brutal political repression. All this while U.S. companies piled up huge profits and while a wealthy elite of Cubans who served the interests of these corporations exercised political power.

The Cuba of today is radically different.

Across the country Cubans have built new factories and industries producing goods needed in Cuba. The standard of living has risen dramatically.

Illiteracy is virtually nonexistent and everyone has the right to a free public education. Over one-third of the population is currently engaged in formal study, one of the highest percentages in the world.

All Cubans are guaranteed free, high-quality health care. Diseases such as polio and malaria have been eradicated and infant mortality is lower than in many U.S. cities, such as Washington, D.C. Life expectancy has increased from under 55 years to over 70.

Workers no longer suffer the social and economic devastation of unemployment. The government provides complete financial support for the elderly and those who are sick or unable to work. Other social phenomena that are products of capitalism such as prostitution, begging, homelessness, and racial discrimination have been eliminated.

Cuban women have also made big strides forward. Before the revolution women were only 9.8 percent of the work force and the big majority of these were domestic servants. Today 32 percent of the labor force are women who work in all branches of the economy, at all different levels — and domestic service no longer exists. Day-care centers have been built throughout the country, abortion and contraception are easily available, and sexual discrimination is against the law. The government has waged an intensive educational campaign against discriminatory attitudes and prejudices and it actively promotes women's participation in all aspects of society.

All these accomplishments are the result of the fundamental changes that came about through the revolution, above all breaking the domination of imperialism, eliminating the rule of capitalism, and creating a planned economy based on meeting human needs.

But while these achievements are so dramatic that even many of the revolution's opponents have been compelled to recognize them, one aspect of Cuba is not so generally known: the involvement of Cuba's people in running their country's affairs; the fact that in Cuba it is the working people who exercise political power.

That is what this book is about.

The speeches collected here trace Cuba's efforts, from the early years of the revolution up to the present, to continually advance the active participation of the working class in running society. Because many readers will be unfamiliar with this period in Cuban history, it may be helpful to review some of the main events.

On January 1, 1959, Cuban dictator Fulgencio Batista fled the country and the revolutionary forces, led by Fidel Castro and the July 26 Movement, came to power. Spearheaded by the guerrillas in the mountains, the revolutionary struggle had the support of the vast majority of Cuba's working people and peasants. Within the cities a widespread clandestine network fought the Batista tyranny. In the countryside the peasants sheltered and supported the rebels. The decisive blow that ensured the revolution's triumph was a massive nationwide general strike.

The new revolutionary government immediately took steps to benefit the Cuban people. Within a few months an agrarian reform eliminated the giant landed estates, many of them U.S.-owned, and hundreds of thousands of peasants gained access to the land. New clinics and schools were set up in the countryside. Rents were cut in half and public utility charges were reduced. The government banned racial discrimination.

Through these and other concrete measures, Cuba's working people and peasants were assured that this was their revolution not only in words, but in deeds.

For the first time millions of Cubans were drawn into active political life, without which these measures could not have been carried out. A nationwide literacy drive was launched, mobilizing a quarter of a million people, mostly youth, to travel to every corner of the island teaching over 700,000 peasants and workers to read and write. New organizations such as women's and farmers' groups were formed to involve these layers of the population in the revolution's tasks. Trade unions were strengthened and reorganized.

While immensely popular with Cuba's working people and peasants, these steps sharpened opposition to the revolution from both the United States government and the former ruling class of Cuba, the capitalists and landowners. These forces began an intense propaganda campaign against the revolution, relying on anticommunism and utilizing the wildest slanders imaginable. They claimed that children were being taken from their parents and sent to Russia, that religion was being suppressed, that the revolution was murdering its opponents. This propaganda was an expression of the sharpening class struggle within Cuba, and of the growing confrontation between Cuba and U.S. imperialism.

At the same time the U.S. government began to wage economic war against Cuba. Commercial credits were denied and the U.S. reduced its purchase of Cuban sugar, eventually eliminating it entirely. The sale of spare parts for Cuba's U.S.-built industries was cut off, as was the shipment of oil — an attempt to paralyze the Cuban economy. Eventually Washington instituted a total economic blockade that covered even foodstuffs and medicines. And trying to strip Cuba of its human resources, the U.S. government encouraged the emigration of thousands of technicians, engineers, doctors, professionals, and skilled workers.

Washington also embarked on military action. In March 1960 President Dwight Eisenhower ordered the creation of a counterrevolutionary mercenary force made up of Cuban exiles, in preparation for an invasion. The U.S. helped organize counterrevolutionary terrorist bands inside Cuba that carried out assassinations, bombings, the burning of crops, and other acts of sabotage. By committing these acts they hoped to terrorize the people and obstruct the revolution's measures such as the literacy campaign and the agrarian reform. During this period the Central Intelligence Agency began to organize assassination plots against Castro and other Cuban leaders.

In response to all these attacks the revolution relied on its chief strength: the support of Cuba's working people and peasants. The people were armed through the creation of the National Revolutionary Militias. Committees for the Defense of the Revolution were formed on a block-by-block basis to mobilize against counterrevolution. Gigantic rallies and demonstrations took place.

Through their participation in struggle the consciousness of Cuba's workers and peasants advanced step by step. They began to understand the decisive role they were playing in their country's history.

Between August and October of 1960, responding to Washington's aggression and the growing resistance of Cuba's capitalist class, the revolutionary government expropriated over $1 billion of U.S. holdings and nationalized many of the major Cuban-owned industries. Cuba was also able to secure the vital assistance of the Soviet Union, which agreed to supply oil to Cuba, purchase its sugar, and provide arms.

On April 16, 1961, on the eve of the U.S.-organized invasion at the Bay of Pigs (known in Cuba as the battle at Playa Girón), Castro openly proclaimed the socialist character of the revolution. The following day thousands of militiamen and regular troops went into combat against the invaders, defeating them in less than 72 hours. This victory helped consolidate the revolution's gains and demonstrated for the entire world its broad base of popular support.

Nevertheless, Cuba still faced giant obstacles. It felt keenly the legacy of underdevelopment. The U.S. economic blockade created drastic shortages of most items. Following Washington's lead all Latin American governments except Mexico broke diplomatic relations. On top of all this, the revolution had the problem of its own inexperience — Cuba's working people now had to learn how to run a country from top to bottom.

One of the challenges the revolution faced from the beginning was that of combatting bureaucratic privilege and abuse. This was an objective problem Cuba's socialist revolution faced, aggravated by the country's underdevelopment and imperialist encirclement.

While the Cubans could not change this objective reality, they did take steps to limit and check the growth of a bureaucratic elite. From the very beginning of the revolution, the revolutionary leadership fought against the emergence of a new privileged social layer. One of its first steps was to prohibit by law the erection of statues or monuments — or the naming of institutions, streets, or cities — for living figures. The Cubans were particularly insistent that privilege and corruption had to be actively fought within the revolutionary vanguard itself. And they sought to eliminate any obstacle that stood in the way of the masses' involvement in the revolutionary process. This commitment was soon to be graphically demonstrated.

Toward the end of 1961, the Integrated Revolutionary Organizations (ORI) was formed by the unification of the three major political groups supporting the revolution: the July 26 Movement, the People's Socialist Party (the old pro-Moscow Communist Party), and the Revolutionary Directorate (a student-based group that had been active in the struggle against Batista). This fusion, led by the July 26 Movement, was an important step in reshaping, consolidating, and expanding the country's revolutionary leadership and creating a new party to help lead the revolution forward.

However, this process ran into trouble. The ORI's organization secretary, long-time PSP leader Aníbal Escalante, attempted to put together a political machine made up of some of his former associates from the PSP. Using his position, he began to appoint his followers to leading positions in the ORI and the government apparatus. The ORI began to take upon itself an increasingly greater role in administrative affairs, rather than acting as the political leadership of the working class.

In March 1962, on behalf of the revolutionary leadership, Castro publicly denounced these practices and explained the danger that bureaucratic abuses posed for the revolution. In a well-publicized speech, contained in this book, he explained that if left unchecked this situation would lead to the ORI's alienation from the working class and to the creation of a new privileged elite. Escalante and some of his associates were subsequently replaced, and throughout the country the ORI was reorganized along lines to strengthen its ties to the working class. Following a proposal by Castro the ORI adopted a new procedure: workers' assemblies were to be held in factories and other workplaces to nominate candidates for party membership. This new feature was to become standard as the ORI eventually became transformed into what is today the Communist Party of Cuba.

The revolutionary leadership's response to the Escalante affair showed its determination to actively combat the inevitable objective pressures and the political errors that would lead toward excluding the masses from political power. During the 1960s Castro and other Cuban leaders referred frequently to the danger that bureaucratization posed to the revolution. They recognized that it was a continuing battle. One of the selections in this volume, a series of editorials from the Cuban Communist Party newspaper *Granma*, summarizes the conclusions reached at that time on the roots of bureaucracy and the methods to fight it.

A turning point in the struggle came in 1970. That year Cuba embarked on an effort to harvest ten million tons of sugar, substantially more than any previous yield in its history. Sugar was Cuba's major export crop and the goal of this drive was both to obtain needed foreign exchange for Cuba's development and to help pay off its growing debt to the Soviet Union. In order to meet the ten-million-ton goal, the Cuban people threw themselves into the effort. Millions participated in voluntary work, planting, cutting, and transporting the sugarcane. The mass organizations and the trade unions mobilized all their forces for the battle. It was a gigantic political undertaking based on the revolutionary spirit of the people.

Nevertheless, the effort ended in failure. Not only did Cuba fail to make the ten-million-ton goal, but the massive diversion of material resources and labor expended in attempting to reach it threw the entire economy into disarray.

This experience forced a reexamination by the leadership of many of the revolution's political and economic policies. One obvious problem was the lack of institutionalized channels for input and decision making by the masses. Many of the difficulties encountered in the course of the campaign were realized by workers involved in the effort. However, they were often unable to transmit their knowledge and concerns to the various administrative bodies. Castro gave the example of a paper factory stalled by the absence of a single cutting blade.

In a historic speech given on July 26, 1970, Castro analyzed the problems, taking full leadership responsibility for the failure, and vowing to "turn the setback into a victory." Among the serious problems he pointed to were a lack of attention to — and consequently a weakening of — the mass organizations, especially the trade unions, and a tendency for the Communist Party to assume an ever larger role in administering the economy and the state apparatus.

A series of measures were taken to correct these weaknesses. Trade union locals held elections as a step toward revitalizing the unions. The Communist Party clarified its role as a political leadership and not an administrative apparatus. The mass organizations were strengthened.

At the same time, the government began to chart a course toward the "institutionalization" of the revolution. This was intended to put an end to the "provisional" period of the revolution by establishing permanent structures and mechanisms for the active participation of the Cuban people in decision making.

Over the next several years this process made significant advances. The judicial system and the executive branch of the government were reorganized. The Communist Party revamped its apparatus and its first congress was held in December 1975, another step in the process that had begun with the formation of the ORI in 1961 and of the Communist Party of Cuba in 1965.

In February 1976 Cuban voters approved a new constitution, the first since the revolution came to power. This referendum culminated a nationwide discussion and debate. Over six million Cubans discussed the document in 168,000 assemblies. Thousands of amendments, suggestions, and other proposals were made, and a number of these were incorporated into the final draft. Codified in the constitution were two of the most important results of institutionalization: the organs of People's Power and the Economic Management and Planning System.

People's Power, the system of elected representative governing bodies, was first introduced in 1974 as a pilot project in Matanzas Province. Based on that experience it was subsequently extended to the entire country. The new constitution specified these bodies as the highest state institutions on the municipal, provincial, and national level. Their functioning is described by Marta Harnecker in *Cuba: Dictatorship or Democracy?* (Westport, Connecticut: Lawrence Hill & Company, 1980), and in several speeches by Fidel and Raúl Castro contained in this present collection.

Municipal People's Power, the governing bodies closest to the population, are based on neighborhood districts that each elect a delegate. These delegates are ordinary working people, well known in their districts. By law every election must have at least two candidates, who are nominated by special assemblies of voters. There are no party slates or political hucksters. Candidates' biographies are posted for all to read and voters select the individual they think will best represent them. Once elected, delegates are subject to immediate recall by their constituents. The municipal assemblies elect delegates to provincial assemblies, which in turn elect representatives to the National Assembly, Cuba's highest state body.

The organs of People's Power are designed to be working bodies that combine both legislative and administrative functions. They supervise — and in some cases directly administer — factories, stores, schools, medical facilities, housing, and other institutions under their jurisdiction.

The individual delegates have the responsibility of representing their constituents; hearing their complaints and concerns, channelling these to the proper bodies, and reporting back decisions made. A special feature of People's Power is the regular scheduling of accountability sessions in each district between the delegates and their constituents. At these meetings delegates must give a full report of their activities and answer questions that are posed to them.

The establishment of People's Power was a big step forward for the Cuban revolution. Previously, even the smallest local institutions — such as restaurants, primary schools, neighborhood clinics, and grocery stores — were directly accountable to government ministries in Havana. This overcentralization and the ensuing paralysis and red tape was a constant source of irritation and frustration to the population. With People's Power, these local institutions became the responsibility of the municipal assemblies. In addition to increasing administrative efficiency, People's Power represents a qualitative deepening of the ongoing effort by Cuba's working people to train themselves to run their society and to develop the democratic institutions to do so.

The other major aspect of institutionalization was the creation of the Economic Management and Planning System. In Cuba, unlike in capitalist countries, the means of production are not the property of individual owners, but are state property belonging to working people as a whole. The government works out a central economic plan and is responsible for its realization. How this plan is developed, what it provides for, and the degree to which it's implemented thus play a crucial role in the country's life.

The Economic Management and Planning System was designed to achieve the most productive organization of the economy, increasing workers' participation in economic decision making. One of the goals that is being increasingly realized is that workers should discuss and vote on the annual plan for their workplace. In addition, the trade unions play an important role in the elaboration of the national plan.

The growing involvement of working people in making and implementing the country's fundamental economic and social policies accelerated Cuba's economic progress during the 1970s. It was also helped by several years of relatively favorable world market prices for sugar and some breaks in the imperialist blockade. During this period new factories were built throughout the country, the economy was diversified, agriculture was increasingly mechanized, and thousands of new technicians, professionals, and skilled workers were trained. The standard of living rose substantially and there was a dramatic increase in the number of items available to consumers. In addition Cuba continued its dramatic progress in expanding and improving the quality of health care, education, and other social services.

All these factors helped lead to a deepening of the Cuban people's support for and confidence in the revolution and its policies.

The revolution was strengthened further by international developments. During the early 1970s Cuba's political isolation eased as a growing number of Latin American governments extended recognition in open defiance of Washington. And the U.S. defeat in Vietnam in 1975 marked a historic turning point in the world relationship of class forces in favor of the working class. This opened up new opportunities for Cuba to act on a world scale to advance the interests of the workers and peasants internationally.

One area where this was reflected was in Africa. In 1974 the Portuguese colonial empire collapsed under the powerful blows of the African masses. The former colonies of Angola and Mozambique won their independence. Angola's independence, however, was soon jeopardized

by a U.S.-backed South African invasion in late 1975. Cuba then decided to take a bold step. At the invitation of the new Angolan government, tens of thousands of Cuban troops were sent to help repel the South African invaders. The Cubans were successful and the South African forces were routed.

Similarly, in 1978 Cuba sent troops to Ethiopia at the invitation of that government. After its revolution, which had overthrown the feudal monarchy of Haile Selassie in 1974, Ethiopia faced a growing threat from the U.S. government. A U.S.-supported invasion by neighboring Somalia led Ethiopia to request Cuban assistance. Once again the Cubans were successful.

These actions greatly enhanced Cuba's prestige in the eyes of the oppressed throughout the world. As a reflection of this new respect Cuba was selected as the site of the 1979 summit conference of the Movement of Nonaligned Countries. As Cuba's head of state, Castro began a term as chairman of that organization, which lasted until 1983.

Two other events occurred in 1979 that had a decisive impact on Cuba: the successful revolutions in Grenada and Nicaragua. After twenty years of isolation, the Cuban revolution was no longer alone in the region. Two other Latin American and Caribbean countries had freed themselves from imperialist domination and installed governments based on the working people and peasants, opening the road to socialism. The Cuban revolutionaries had always recognized that the fate of their revolution was ultimately bound up with its extension to the rest of the hemisphere. This understanding was the basis of Cuba's long-standing solidarity with revolutionaries throughout Latin America, symbolized by Che Guevara's unsuccessful guerrilla campaign in Bolivia in 1967.

Cuba immediately extended assistance to Nicaragua and Grenada. Hundreds of thousands of Cuban doctors, medical technicians, teachers, construction workers, and other technical personnel volunteered their services and many were sent to these two countries. Cuba also did its best to mobilize political support for Nicaragua and Grenada in the face of the U.S. government's efforts to destabilize and overthrow their revolutions. Washington clearly recognized the significance of these developments, and the threat they posed to U.S. economic and political domination in Latin America and the Caribbean. The advancing revolutionary struggles in El Salvador and Guatemala highlighted this only too clearly. Cuba made it clear that it would consider an attack by the U.S. against Nicaragua or Grenada as an attack against itself.

At the same time that it took measures against Nicaragua and Grenada, Washington escalated its threats and aggressive actions against Cuba as well. It stepped up the U.S. military presence at Guantánamo, created a Caribbean naval task force, increased the number of spy flights, tightened trade restrictions, and put into effect a new ban on travel to Cuba by U.S. citizens. Within the U.S. government there was talk of imposing a complete naval blockade, and even of an eventual U.S. invasion.

This growing danger of renewed U.S. military aggression against Cuba, combined with the still-real economic underdevelopment, created the context in which a new round of the political battle to preserve and deepen the revolution was fought. In a move to educate and prepare the Cuban people to meet the test of the deepening confrontation with imperialism, a new campaign was begun in 1979 against administrative laxness, "buddyism," privilege taking, and a flagging political consciousness among a section of the population in the face of the economic and political pressures of imperialism.

In several speeches printed in this book, Raúl Castro denounced "the presence of indiscipline, lack of control, irresponsibility, complacency, negligence, and buddyism, which, in addition to aggravating many problems, prevent others from being solved and generate justified irritation on the part of broad sectors of the population."

As he explained, "I note in the conduct and expression of certain diverse elements of our present-day society signs of that same weakness, of the poverty of spirit and timid psychology of the faint-hearted which flourishes in times of trouble. . . . It comes as no surprise that among those inclined to fall prey to defeatism are those who avoid facing up to problems because they are more concerned about retaining the positions they hold than about the needs of the people they are supposed to serve."

Only the workers could solve these problems, he added. They "must fight against all signs of indiscipline, against the widespread practice of letting people get away with things, against giving special treatment to friends, against weak management and some tamed trade union leaders, against the workers themselves who come late or skip work, and against all signs of individualism and misuse of social property. . . . The order of the day is to be *demanding*."

The significance of this campaign became clear the following year with the exodus of 125,000 Cubans to the United States in the spring of 1980. This emigration and the Cuban people's reaction to it are referred to in several speeches in this collection.

Cuba's policy has always been that building socialism is a voluntary undertaking, "a task for free men and women," in Fidel Castro's words. It has therefore not put obstacles in the way of those wishing to leave. The United States government, on the other hand, has — from the first days of the revolution — used emigration from Cuba as a political weapon, granting or refusing visas based on which of these would put more pressure on Cuba at any given time. Since the early 1970s Washington consistently refused to grant visas to all but a handful of Cubans

wanting to leave, all the while encouraging them to leave illegally —
hijacking boats and planes, and occupying the embassies of various
countries. After many such provocations, culminating in the much-pub-
licized 1980 incident at the Peruvian embassy that left a Cuban guard
dead, the Cuban government finally decided to take action: it turned the
tables on Washington — which was trying to make it seem as if it were
Cuba that was responsible for denying visas — and proceeded to au-
thorize U.S. boats to come to the port of Mariel and pick up Cubans
wishing to leave.

Those who left were tempted by the greater availability of consumer
goods in the U.S. Many were anxious to flee from the growing danger
of renewed U.S. military aggression as the revolutions in Central
America and the Caribbean deepened. Among those who left were also
a layer of professionals and government functionaries who had in the
past masqueraded as revolutionaries.

Spontaneous demonstrations in support of the revolution and in repudiation of the *escoria* ("scum") erupted throughout Cuba. As a show
of the revolution's strength the government organized several gigantic
outpourings. On April 17, 1980, one million people demonstrated in
front of the Peruvian embassy, where ten thousand people wanting to
leave Cuba had gathered. On May 1, 1.5 million attended a rally to hear
the revolution's leaders. And on May 17, five million Cubans — half the
country's population — demonstrated in cities throughout the country.
Those millions were also demonstrating their commitment to the revolution's political course, that of subordinating Cuba's interests to the revolutionary struggle worldwide. And they were telling the U.S. government that they were not afraid of its threats.

The whole experience strengthened the revolution and deepened the
Cuban people's commitment to it. In Castro's words, "The people demonstrated that their strength, unity, awareness, fighting spirit, and discipline were unbeatable. . . . The masses were tempered and tremendously strengthened in the struggle, and their spirit of patriotism and defense of the principles of socialism and proletarian internationalism were
deepened. The struggle also boosted production and discipline and
helped us find solutions for our own internal weaknesses. . . . We
consider the battle that the masses waged . . . to be one of the most important political, ideological, and moral victories the revolution has won
in its entire history."

Cuba took a further step in response to the growing U.S. threats by establishing the Territorial Troop Militias. (The previous militias had been
gradually incorporated into the regular armed forces and reserves.) Over
half a million Cubans were enrolled — men and women, old and young
— and another million who volunteered could not be accepted because
of a lack of weapons.

In addition to being an important tool for the country's defense, the creation of the militias was a further demonstration and a deepening of the Cuban people's participation in the revolutionary process. Castro explained its significance in the following terms: "The exploiting classes have always opposed arming the people. How can an exploitative society arm the people? How can an exploitative society give arms to the workers, peasants, and students, when we read that workers are involved in constant strikes and struggles, as well as the peasants and students? If an exploitative society were to arm the people, it would disappear in a question of weeks, days, or hours. . . . Only a people's revolution can arm the people."

*   *   *

The speeches contained in this book show that although the Cuban leadership's basic thinking has developed and progressed since 1959, its fundamental political approach has been consistent over the years.

One example of this is Cuba's commitment to the active involvement and participation of the working masses in all areas that affect their lives, to the expansion and deepening of genuine democracy. The Cubans explain that democracy is inconceivable under capitalism, where a tiny minority control the means of production and therefore have the power to determine the direction in which society will move. Real democracy begins with the creation of a government that is based on and defends the interests of the vast majority who produce all of society's wealth: the working class and the small farmers. As Raúl Castro explained, "When a state like ours represents the interests of the workers, regardless of its form and structure, it is a much more democratic state than any other kind that has ever existed in history, because the state of workers, the state that has undertaken the construction of socialism, is, in any form, a majority state of the majority, while all other previous states have been states of exploiting minorities."

Although the system of People's Power was not created until 1976, it would be wrong to assume that democracy did not exist prior to that. In Fidel Castro's words, "the first sovereign action by the people was the revolution itself," where the Cuban people took their country's destiny into their own hands. The revolution's defense in its early years was an expression of this democratic character, as working people by the millions mobilized in the face of U.S. attacks and domestic counterrevolution. Throughout every stage of the revolution the mass organizations — such as the Committees for the Defense of the Revolution, the women's federation, the farmers' organizations, and the trade unions — have been channels for "people's power." The Cubans developed the procedure, for example, of these organizations discussing, debating, and voting on major pieces of legislation proposed by the government.

But it's not enough to simply create the formal channels for democratic decision making. Working people must be trained to govern. Cuban revolutionaries refer to Lenin's statement that "We must teach the people, down to the humblest sections, the art of governing and administering the state, not only through books, but through immediate practical application everywhere of the experience of the masses." They have attempted to apply this concept through the trade unions, the mass organizations, and People's Power. And it is why they put so much emphasis on formal education, as shown in the literacy drive, adult education programs, and the massive expansion of the entire educational system. All this helps raise the general technical, cultural, and political level of society as a whole, a necessary component of the expansion of democracy.

Another side of the educational effort is promoting the development of a new social consciousness. Castro explained it the following way:

"Under capitalism the thing uppermost in a man's mind is survival, health, his children. If he's the head of a family; if one of his loved ones is sick, he's hounded by the thought of not having any money; he's hounded by all the fears on which capitalist labor discipline is founded. In other words, under capitalism, it's the subhuman standard of living that disciplines the workers.

"Such motivations don't exist in socialism; in socialism money isn't essential in facing these problems. The important things, the problems that — logically enough — are of vital importance to the workers are solved by the entire society.

"That is why the contribution made by the consciousness of the workers, by the political culture of the workers and by their attitude, becomes an irreplaceable element in socialism, since the workers' motivations are of a different character.

"Naturally, in socialism, man becomes fully identified with the means of production, with the country's sources of wealth, with the country's future, with the country's political process, with the country's political problems. In other words, the worker becomes the master of his country's wealth and the master of his country's destiny.

"In socialism, however, moral factors, the factors of consciousness, the factors of culture, are essential."

Cubans often refer to the example of Che Guevara, who frequently dealt with the importance of creating a "communist consciousness." Guevara is also seen as an example of Cuba's internationalism, the idea that the Cuban revolution is only one part of — and subordinate to — the worldwide struggle for socialism.

In this light Cubans consider it a duty to make whatever sacrifices are necessary for the revolutionary struggle internationally. As Castro stated in 1975, "The starting point of Cuba's foreign policy . . . is the subordination of Cuban positions to the international needs of the struggle for socialism and for the national liberation of the peoples." It is a source of pride, for example, that tens of thousands of Cuban workers are currently serving overseas in over thirty-five countries as health workers, teachers, construction workers, technicians, and military personnel.

One theme that appears repeatedly in this collection is the struggle against bureaucratic functioning. To the Cuban revolutionary leadership this is a fundamental question. In an interview printed in this volume, Cuban leader Carlos Rafael Rodríguez terms bureaucracy "one of the permanent dangers of socialism." In his words, it "consists in substituting for the masses in the decision-making process, at whatever level, in imposing an administrative or political apparatus on the workers without taking into account either the workers or their organizations."

The Cubans say that much of what they have learned in this regard comes from Lenin's writings about this problem in the early years of the Soviet Union. Lenin believed this problem stemmed from the economic and cultural backwardness existing in the Soviet Union combined with the pressures resulting from encirclement by world imperialism. While strong measures could be taken, the problem could not be fully solved short of the victory of world socialism, the establishment of economic planning on an international scale, and a consequent material abundance greater than anything capitalism can or has been able to provide. What was important in Lenin's view was to find ways to limit and contain the pressures toward the bureaucratization of the revolution — understanding that these pressures would be constantly bred by scarcity and other survivals of capitalism. He indicated that it could be fought through educating and mobilizing the workers around the real revolutionary challenges they faced.

Following Lenin's death a bureaucratic caste composed of government functionaries, party members, and military officers who benefitted from substantial institutionalized material privileges emerged in the Soviet Union. It came to monopolize political power and pushed the working class aside. Its political outlook was based on subordinating the advance of the world revolution to the maintenance of the status quo, to preserving its privileged position. The party Lenin had built was destroyed, its leadership physically liquidated, and the Communist Party became an instrument of the bureaucracy, not the working class either in the Soviet Union or internationally.

The Cubans have learned from these and other experiences. As the speeches in this book show, from the beginning the revolutionary leadership has been conscious of how underdevelopment creates continual pressures toward bureaucracy. Over the years they have actively fought this danger both in what they say and what they do. In Cuba there have never been special material advantages for managers, government functionaries, or party members. There are no special ration cards or special stores as exist in other countries where capitalism has been eliminated. Although there are salary differences for different types of jobs, these are held to certain limits; and the differential is further lessened by the number of free services that exist and the low prices Cubans pay for basic necessities. The tendency in Cuban society is toward greater, not lesser, equality.

In addition, the revolution has taken other steps to prevent a gulf developing between the working class and the state and party apparatus. These include the active role of the trade unions and workers' assemblies in economic decision making, the administration and supervision of local institutions and enterprises by People's Power, and the method of having workers nominate candidates for party membership. The party itself has made big advances in its efforts to have its composition reflect the growing political consciousness of Cuba's working class. It has recruited to its ranks a whole new generation of workers, and has increased the percentage of party members who are working in production and those who are women. Through all its institutions and policies, the basic approach of the revolution is to draw the working masses into active political life, not away from it.

The Cubans have also recognized that the problem of bureaucracy needs to be combatted politically and ideologically as well. The revolution has gone through many experiences which are chronicled in this volume, from the Escalante affair in 1962 up through the 1982 battle against corruption. Throughout, the revolutionary leadership has pointed out the political pressures that promote the growth of bureaucracy.

As Raúl Castro indicated in 1979, it is above all demoralization, discouragement, a lack of faith in the working class in Cuba and internationally, and a faint-hearted cowering before the power of the imperialists that must be fought. The Cuban leadership's approach has been to politically educate the masses about their own class interests, inspire them to push ahead in carrying through the revolution's tasks, and to continually point to Cuba's responsibilities to aid the struggles of workers and oppressed throughout the world, regardless of the risks to Cuba.

The Cubans' political orientation throughout more than twenty years has taken on added importance today. In Nicaragua and Grenada the revolutionaries are grappling with many of the same problems and tasks Cuba faced: organizing, mobilizing, and leading the masses to carry through measures in their own interests; developing the political consciousness of the working class and peasants through this process; combatting corruption, privilege, and bureaucratic arrogance; and expanding the proletarian leadership of the revolution. These revolutionaries have closely studied Cuba's experiences and have learned important lessons from them.

Likewise, the U.S. government and its allies see in Nicaragua and Grenada — and in El Salvador and Guatemala — the spector of "new Cubas" springing up throughout the hemisphere. They are marshalling their forces to try to prevent this from happening.

The example of the Cuban revolution is thus at the center of the growing confrontation in the Caribbean and Central America between the U.S. government and the advancing revolutionary movement of the area's workers and peasants. This fact makes the publication of this book all the more timely.

*   *   *

This is the second volume in Pathfinder Press's series of speeches by Fidel Castro. The first volume, *Fidel Castro Speeches: Cuba's Internationalist Foreign Policy 1975-80,* dealt with that aspect of Cuban policy. The present volume covers Cuba's fundamental domestic policies and spans a broader range of time.

This book also contains several speeches by other leaders of the revolution, speeches that are important in tracing the development of Cuba's policies. This reflects the reality that, contrary to many assertions, Cuba does not have a "one-man" leadership. Fidel Castro is the main figure in a strong leadership team that has developed over the years. The major speeches and policy statements by Fidel Castro, Raúl Castro, and other leaders reflect the collective thinking of this leadership as a whole.

A number of the speeches in this collection are reprinted in full. Because of space considerations, however, others have been abridged. In some cases sections have been omitted from speeches that deal with questions outside the immediate scope of this volume. Wherever deletions have been made these are indicated by a line space.

Except where otherwise indicated, all translations are taken from the English-language *Granma Weekly Review,* the official organ of the Central Committee of the Communist Party of Cuba. To ensure accuracy, these have been checked against the text of the Spanish originals and corrections have been made where necessary. Other minor editorial changes have been made for clarity and stylistic consistency.

To assist the reader each speech contains a brief editorial note providing background information.

Michael Taber
February 1983

This Is Democracy

May 1, 1960

NOTE: On May 1, 1960, in the midst of escalating U.S. threats and a growing number of counterrevolutionary incidents, a massive May Day demonstration was held in Havana. Below is the major part of Castro's speech, given in the Civic Plaza (now the Plaza of the Revolution) following the march. It is reprinted from the pamphlet "Labor Day Address About the Destiny of Cuba" (Havana, 1960).

Distinguished visitors from Latin America and from all over the world; Workers, farmers, students, members of the militia, professionals, youth brigades, all Cubans:

On other occasions we have met together in great meetings — sometimes to defend our country from slander; other times to commemorate some patriotic anniversary; other times to protest against some aggression. But never before have the people assembled together in greater number or in a meeting so significant as today's, a day on which we observe International Workers' Day and therefore the day of the Cuban workers, as well as the day of the Cuban farmers, the day of all those who produce, the day of all the humble among the people of our country. Workers' Day not only honors those who work with their hands or with their minds, producing material goods or lending services to their country, but also in this decisive hour, Workers' Day honors those on whose shoulders rests the defense of the nation and the defense of the revolution.

This is also the day of the rebel soldiers, of the heroic fighting men of the revolutionary army. It is furthermore the day of all the members of the Revolutionary Armed Forces and the day of the revolutionary militia, because the soldiers of the Rebel Army are also farmers and workers. Therefore today is the day of all the revolutionaries, of all revolutionaries united, because in unity lies and will always lie the success and the strength of our revolution.

Today's gathering not only demonstrates that the great majority of the people support the revolution — in case there were to remain any doubt among those who are so naive as to take pleasure in deceiving themselves or in allowing themselves to be deceived. There is something still more important: this great majority of the people is organized.

Today it is an organized people who have met together. That is why we are stronger this year than we were last year. The revolution not only has the majority but also has organized that majority.

And this fact, to which all of us today have been witness, this truly impressive and unforgettable event, proves the capacity of the Cuban people.

Even a few months ago not a single militia unit — neither worker nor farmer — was organized. The appeal to organize the militias began in the month of October, exactly October 26, as a result of the rally of protest against the aerial incursion that cost more than forty victims among our citizens.* Six months ago we did not have a single workers' militia. Six months ago the workers did not know how to handle arms. Six months ago the workers did not know how to march. Six months ago there was not a single company of militias to depend on to defend the revolution in case of aggression. And in only six months the militias have been organized, have been disciplined, and have been trained.

Our people were not, nor are they now, a militaristic people. Our people have never been nor will they ever be a militaristic people. There was no military tradition in our country. Cuba was not Prussia. Cuba is a country eminently peaceful and civil minded. In Cuba we despised marching and uniforms and arms, because for us these were always the symbols of oppression and of abuse, the symbols of privilege, the symbols of mistreatment. Arms and uniforms have been hateful to us. Nevertheless, in six months we have organized and trained more than a thousand companies of workers' militias, student militias, and farmers' militias. This formidable organization that paraded here today, built in only six months, shows what the people of Cuba are able to do.

Those who underestimated our people believed that we were people incapable of organizing ourselves. They believed that we were incapable of unity. Those who underestimated us believed us to be — as they believe our sister nations of Latin America also to be — a helpless nation that would submit easily. They believed we were going to be victims of disunity, of unpreparedness, of the incapacity to organize ourselves. They believed us to be incapable of defending ourselves and no doubt they even considered us to be too cowardly to defend ourselves.

However, what has been accomplished proves the opposite. What has been accomplished in so short a time demonstrates the extraordinary qualities of our people and shows what our people can do.

But why is it that today every citizen whose heart holds love for his country and his people, every citizen who has enough sensitivity for his fellow man, enough moral consciousness and enough dignity to feel —

---

*This refers to an October 21 raid by a B-25 bomber originating in Florida.

and to know what is — a sense of justice, today wants to belong to a corps of the militia, today wants to know how to handle arms? Why has every citizen learned to do things that he never had done before and to become organized like this?

What is it that has made our people form militias? What is it that has made the workers, the students, the farmers, the doctors, the women as well as men, form militias and learn how to handle arms? What is it that has converted us into a Spartan people? What happened so that when a worker finished his daily eight hours he goes to march three or four hours and marches at night, marches in the rain, or sacrifices his weekly day of rest to learn how to handle arms? What is it that moves him to make such a sacrifice not on one day, but on many days, and continually during many months?

To what should be attributed this fervent effort of Cubans? Simply to a reality: the reality that the nation is in danger, the reality that the nation is threatened. True as it is, difficult as it is, this knowledge should not discourage anybody. It is a reality that we need to defend ourselves. In stating this we do not lie nor exaggerate. We have never lied to the people and above all, we will never withhold realities from the people.

Many things we have had to learn, many things we have all learned, all of us without exception. Today, for example, as the organized units of the people filed back and forth in endless numbers to march for seven consecutive hours, today while we have had an opportunity to see the tremendous strength of the people, while we have had the opportunity to see the incomparable and invincible strength of the people, we asked: But is this people today the same as the people of yesterday?

How is it possible that a people with such tremendous and extraordinary strength should have had to endure what our people have had to endure? How was it possible, with the tremendous strength of hundreds of thousands of Cuban farmers, and the tremendous strength of more than a million Cuban workers, and the tremendous strength of hundreds of thousands of young people like those who paraded today in the ranks of the patrols and the student militias? How was it possible? How can they be the same men and women as yesterday?

Since these citizens who paraded by here today are the same citizens that made up our people just a few years ago, how is it possible then that we should have had to suffer such extreme abuse? How is it possible that so many hundreds of thousands of families in our rural areas lived in conditions of starvation without land and were so exploited, as victims of the most heartless exploitation by foreign companies that lorded over our land, while those almighty who gave orders were those who in most cases not only had never planted a seed on our land but furthermore had never even seen our land?

While so much courage was in the hearts of our people, how was it possible to abuse our workers so? How was so much exploitation possible? How was so much crookedness, so much theft, so much plundering of our people possible? While we had so much strength, how was so much crime possible? How was it possible for a handful of men, a band of mercenaries, or a plague of petty politicians to dominate our people and direct the destiny of our people during half a century?

How was it possible for our people to have to pay a price so high that to give us a clear notion of it we would need to see united together here in a square many times bigger than this the millions of Cubans who were left unable to read or write, the hundreds of thousands of children who died without seeing a doctor, the ocean of suffering and anguish, of hunger and misery, of abuse and humiliation that the sons and daughters of this land had to endure because of poverty, or because of illiteracy, or because of their color, or because of their sex.

Ah, our people had reserves of extraordinary energy and extraordinary strength, but we did not know it, or we had not been permitted to draw that strength together, to organize it. And therefore, the privileged and educated minorities were able to do more with the help of alien interests than our people were able to do with their tremendous reserves of strength.

That has been the great lesson of this day, because never so much as today have Cubans had the opportunity to see our own strength. Never so much as today could the Cuban people have an exact idea of their own strength. The endless stream of columns marching for seven hours has been necessary so that our people should have a concrete idea of their own strength. And this great lesson should be an unforgettable lesson for us.

First, the children and young people marched, opening ranks. Then the soldiers of the Rebel Army marched. Then the farmers' militias marched. Then the militias of Latin America marched, with the flags of their respective countries. Then the student militias marched, and finally the workers' militias marched — first women, then men, and behind or around the militia units, the people. What formidable training! The people have been made conscious of their strength and the people have learned what constitutes strength. [*Applause*]

The soldiers alone, the soldiers who paraded here today, constitute a force, but only a single force. The farmers alone constitute a force, but only one force. The students alone make up a force, but no more than one force. The workers alone make up a force, but a single force. The nations of Latin America represented here today constitute a force, but each one of them separately is a single force.

Before, the tactics of those who used to rule over our destiny consisted of dividing us and of setting one force against another.

They set the soldier against the farmer. They set the interests of the farmer against the interests of the worker. They set every faction of the people against the other factions as part of an international strategy of the big reactionary interests of the world. They set sister nations against each other and they set the various sectors of each nation against each other to serve the privileged classes.

They set one group of the lower classes against another group of the lower classes. They took a poor farmer and made him a soldier. Then they corrupted this soldier and made him an enemy of the worker and an enemy of the farmer.

They weakened the people by their practice of setting one humble sector against others. They divided the people into petty political parties that brought no guidance to the nation. [*Applause and shouts of "Out with them!"*] They divided the ignorant and misled people into factions supporting unscrupulous and greedy politicians. Thus they weakened the people. Thus they confused the people and thus the apparatus of the government with its rigid and reactionary institutions destroyed all hope, all possibility of progress for our society. Every means to teach ideas — the movies, the majority of the press, the centers of learning, and all the administrative apparatus of the state — were at the service of this policy of oppressing and weakening the people.

That was what used to happen. What was May Day in those days? The workers used to be almost unable to walk under the weight of all the posters that they carried on their shoulders every May Day. Today, the workers have not brought a single demand.

May Day was an opportunity for the workers to parade carrying posters, in the hope of satisfying those demands or some of those demands. May Day used to be, actually, a mockery for the workers. The next year they had to return once again carrying the same posters with the same demands.

Nothing that they attained was granted to them graciously. Anything they attained was granted to them only after a grueling fight, after strikes and organized movements demanding wage increases. The worker knew that he had to fight. The worker had to keep up a constant fight in order to obtain some small benefit in the economic order. He had to fight so that his most elemental rights would be respected.

Therefore, every May Day they had to come carrying their demands. What else could they do? The worker knew that what he did not do for himself nobody else would do for him. The worker knew that what he did not win by his own work nobody would win for him. You, worker; you, farmer, always worked for others. You did your own work and the work of others. You — worker, farmer, doctor, intellectual worker, and all the rest of you workers — did your own work and the work of others.

But nobody every worked for you, farmer, nor for you, worker. You gave everything with generosity, you gave your sweat and your energy.

You gave your life. Many times you denied yourselves your hours of rest. You gave to everybody, but to you nobody ever gave anything. What you did not do for yourselves, nobody would ever do for you. You were the majority of the people. You, the farmers, the workers, the youth, were the majority of the people. You who produce, you who made sacrifices, you who work, you were always and you are today and will be tomorrow, the majority of the people. But you did not govern. You were the majority, but others governed in your stead and governed *against* you.

They invented a democracy for you — a strange, a very strange democracy, in which you, who were the majority, did not count for anything. Although you, farmer and worker, were the ones who produced the majority of the wealth and — together with the intellectual workers — produced *all* the wealth, many of you who produced everything did not even have the opportunity to learn to sign your name.

They invented a strange democracy for you — a democracy in which you who were the majority did not even exist politically within society. They spoke to you of civil rights. In that situation of civil rights your child could die of hunger before the unconcerned glance of the government. Your child could be left without learning to read or write a single letter and you yourself had to go sell your work at the price that they wanted to pay you for it and whenever anybody was interested in buying it from you.

They spoke to you of rights that never existed for you. Your children could not be sure even of the right to a school. Your children could not be guaranteed even the right to a doctor. Your children did not have the guaranteed right even to a piece of bread, and you yourself did not have the guarantee even of the right to work.

They invented for you a democracy that meant that you, you who were the majority, did not count for anything. And thus, despite your tremendous force, despite your sacrifices, despite your work for others in our national life, despite the fact that you were the majority, you neither governed nor counted for anything. You were not taken into account.

And that they called democracy! Democracy is where the majority governs. Democracy is that form of government in which the majority is taken into account. Democracy is that form of government in which the interests of the majority are defended. Democracy is that form of government that guarantees to man not just the right to think freely but the right to know how to think, the right to know how to write what he thinks, the right to know how to read what is thought by others. Democracy guarantees not only the right to bread and the right to work but also the right to culture and the right to be taken into account within society. Therefore, *this* is democracy. The Cuban revolution is democracy.

This is democracy, where you, farmer, are given the land that we have recovered from usurious foreign hands that used to exploit it. Democracy is *this*, where you, the sugar plantation workers, receive 80,000 *caballerías* of land in order that you shall not have to live in *guardarrayas*.*

This is democracy, where you, worker, are guaranteed the right to work, so that you cannot be thrown out on the streets to go hungry.

Democracy is *this*, where you, students, have the opportunity to win a university degree if you are intelligent, even though you may not be rich.

Democracy is *this*, where you, whether you are the child of a worker, the child of a farmer, or the child of any other humble family, have a teacher to educate you and a school where you can be taught.

Democracy is *this*, where you, old person, have sustenance guaranteed after you can no longer depend on your effort.

Democracy is *this*, where you, Black Cuban, have the right to work without anybody being able to deprive you of that right because of stupid prejudice.

Democracy is *this*, where the women acquire rights equal to those of all other citizens and have a right even to bear arms alongside the men to defend their country.

Democracy is *this*, in which a government converts its fortresses into schools, and in which a government wants to build a house for every family so that every family can have a roof of its own over its heads.

Democracy is *this* — a government that wants every invalid to have a doctor's care.

Democracy is *this*, that which does not recruit a farmer to make a soldier out of him, corrupt him, and convert him into an enemy of the worker or into an enemy of his own brother farmer, but, rather, converts the soldier into a defender of the rights of his brothers, the farmers and the workers, instead of converting him into a defender of the privileged classes.

Democracy is *this*, that which does not divide the humble people into factions by setting some against others.

Democracy is *this*, in which a government finds the force of the people and unites it. Democracy is *this*, that which makes a people strong by uniting them.

Democracy is *this*, that which gives a gun to the farmers, gives a gun to the workers, gives a gun to the students, gives a gun to the women, gives a gun to the Black people, gives a gun to the poor, and gives a gun to any other citizen who is willing to defend a just cause.

Democracy is *this*, that which not only takes the rights of the majority

*One *caballería* is equal to about 33 acres. *Guardarrayas* were roadside shacks lived in by many landless peasants.

into account, but also gives arms to this majority. Only a government truly democratic can do this. This can be done only by a government truly democratic, a government where the majority governs.

A pseudodemocracy will never be able to do all these things. We would like to know what would happen if a gun were given to every Black person in the South of the United States, where so many times Blacks have been lynched. What an exploiting oligarchy will never be able to do, what a military caste of the kind that oppresses and plunders nations will never be able to do, what a government of minorities will never be able to do, is give a gun to every worker, to every student, to every young person, to every humble citizen, to every one of those who make up the majority of the people!

But all this does not mean that the rights of others are not taken into account. The rights of others count just as the rights of the majority count, to the same extent that the rights of the majority count. But the *rights* of the majority should prevail above the *privileges* of minorities.

This true democracy, this democracy to which no one can object, this sincere and honest democracy, is the democracy that has existed in our country since January 1, 1959. This democracy has been expressed directly in the close union and identification of the government and the people, in this direct relationship, in this working and fighting in favor of the majority of the country and in the interests of the great majority of the country. This direct democracy we have excercised here has more purity, a thousand times more purity, than that false democracy that uses all the means of corruption and fraud to falsify the true will of the people.

Our democracy today has prevailed in this direct way, because we are in a revolutionary process. Tomorrow will be as the people desire. Tomorrow will be as the necessities of the people demand, as the aspirations of our people demand, as the interests of our people demand. Today there is a direct relation between the people and the government.

When the revolutionary process has gone far enough and the people understand that we are advancing toward new procedures — and the revolutionary government will always understand this just as the people understand it — then the people and the government will adopt whatever procedure the circumstances of a consolidated and victorious revolution demand of you and of us.

Here nobody is in public office because of ambition or pleasure. Here we are only fulfilling our duty. All of us are in the same position and attitude of sacrifice. All of us have the same willingness to work. All of us are joined in a single purpose, which is to serve our cause.

Our enemies, our detractors, ask about elections. [*Prolonged shouts of "Revolution!" "Why elections?" and "We've already voted for Fidel!"*] Even one Latin American leader, chief of state of one Latin

American nation, has declared recently that the Organization of American States should be made up of only those countries whose leaders are chosen by electoral processes. As if a true revolution like this in Cuba could come into power disregarding the will of the people! [*Shouts of "Never!"*] As if the only democratic procedure for taking power were the electoral processes so often prostituted to falsify the will and the interests of the people and so many times used to put into office the most inept and most shrewd, rather than the most competent and the most honest.

As if after so many fraudulent elections, as if after so much false and treacherous politicking, as if after so much corruption the people could be made to believe that the only democratic procedure for a people to choose their leaders was the electoral procedure. And as if *this* procedure were not democratic — this procedure through which a people choose their leaders not with a pencil but with the blood and the lives of 20,000 fellow patriots, struggling without arms against a professional and well-armed army, trained and outfitted by a powerful foreign country.

The people of Cuba broke their chains and by breaking the chains that enslaved them, they put an end to privileges, they put an end to injustices, and they put an end forever to the practice of criminal abuse of the people.

The people of Cuba have begun a truly democratic phase of progress, of liberty, of justice. If there is any process in which the incompetent fall behind, if there is any process in which the crooked fail, that is the revolutionary process.

In the revolutionary process, virtue opens a way for itself, merit prospers, and conniving, greed, and cheating fail. In a process of revolutionary struggle, as in no other struggle, only the firm — those with true convictions and absolute loyalty — can stay in the ranks.

And a revolutionary process does not mean only the insurrectional phase of the war. The real revolution comes later. The rebellion of our people brought about the war. The creative spirit of our people has brought about the revolution.

For this reason we said that in Cuba a true democracy is very much at work, despite the allegations of the enemies of our revolution.

At this time what is the principal job we Cubans have ahead of us? What is it that every Cuban should know today? Why is our job fundamental now? What are the reasons for which our country sees itself threatened by aggression? What has the revolution done but good to its people? What has the revolution done but justice? What has the revolution done but defend the interests of the large majority of our people, of the most humble classes of our country — those who constitute the immense majority and who not only make up the majority with a right of their own to count in the destinies of our country but who, furthermore, are also the part of our country that has suffered most? What has the revolution done but defend those who are not only the majority but are furthermore the exploited part of our country?

Where is the crime in fighting for the people? Where is the crime in wanting the farmer to have land? Where is the crime in giving land to the farmers? How is it a crime to fight for the people, to do what the revolution has done for the people? What the revolution has done for the people is given testimony by the presence here of this crowd, a crowd of flesh and bone, real men and women of the people who came here spontaneously, who came here paying their own expenses, who came here from different places by traveling all night long and marching for a whole day, standing on foot during an entire day under the sun, without drinking water, without eating. The presence of such a great crowd is the best proof that the revolution has fought for the people.

It is not possible to destroy a revolution like this — a revolution with such extraordinary support from the people, a revolution that defends a cause so just, a cause that has the solidarity of all the men of revolutionary thinking of the American continent.

The most reasonable, the most sane, the most intelligent thing that could be done by those who do not want to resign themselves to this revolution would be exactly to resign themselves, because this revolution is a reality. It would be intelligent for them to leave us in peace. Otherwise, in the senseless attempt to destroy the revolution, they will lose much more than they have already lost.

Realities do not arise in the world through someone's whim. Revolutions, real revolutions, do not arise by the will of one man or one group. Revolutions are realities that obey other realities. Revolutions are remedies — bitter remedies, yes. But at times revolution is the only remedy that can be applied to evils even more bitter. The Cuban revolution is a reality in the world. The Cuban revolution is already a reality for the history of the world.

The Cuban revolution is a reality just as the people's support of it is a reality, just as the guns that can defend it are realities, just as the men who are willing to die for it inside Cuba and outside Cuba are realities.

In case of aggression against our country, under any pretext, by any power or by any group of nations, that may be ensnared by any maneuver, aggression against our country will mean war not only against our people but also against every Cuban anywhere and it will be a struggle against the friends of Cuba — all those who are willing, wherever they may be found, to fight for Cuba.

In declaring our determination to fight we are as sincere as when we state that we are longing and striving to see our dreams converted into realities.

To speak more clearly would be impossible. Furthermore, so that nothing should be left unsaid, all Cubans should be reminded that we should always be alert, and that we do not know how many years we must be alert. That is the price we must pay for the work we have set out to do. Always alert, against any aggression, whether by surprise or with advance warning. Always alert and willing to fight wherever we find ourselves.

Every soldier of the Rebel Army and every revolutionary soldier, always alert. Every member of the militia, every farmer, every worker, every student, every young person, every man and every woman, every old person and every child, always alert.

Always alert, in every circumstance, in every condition. Always ready to resist any attack, without faltering, always determined in spirit. What no one can ever crush is the spirit of the Cuban people. No people will be subjugated if their spirit does not yield, if their will is not destroyed.

Always alert and ready to fight, to fight with whatever we have at hand, to fight wherever we find ourselves.

Always remembering to resist, to fight against any aggression, always determined to win or to die. [*Applause and shouts of "Patria o muerte!"*] Always alert and willing to fight, whatever may happen, whatever may befall us. Always alert and willing to fight, no matter who may be missing, no matter who may die.

Our revolution would not be destroyed if the enemy should deprive one of us, two of us, or three of us, of our lives. If a leader falls, the duty immediately and without argument of any kind is to replace him with another leader. If a leader falls, whoever the leader may be, immediately another will fill his place.

On an earlier occasion, when the circumstances were not those of today, we gave our opinion and the people made a decision. If the prime minister should at any moment ever be missing among you — [*Shouts of "No!"*] The question is not whether or not you want this to happen. The question is that everybody should know what they should do in every circumstance, and what concerns us is that the people should know what to do in every eventuality.

It is our duty to the people to repeat: If the prime minister should ever fail to be among you, that is, if the enemies of the revolution should carry out an aggression, it is realistic and it is important only to know what must be done — to know that you have immediately a substitute for the prime minister. You are going to say who.

Already in that previous rally I proposed Raúl [Castro] for prime minister if the prime minister should ever be missing. [*Prolonged ovation*] If both of us should fail to be with you, the president of the republic will meet with the council of ministers and designate another prime minister. It is necessary to be prepared for all possibilities.

When a nation undertakes a job like the one the Cuban nation has undertaken, when a small country like Cuba has powerful adversaries such as Cuba has today, all the possibilities should be foreseen, and the people should know what it is that they have to do. What they have to do, above all, is know that our country can never be divided in the face of an enemy action. The reaction of the people is always to close their ranks.

When a small nation like ours takes upon its shoulders a job like the one that we have taken upon our shoulders, they must always know what to do. And if we conduct ourselves well, it does not matter that we are small. If we know what to do, we will win because victory always goes to those whose cause is right, to those who know how to uphold their rightful cause, and know how to fight for their rightful cause. We can be sure that if we do what we have to do, we will win.

So, on this May Day, what remains for us to do is reaffirm that purpose, that purpose of all of us — to continue to fulfill our duty, in our positions, and to ask that everybody else do the same. To express our faith in the destiny of the nation, our faith in the solidarity of the sister countries of the continent. We are fighting for all of them because they will learn from our experience. They will learn from the success that we have, and they will learn even from the errors that we make.

So, our mistakes as well as our successes will be useful to our sister nations. We have faith in the solidarity of these sister nations and faith in the solidarity of all the peoples of the world.

May all the visitors here go tell our sister nations of Latin America what Cuba is today. May our visitors go repel the lies that are written about this generous and noble land. Tell the people of Latin America that the people of Cuba are not here in this Civic Plaza because they follow anybody, but that they are here for profound reasons, that the Cuban people are here because since the revolutionary government began, we have fulfilled our promises to the people and the people are loyal to those who are loyal to them. The people have faith in those who have faith in them.

Let our sister nations know that here there is a Spartan people. Of us can be said what the gravestone said in the Pass of Thermopylae: "Go tell the world that here there lie 300 Spartans, who preferred to die rather than surrender."

That is what Latin America expects of us. That is what the world expects of us. And we will know how to respond to the friendship and the solidarity that we have received.

Soldiers of the Rebel Army, militia members, farmers, workers, students, young people, all of you, let us take a pledge together:

We raise our Cuban flags, we raise our rifles, we raise our machetes, to swear that we will keep our promise:

Patria o muerte! [Our homeland or death] [*Prolonged ovation with the masses holding flags, rifles, and machetes in the air*]

Against Bureaucracy and Sectarianism

March 26, 1962

NOTE: The fusion of the July 26 Movement, the People's Socialist Party (PSP), and the Revolutionary Directorate at the end of 1961, which created the Integrated Revolutionary Organizations (ORI), was an important step in forging the vanguard of Cuba's working class. However, the policies encouraged by the ORI's organization secretary, long-time PSP leader Aníbal Escalante, soon endangered the process of unification, posing a threat to the revolution itself.

Escalante began to appoint supporters of his from the old PSP — some of whom had been at best minimally involved in the struggle against Batista — to important posts in the party and state apparatus. At the same time he belittled the revolutionaries that had come from the other two organizations. A tolerant attitude toward special privileges for party members and government functionaries began to grow among this layer. The ORI units that were formed often had few ties to the workers.

On March 26, 1962, Castro gave a televised speech, printed below, criticizing Escalante and pointing to the dangers that bureaucracy and sectarianism posed for the revolution. The leadership subsequently removed Escalante from his post and reorganized the ORI. On Castro's proposal workers' assemblies were held throughout Cuba to nominate candidates for ORI membership. This procedure was to become standard in the future.

In May 1963, the ORI became the United Party of the Socialist Revolution, and in October 1965, the Communist Party of Cuba.

Escalante subsequently filled various diplomatic assignments in the Soviet Union and Eastern Europe. After returning to Cuba several years later, he organized a secret grouping composed of his former political associates, including two members of the Communist Party's Central Committee. This grouping — later termed the "microfaction" — disagreed with Cuba's revolutionary policies. But its members did not seek to have an organized discussion within the party about their differences. Instead they attempted to convince the governments of the Soviet Union and various Eastern European countries to put pressure on Cuba.

Despite repeated warnings to cease this activity they persisted in their course. In early 1968 Escalante and a number of his associates were ar-

rested, tried, and convicted for a series of acts, including distributing secret government documents and actively seeking to undermine Cuba's relations with other governments. Escalante was sentenced to fifteen years' imprisonment, serving most of his time on a state farm before his early release. He died in 1977.

The following are excerpts from Castro's 1962 speech. The complete text is contained in Selected Speeches of Fidel Castro, *(New York: Pathfinder Press, 1979).*

To begin with, I would like to refer to a saying of Lenin, that the attitude — that is to say, the seriousness of purpose — of a revolutionary party is measured, basically, by the attitude it takes toward its own errors. And in the same way, our seriousness of purpose as revolutionists and as members of the government will be measured by the attitude we take toward our own errors.

Of course, our enemies are always alert to know what those errors are. When those errors are made and are not subjected to self-criticism, our enemies take advantage of them. When those errors are made and are subjected to self-criticism, they may be used by the enemy, but in a very different way. Because in the former case our errors would not be corrected and in the latter they would be. That is why we have decided to take a forthright and serious attitude toward our own errors.

In this regard, the group of revolutionary comrades who had begun serving as members of the Directorate of the Integrated Revolutionary Organizations have been conducting a wide-ranging discussion. We have been making a serious analysis, an honest analysis, a deep analysis of this whole process, from January 1, 1959, to the present. We have been analyzing all that has been done, the good things that have been done and also the errors that have been made.

Accordingly, we have submitted to a process of analysis this whole stage of the formation of the Integrated Revolutionary Organizations. This is not a simple problem. This is not an unimportant problem because, simply, it has to do with the political power of the revolution; it has to do with the methods of the revolution; it has to do with the ideology of the revolution.

The revolution — everyone is aware of the characteristics of its whole development, of its origin, of the historic moment in which this victorious revolution takes place; of all the circumstances characterizing the process, of the forces which participated, of the different tendencies which struggled to make their point of view prevail within the revolutionary process. In short, all of this is common knowledge.

The revolution clashed with a variety of ideas that were established in our country, ideas which had been inculcated in our country by the forces of reaction, by the forces of imperialism; ideas which were spread by the enemies of progress. They were a whole series of false ideas, of conservative ideas, of counterrevolutionary ideas really, which had the strength of habit, which had the strength given them by years of existence. In some cases they had the strength imparted to them by decades of existence — or even of centuries.

These ideas had the strength of superstition. They had the strength of a series of conventional lies. They had the strength of a series of slogans which are given to the people as unquestionable truths, a series of dogmas of an economic nature, of a political nature, of a social nature, which had been inculcated for decades by the mass media, in books, in the universities, in the secondary schools, by the political parties which were beholden to the ruling classes.

The new ideas of the revolution clashed with the strength of all those ideas. Wherein lay the strength of the ideas of the revolution? Was it in the publicity which had been given to these ideas? Was it in the political parties which could have been organized to spread these ideas? Was it in the existing newspapers, on the radio and television stations? No. The strength of these new ideas, that is, of the revolutionary ideas, dwelt in the economic and social reality of our country. These ideas represented truths, truths which had to confront reality, truths which had to confront the lies of the enemies of the exploited classes, truths which simply had to win acceptance.

Why did the truths of the revolution win acceptance? They won acceptance simply because these truths, these ideas, answered the great desires of the masses; they answered the needs of the masses. And that is why all the lies began to crumble; why all the lies of the bourgeoisie began to crumble; why the lies of the reactionaries, of the landlords, of the imperialists, began to crumble. All their conventionalism, all their lies were slowly defeated by the overwhelming advance of the revolutionary ideas which represented the interests of the exploited masses.

But that marked a period of struggle, a difficult period of struggle. The masses were slowly won over to revolutionary ideas. In that struggle everyone took a position. Not everyone was won over to these revolutionary ideas. Some took a certain position toward revolutionary ideas and others took other positions, that is, depending on the revolutionary ideas. This is a process which cannot be cut short. This is a process in which opinions and the different classes of the nation cannot be sliced neatly because it is a very complicated one. It would be necessary to analyze the reasons why some reacted in one way and some in another.

Behind it all were class interests. The peasant, the worker, the poor citizen, the poor family, reacted according to their class interests. The rich, the latifundists, the owners of big stores, the bankers, those who had been educated in the ideas of the imperialists — ideas which more-over responded to their own interests — reacted differently.

And there were some who held opinions which were not in accord with the interests of their class. There were people of the poor, humble classes so confused by lies, by superstitions, that they reacted against their own class interests. There were people who, although they could not be considered as belonging to an exploited class, nevertheless reacted favorably toward the revolution. There were untold numbers of young people who were not yet politically well-grounded, but who pos-sessed an excellent attitude, great qualities — a great spirit of rebellion, a great sense of justice, of equality, a great understanding of the new, a great readiness to accept revolutionary ideas — who, however, had not developed sufficiently.

All these facts marked a great struggle; they marked a struggle be-tween ideas. Which ideas came out victorious? The revolutionary ideas were victorious; the ideas of the masses came out victorious; the new truths of the revolution came out victorious. All lies, all dogmatism, all falsehoods, all hypocrisy were defeated.

Does this mean that that struggle has ended? No, that struggle has not ended. The struggle assumes very different forms, very subtle forms at times. That is to say that in the first great battles between the new and the old ideas, the new ideas, the revolutionary ideas, have come out vic-torious over the old ideas.

The revolution became a powerful ideological movement. Revolu-tionary ideas slowly won the masses over. The Cuban people, in great numbers, began to accept revolutionary ideas, to uphold revolutionary ideas. That ardor, that rebelliousness, that sense of indignant protest against tyranny, against abuse, against injustice, was slowly converted into the firm revolutionary consciousness of our people.

Revolutionary ideas did not become the consciousness of a minority, of a group. They became the consciousness of the great masses of our people. Whoever doubts it, let him recall the Declaration of Havana, the Second Declaration of Havana, the presence there of a million Cubans; the enthusiasm with which those one million Cubans supported the rev-olutionary ideas, radical ideas, truly advanced ideas, contained in that Second Declaration of Havana; the enthusiasm with which they sup-ported them, the evidence of political judgment they displayed as they hailed the value of each sentence.*

What did this show? That the masses had become revolutionary; that

---

*The First and Second Declarations of Havana were each read to rallies of over one million people on September 2, 1960, and February 4, 1962, respec-tively. They laid out the need for revolution throughout Latin America.

the masses had embraced Marxist ideology; that the masses had embraced Marxism-Leninism. That was an unquestionable fact. The camps had been defined; the enemies had declared themselves as such; the laboring masses, the peasant, the student masses, the masses of the poor, the underprivileged masses of our nation, significant portions of the middle class, sections of the petty bourgeoisie, intellectual workers — made Marxist-Leninist ideas their own, made their own the struggle against imperialism, made their own the struggle for the socialist revolution.

That was not the product of a whim; that was not something which was imposed upon the masses. The revolutionary laws themselves, the very accomplishments of the revolution, began to win the masses over to the revolution. They began to convert the masses into revolutionary masses. There were a whole series of accomplishments which began with a series of laws that benefited the people. All the laws benefited: the reduction in telephone rates, the cancellation of the corrupt contracts which the companies had obtained under the protection of the tyranny; the urban reform laws, the rent laws, beginning with the laws reducing rent and then the reduction of the price of building plots, then the urban reform law; then there were the agrarian reform laws; then the laws nationalizing foreign businesses and later the laws nationalizing large businesses. These became milestones marking the course of the revolution, marking the advance of the revolution, of the people.

The people developed rapidly — the people became more revolutionary by the day. When the danger of invasion began to threaten our country, when it even was thought possible that an attack would be made by the powerful forces of imperialism, when we became aware of that danger — because we will have to consider the possibility of such an attack for a long time to come — the people were mobilized. They became members of the militia. Thousands upon thousands of young men became antiaircraft artillerymen; thousands upon thousands of workers, of poor people, became antitank gunners and artillerymen of various types; hundreds and thousands of men and women enrolled in the battalions. They enrolled in the combat units and they prepared to fight, if necessary, one of the greatest battles, one of the most heroic which any people could engage in.

This means that our people were prepared to take all the risks, to suffer all the consequences of their revolutionary stand, to oppose imperialism resolutely, without wavering. They were all willing to die, if necessary, in defense of the revolution and in defense of the homeland. Who will deny the enthusiasm with which the masses carried out many tasks, such as volunteering for work? They responded to every call that was made to them, to every mass meeting, to every patriotic gathering, to every revolutionary gathering.

So that when the cowardly attack of April 17 — or of April 15 came, when airplanes, which came from foreign bases attacked various places in our country; when we went to bury those comrades who had died that day, as we had gone before to bury other comrades, as we had done a few months before to bury the victims of the steamer *La Coubre*,* other victims of reaction, of imperialism, of the reactionaries, of the exploiters; on the eve of the battle with the imperialists — for it was not done after the battle — the socialist character of the revolution was announced; we proclaimed what was already a fact.

And who can deny it — the overwhelming enthusiasm with which the masses of workers assembled there and formed into militia battalions, raised their rifles and resolved to fight, resolved to give combat? Who can deny the heroism with which the soldiers, members of the militia, men and women, fought? Who can deny the heroism with which the people fought the mercenaries at Playa Girón? Who can deny the selflessness, the disregard for their lives, which the men showed when they threw themselves against tanks, against enemy machineguns, as they advanced steadily across open terrain, in the face of danger from enemy bombers, advancing steadily in the face of the enemy's air attacks, despite casualties and deaths caused in their ranks by the enemy's aircraft and the enemy's shells? Who can deny this? A look at the number on the casualty list will suffice to make us understand the enthusiasm and selflessness with which the masses threw themselves into the fight. There they were, filled with enthusiasm, fighting consciously for the socialist revolution.

What does this mean? This means that a great qualitative change had taken place in the masses: they had become revolutionary masses. That is a positive fact, an undeniable fact. Whoever doesn't see it that way is nearsighted. Whoever doesn't see it that way is blind. Whoever doesn't see it that way is simply an idiot.

If that was a truth which was self-evident, could we then apply methods which were applicable to other conditions? Could we convert into a system those methods which the needs of the struggle in a specific phase demanded — could we convert that into a system? Could we turn that policy into a system? Could we turn those methods for the selection of comrades for various administrative posts into a system? We could not turn those methods into a system!

It is unquestionable, and dialectics teaches us, that what in a given moment is a correct method, later on may be an incorrect one. That is what dialectics teaches us. Anything else is dogmatism, mechanism. It is a desire to apply measures which were determined by our special

---

La Coubre, a French merchant ship carrying ammunition from Belgium, was blown up in Havana Harbor March 4, 1960, killing 100 people.

needs at a given moment to another situation in which the needs are different, in which other circumstances prevail. And we turned certain methods into a system and we fell into a frightful sectarianism.

What sectarianism? Well, the sectarianism of believing that the only revolutionists, that the only comrades who could hold positions of trust, that the only ones who could hold a post on a people's farm, on a cooperative, in the government, anywhere, had to be old Marxist militants. We fell into that error partly unconsciously; or at least it seemed that all those problems brought about by sectarianism were problems which were the product of unconscious forces, that they came about with a fatal inevitability, that it was a virus, that it was an evil which had become lodged in the minds of many people, and that it was difficult to combat. It was truly difficult to combat until that virus manifested itself as a disease.

There are those who suffer from the flu, but it has been incubating inside of them for ten days and they become aware of it only when they are unable to speak. There are those who incubate a tetanus infection — I don't know if for fifteen or twenty days, the doctors should know how long it takes — they carry it inside of them but they never receive a single injection until the moment the infection manifests itself, until the moment they are already suffering from the disease.

We often asked ourselves: What could be the reason? Where lies the reason for that implacable, untiring, systematic, sectarian spirit which is found everywhere, which is found on all levels, which is found wherever one goes? What are the causes, the roots of this sectarian spirit? For it was difficult to believe that that spirit sprang inevitably solely from a series of circumstances.

The comrade who was authorized — it is not known whether he was invested with the authority or whether he assumed it of his own accord, or whether it was because he had slowly begun to assume leadership on that front, and as a result found himself in charge of the task of organizing, or of working as the secretary in charge of organization of the Integrated Revolutionary Organizations. The one who enjoyed everyone's confidence, who acted with the prestige given him by the revolution, who, while speaking with the authority of the revolution because he spoke in its name and in the name of the other comrades of the revolution, the one who despite this fell, who regrettably, most regrettably, fell into the errors we have been enumerating, was the Comrade Aníbal Escalante.

This is not an easy task for anyone. It is not an easy matter for us to discuss and to explain all of these problems. Does it pain us? Of course it does. We cannot look upon Aníbal Escalante as we have upon other men who once were part of the revolution and then betrayed it.

Aníbal Escalante was a Communist for many years. In our opinion he was a true Communist, an honest Communist. Has Aníbal Escalante become an anticommunist? A capitalist? No. A proimperialist? He has not become a proimperialist. Has he betrayed the revolution by going over to the enemy's camp? No, he has not betrayed the revolution by going over to the enemy's camp.

Aníbal Escalante has for a long time been our comrade in carrying out tasks related to the direction of the revolution. It has been more difficult still for those who, being Communists, worked closely with him not for one, not for two, not for three but for ten, twenty years; during years that were difficult ones for the Communists, when the harassment was great, when they were heavily attacked, when the slanders were many, when the campaigns, the efforts to isolate them, to surround them, to destroy them were great. Anyone can understand what I mean by seeing how Communists are treated in the United States today. How their leaders are treated. The Communist worker loses his job; he is persecuted; they try to starve him to death. Or they do to him what they did to Henry Winston, who was locked up, mistreated, until, in a display of hypocritical kindness, he was released from jail — a blind man, physically destroyed. You all know how in the capitalist countries Communists are treated with hate, with cruelty.

Aníbal Escalante passed through that whole period and saw his fondest dreams, what he had only seen as a hope, as an ideal of his worthy ideas, as an opportunity to transform our country from a semicolonial country, oppressed by imperialism and capitalism, into a socialist country. He saw all this come true. Nevertheless, Aníbal Escalante erred. Aníbal Escalante, the Communist, made grave mistakes. But this should not surprise us for the Communists are human and they make errors! Is this perhaps the first time? No, the Communists have erred many times. Throughout the history of the movement, of the very international communist movement from the time that it sprang forth in the ideas and in the books, in the efforts and in the work of Marx and Engels, until the time that under Lenin it succeeded in establishing the first workers' government, it made great mistakes.

Many deserted Marxism, many attempted to revise Marxism; many made incorrect applications of Marxism. Leninism is necessarily forged in the struggle against the revisionists, against the pseudo-Marxists or mistaken Marxists.

Being a man like any other and, like any other human being, prone to error, Comrade Aníbal Escalante made great mistakes.

We reached the conclusion, we were all convinced, that Comrade Aníbal Escalante, abusing the faith placed in him, in his post as secretary in charge of organization, followed a non-Marxist policy, followed a policy which departed from Leninist norms regarding the organization of a workers' vanguard party, and that he tried to organize an apparatus to pursue personal ends.

We believe that Comrade Aníbal Escalante has had a lot to do with the conversion of sectarianism into a system, with the conversion of sectarianism into a virus, into a veritable sickness during this process.

Comrade Aníbal Escalante is the one responsible for having promoted the sectarian spirit to its highest possible level, of having promoted that sectarian spirit for personal reasons, with the purpose of establishing an organization which he controlled. He is the one responsible for introducing, in addition, a series of methods within that organization which were leading to the creation not of a party — as we were saying — but rather of a tyranny, a straitjacket.

We believe that Aníbal Escalante's actions in these matters were not the product of oversight nor were they unconscious, but rather that they were deliberate and conscious. He simply allowed himself to be blinded by personal ambition. And as a result of this, he created a series of problems, in a word, he created veritable chaos in the nation.

Why? It's very simple. The idea of organizing the United Party of the Socialist Revolution, the idea of organizing a vanguard, a vanguard party, a workers' party, meets with the greatest acceptance among the masses. Marxism has the full support of the masses; Marxism-Leninism is the ideology of the Cuban people.

The establishment of the Marxist-Leninist party as the workers' vanguard party has the full support of the people. The people approve the principle that that party should have the direction of the revolution in its hands. The people accept this basic principle of Marxism-Leninism. In such a situation, when all the people accept this principle, it was very easy to convert that apparatus, already accepted by the people, into an instrument for the pursuit of one's personal ambitions. The prestige of the ORI was immense. Any order, any directive coming from the ORI was obeyed by all. But the ORI was not the ORI.

Comrade Aníbal Escalante had schemed to make himself the ORI. How? By the use of a very simple contrivance. Working from his post as secretary in charge of organization he would give instructions to all revolutionary cells and to the whole apparatus as if these instructions had come from the National Directorate. And he began to encourage them in the habit of receiving instructions from there, from the offices of the secretary in charge of organization of the ORI, instructions which were obeyed by all as if they had come from the National Directorate. But at the same time he took advantage of the opportunity to establish a system of controls which would be completely under his command.

This policy was accompanied by that sectarianism which had been encouraged to the limit, a sectarianism which tended to create conditions favorable to the achievement of those aims. And being in a position to carry it out, since he also had the task of individually organizing all the revolutionary cells, a policy of license was encouraged rather than one of discipline, restraint, strict adherence to standards on the part of the organization's militants. Rather than this, a policy of permissiveness was encouraged. Since a correct policy, adjusted to those functions proper to a workers' vanguard party, did not fit with these plans, a policy of privilege was promoted. He was creating conditions and giving instructions which tended to convert that apparatus not into an apparatus of the workers' vanguard, but rather into a nest of privilege, into one which tolerated favoritism, into a system of immunities and favors. Slowly he began to pervert completely the role of the apparatus.

In other words, the predominance and preponderance of the nucleus had to be created.* There had to be a confusion of ideas. The idea is that the Marxist party gives guidance, that the workers' vanguard Marxist party directs the state, a leadership which it can exercise only through the use of certain channels, and after receiving guidance emanating from the National Directorate. He attempted to establish a directorate on all levels. That is, something more than a directorate on all levels: a participation of the political apparatus in administrative matters, on all levels whence, with a frightful, deplorable, and shameful confusion, the criterion was established that the nucleus gave all orders, that the nucleus could name and remove administrative personnel, that the nucleus governed.

And, as a result, a veritable chaos, a veritable anarchy was being introduced into the nation.

That, of course, is far removed from the idea of a workers' vanguard party, of a Marxist-Leninist party.

On the other hand, on the level of the secretary in charge of organization, it already was impossible for a minister to change an official or to change an administrator without having to call the office of the ORI, because of habits which the comrade — by deceiving government officials, by making them think that he was acting under instructions from the National Directorate — tried to establish and succeeded in establishing to a large degree.

The nuclei decided and governed on all levels. When a ministry faced a problem, instead of solving it themselves, they would refer it to the ORI. This was so much so that if a cat gave birth to a litter of four kittens it was necessary to refer the matter to the ORI so they might decide upon it.

In other words, there no longer was a subject, a question, a detail, which did not first have to be discussed in the offices of the ORI. And

---

*The nucleus was the basic unit of the ORI (and later of the Communist Party of Cuba), existing in workplaces, military units, etc.

many ministers would go there to discuss their problems; and undersecretaries no longer discussed the ministry's problems with the minister, instead they went to the offices of the ORI; and a security officer would no longer go to the offices of the security force, he went instead to the ORI.

Because of this there developed form top to bottom — don't imagine that this happened in a matter of weeks, it took months to develop — a truly abnormal, truly absurd, intolerable, chaotic, anarchic process; people were possessed of a mania for giving orders, of an eagerness to decide all problems.

And what was the nucleus? Was it a nucleus of revolutionists? The nucleus was a mere shell of revolutionists, well versed in dispensing favors, which appointed and removed officials. And, as a result of this, it was not going to enjoy the prestige which a revolutionary nucleus should enjoy, a prestige born solely from the authority which it has in the eyes of the masses, an authority imparted to it by the example which its members set as workers, as model revolutionists. Instead of coming from these sources, the authority of the nucleus came from the fact that from it one might receive or expect a favor, some dispensation, or some harm or good. And as was to be expected, around the nucleus conditions were being created for the formation of a coterie of fawners, which has nothing to do with Marxism or socialism.

And chaos reigned under those conditions. These are not the functions of the revolutionary nucleus. This is a perversion of the principles of Marxism-Leninism. This is a frightful confusion of socialist ideas. To begin with, this serves to create chaos, disaster, a monstrosity. A workers' Marxist-Leninist party directs the state, but it exercises this through proper channels; it exercises direction of the state through the National Directorate of that party, which has jurisdiction over the political apparatus and the public administration.

What is the function of the party? To orient. It orients on all levels; it does not govern on all levels. It fosters the revolutionary consciousness of the masses. It is the link with the masses. It educates the masses in the ideas of socialism and communism. It encourages the masses to work, to strong endeavor, to defend the revolution. It spreads the ideas of the revolution. It supervises, controls, guards, informs. It discusses what has to be discussed. But it does not have authority to appoint and to remove officials.

It is to be expected that if the revolutionary nucleus has within it the best laborers, the best workers, then it is logical that when an administrator wants to choose a foreman or someone for any type of responsible position, he will find that person within the nucleus, because the nucleus will have gathered the most competent, the best. But the choosing will be done by the administrator, not by the nucleus. The nucleus does not have to choose officials. This is something which we learned to expect from the PAU [United Action Party], from the PUR [Revolutionary Unity Party], from the old Liberal Party, from the Conservative Party, from any old corrupt political party.* But this is something which we do not expect from a workers' vanguard party. This is, simply, a reinfection of old political vices which our nation has lived through. This is not the responsibility of the nucleus.

The best revolutionists, the best workers, should be in the nucleus. The party should not weaken itself in order to buttress the state apparatus. The state apparatus must develop its own officials from the ranks. It does not have to have recourse to the nuclei in the people's farms, in the cooperatives. It does not have to bring in the official from the outside; that person should simply be promoted from among the workers.

In any group of five hundred workers, anyone may be sure of finding at least five generals, ten musicians, twenty artists. The fact is that in any mass of workers one will find an infinite variety of intelligence, of talents, of merit.

Where is the person who considers himself a Marxist who can deny that among the masses one will find represented all forms of human values, all human resources, all intellectual capacities? And who will believe that the possessors of these intellectual capacities, of these merits, must be promoted by the nucleus? The nuclei must work with all the masses. They must educate the masses. But when a personnel manager is to be appointed, when an important post is to be filled, there is no need to go to the nucleus for it to pick him. He must be picked from among the masses; he must be promoted!

That is the task of the manager; that is the task of the state administration. The personnel for the functioning of the state must be chosen from the masses themselves, and all work centers should choose their personnel from the masses of workers; they should base the promotions of their managers on the qualities they display as workers, according to their abilities. If not, it would become a problem of political chicanery, it would become a prize which someone could award. The nuclei would begin to be infested with flatterers and fawners, with position seekers. That is not the function of the nucleus! The nucleus has other tasks. Its tasks are different from those of state administration. The party directs; it directs through the party as a whole, and it directs through the governmental apparatus.

Today an official must have authority. A minister must have authority, an administrator must have authority. He must be able to discuss

*These were some of the bourgeois political parties that existed during Batista's rule.

whatever is necessary with the Technical Advisory Council. He must be able to discuss with the masses of workers; with the nucleus. But the administrator must decide; the responsibility must be his.

The party, through its National Directorate, endows the administrative personnel with authority. But in order to demand an accounting from them, it must endow them with true authority. If it is the nucleus which decides, if it decides at the provincial level, or at the level of the work center, or at the local level, how then can we make the minister responsible for these decisions? He cannot be made responsible because he has no power.

The minister has the power to appoint, to remove, to appoint within the norms established by the rules and the laws of the nation. But at the same time he is charged with responsibility; he is responsible to the political administration of the revolution for his actions, for his work. In a word, he must give an accounting of his stewardship. Now, to give an accounting he must have powers.

In Cuba, as a result of this chaos, of this irregularity, of this monstrosity, no minister, no official, no administrator had power. He had to go to the nucleus to discuss it. And we are going to give an example of this which Comrade Carlos Rafael Rodríguez gave me today.

He found it necessary to remove — a matter which we discussed, but which did not need to be discussed — to remove the person in charge of a corporation, the Meat Corporation, because he considered him incompetent, for he was a person who really had the ability to manage only a small business, and did not have the ability required to handle the responsibilities of a gigantic undertaking like the Meat Corporation. What happened? He called him in; he informed him that he would be sent to another job which was more in consonance with his abilities. And what did the comrade do? He went to the nucleus in the INRA [National Institute of Agrarian Reform] to charge that a grave injustice had been done him, and to demand that the matter be discussed with Carlos Rafael.

What a fix we'd be in! I mean that our goose would be cooked if we followed such procedures! What a sorry mix-up! To do this is to mistake the nucleus for a clique of gossipers. To do this is to mistake the nucleus for a privileged gang, for dispensers of patronage. And that habit of thinking had been introduced into the Integrated Revolutionary Organizations.

No minister could decide anything, because if the matter was not discussed with the nucleus, the offices of the ORI would have to be called. Can we imagine such a monstrosity? Can we imagine such an absurdity? Comrades, can we imagine such a mess?

Things must be called by their right names. This does not mean that we are speaking with hate, nor harshly about anyone. We should analyze, censure, criticize seriously all these things.

It is logical to expect that the enemy will take advantage of these errors to sow confusion, to go about saying that the Communists have taken over; that Fidel had been replaced by Blas [Roca] or by Aníbal, or by someone else, and Raúl by another, and so on about everyone else.

Comrades, our enemies take advantage of our own errors, our enemies take advantage of our own stupidities. Do you want to know the reason for all those rumors? It was that obsession with command, that mania for giving orders, that mania for governing which took possession of a certain comrade together with a sectarianism promoted to unheard of extremes.

Was this power real? No, it was not a real power; it was a power in form only; it was a fictitious power. There was no real power in the hands of that comrade. Fortunately, there was no real power! The real power did not rest there. The real power of the revolution cannot simply be usurped in that fashion. It cannot be circumvented in that way, comrades. That is a ridiculous and idiotic attempt at circumvention!

But behind that there plainly was an obvious intent. Of course, that type of evil cannot be developed in our country because our country is not prone to being meek or to being tamed. Nor are revolutionists so inclined — the large number of revolutionary comrades. But through the use of deception, the attempt was made to create conditions suitable for permitting the imposition of a tyranny, of a straitjacket, of an apparatus for the serving of personal ends which, later on, would wipe out the old and new values of the revolution.

When a whole people becomes revolutionary, when a whole people, that is to say, when the immense majority of our people, embraces Marxism-Leninism, how absurd is it then to fall into the sectarianism of the "old militants"; to boast about the number of years of one's militancy; to see it manifest itself in the work centers! And then for everyone to become aware that it was more than a verbal sectarianism, that in order to hold a post of personnel director, to be able to fill certain posts in factories or in offices, the best-paid jobs, one had to belong to that sect. I do not mean by this that I am calling the old Marxist-Leninist party a sect; rather I call the spirit which they created, or which was created after integration, the spirit of a sect.

What hope remained for the great mass of laborers, for the great mass of workers? What kind of situation did millions of citizens find themselves in? For, while the old Communists had been only a few thousand, the people, who had embraced the cause of Marxism-Leninism, had been integrated by the millions.

It requires little intelligence — if a little is all one has — to realize that application of such a policy upon someone's flaunting his record of militancy, accompanied by the fact that lack of that stamp of approval in that sect was enough to leave people without the least hope of being chosen for anything, either for a post as technician, for a responsible post on a state farm, on a cooperative, in municipal or provincial government, in the JUCEI [Coordination, Application, and Inspection Council], or in the national government. The folly, the idiocy, the negative nature, and the stupidity of such a policy then became obvious.

To what did such a state of affairs give rise? To vanity, to a domination of influence, to privilege. What would this engender but conditions which would earn the old Communists the antipathy and the suspicion of the masses? What else would it produce but the conditions which, moreover, were going to lead an old Communist to take the wrong course, the wrong road in his life, in his work, in his attitude?

Add to this the indulgence of errors. Add to this the fact that if an old Communist made mistakes, nothing was done to him; he was not removed from his post, nor was he disciplined in any way; on the contrary, his errors were tolerated, no matter what the error, the abuse, or the injustice committed.

Of course, that was not a policy applied to the masses, nor was it generalized, but it was an established method for the indulgence of all faults: to create a caste spirit, to create a clique spirit, because all of that fitted very well with a policy which aimed at creating an apparatus for the satisfaction of personal ambitions and aims. It is evident that not only was the privilege of a sect created but also indulgence of all faults; comrades were appointed to many posts who, in many cases, lacked the capacity to fill them. This was not so in other cases, let us be fair.

Those were the results. It was natural that a feeling of great personal power was created, and this was so much so that some comrades had lost all sense of control. They imagined that they had won the revolution in a raffle. At least, that is the way they acted, forgetting the blood which was spilled, the sacrifices which this revolution had cost.

Very well, then. How could such things happen in a party? There you have that matter which has been discussed so much, the problem of the cult of personality. Perhaps an example of what we, or at least of what I understand as the cult of personality could serve as the subject of a good lesson for political instructors to give the troops and for principals to give in the schools, which has nothing to do with the prestige of the leaders, which has nothing to do with the authority of the leaders, as it seems that some, thinking in reverse, have thought. Who thought about the things that were happening, things which were not so difficult to see? Recently, we could, at least, see this phenomenon in operation. Most likely there were some who thought that these problems had to do with us; who thought that we had to be watched to see if we were likely to fall into the errors of the cult of personality.

Of course, such an idea, such a doubt, never entered our minds, because we know that those problems do not exist in our country, rather the reverse. Now I ask myself: Why did we argue so much about this problem, if we were incapable of seeing what was happening before our noses? Certainly this problem did not arise from the danger that the prime minister of the revolutionary government would allow himself to be seduced by the cult of personality.

Whether we wanted to or not, even if we ourselves did not want to, they do not interest us, honestly; those problems do not interest us personally. They interest us only from the point of view of whether or not they can do harm or good to the revolution, whether they can be useful or useless to the people, to the present generation, the coming generations.

But for the benefit of those through whose minds there might pass the thought that we could even remotely be suspect of having such inclinations, it is good to recall certain deeds, certain deeds as evidenced by the fact that we waged a war, we led it, we won it, and there are no general's stars on our shoulders and no medals hang from our chests. And the first law that we proposed when we assumed governmental power prohibited the erection of statues — these problems related to the cult of personality were not discussed as much then as they are now — but out of deep conviction we proposed prohibiting the erection of statues of living persons, naming streets after living persons and, what is more, that the placing of our portraits in government offices be prohibited by law. This we did from deep conviction, from deep revolutionary conviction. Was this demagogy? No. We acted this way from profound revolutionary conviction.

Great responsibilities fell on our shoulders. The masses of our country placed great powers in our hands which we have shared with others as it was fitting that we should do, as it was correct for us to do, as it was our duty to do.

I believe sincerely and firmly in the principles of collective leadership but no one forced me to do so, rather it came from a deep and personal conviction, a conviction with which I have known how to comply. I believe what I said on December 2:* I believe in collective leadership; I believe that history is written by the masses; I believe that when the best opinions, the opinions of the most competent men, the most capable men, are discussed collectively, that they are cleansed of their vices, of their errors, of their weaknesses, of their faults. I also believe that neither the history of countries, nor the lives of nations, should be de-

---

*On the night of December 2, 1961, Castro gave a televised speech declaring his adherence to Marxism-Leninism and outlining the principles for the Integrated Revolutionary Organizations.

pendent on individuals, on men, on personalities. I state that which I firmly believe.

Why do I make this clear? Very well, because we have also made, among others, this error. We have many things to discuss about the problems of Marxism, about the whole rich and vital history of Marxism, about the struggle of Marxism against the revisionists, against the perverters of its principles. We have much to learn from Lenin, much to learn from the history of Marxism from its beginnings to the present day.

Many times in the schools, in many places we have discussed this same subject of the cult of personality excessively, to our way of thinking. Not because it bothers us, comrades. As far as we are concerned people can discuss these problems till they breathe their last; it doesn't bother us.

But I ask myself the following question: Why have we been discussing a problem so much which was not our problem but the Soviet Union's? All right. We should be well informed. We should inform, discuss, if they are problems which have to do with the experience of Marxism, but we didn't have to turn it into the central theme of our discussions. For we have much more important things to discuss and this means that we are doing something like the following: that we are waging a campaign against the bubonic plague when, instead of the bubonic plague, there is malaria and poliomyelitis. It is true we don't want to be attacked by the bubonic plague, and we should be vaccinated against it and take the necessary measures and, in addition, we should know what the bubonic plague is. But when we have to fight we should fight against malaria and poliomyelitis, which are the actual and present ills.

Those evils have not been a threat in our country. The only danger there was was the one we did not see. How blind we were! What a difference between theory and practice! What a good lesson! Much discussion was conducted on a subject while, all the time, we ran the risk of misleading many people and yet, no matter how much we discussed the subject, we did not see the evil that was close by.

Many were saying: "The cult of personality — is the same thing going to happen here as in the Soviet Union? Could the prime minister be one of those who will have to be watched to prevent his falling into the evils of the cult of personality?"

Very well. I don't think that there was a show of bad faith in this, nor anything like it. I am sure that the problem here was not one of a lack of information. These matters were amply discussed. But the point is that there are many people around who are on the wrong track; there are many people who are confused as to what are the most timely subjects, the most basic. We lack skills; we exercise no care and we get off the right track. That is why we take the wrong train.

To my mind many of those rumors, all those campaigns, and this whole problem that was taking shape within our country has to do, in part, with the undue discussion of a subject which should not have been the principal subject of our discussion.

And it is clear that what took place in an unconscious and spontaneous manner aided in the creation of the other problem, of the other phenomenon: the destruction of the prestige of the revolution. Why? For the more prestige the revolution has, so much the better; the more voices the revolution possesses that speak with authority, so much the better. For it is not the same to have a choral group of ten people as it is to have one of three hundred. When you see a choral group of ten members it is good, but one of three hundred voices is much better, more beautiful, more excellent. If we have one leader, two, ten, with prestige, we should have more leaders with prestige. We should not destroy those leaders who have prestige. What happens if we destroy them? Then, unfortunately, when difficult times come the people do not have anyone in whom to believe. When we have to face situations similar or worse to what we faced at Playa Girón, when all at once we have to face situations ten times worse than what we faced at Playa Girón, then we have to speak with the people; we have to appeal to the people's faith.

And what do we gain by sowing the slightest doubt? What do we gain by destroying the prestige of the revolution?

Of course, I do not place the least blame on any honest revolutionist, on any of the many comrades, on any of those who have spoken on this subject. No, but I understand, comrades, that conditions were being created that, unfortunately, that discussion . . . the same thing would result if we started now discussing things which must be discussed later on. For to discuss them now would cause damage. They would not be in consonance with present needs.

Later on we will discuss other problems which existed at the time those discussions were undertaken for, unfortunately, they coincided with certain campaigns which were directed against certain comrades, campaigns which were being conducted in a very subtle manner, certain campaigns that were directed against the prestige of certain well-known and very valuable comrades which sprang from the same problem that we have posed; a series of subtle campaigns directed against a number of very valuable comrades of the revolution, conducted, comrades, by those who were promoting the same sectarian policy.

How did this affect the masses? Well, clearly this discouraged the masses. Did this turn the masses against the revolution? No, the masses did not turn against the revolution, the masses are with the revolution and they will always be with the revolution, in spite of errors. But this cooled the enthusiasm of the masses; this cooled the fervor of the masses.

How did this affect the political organization of the revolution? Very simply, comrades. We were not creating an organization; I already said that we were preparing a yoke, a straitjacket. I'm going to go a little further: we were creating a mere shell of an organization. How? The masses had not been integrated. We speak here of the Integrated Revolutionary Organizations. It was an organization composed of the militants of the People's Socialist Party.

The rest of the organizations, the Student Directorate, the July 26 Movement, what were they? Were they organizations which had an old organized membership? No. They were organizations which had great mass support, they had an overwhelming mass support. That is what the July 26 Movement was; that is what the other organizations were. They enjoyed great prestige, great popularity. These people were not organized into an organization.

If we are going to form an organization, an integration, and we do not integrate the masses, we will not be integrating anything; we will be falling into a sectarianism like that we fell into.

Then how were the nuclei formed? I'm going to tell you how. In every province the general secretary of the PSP was made general secretary of the ORI; in all the nuclei, the general secretary of the PSP was made general secretary of the ORI; in every municipality, the general secretary of the PSP was made general secretary of the ORI; in every nucleus, the general secretary — the member of the PSP — was made general secretary of the nucleus. Is that what you would call integration? Comrade Aníbal Escalante is responsible for that policy.

What resulted from this? What consequences did it have? All that we have done to fight against anticommunism, the ideological struggle, the incessant explaining, which slowly destroyed anticommunism — for anticommunism, as we ourselves have said, engendered sectarianism in its turn, because the isolated, harassed Marxist-Leninists tended to protect themselves closely within their own organization, to shut themselves up in their organization.

Very well. Those are the consequences of anticommunism, of harassment; they engender sectarianism. Once anticommunism is wiped out, if extreme sectarianism still remains, it will once again give rise to anticommunism and to confusion. Because many people will ask: "Is this communism? Is this Marxism? Is this socialism? This arbitrariness, this abuse, this privilege, all this, is this communism?"

"If this is communism," they will say along with the Indian Hatuey, "then . . . " When the Indian Hatuey was being burned at the stake, a priest came up to him to ask him if he wanted to go to heaven, and he said, "No, I don't want to go to heaven if heaven is all of this." Do you understand me? I have to speak clearly.

No one should have the slightest doubt, and I think that anyone who has it now must be completely crazy — let's use that word. At the present time I must speak with extraordinary objectivity, but with an extraordinary objectivity, frankness, loyalty, honesty, keeping back nothing. Because we will make sure that our words will not be misunderstood, comrades.

Very well then, that sectarianism fosters anticommunism anew. What Marxist-Leninist mind could think of employing — when the socialist revolution is in power — the methods employed when Marxism-Leninism was not in power, when it was completely surrounded and isolated? To isolate oneself from the masses when one is in power, that is madness. It is another matter to be isolated by the ruling classes, by the exploiters, when the latifundists and the imperialists are in power; but to be divorced from the masses when the workers, the peasants, when the working class is in power, is a crime. Then sectarianism becomes counterrevolutionary because it weakens and harms the revolution.

What should be the ideal of a Marxist-Leninist? "These are my ideals, this is my cause." For many years we were but a handful — ten thousand, fifteen thousand, those who were truly Marxist-Leninists. How then, at the very time in which that same cause, his cause, his standard, his ideal, is the ideal of three million Cubans, is he going to isolate himself from the masses and act exactly as he did when there were five thousand, ten thousand, or fifteen thousand? That is a gigantic error. To fall into an error of that nature is a crime, a counterrevolutionary crime. How can we do that when we can count on the strength of the masses?

The organizational framework for those masses must be built. That framework must be built with new forces, with new cadres, not with a reduced number of cadres as when the organization was very small, when the Marxist-Leninist party had a few thousand adherents. When Marxism-Leninism has millions of adherents in our country, the framework for those millions must be built. To do otherwise is, as we have said on other occasions, like wanting to empty the Cauto River — I mean, like wanting to empty the Amazon River into the Cauto River, like wanting to empty a vat into a cask and like wanting to build a forty-story building on top of a building having only two stories. It would come crashing down, comrades! It would mean isolation from the masses!

And we have fallen into that error. From the Marxist-Leninist point of view that is a grave error, an unforgivable error, an error which must be corrected.

What was the result of this? Very simply. The organization of the revolutionary nuclei was begun, but the nuclei were secret; they were secret. Can you conceive of secret contacts with the masses? And can you conceive of forming a secret nucleus exactly as it would have been formed under Batista: That is to say, nuclei which the masses did not know?

And then, what did we do? Well, in a work center with 5,000 workers we had a nucleus with seven members. Begging Comrade [José] Llanusa's pardon I am going to cite the case of the Sports Palace.

Garrucho and two women to whom he gave employment — Who is Garrucho? We are not going to argue over who Garrucho was. Garrucho was elected councilman on the PUR ticket in the year 1954. Then the branch of the People's Socialist Party of Regla made an error, to our way of thinking — we should speak with frankness for we are neither accusing nor blaming anyone, nor anything like it. Let us forget all that. Now we should all speak about all things without prejudice, without vacillation. They erred because he repented, because the man said that he was willing to resign. And then he was made a member of the People's Socialist Party. Well, then he was allowed to remain at his post. I don't know, but to my mind that was a wrong tactic for the branch to use — it was the branch, not the party — but the fact is that that man filled the post of councilman up to the very thirty-first of December [1958].

Then all of a sudden, in spite of the hatred in which the councilmen of the PAU and the PUR were held, and all that had anything to do with them, we find that man promoted from councilman — hero of the PUR to revolutionary leader. Very well. This could be explained. It was the result of an error. It is undeniable that it was an error to admit him. It is the same as — well, why should I cite examples? I have one but I do not want to remember those poor people now, for I am going to hurt them for no reason at all.

Well then, Garrucho ended up in the INDER [National Institute of Sports, Physical Education, and Recreation]. He brought a secretary and another girl to work there. I believe they are excellent girls; nothing is known against them. And there Garrucho turned out to be an important functionary. He was sent from the office of the provincial government or from who-knows-where to Llanusa and he was given an important post.

When we went to see the kind of nucleus that the INDER had, we found that it consisted of seven members out of four hundred employees. And there were twenty or thirty excellent, superb people, and they were only seven: Garrucho, the two women, Llanusa, his secretary, and two old Communists, Ezequiel Herrera and Pancho López. That was the nucleus. That was our contact with the masses there, our secret contact with a mass consisting of four hundred employees. Would you call that a political apparatus?

Very well, Llanusa formed part of the nucleus because he was Llanusa and he was the director of the INDER, and I believe that Comrade Llanusa has a right to belong to the nucleus. As to the secretary, well I believe she belonged because she was Llanusa's secretary, although I understand that she is an excellent girl. But there were others who were not lucky enough to be Llanusa's secretary. There were other excellent girls there but since they did not enter with Garrucho they could not form part of the nucleus. And there were two old Communists there. One, Ezequiel Herrera, an excellent worker, who was proclaimed as a model worker there by the masses. What a joy, what a feeling of satisfaction we experienced when we saw a member of the nucleus proclaimed there a model worker by the masses! That was Ezequiel Herrera. Pancho López was also proclaimed a model worker. I understand that he ended up there after a bit of trouble in the G-2 [security police] or some other place. But Pancho was also there. They say that he is a good comrade. But he was there in the nucleus. He was one of the "seven privileged ones of the nucleus."

And who was Ezequiel Herrera? They say that Garrucho himself had proposed replacing him with one of his own cousins even though he was an old militant. That is what Comrade Llanusa told me. I don't know if he will confirm it. We are not going to — everything that is said here, has good witnesses to support it, so there is no danger that we are going to invent anything here.

Then we went to Ambar Motors. Now Ambar Motors is a place which has a larger proportion of workers than the INDER does. We were going to have a meeting. The nine-member nucleus had been formed there also. Well, what is the use of talking?

The nucleus consisted of nine members using the same system: the comrade director, the secretary of the director, the director's brother-in-law. Of course, I want to point out that the director's brother-in-law is a good comrade who is recognized as such by the workers there, but it comes to the same thing.

We went there to exchange a few opinions with the members of the nucleus and out came the head of personnel, in a work center like that one, which is filled with workers dressed in sweatshirts and overalls smeared with grease, a head of personnel wearing a "cute" shirt with loud colors and a pair of white pants. And he was a member of the nucleus! What the blazes! They were completely separated from the masses.

What happened? The following happened: they took out the old militants and made them part of the administration — head of personnel, director. Later, when they formed the nucleus — since they once again made use of the old militants — they made that commission of directors a part of the nucleus. The members of the nucleus were old militants and all were directors. There was no one from the masses in the nucleus. It was an administration nucleus.

These examples illustrate the errors we have committed. Well, what was happening as a result of these things? The Ministry of Industry rewards sixty to one hundred workers every month; of the present sixty, only five were members of the revolutionary nuclei. The average runs from five to ten members of the revolutionary nuclei. Five to ten percent out of every one hundred workers. Is this not so, more or less? From five to ten out of every one hundred prize-winning workers. We had fallen, then, into all those errors. Those are the things which we, all of us, the old as well as the new, joined together in a common purpose, must rectify.

We said, "Well, we have to rectify that situation. That is not the proper way to maintain contact with the masses." Why then, despite this situation, were we able to mobilize so many people so often? We were deceiving ourselves. It was not through that shell of an organization that we were able to accomplish that. It was through the means at the disposal of the revolution for mobilizing the masses: through the radio, television, the press — through all of those means. When we discussed all those matters with Comrade César, he expressed the opinion that there existed through those media a tremendous power for the mobilization of the people, a direct means for the mobilization of the masses. That shell of a party did not mobilize the masses.

We would be in some fix if we had to depend on that mere shell of a party during an enemy attack. It was a mere shell of a party. There were very good comrades in it. I am not going to go into — later on I am going to speak about the old Communists, about all those things; of how we have to view this objectively, calmly, honestly, fairly, justly.

But of course, that was not an apparatus for the mobilization of the masses. There really existed a great power for mobilization through the Commission of Revolutionary Orientation, a great power existed, basically, through those means which the revolution has for mobilizing the masses. But no proper means for maintaining contact with the masses existed and that responsibility belonged to a workers' vanguard party.

Then we simply have to integrate the masses. We had organized a few ORI, Integrated Revolutionary Organizations, and the masses, who are revolutionary masses, and who are the ones who make history, were not integrated, because there were no members who were from the masses, no one, no one from the masses. That is how the Integrated Revolutionary Organizations were formed.

I am sure that any communist, any citizen, old or new, anyone who thinks, agrees that this is an error. Not what we are doing today. Today we are not arguing about communism and anticommunism, nor about what ideological road to take. The revolution is irrevocably defined as Marxist-Leninist and we are making this self-criticism of our errors within the framework of Marxism-Leninism. Let no one suffer from any fantasies or engage in any illusions on this score. Do not imagine that we are going to take a single step backwards. No, on the contrary, we are going to move forward! [*Ovation*]

I was going to say just at the moment that you interrupted me that we are going to advance greatly. We are going to take long strides forward and we are going to do so precisely by rectifying our errors.

We are discussing here — we are engaged in self-criticism as Marxists, comrades, as Marxist-Leninists. Let the enemy say what he likes; it is not to the enemy's advantage that we hold this discussion; it is not to the enemy's advantage that we make this correction. This correction is only salutary and it will benefit the revolution.

That is, that we had made all these errors. We have to be a workers' vanguard party. We have to govern in the name of the working class, and we are making the aims of the revolution come true, and we are governing this country in the name of the working class, of the laboring class.

Our party has to be organized using Marxist methods, not by the methods of Louis XIV. Again I repeat a little expression which I have used at some meetings. These are the methods of Louis XIV: "Presto, I am the party. Presto, I begin to name the members of the party."

No, that is not democratic centralism nor anything like it. Democratic centralism is a very different thing. It is a leadership which organizes a party using Marxist-Leninist methods of selection, of work. What does it look for? It tries to gather within that party the best of the people, the best of the working class. The best workers in the country should be members of that party. Who are they? They are the model workers, the model laborers, who are in abundant supply.

In other words, the first requirement for belonging to the nucleus is to be a model worker. One cannot be a builder of socialism, nor a builder of communism, if one is not an outstanding worker. No vagrant, no idler, has any right to be a member of the revolutionary nucleus.

Very well now, that is not enough. Our experience during the course of this meeting has provided us with many interesting examples. He has to be an exemplary worker, but in addition he must accept the socialist revolution; he must accept the ideology of the revolution; he must want, of course, to belong to that revolutionary nucleus; he must accept the responsibilities which go with membership in the revolutionary nucleus. But, in addition, it is necessary to have led a clean life, that is to say, that one must never have served the tyranny as a soldier, as a policeman. Of course, there were people who had been members of the army who had been imprisoned for a long time; these cases are different.

There are special cases, of course, which are not like that of Garrucho. Garrucho was a councilman up to the very end, and I believe that he is a hero because only a hero could pretend to be a Batistiano for so long. If he was not really one, he deserves a medal.

But, well, what I want to say is the following: to have led a clean life;

not to have any record as a Mujalista,* as a Batistiano; not to have been active in the PAU, in the PUR; not to have belonged to the armed forces of the tyranny, to the SIM [Military Intelligence Service — Batista's secret political police], or to any of those groups. That worker's life must be free from that type of stigma.

This is interesting because recently, in a meeting, in — I believe that it was the Aspuru hardware store — in that meeting the workers were choosing the model workers, because masses are perceptive, they have a sense of justice that in every meeting at which we have been present, and in all other meetings, manifests itself in the choosing of some old militant from among the masses, because he stands out as a great communist, as an excellent worker.

The masses have a great sense of justice. Sometimes someone who has a bad record is chosen and the masses immediately bring this out. There have been cases where people who have bad records have been proclaimed as model workers. In some cases they have unfortunate records. Unfortunately such things happen. But in the meeting to which I am referring it so happened that the masses named an individual as a model worker. A worker got up from the multitude and said, "This man was a Mujalista." Then the man defended himself by saying that he had not been a Mujalista, and he confessed to having been a follower of Batista.

And in spite of this the masses said that he should belong to the nucleus. Such a mass of workers is confused and should be oriented. This means that it should be explained to them that such a man cannot belong to the nucleus for whoever says that he was a follower of Batista is saying that he agreed with all the crimes, with all the murders, all the tortures which Ventura, Carratalá, and all those criminals committed.† This has to be argued with the masses. That is the duty of the party organizers and they must say "No!"

Because, after all, the masses are not going to elect the nucleus; the party is not an elected party. It is a "selection" which is organized through the principle of democratic centralism. Now, the opinion of the masses must be taken into consideration. It is of the utmost importance that those who belong to that revolutionary nucleus have the complete support of the masses, that they enjoy great prestige with the masses.

We have been witnesses to truly moving cases. We have arrived at a meeting and asked for a list of fifteen comrades. We have asked that the masses point out those whom they consider to be model workers. They

---

*Supporters of Eusebio Mujal, head of the Central Organization of Cuban Trade Unions under Batista, who was loyal to the dictatorship.

†Capt. Estéban Ventura and Lt. Carratalá were notorious torturers under the Batista regime.

have stood up there and proposed certain names. And there are many methods for inventing tricks, hoaxes, fixed meetings, but the methods used by a resourceful parliamentarian make all that impossible.

When we asked them, "Do you believe that there remains the name of someone here who, because of his merits, it would be a pity to leave off the list?" They proposed a worker, a young comrade, a Black. I believe that his name was Juan Antonio Betancourt. They pointed him out.

That extremely modest worker got up. He is quiet, shy. He got up on a stool and they began to ask, "Why do you think, comrade, that this man is a model worker?" And they began to explain, and a worker with the look of honesty about him said: "Look, I was a dissatisfied worker. I was unhappy with the revolution. I was transferred to this work center. Comrade Juan Antonio approached me, he spoke to me many times. He explained things to me over and over again. He did so much; he acted so well; he was such a good comrade; we saw this comrade always work with such determination; we saw him do so many things — this comrade came to work even when he was ill — that this comrade succeeded in convincing me, in persuading me. Today I am a worker who understands the revolution, a worker who supports and defends the revolution."

Another worker got up and said: "I would like to add to that. I was a worker who used to be absent quite often. I used to work on the outside because I earned more money. I used to earn two or three pesos more by working on the outside. Juan Antonio approached me; he spoke to me every day; he explained to me that I was hurting the revolution; that mine was not an honest attitude; that I was harming the work center; that I was harming the working class; that I was harming my homeland. And then I was never absent again from my work center; I was never again an absentee worker."

Another one got up and said: "Juan Antonio suffers from a gum condition. He has such and such a problem and sometimes his face has been swollen for two weeks and he has never been absent from work."

Another worker stood up and said: "This comrade was once a painter. Later he began working in one of the offices. One day we arrived here with fifteen cars which had to be painted. It was urgent that those cars be painted and this comrade said, 'Don't worry, just wait until I finish my work.' When he finished his office work he spent long hours until he had completed the painting of all the cars. And this comrade will just as readily work fifteen or twenty hours."

While the masses were explaining those virtues, the qualities of that worker, one could not help but be impressed by all that was said, by all that recognition.

Then I asked a worker, "What do you think of this worker? Do you think that he is a better worker than you?"

And he said, "He's ten times better than I" — he was a young man. "And do you hope to be like him? Do you think that you will be like him some day?"

And he said, "Perhaps I will. Perhaps if I improve myself, if I work, perhaps some day I will get to be as good a worker as he."

These are the men whom we have to recruit! If that worker has a clean record, if he was not a Batistiano, if he was not a Mujalista, if he does not have a bad record, we must win that man over to our side, we must send him to school, we must teach him Marxism-Leninism, for such men possess the most excellent, the most valuable raw material for the making of a builder of socialism, of a builder of communism.

How are we going to build socialism and communism, which means work, which means the giving of oneself over completely to the work of society, without the men who are willing to work all the hours necessary, to make the necessary efforts, who go to work even when they are ill, who are never absent, without that type of worker of which the masses can give us many examples? That type of worker who is a militia-man, who is never absent when sugarcane has to be cut, who never misses guard duty, who is the kind of comrade who encourages others, who is recognized by the masses as a worker-hero, as a model citizen. We have to recruit such men as these. We must recruit all the revolutionists, old and new.

How could we keep the masses out? How could we divorce ourselves from the masses? There are many model workers among the old revolutionists who are recognized as such by the masses. There are others who are not model workers. There is no reason why there should be disagreement with this because being a communist does not endow one with a hereditary title nor with a title of nobility. To be a communist means that one has a certain attitude toward life and that attitude has to be the same from the first day until the moment of death. When that attitude is abandoned, even though one has been a communist, it ceases to be a communist attitude toward life, toward the revolution, toward one's class, toward the people. If this is so, let us then not convert that into a hereditary title!

We have fallen into that error. We have fallen into a problem of castes, not into one of classes, comrades. Let us not give up the principle of class in order to fall into the problem of castes, into that of titles of nobility, into that of privileges, into that of sectarianism, comrades. Every good Marxist, every good communist must understand this.

What spirit moves us to make these criticisms? Do we do this to bring about a change of opinion, to create an unfavorable opinion in regard to the old Communist militants? No, comrades, never. On the contrary, we do not want to expose so many good Communists to the blame and to the scorn to which bad methods, methods which are not communist methods, to which a sectarianism which is neither Marxist nor Leninist, will expose them. Because such methods bring discredit and tend to spread. And they tend to make the masses regard all Communists as they do that bad one, and not as they do the good ones, as they do so many Marxist militants.

We make this criticism, this self-criticism of criticisms, in which we are all to blame for the way in which these events have developed, simply to overcome these errors so that the revolution may free itself from these errors, so that we may proceed to the formation of a true vanguard party, a true Marxist-Leninist organization, which will march at the head of the working class.

Let us not confuse the functions of that organization with the administrative functions of the state apparatus. It so happened that we had established a principle of interference on all levels which was destroying the apparatus of the socialist state. And the socialist state has to function with great efficiency. How could we destroy that apparatus? How could we create such confusion? We must come out of that confusion.

We have been harsh today. We felt that it was necessary to be so, that it was healthy to be so. Because, comrades, we feel that from this moment on, comrades, all differences between the old and the new, between those who fought in the Sierra and those who were down in the lowlands, between those who took up arms and those who did not, between those who studied Marxism and those who did not study Marxism before, we feel that all differences between them should cease. That from this moment on we have to be one thing alone. And rather than be like that woman who they say kept looking — who the Bible says — kept looking toward that lake, toward that city which had sunk, and who was changed into a pillar of salt.

We cannot be changed into a pillar of salt, looking back at what we have done, contemplating, enjoying what we have done. We must look forward, comrades! That is the only proper attitude for us to have, which all honest men should have, which all honest revolutionists, old and new, should have without reservations of any kind, without regrets of any kind, without mistrust of any kind. All of us, embracing our cause, our revolution, the historic mission of this revolution, embracing Marxism-Leninism, which is the ideology of the working class, which is a science. Embracing Marxism-Leninism, which possesses all the attractions which a true revolutionary theory, a true revolutionary science, possesses. It is extremely rich and from it we can extract extraordinary lessons; in it we have an extraordinary instrument for struggle, an incomparable cause, the best cause for which to fight, the best cause for which to die, a cause which can be identified only with the spirit which is most profoundly human, most profoundly just, most profoundly generous, most profoundly good.

The enemy tries to present Marxism as something bad, as something unjust. No! Never allow them to confuse the masses by using the errors of those who act badly, of those who are wrong!

Our people today have the good fortune of being able to rely on a triumphant revolution with its power based on the masses. It has the good fortune of being able to rely on a revolutionary ideology, irresistable, invincible, a thousand times superior, infinitely superior, to the ideology of the reactionaries, of the exploiters; an ideology enriched by a century of struggles, enriched with the blood of workers, with proletarian blood, with the blood of heroes spilled in the defense of justice's cause, in defense of the cause of the equality of man, in defense of the brotherhood of man!

That is our cause. That is our standard! That is why we should feel proud, proud of being Marxist-Leninists, proud of being honest, proud, comrades, of having the public spirit and the honesty to discuss here — publicly — our errors, to discuss them as we have discussed them, together, proud of solving them, as we have solved them, together; proud of appearing, as we are appearing here before the masses in order to explain to them, to explain to them in general terms, the basic measures taken — the dismissal of the comrade whom we consider responsible for these deeds, measures concerning the Directorate and the offices of the secretary in charge of organization; the measures we have taken, the increase in the members of that National Directorate so that there may be included in it all the historic names, all the comrades who, because of their merits, in one way or another, are worthy of belonging to that National Directorate!

If we do the same on all levels it will strengthen us, it will make our revolution more powerful. It will make the people's faith in the revolutionary leadership firmer. It will make the faith of all the revolutionists of the world in us greater. It will make the faith of all the revolutionary organizations of Latin America in the Cuban revolution greater. Why? Because the fact that we know how to make corrections will give the Cuban revolution prestige. It will give the Cuban revolution all the strength which organizations have when they know how to purify themselves of evils, when they know how to correct their errors, when they know how to overcome their difficulties!

Rest assured, comrades, that by doing this our revolution will be invincible. Rest assured, that by doing this there will be no force in the world which will be able to defeat our revolution, and I repeat here what I said once when we arrived at the capital of the republic: "We have overcome our own obstacles. No enemies but ourselves, but our own errors, remain. Only our own errors will be able to destroy this revolution!" I repeat it today, but I add that there will be no error which we will not oppose and that therefore there will be no error which will be able to destroy the revolution! There will be no errors which will not be overcome, and that is why our revolution will be invincible!

The Struggle Against Bureaucracy:
A Decisive Task

Editorials from 'Granma'

March 1967

NOTE: Many of Castro's speeches during the middle and late 1960s dealt with the danger of bureaucracy and the need to fight it. In March 1967, a series of editorials appeared in Granma, *the daily newspaper of the Communist Party, analyzing in more detail the nature of bureaucracy and the significance of the fight against it. Nelson P. Valdés, a prominent historian of the Cuban revolution, has attributed these editorials to Armando Hart. Hart had been a leader of the July 26 Movement. In 1967 he was the organization secretary of the Communist Party of Cuba.*

The following articles have been reprinted from the March 5 and March 12, 1967, issues of the English-language Granma Weekly Review.

I. A Purely Bourgeois Institution

The struggle against bureaucracy is of decisive importance in the progress of the revolution. Fidel Castro has given this definition: "The struggle against the bureaucratic mentality is almost as difficult as the struggle against imperialism itself. More difficult than the struggle against the landowners, of course, since these were the minority, and there are many more people with bureaucratic mentalities than there were landowners in this country."

This is a long and complex struggle that cannot be won in one day. The mere establishment of revolutionary measures and laws is not enough. Action is necessary on the part of the masses and the party, as well as the constant application of a policy based on the principle of maximum reduction in numbers and maximum increase in efficiency. As Fidel has said, ". . . the only way to lend dignity to administrative work is to liberate it from bureaucratic concepts and methods."

Bureaucracy is a legacy from the capitalist system. Its complete and radical elimination is fundamental in achieving the complete triumph of the revolution.

Only if we are clearly aware of the danger posed by the existence of the petty-bourgeois mentality within the state apparatus can we properly understand, in all its magnitude, the importance of this key struggle in a country such as ours that proposes to achieve the maximum aims of revolution: the construction of the communist society. This is why we cannot detain ourselves in a mere struggle against the most obvious, quantitative aspects of this evil. We could make the mistake of reducing all of the personnel in a given place without taking their methods of work into consideration, thereby, even with a minimum of employees and functionaries, permitting bureaucratic work to continue and allowing obstacles to action to prevail, along with divorce from the masses and from the real problems at hand. This is well known by all who have thought over this matter. What does this ideological origin reveal? It reveals that the problem of bureaucracy has ideological origins, that it originates in a concept and a mentality, not only of excess administrative personnel. Fidel Castro expresses this clearly when he says, ". . . the principal cause is the petty-bourgeois mentality, the lack of awareness of the importance of a country's human resources, of a country's material resources."

Since this is the case, we must complement the struggle against bureaucracy's external manifestations — such as the proliferation of administrative personnel, inertia, red tape, the "run-around," etc. — with ideological struggle against the concepts that engender these evils, against the petty-bourgeois mentality within the revolutionary state.

This editorial, as well as those that will be appearing during the next few days, proposes to collaborate in this struggle.

Where and when did bureaucracy arise? In what social system did it originate? This is the first question we must analyze, because bureaucracy is not a product of our society, but rather one of the most unsavory holdovers from the past that we have had to deal with. The rise of bureaucracy is closely related to the capitalist system. Its development has taken place parallel with that of the bourgeoisie in its rise to the position of the ruling class in contemporary capitalist states. Although in former societies there did exist some incipient forms of bureaucratic work, such as that of functionaries, scribes, and priests, it cannot be said that a highly developed bureaucracy existed under slavery or feudalism. Why not? Because in those societies, such activity did not favor the growth and consolidation of a social stratum that would exercise power in the name of the ruling class. But such a parasitic stratum does exist in bourgeois society. The basis for its existence is the greater complexity in administration and government demanded by the centralized bourgeois state — which involves multiple forms of mercantile and financial relations determined by an active domestic and world trade requiring numerous controls; a government with a complex fiscal system; and finally a state apparatus with forms of organization that must necessarily be complex in view of the veiled character of exploitation in bourgeois society.

Bureaucracy also constitutes the most negative product of the division between manual and intellectual labor.

This division between the productive work of society and that of the members of the ruling class — whose work is dedicated to political or cultural activities — arose at the onset of class society. The slave system's ruling class, owners of great extensions of land and slaves, was exempt from all physical productive work. This they relegated to the great masses of the people, considering it "unworthy of true men." This also was a characteristic of the feudal regime, in which the landowning aristocracy considered the work of the agricultural serfs as unfit for them.

Under capitalism, this division is sharpened to even greater extremes by the bourgeoisie. Bureaucracy, a bourgeois creation, is profoundly steeped in this attitude toward manual labor. Educated in the petty-bourgeois ideology, bureaucrats disdain productive activity and consider themselves an intellectual stratum on a level with the bourgeoisie, situated above the working people.

Indeed, it must be stressed that even if we go so far as to classify bureaucratic work as "intellectual," if it is "intellectual" at all, it is one of the most simple and mediocre forms of intellectual work. Of this there is no doubt. There is nothing creative about bureaucratic work: deviation from the beaten path of routine can cost any functionary or employee his job.

There are other products of the division between physical and intellectual work that can be considered as historically necessary, since they have played a very important role during class society in the development of science, art, and literature. But bureaucracy, on the contrary, is a sterile entity that can claim no important accomplishment in the history of human culture.

Where could the bourgeoisie discover a social base to use in the establishment of this bureaucratic stratum? The bourgeoisie had no interest, nor were they in the position, to take over intermediate posts in government and business, since they were busy with the running of their own private affairs. They reserved high offices in the state and business for themselves. Therefore, they needed a specified sector of society to be used as instruments in the running of government matters and the management of the companies they owned, with the purpose of organizing, controlling, and administering their exploitation of wage earners. Moreover, the bourgeoisie, although they were masters of the nation's economy, were a rather small group numerically. A wider social stratum was required to give them support, one allied to their own interests, which could be used in the exercising of their dictatorial class power as a direct instrument against the working classes. The creation of a bureaucratic stratum was one of the solutions seized upon to fill this need. Together with the bureaucracy, we also had the "labor aristocracy," set up with the same end in mind, the strengthening of the bases of power and the extension of social influence.

Both the bureaucracy and the labor aristocracy in a bourgeois regime became mere extensions of the capitalist class into the petty-bourgeois sectors and the proletariat. Both groups served as supports to the dominant power, carrying on political maneuvering, causing division in the ranks of the proletariat, and hampering any kind of popular movement.

In the early days of capitalism this stratum was drawn from middle-class urban groups whose position was neither that of the feudal aristocrats nor of the workers and poorer artisans. In this environment the bourgeoisie created and nurtured the appropriate ideology and outlook on life. It developed a petty-bourgeois mentality in this social sector.

This was achieved through a hierarchy of officials and employees. Each of these was subject to the authority of an immediate superior, and all were trained to stick to routine work, obey more or less inflexible rules and regulations, and to abhor the introduction of innovations. They sought security and rank in society, which would give them certain "respectability," placing them above the working class.

This gave rise to the criteria of the bureaucratic post as a profession, and the concept became ingrained that the duty of one holding such a post was to blindly abide by the orders of superiors in the hierarchy. The bureaucrat was given the guarantee of a secure livelihood in exchange for his absolute submission to the bourgeoisie's planning. This explains why bureaucracy was born and grew identified with the capitalist class ideology, possibly to a greater degree than any other sector of the petty bourgeoisie.

Bureaucrats were formed by the division between manual and intellectual work. They were trained to completely ignore and despise production and those who made it possible.

What is bureaucracy?

As Lenin points out, it is "the particular stratum which holds power in its hands." It is the intermediary entrusted by the dominant class with the handling of affairs of state and administrative work in capitalist enterprises; an intermediary which reflects faithfully the thinking and the conceptions of the capitalist class. That is, in a bourgeois regime bureaucracy constitutes a social stratum playing a role subordinate to the political and administrative authority of the dominant class. It is an intermediary stratum that executes the decisions of the bourgeois dictatorship. It is the administration of power by employees and officials placed between the capitalists and the working masses. This stratum is invested with power and government by the exploiting classes whom it serves.

Therefore, we should define bureaucracy on the basis of its relations with the capitalist class and its participation in the government of that class, rather than on the basis of its concrete administrative functions.

We have analyzed the origin of the bureaucratic stratum, have determined at what moment in history it arose, and have shown what classes it merged with: This proves Lenin's idea that, " . . . every bureaucracy by its historical origin, its contemporary source, and its purpose, is purely and exclusively a bourgeois institution."

Engendered by and serving the interests of the bourgeoisie, bureaucracy reaches the zenith of its reactionary, antipopular nature under imperialism.

Impersonal bureaucratic functions reach their highest degree of dehumanization. There is a veritable army of clerks and offices, acting as a machine of international oppression.

The phenomenon that had appeared with the rise of capitalism grows more pronounced: in industry, in commerce, in the trade unions, in social institutions — on every level bureaucracy manifests itself and becomes entrenched. Its end is always the same: alienation of the worker — turning him into an object, a cipher, one more item of merchandise — encouraging the exploitation of man by man.

In underdeveloped countries, the problem of bureaucracy takes on very particular characteristics. It is tied to and facilitates exploitation by foreign monopolies; it is steeped in the imperialist ideology and often comes into conflict with the interests of the nation itself.

Servitor of neocolonial governments, bureaucracy is allied with administrative corruption and the sinecures typical of countries under the national domination of militarists and land barons.

It no longer serves only as a social bulwark of the bourgeoisie, but has become an international mainstay of imperialist policy and exploitation.

While this may not be so in each and every case, it is a widespread reality affecting bureaucracy in underdeveloped countries.

The bourgeois states formed their armies in keeping with their particular organizational concepts. The armies of the capitalist states took on a bureaucratic structure. The growing use of artillery, complex troop movements, the formation of enormous armies, required the presence of an extensive apparatus of officers, liaison men, and many other command cadres, directed from the top down through the hierarchy.

In the era of bourgeois revolutions, these armies represented a force superior in organization to the feudal forces. Obviously, the methods brought into play were not the only determining factor; many others determined the superiority of the bourgeois armies over their feudal counterparts. But the establishment of bureaucratic methods in modern armies is sufficiently important for us to pursue the matter further.

Side by side with expansion of its sphere of action and development in its highest stage — imperialism — capitalism needed to augment its entire military apparatus, to create a large war industry, and to operate transports that could move its armies anywhere. As this took place, the bureaucratic structure of the armies expanded.

The military forces of any imperialist nation have thousands of command cadres; there are modern armies that need seven men in the rear to back up three men in the front lines.

Besides the administrative or command function realized by this entrenched bureaucracy in the armed forces, it also fulfills the function of a stratum closely tied to the military caste and to the monopolists of the regime; that is, from the army, this stratum serves the political interests of the most reactionary class.

Bourgeois ideologists claim that there is no organization technically superior to that of an imperialist army, and they point to the structure of modern armies as an example of the efficiency and superiority of bureaucratic methods.

But history teaches us something else. The peoples who fight for liberation organize their armed forces without resorting to bureaucratic techniques.

We are not going to enter upon an analysis of all the factors moving the struggle forward nor all the elements present in a victory in a war of liberation. We only wish to stress that there exist organizations which are not constituted bureaucratically and which are capable of standing up to armies set up with the highest techniques of bourgeois organization.

To take only a few examples, we have the war of liberation of the Algerian and Vietnamese peoples against the French army, and the present battle of the Vietnamese guerrillas against the hierarchically superorganized forces of the imperialists.

The armies of the underdeveloped countries are characterized by their swollen staffs.

In an article entitled "Latin American Viet Cong" in the Canadian newspaper *Toronto Star*, appearing on November 5, 1966, it is stated:

"U.S. officials in Guatemala City are astonished at the rapid tendency of Guatemalan officers, returning after months of tough training in the United States, to develop large stomachs and settle down in easy, secure office jobs which they do not seem to want to relinquish."

The article later describes the Guatemalan army as: "An overgrown corps of top-ranking officers, with 400 out of the 1,000 officers assigned the high rank of colonel."

This army has tried and failed on numerous occasions to destroy the popular forces organized into guerrilla detachments.

Of course, this bureaucratic tendency typical in all spheres in under-developed countries is not the essence of the phenomenon, but it is one of its most injurious manifestations. It is an element that comes to have a determining character in the decomposition of these regimes.

We Cubans know this situation very well. The proimperialist army of the tyranny was completely rigid in structure. Among the consequences of the decomposition of the capitalist system under the exploitation of Yankee capital was the bureaucratizing of the army, a sort of fossilization, an inability to face a new form of struggle. Our Rebel Army — the popular forces — dispensed with everything superfluous, conducting the war in a direct, very concrete way, bringing into play a nonbureaucratic organization that showed organizational superiority over the bureaucratic military apparatus.

We can draw a conclusion from the confrontation of the liberation forces, based on the incorporation of the masses, with the traditional armies: it is possible to transcend bureaucratic ways of organization. There are organizational forms which are far more efficient than bureaucratic ones.

In socialism, the incorporation of workers via the militias — the revolutionary origin of the armed forces — and the system of an army of technically trained cadres, with large numbes of young men coming in through conscription makes possible an army free of the evil of bureaucracy.

II. The Danger of Bureaucracy as a Special Stratum

We have been analyzing the more obvious and immediate aspects of bureaucracy in our country, which we have fought and will continue to fight tirelessly. But it is also necessary to ponder deeply the problems posed by the existence of a bureaucratic stratum to the process of constructing socialism and communism. This is a phenomenon of universal validity. It is a danger we must abolish from our country since the complete success of the revolution depends to a great extent on its elimination.

Bureaucracy, without any doubt, constitutes a special sector with a specified relationship to the means of production. We can affirm that with the triumph of the socialist revolution *bureaucracy acquires a new character*.

On what basis do we affirm this? Under capitalism bureaucracy holds the same positions and apparently has the same relationship to the means of production. Nevertheless, in such a regime, it plays a subordinate role to the administrative and political power and authority of the dominant class, the bourgeoisie.

Capitalist bureaucracy is made up of public employees and the functionaries and employees of private enterprises. Neither group is directly concerned with political or governmental policy. In fact, public functionaries and employees, as well as those in private enterprise, are trained to think of their activity as a specialized professional function, removed from politics, and even to view political activity with a certain disdain. Thus capitalist bureaucracy serves as an *intermediary*, totally submissive to the domination of the bourgeoisie.

But what happens following the triumph of the revolution? In the first place, all of the formerly dispersed bureaucratic apparatus is vertically redeployed into the state apparatus and, to a certain extent, organized and strengthened. If we add to this the problems of lack of experience and knowledge on the part of revolutionaries, the tendency toward centralization or the application of bureaucratized foreign patterns, it is clear that bureaucracy *will grow, develop, and gain strength* during the early years of revolutionary power.

However, there is much more to the question than this. In addition to greater organization and growth in size, *bureaucracy takes on a new character in its relationship to the means of production and, therefore, to political activity as well.* When the revolution triumphs and the direction of the economy passes into the hands of the state, bureaucracy intervenes in the administration of production, in the control and governing of the material and human resources of the nation.

Minor functionaries, who previously were not entrusted with making decisions on political and administrative questions, move into posts which require political decisions and decisions affecting the means of production. That is, a change occurs in their relation to the entire life of the nation.

The fact that many workers begin to hold administrative posts does not give a class content to state administration. On the contrary, when a worker or farmer takes over an administrative post, he is in danger of being influenced politically and ideologically by this administrative job, of becoming one more bureaucratic functionary. A worker transformed into a position of authority in the direction of production is not necessarily thereby transformed into a leader of the working class.

As long as the state exists as an institution and as long as organization, administration, and policy are not all fully of a communist nature, the danger will continue to exist that a special stratum of citizens will form in the heart of the bureaucratic apparatus which directs and administers the state. This apparatus has a given relationship to the means of production, different from that of the rest of the population, which can convert bureaucratic posts into comfortable, stagnant, or privileged positions.

And this is the most profound and serious problem to be considered in the campaign against bureaucracy!

Socialism and communism are not spontaneous phenomena. Arrival at these higher stages of social development is achieved by following a correct policy and orientation. The fact that a revolution triumphs and proclaims its intention to construct a new society is no guarantee that this society will become a reality.

To achieve socialism and communism two factors must be combined: the development of the new man with new awareness and attitudes toward life, and the advance of technology to a level which will multiply productivity and bring about abundance of material goods. In order to reach this high goal in human society, a policy consistent with the principles of Marxism-Leninism, with the concepts developed by Marx, Engels, and Lenin and other great leaders of the working class, is essential. A policy which will lead to the disappearance of the concepts and ideology of the exploiting classes and of the petty-bourgeois mentality is essential. This demands the existence of a party which is *always youthful, always alert, never stagnant*. The party must be ever creative and united with the masses, never a party which is simply resigned to repeating what has been done by others without first evaluating this critically in the light of the concrete situations under which it must exercise its function of leader and guide.

Starting on the road to communism is no guarantee of arrival. At the least, it could happen that the revolution's ascendant movement might be frustrated and that stagnation and decomposition might appear in the earliest stages of the process.

A number of factors are involved in this problem which, taken as a whole, depend upon the general conception that is held of how socialism and communism are to be constructed.

If we allow certain categories characteristic of the capitalist system to survive within the organization and development of our economy, if we take the easiest way out, using material interest as the driving force in the construction of socialism, if merchandise is held up as the central core of the economy, if the presence of money remains omnipotent within the new society, then selfishness and individualism will continue to be the predominant characteristics in the consciousness of men and we shall never arrive at the formation of the new man.

And if such concepts prevail within the society, if an individualistic and petty-bourgeois ideology survives, a bureaucratic mentality will likewise survive, together with a bureaucratic concept of administration and politics, *but with the aggravating factor that now this concept will prevail among a special stratum of men whose relation to the means of production and political decisions places them in a position of leadership*. Thus there is nothing strange about the fact that the desire to belong to this bureaucratic stratum of society is kept alive or that this becomes a material objective for those seeking comfort and privilege.

If the party does not win this battle over bureaucracy, if this danger is not eliminated through the formation of the new man and the application of an unyielding policy consistent with Marxist-Leninist principles, the party will end by bureaucratizing itself. And a party which stagnates is a party in decomposition.

What does this mean? What occurs if the party organization sinks into this bureaucratic morass? When that occurs, a special stratum consolidates itself in the administration and direction of the state and in political leadership, a special stratum with aspirations toward self-perpetuation that draws constantly farther away from the masses, divorced from fruitful productive labor and from those who perform it, to become a privileged body, incapable of impelling the people forward, incapable of leading the consciousness of the people toward higher levels.

And when this occurs the construction of socialism and communism has already been abandoned.

As long as certain functions of an administrative nature, necessary in the transitional period, continue to exist, certain measures can be taken to aid in the avoidance of this danger. One of these is to maintain mobility in the posts of administrative officials and public employees, to prevent their becoming fossilized and to avoid the formation of a special stratum of society.

The apparatus for the direction of the state must be kept simple and at the same time dynamic, informed in the technical processes involved in production, capable of coordinating efforts, of stimulating activity, and of inspiring the spirit of work in those who function under its leadership.

Danger also exists that, within political organizations and the party itself, a special category of citizen may be created among profesional cadres, differentiated from the rest of the population. This is a danger that must be assessed and taken into consideration, because the historical and social process is a result of certain laws and principles which we must understand extremely well or we run the risk of falling into grave errors.

The way to avoid functionaries and administrative cadres within the party becoming a special sector of society is by confronting them directly with problems of production. This danger will be avoided to the extent to which the cadres face up to the concrete tasks of agriculture and industry in the closest possible contact with production itself. And this rule is valid for functionaries and administrative employees, as well.

In our own present reality, since the party is a product of the revolution and grew out of the revolution, the need has arisen for the party cadres to dedicate themselves to tasks of production and management in the most direct and immediate form. They must be in contact with technical problems as they come up in the fields, on state farms, in industrial plants. We are aided in this task by the fact that our party is young, without professional experience in most cases.

Thus, measures are being taken within the party to avoid the development of a special stratum of professionals, which in any case should always be *as limited and reduced in size as possible*, and as close as is possible to production. We will be helped in this task by the constantly increasing trend toward the formation of new cadres, which will provide greater movement among them from production to the party, and from the party to production.

III. An Obstacle to Revolutionary Action

In January 1959, the revolution found itself confronted with a society characterized by vestiges of feudalism in agriculture, incipient capitalist development, extensive domination of our economy and commerce by imperialism, and an extraordinary concentration of the population and administrative apparatus in Havana, contrasting with neglect, depopulation, and misery in the countryside.

Alongside the large U.S. companies had developed a great variety of small enterprises such as insurance companies, banking agencies, businesses, private health institutions, private schools, etc., staffed with administrative personnel to assure their operation: traveling salesmen, bill collectors, publicity agents, office workers, etc.

The proimperialist, bourgeois-latifundist Cuban state was corrupt to its very core. Daily, new posts were created and public offices multiplied to favor elements allied to the regime in power. Those who held government office prospered on public funds. *Botellas* (fictitious posts with salaries attached), embezzlement, and graft were common from the office boy right up to the chief of state.

That pseudoadministrative apparatus was consolidated into an enormous bureaucratic army. It was for many — and quite markedly so in a country like ours, without job possibilities for hundreds of thousands of men and women — a hope, a goal. Institutions designed to train people in unproductive tasks sprang up all across the nation: business schools, typing and secretarial academies. This mentality was deep rooted among the petty bourgeoisie.

The revolution did away with graft and *botellas*; it wiped out administrative corruption and conducted a general clean-up campaign in public administration. This was one of the important achievements at the beginning of the revolution. But obviously the young revolutionary power could not at that time eliminate the bureaucratic concept, the petty-bourgeois spirit in the administration of a state designed to serve the interests of the workers and farmers.

Later we had to confront the phenomenon of bureaucracy within the process of constructing socialism and communism. The experiences gained in this struggle and the pitfalls that have come to light are of extraordinary importance and should be food for thought for all revolutionaries in our country, especially for party members.

With the nationalization of the major foreign and national enterprises, this immense bureaucratic army, until then scattered, became state employees and functionaries. Many of them, those closest to the bourgeoisie and to Yankee imperialism, chose to leave the country. In contrast, the revolution offered men and women of the people opportunities to hold these positions, in many cases as a way — a poor way — to alleviate the serious problem of unemployment and the lack of job sources.

At the same time the need to control the different enterprises and organizations — many of which were new, products of the revolutionary process — led to the development of a policy of centralization which resulted in the excessive growth of central administrative organisms, such as consolidated enterprises and ministries. In this, an important part was played by the inexperience of many revolutionary leaders placed in positions of responsibility, who did not know how to organize or administer efficiently. In trying to solve the problem of poor functioning, constant backlog, lack of controls, and bureaucratic shackles, they could think of nothing better than to create new departments, increase office personnel, appoint more and more functionaries, and constantly invent new forms to fill out.

All they accomplished was to add more fuel to the fire. And who got burned? The people.

Another element aiding the development of bureaucracy in the first few years of the revolution was the introduction of some administrative systems and organizational procedures, copied from countries of the socialist camp, that were weighted down with bureaucracy. At the same time, we lacked sufficient experience and a sense of criticism, which led us to accept as good, structures from economically advanced countries that did not correspond to our needs, to the situation of a country just undertaking its development.

Fidel has pointed out that perhaps the greatest merit of this generation of revolutionaries has been to accomplish all these successes in production, education, and defense despite our own ignorance. Lenin also stressed that if revolutionaries, on assuming the responsibilities of power, do not have the background and concepts to oppose bureaucracy, it will continue to dominate because of its greater background and superior knowledge of "how to do things" — naturally, according to the capitalist pattern. Something like that happened in our country. Bureaucracy, to a certain extent, imposed its background of experience on us, its concepts of how to organize the new state, and what institutions are necessary. As Fidel pointed out in his address at the closing of the conference on the long-range sugar production plan in Santa Clara, "at first we imitated everything done by the bourgeoisie, the capitalists, the old state. That's true. Unconsciously we were influenced by the idea that a ministry was a ministry and a minister a minister, that an office was an office and an organizational diagram an organizational diagram, and so the world advanced. And the world advanced, and everybody retained this concept, followed these ideas."

As can be seen from what our prime minister said, bureaucracy in a socialist state has much to do with our conception of that state. It has much to do with the economic categories prevailing in that society. It has a lot to do with the structures that are created within that state. Bureaucracy was born with capitalism. Its origin closely links it with the existence of a mercantile economy, with the commercial operations and tax system of the bourgeois financial system.

For the gradual elimination of bureaucracy we must transform the state apparatus inherited from capitalism into an instrument appropriate to socialism. This requires gradual elimination of the activities of those categories that our society has inherited.

We are therefore trying to simplify operations between state organizations as much as possible. We are trying to eliminate mercantile operations between organs of the socialist economy. We will be inflicting decisive blows on bureaucracy to the extent that our economic concepts shake themselves free of the norms and methods regulating the capitalist economy and we adopt truly revolutionary measures on our path toward communism. What would happen in our country if we permitted each enterprise to buy from and sell to other state organizations, conduct private accounts, divide profits, and pay taxes to the socialist treasury, or if we gave encouragement to a mercantile type of economy? We would never rid ourselves of bureaucracy! On the contrary, it would grow right along with the growth of our economy.

Valuable orientation on many essential problems in organization of the new revolutionary state can be obtained through the profound study of Marx's conclusions on the Paris Commune and Lenin's original statements on the soviets of workers, peasants, and soldiers.

These statements essentially indicate the need not only for a new type of state, but for an agile, simple executive state, without a huge central apparatus, without bureaucracy, and with permanent and direct participation by the workers. All the great founders of Marxism-Leninism coincide in this view. This is what Lenin had in mind when he said: "The essence of the question lies in *whether the old State apparatus* (tied by thousands of threads to the bourgeoisie and filled to the core with routine and inertia), *is to be maintained or destroyed*, replaced by a completely new one. The Revolution must consist not in having the new class command and govern with the help of the old State apparatus, but in destroying that apparatus and governing with the help of a completely new one."

"We must teach the people, down to the humblest sections, the art of governing and administering the state, not only through books, but through immediate practical application everywhere of the experience of the masses."

Lenin himself expressed important views such as rejection of all veneration for ministries, and their replacement by work commissions, by teams of specialists and technicians.

Bureaucracy engenders bureaucracy. An overgrown central apparatus continually demanding reports and data, much of which is meaningless for practical purposes and determining concrete measures, engenders the need to staff the lower level of the hierarchic structure with a shocking number of employees and functionaries. Therefore, a decisive aspect of the direct, immediate struggle against bureaucracy is an analysis of organization. For in many cases the problem does not consist simply in analyzing exactly what work is done by each individual employee or official. What we must also concern ourselves with is whether that office, that department, that branch or enterprise itself should exist at all.

We must check each paper, each form, and ask ourselves what purpose it serves. We must check the function of each employee and official, what he does, the whys and wherefores of his work. And together with this, we must analyze the entire structure of our state, from the organization and operation of each department to entire branches and ministries.

Bureaucracy leads to a brake on revolutionary action. Perhaps this is one of its most serious immediate consequences.

Hemmed in by a rigid and inoperative hierarchy, no one dares to decide, to act, to solve problems. "I have to take this up above," is an eloquent and all too familiar answer. The bureaucratic conception suffers from a generalized malady: lack of confidence in the masses, lack of confidence in the grass roots — the level at which real production takes place, where the revolution's great goals are decided. Thus, practical executive decisions are reserved in many cases for immediate or central echelons, where at times they are put off indefinitely.

Our policy must be directed toward bringing those in leadership as close as possible to production units. This is extremely important for agricultural production in particular, where rapid decisions are essential due to unpredictable factors such as rain. As our commander in chief pointed out: ". . . agriculture cannot be directed with abstract ideas, agriculture cannot be directed in an abstract manner. Agriculture can only be directed right there in the province, at the farm aggregate, on the individual farm, on the lot. For there is where all the headaches are, all the problems. . . ."

The bureaucrat, on the other hand, is an alienated being. He shuffles around among forms, memorandums, orientations, and plans; he substitutes "discussion" for "action." Solutions are put off while problems are chewed over on all levels, going from one department to another. Thus, many times the real, practical problem, the problem affecting the people, is relegated to a secondary plane, forgotten, and attention is concentrated on papers, plans, discussions, and "levels" that supposedly exist to solve it.

The bureaucrat turns means of solving problems into ends, objectives of his work. This causes him to work in an impersonalized manner, and he becomes detached from the real needs of the country. He completely loses the political sense of his work and draws away from the masses.

Bureaucratic work lacks sensitivity to human beings; it is characterized by inability to analyze a situation from a political standpoint. Its very conception makes it dogmatic and mechanical to the core.

Bureaucracy perverts methods of revolutionary work: it turns collective leadership into a convenient means of disclaiming individual responsibility; criticism and self-criticism shift from methods of overcoming deficiencies to superficial confession and self-absolution of errors. New and revolutionary work principles cannot be carried out where this petty-bourgeois conception exists.

One of the greatest damages produced by bureaucracy is in its repercussion on the workers — not only production workers, but also many administrative employees, victims themselves of the bureaucratic system. As for workers and farmers, bureaucracy hits them by affecting production and frequently affecting distribution of consumer articles or the provision of services needed by the worker and his family.

What could be worse than for a worker or farmer to see problems that he understands and knows how to solve — in many cases simple matters — remain unsolved or badly handled because of bureaucratic functionaries and procedures?

What is more likely to dishearten those who must make the greatest effort to produce the nation's wealth? What is so capable of affecting the workers' faith and confidence in their revolution?

Many times a body gives instructions that "must be fulfilled," and although in practice, in real life, at the grass roots, these are way off the mark from what is needed, the mental make-up of the bureaucrats comes into play and forces its will. The result: failure, discontent, nonfulfillment, astonishment — and "meetings for analysis" with an abundance of "self-criticism."

Bureaucracy causes us more damage than imperialism. Imperialism is an open and external enemy. Bureaucracy corrodes us from within and attacks the healthiest, firmest elements of the masses, those who must suffer the most from it. It is clear that our people have an extraordinary sensitivity in detecting these problems and full confidence in the leadership of the revolution. Our people do not believe in the omnipotence of any bureaucratic functionary.

They react immediately when something goes wrong, when it is necessary to discover and fight these errors of administrative overgrowth. For that reason the masses and our party, their vanguard, must lead the constant, stubborn battle against bureaucracy.

Bureaucracy also permeates numerous social sectors whose work is not in itself bureaucratic. In other words, bureaucracy is not limited to administration only, but transcends this, corrupting other spheres of work.

The work of a teacher, for example, is not in itself bureaucratic. It may even be considered an indirect form of productive work, since it trains the future productive members of society to handle technology. Education provides people with a new social awareness and prepares them for life. In other words, the work of a teacher is of exceptional value for society: it is at once creative and formative. Now, what happens when we swamp a teacher with a torrent of circulars, forms, and other bureaucratic manifestations? We often succeed in turning him into a bureaucrat. He begins to feel that the most important part of his job is to fill out all of the forms correctly, and loses sight of his real role in the training, study program, and progress of students. He falls prey to formalistic detail — to bureaucracy.

Those who direct education in our country are waging an all-out offensive against bureaucracy. This struggle is decisive for achieving good quality in teaching, which runs the risk of being thwarted, held back, and sidetracked by the petty-bourgeois and bureaucratic mentality of certain functionaries in education.

This same bureaucratizing process may affect a restaurant worker, a train conductor, an agricultural expert — in short, any worker. The bureaucratic concepts and mentality of the hierarchy above him can thwart the worker's ability to think, create, and reason, as well as dampen his eagerness to solve problems, rendering him a simple robot that executes orders, circulars, and instructions: annihilating him as a man, recreating him as a bureaucrat.

In other words, the bureaucratic mentality, in practice, is a corrosive acid that penetrates and perverts the most important activities in the life of a country: the economy, education, culture, and public services.

Because they are well aware of this reality, those at the helm of education, production, and other principal fronts of the revolution, led by Fidel Castro, are waging steady combat against this. As Fidel has said, "When we say bureaucracy — and let's clearly understand this — we do not mean administration; but rather the overextension of administrative work, the massive, useless, parasitic, and unproductive concentration involved."

We must not underestimate the importance of administrative work. An agile, dynamic administration, based upon direct participation in technology and the concrete problems of production, is of extraordinary political value.

It is true that our administration needs accountants and office workers of the highest caliber, but what is essential is that revolutionary administration be in the hands of technicians and economists who really understand the productive process. The value of administrative work can be truly appreciated only when it is based upon the technical processes of production at the grass roots. This is what we are striving toward.

The struggle against the petty-bourgeois and bureaucratic mentality must not categorically reject the necessity and importance of organization and control in productive activities and social services.

Our immediate struggle is to reduce the personnel working on these fronts to a bare minimum, instilling in that personnel a new outlook stressing technology, stressing the real problems of the masses, concentrating on revolutionary action and flexible, ready means of solving problems. In short, a new, dynamic, and aggressive style of work must be developed. Along with this, the struggle includes maximum simplification of the structures of the state apparatus as well as achievement of maximum efficiency from minimum personnel.

One of the major tasks included in the struggle against bureaucracy is to find enthusiastic, tireless individuals capable of carrying out the plans of the revolution. We do not propose a sporadic, chance discovery of such people, but rather a very concrete policy designed to produce such people with an aggressive, direct style of work. We are going to depend less on schemata, on theoretical organization, and instead place our trust in the practical and executive ability of people who carry out and control plans efficiently without resorting to a bureaucratic apparatus.

Experience has taught us that there is no better control than that guaranteed by a job headed by someone capable, steeped in the revolutionary spirit, and eager to further the construction of the new life. More can be accomplished by one revolutionary cadre, linked with the masses he directs and fully dedicated to the problems of production and technology, than all the organizational diagrams, forms, and bureaucratic "brain trusts" put together.

One man with executive ability, directing a plan with a spirit of unwillingness to put up with obstacles, is worth more than any traditional form of control.

Ample experience has taught us that it is necessary to place our most competent cadres, with the exception of those engaged in some centralized jobs, as near as possible to the actual process of production or public services.

The example of our leading revolutionary figures, principally Fidel Castro, stands before us. All of us must become steeped in this new approach. This consists in working with concrete realities, going to state farm after state farm analyzing each problem in all possible detail, orienting, discussing, conversing with the workers themselves, living their problems and difficulties.

Of course, in order to do this properly, we must have a very thorough knowledge of the technical problems of agriculture and industry. It is the most difficult road, but, without a doubt, the most effective, economically and politically.

IV. A Long, Tenacious Campaign

No one should deceive himself about the revolution's campaign against bureaucracy. It is not a battle that can be won in a few months' time. It is a complex and difficult task with certain practical operative aspects which can be dealt with directly and immediately. However, there are ideological aspects involved as well, and this is where it is much more difficult to triumph rapidly. It will be necessary to mobilize all the revolution's resources, our labor movement, women, and young people, all under the leadership of the party, for an effort to strike out against bureaucracy on all fronts, in all its manifestations.

The fact that this is an ideological struggle does not mean that the problem can be solved with propaganda campaigns, through the proclamation of slogans or political phrases.

In addition to the always-necessary information campaigns, serious work must be undertaken among our masses to help them develop a full understanding of just what this top-heavy phenomenon and this petty-bourgeois mentality truly represent within our revolutionary state.

We must confront this bureaucracy directly with a militant working-class spirit. Past experience in struggle against this evil indicates that bureaucracy tends to operate as a new class. Certain bonds are formed among bureaucrats themselves, close ties and relationships characteristic of every social class.

They work hand-in-glove protecting each other against revolutionary rules and regulations. If the party and revolutionaries in general let down, if they lower their guard for a single moment, bureaucracy tends to spring up again, regulations are violated, and once more the same group installs itself in places of influence. And this occurs because bureaucratic functionaries have nothing to defend except their own positions and these they defend as would any class.

We must launch a program of revolutionary action against all this and prepare ourselves for a day-by-day, month-by-month struggle. And this combat must be continued as long as necessary, until this impediment to the revolution's progress is completely eliminated. Specifically, first consideration and highest rank must be given to those who are doing productive work, to technicians, to workers and farmers alike. For they are the ones who are doing the most useful work, and the hardest work as well. Their efforts will go farthest in solving the problems fundamental to the construction of socialism.

The advocates of such an ideology, an alien ideology, inadmissible under socialism, must be sought out and ousted from their posts. And care must be taken to assure that bureaucratic "solidarity" does not substitute the old practice of "kicking people upstairs" for one of transferring them to similar jobs.

The increase in new administrative posts must cease. Infractions of revolutionary norms must be detected and sanctions applied.

We must track down every printed form to see what it really is like, what it solves, and what end it serves. We must simplify supervision to the maximum. And whenever possible, participation of the masses in the selection of administrative personnel should be encouraged.

Commitments to the masses must be strengthened in place of commitments to a bureaucratic hierarchy alone.

We must continue to develop our policy of promoting new cadres based on political considerations. While this policy advances, administrative posts must be rotated. A principle of mobility must be put into effect in order to prevent job rigidity, a tendency to settle in and consider oneself "indispensable."

The Havana provincial committee of the party, together with students from the Revolutionary Instruction Schools, has been carrying out an investigation of cases of failure to enforce the government's labor policies.

These investigations have revealed a number of irregularities which the Ministry of Labor is now studying with the idea of applying the necessary sanctions. Those who have committed infractions of regulations laid down or general orientations must be subject to sanctions. This is one of the measures which must be adopted in our campaign against bureaucracy.

Thus, under *party supervision*, the Havana provincial committee and the Ministry of Labor are studying the stabilization of the entire system of employment practice and considering what measures are required for strict supervision of the naming of new personnel in administration, services, and production in general.

It is absolutely vital that the Ministry of Labor lay down exact labor rules and regulations and that these be adhered to most precisely. For, as we have stated, excess of administrative personnel is one of the more obvious manifestations of bureaucracy.

It is absolutely essential that all of the nation's work centers and each and every administrative office have only the minimum indispensable personnel needed to carry out their functions. Accordingly, it has been decided that a very reduced number of persons, an absolute minimum, may have the authority to employ additional personnel or put new workers under temporary contract. Moreover, this minimum must be determined by the actual operational problems at service and production centers.

And this reduced group of functionaries authorized to contract new employees must have an absolutely clear conception of what bureaucracy means.

All those who have the authority to hire new employees must be comrades fully aware of what the antibureaucratic campaign means. Party branches on all levels must develop this awareness. Administrative leaders must delve deeply into the subject. It will never be enough merely to deal out sanctions. What we must do is develop the social consciousness and sense of responsibility of those authorized to appoint personnel. Moreover, at work centers throughout the nation, workers should seriously discuss what the campaign against bureaucracy signifies, where its roots lie, and a campaign without quarter must be launched against any who break those administrative norms. That is why worker participation, under the guidance of union locals and members of the party, is a cardinal factor.

The party nuclei have, among other duties, the responsibility of making a profound study of the ideological roots of bureaucracy in order to increase antibureaucratic consciousness in the masses and to make certain that every center of work is fulfilling party policies in this important campaign.

Vigilance on the part of communists and workers in the application of employment practices is very important in the fight to do away with excess personnel and eradicate violations of employment policy in general.

The greatest concentration of bureaucrats and consequently the greatest stronghold of the petty-bourgeois spirit is in metropolitan Havana. The investigation results show that there is a total of nearly 74,000 employees and administrative officials with a yearly salary fund of $140 million. That is why our main battle against this evil within our state apparatus must be carried out here, following a revolutionary policy and in such a way that no one need feel worried or insecure about their future.

Thus, the struggle against bureaucracy has become the most important task for our party in the capital.

Because of its importance and the vigor it has gathered, the struggle against bureaucracy has come to be a veritable revolution within the revolution. It is, possibly, the kind of revolution that has never before taken place anywhere. This is the revolution that lies ahead of us and we can carry it out successfully insofar as we can combine the struggle *against* bureaucracy and the struggle *for* self-improvement, technological training, and massive participation in the tasks of production, especially agriculture.

The development of agricultural and cattle-raising programs in the various provinces and the consequent demand for technicians result in a permanent deficit of technicians and workers on every farm or farm aggregate in our country. On the other hand, an increase in educational plans and the extension of important public services offer a wide field for self-improvement and for incorporation into more useful work, which will result in greater satisfaction and moral stimulation for those who participate in it.

The greatest thing that Havana and other large cities can do for the countryside is to offer the services of technicians, economists, and labor power in general.

Administrative and directive officials must be incorporated, actively and in a spirit of militancy, into this battle. Nothing will reflect so clearly their capacity to occupy positions of responsibility as a clear awareness of and a determined attitude toward these problems.

In many instances, these comrades have become the victims of a situation which has condemned them to routine and inertia. Their only way to give their work a new meaning and a new style is to join the front ranks of the battle against bureaucracy.

And at the head of this battle, setting the example, will be militants of the party.

Party bodies in the province of Havana have started a movement to incorporate hundreds of Communists now doing administrative work in the capital, into the tasks of agriculture. Six hundred Communists in the capital have registered for agricultural work. Many of them have a certain amount of technical skill and political development. This is a very important step in the struggle against bureaucracy and a significant contribution to the work of agriculture.

Communists and workers in work centers who have registered for agricultural work must consider, when they are called, whether it is necessary for these industrial or administrative centers to hire new personnel to substitute for them.

Communists already doing agricultural work as well as the workers who stay behind must demand that no new personnel be hired unless it becomes absolutely imperative.

Party workers should be assigned to work at the base, that is, on farm lots and cattle-rotation pastures, as these are places where the battle of production is either won or lost.

The movement of city militants of a higher cultural and ideological level to the country can be a factor of extraordinary importance for the strengthening of the party in each lot, department, or farm. This is the honorable and revolutionary task confronting Havana party militants, since the party must be strengthened on the farms, where it is still weak.

The correct thing would be to have a party nucleus in each farm lot. Until this becomes a reality we cannot speak of an organized party in agriculture. The incorporation of hundreds of party militants from unproductive sectors in the capital will be a great contribution to this task of organization.

Thus we will strengthen our party membership and we will be prepared to send thousands upon thousands of workers to a more dignified, useful work, urging them toward a higher education and technology, and investing their new activity with a new context that will be a source of satisfaction and happiness for those who have been the victims of a system that chained their energies to sterile, enervating work.

Certain expressions of bureaucracy take on frankly negative aspects. One of them for instance, is the employment of young people in bureaucratic, unproductive work. This constitutes a crime against the future of these youths as well as against the interests of the revolution.

Young people should either be studying, doing productive work, particularly in agriculture, or serving in the Revolutionary Armed Forces (FAR). It is hard to conceive that a young person today should fail to participate in one or more of these activities.

Our duty and our policy should be not to hire any young person for unproductive work. As a matter of principle, we should struggle hard to implement this concrete policy. It should be the task of every party and Young Communist organization in each province, region, or municipality to check the activities of every young person; what he does, where he works, and where he studies. And to struggle, permanently and systematically to have these people study, serve in the FAR, or do productive work, if possible in agriculture. The Young Communist League plays a leading role in this battle, directing and leading the young people toward agricultural work. In the Camagüey and Isle of Pines agricultural programs, in places such as Juraguá, all through our countryside, this accurate policy constitutes a significant factor in the eradication of the bureaucratic concept and in the formation of the new man. It means the materialization of the principles set forth by our commander in chief in the sense of more "ruralization" and less "urbanization."

A study must be made at each production unit to decide if it is absolutely necessary that the young people going into agricultural work be replaced. This is a task for the appropriate administrative organism. However, the working masses, inspired by the example of the Communists and the young people must demand that no personnel be hired unless their services are indispensable to production or the service in question.

Our attack on bureaucracy within the state includes taking the necessary measures for the education of future generations under quite different principles, principles that will make them impervious to the petty-bourgeois spirit. The "school goes to the countryside" program is a very good example. Every year, thousands of young people combine education with participation in productive agricultural work. As Fidel has pointed out, in the formation of our children, this principle must be applied beginning in early childhood. Only thus will we be able to eliminate the "dead weight" of bureaucracy as an ideological factor within the new society.

On the other hand, the immediate, direct attack on this evil has entered a new stage. The Commissions for Struggle Against Bureaucracy are now on the offensive, with a new spirit and a new force. Serious and careful work lies ahead: that of simplifying to the nth degree all structures, paper work, and regulations within the revolutionary state. This will require the examination of every instrument of administrative power, since many of them correspond, in essence, to a society that no longer exists in our country. This analysis will be the determining factor in deciding whether or not the departments, branches, and even ministries and state organisms of our central apparatus are really needed.

The work of the officials must be made more concrete and direct, closely bound up with production and given content directed toward technology and control.

A great step forward would be on-the-spot technical and control teams which would help organize work centers without the need of hierarchies and bureaucratic echelons.

The wars of liberation have given us great lessons. We have already cited some of these.

There are superior forms of organization, based on different principles, which have given rise to methods far more efficient than those stemming from the bureaucratic structures typical of bourgeois military institutions, beloved example of ideologists of capitalism.

The revolution is now on the offensive in its war against bureaucracy. We are making advances in our struggle, supported by the masses and our party.

It will be a long fight. We cannot let down our guard for one single minute. But we will do away with the danger of a special stratum within our revolutionary society. We will confront this danger with the formation of a new man and victory will be ours.

In order to succeed, we must increase the awareness of our entire nation. It is only when the young cadres and workers in general have acquired an ample, profound understanding that we will win this decisive battle, that is, that we will be victorious in the revolution that is yet to be made: the antibureaucratic revolution!

1970 Self-Criticism:
Speech to the Federation of Cuban Women

August 23, 1970

NOTE: In 1970, Cuba set itself the goal of harvesting ten million tons of sugar. In spite of the massive effort channeled into the drive, the final total fell a million and a half tons short, and the process of putting every resource into the drive disrupted the entire economy. The campaign's failure highlighted many of the revolution's weaknesses.

Castro's July 26, 1970, speech analyzed in detail the reasons for the failure, taking full responsibility on behalf of the country's leadership.

"Above all, we want the people to be informed," Castro stated. "We want the people to understand. We want the people to gird themselves for battle. This is because our problems will not be solved by means of miracles performed by individuals or even by groups of individuals. Only the people can perform micracles.

"There are objective difficulties. Some of them have been pointed out. But we aren't here to discuss the objective difficulties. We must discuss the concrete problem and man must contribute what nature or our means and resources have not been able to provide. It depends on man. Men are playing a key role here and especially the men in leadership positions.

"We are going to begin, in the first place, by pointing out the responsibility which all of us, and I in particular, have for these problems. I'm not trying — or anything like that — to assign blame that doesn't also belong to myself and to the entire leadership of the country. Unfortunately, this self-criticism cannot be accompanied by other logical solutions. It would be better to tell the people to look for somebody else. It would be better, but it would be hypocritical on our part.

"I believe that we, the leaders of the Revolution, have cost the people too much in our process of learning. And, unfortunately, our problem — not when it is a case of the Revolution; the people can replace us whenever they wish — right now if you so desire! (SHOUTS OF "NO!" AND "FIDEL! FIDEL! FIDEL!") One of our most difficult problems — and we are paying for it dearly — is our heritage of ignorance."

Castro went on to point to the need to democratize the revolutionary process and seek greater involvement of the population in all the differ-

ent tasks of the revolution. One of the tasks he outlined was strengthening the trade unions and the mass organizations.

Following this speech, a deepgoing discussion took place throughout Cuba and Castro gave several widely publicized speeches analyzing these problems throughout the summer and fall of 1970. One of these was to a rally celebrating the tenth anniversary of the Federation of Cuban Women (FMC), an organization whose task has been to draw women into the revolutionary process, playing important roles in education, health care, and encouraging women to join the work force. More details on the FMC and its work can be found in Women and the Cuban Revolution, *edited by Elizabeth Stone (New York: Pathfinder Press, 1981).*

Below is the major part of Castro's speech, reprinted from Granma Weekly Review, *August 30, 1970.*

Comrades of the Federation of Cuban Women:

This is really a very meaningful ceremony. It reflects a job well done, [*Applause*] an efficient and adequate development of a revolutionary force.

[FMC President] Vilma [Espín] explained that in January 1961, a few months after the FMC was established, it had 17,000 members. Now, by this anniversary, its membership has grown to 1,324,751. [*Applause*] The figures are impressive, but they aren't the most impressive thing. We should say that the most impressive thing is the quality of this growth. [*Applause*]

There has been a qualitative as well as a quantitative growth. [*Applause*]

The organization, all the grass-roots organizations or delegations total 27,370. One hundred and twenty-nine thousand, nine hundred and ninety-one women are participating in the leadership of these grass-roots-level organizations, and 89,169 as activists.

These are very impressive figures, which is why they are easy to remember.

Nearly 130,000 women are in positions of responsibility in their grass-roots-level organizations. They are not professional leaders, but comrades who are responsible for the activities of the federation there in their fundamental units.

This indicates the value of a mass organization in a revolutionary process and the value of the mass organizations as the best schools available to a revolutionary process for forming and training leaders and cadres.

Several of the comrades who are today in the national leadership and the national departments began at the grass-roots level.

One very interesting fact is that 24,712 comrades in leadership positions in the federation are studying. That is, 24,712 women cadres are improving their educational levels. This is apart from the 83,621 women who are studying to finish the sixth grade and 51,730 others who are studying dressmaking. And since we've mentioned the dressmaking schools, there's another figure which is also impressive, as it reminds us of when the first, tiny school of this kind came into being. It is that 94,796 — almost 100,000 — women have been graduated from these schools. [*Applause*]

This shows how a constant effort bears fruit — with nearly 100,000 women graduates of these schools. This is important not only from the social, human, cultural, and self-improvement points of view; it is also very important from an economic point of view, as it helps solve the problems of the clothing industry. Many women are employed in it, and the fact that such a large number of women have learned dressmaking and now make their own clothes and, in many cases, those of their relatives, gives an idea of the economic implications involved. Because, regardless of how mechanized this industry may be, the vast number of items needed will always require a large number of workers. Moreover, even with modern machines, production is still not high enough, and thousands of women are needed in these shops. When more raw material is available — that is, more cloth — when the revolution has more cloth available, the importance of having such a large number of women trained in this skill will be apparent to all.

Scores of comrades are also being trained in the self-improvement schools and in the schools of general education and technical knowledge. This will enable them to acquire the knowledge needed for work in many fields of endeavor.

It is very important — I repeat — that so many of the organization's leaders should be studying — and studying at the cost of great effort and sacrifice, amidst difficulties.

They have just a few hours available every day in which they can increase their knowledge. This shows us that the revolution has extraordinary resources available and will have even more resources available to the extent that this policy is continued, for this injects necessary resources at the spot where the revolution is usually weakest — which is the capability of the men and women in leadership positions.

Lack of knowledge, of training, and of organizational ability is one of the most serious problems facing a radical and far-reaching revolutionary process, such as ours, which brings about a total change in the mode of production and type of society. Those who were on the bottom are placed on top, and those who were on top go down — and out. [*Applause*].

We don't say that they simply go down; it would be more accurate to say that they have gone by the wayside. Certainly they have gone to other countries.

In the old society there were trained people who ran a factory with a whole slew of accountants, lawyers, technicians, and offices. Others ran two factories. Others ran a big store. Others, a small store. Still others, a medium-sized store. The most powerful had two, three — up to ten — sugar mills. These were the most powerful financiers. And now the country has to run 153 sugar mills. What I mean to say is, the task is really tremendous.

When those from the bottom rise up, they have to run things on a much bigger scale than was ever done by any of those who were on top before. Problems become really huge. And the country must carry out this task without any experts, without any personnel with experience in running any of these units. When the time comes to organize on the regional, provincial, and national levels, we are faced with this problem. And this is true not only of the sugar industry, but of all fields of endeavor — transportation, services, construction.

For a people that carries out such a total transformation, this, beyond any shadow of a doubt, is the greatest problem — though not the only one.

In our opinion, the FMC in these ten years has provided a magnificent example of what can be done, of what can be done with a correct method and policy.

To this we must add that the very content of the work of the organization has undergone a vast change from the time it tackled its first tasks to the present; there is a big difference between the first tasks with which the organization was entrusted and those it is carrying out today. We are truly amazed by the evolution undergone by this work, because it encompasses so very much more now than it did on that August 23, 1960, when even we could not grasp to what extent it would grow. And it is still continuing and will continue to develop. [*Applause*]

There are new tasks. We have mentioned some of the tasks in relation to organization: the number of grass-roots organizations and the growth of the organization itself. We also spoke of some tasks in relation to education, but the tasks involved in that field are many, many more than those we have mentioned.

In 1960 — when there was an excess of labor power — the task of incorporating women into work was not given priority, yet this is one of the activities given the greatest emphasis by the federation in the past few years. In 1969 a total of 113,000 women were recruited for work, and everything indicates that the figures for 1970 will be much higher.

Of course, it is necessary to be aware of our great difficulties and limitations in the material order to fully appreciate the merit of such a vast incorporation of women into productive work — an incorporation which, unfortunately, cannot be maintained in many instances, as a result of those very limitations, but which, nevertheless, gives us an idea of the effort that has been made.

There are other activities such as those pertaining to the Department of Social Services, many of which are completely new tasks; take, for example, social work, the health brigades, the debates on public health, vaccination against tetanus, hygiene and neighborhood face-lifting campaigns, the social aid plan, classes to teach mothers how to care for their children, maternity recovery centers, and homes for the aged.

All this is part of the new work of the federation, and there is increased activity in the field of education, as well. Initiatives are taken, such as those concerned with the organization of brigades in the Militant Mothers for Education movement — which in our opinion, has tremendous possibilities.*

What does all this show us — all these tasks — what is the principal lesson to be gained from all this?

It reveals to us all the possibilities latent in this organization and the mass organizations. It shows us an excellent way; an excellent revolutionary, democratic way.

On one occasion we said that the women's movement constituted a revolution within the revolution. Today we may add that the mass organizations in general, as revolutionary vehicles of the masses, as formidable instruments of progress, also constitute a revolution within the forms of development of our revolutionary process.

It is quite probable that we are barely scratching the surface of such fantastic possibilities, because already the masses, in an organized way, are beginning to tackle an endless number of tasks which are of vital importance to all of society.

The work that is being done with the school councils, the support to education and health (activities which are still included as services), the support to production and the direct participation in the solution of those problems — all these things are pointing to a very interesting way — perhaps the best way, the very best way — to overcome the difficulties that still lie ahead.

Several days ago, on July 26, we spoke of and emphasized our problems. We pointed out neither the objective difficulties — which cannot be denied and we do not deny — nor the achievements of the revolution — which cannot be denied and we do not deny. Instead, we concentrated on what, in our opinion, should be pointed out: our mistakes.

---

*The Militant Mothers for Education is a movement composed mainly of housewives, whose tasks are to check on students' attendance, help children in collective and individual study, help in the upkeep of schools, and when necessary do substitute teaching. Hundreds of thousands of women participate.

If we devoted ourselves to gauging the scope of the objective obstacles, we would always find some justification for minimizing our deficiencies; if we devoted ourselves to gauging the magnitude of the successes scored by the revolution, the same thing would happen — it would only serve to cover up our deficiencies.

Our successes have been mentioned quite often. And, of course, successes mean added encouragement. Today, you are encouraged by the successes attained during these past ten years. [*Applause*] However, our people have reached such a degree of maturity that it is possible to speak too, without the slightest fear, of our deficiencies. Our people have reached such a degree of maturity that they no longer need to have their victories pointed out in order to feel stimulated and ready for action.

Some of the enemies of the revolution — especially those encouraged by the reactionary news agencies — came close to believing in the failure of the revolution or believing that our mention of deficiencies was a kind of swan song for the Cuban revolution. Even reactionaries of the lowest order — exploiters, some of the most notorious proimperialist elements in the hemisphere among them — tried to take advantage of the courageous statements made by our revolution; of that courage displayed by our people when faced by any problem; of that sincerity, loyalty, and respect for truth which characterizes our revolutionary process [*Applause*] to try to sow confusion among the peoples and even try to bring pressure to bear on the political processes taking place in other countries.

Then they accuse us of interfering in the affairs of others, when it is they, the most shameless reactionaries, who, without any scruples whatsoever, keep trying to present the Cuban revolutionary process as a part of the problems of other countries.

We believe that we serve the cause of the other peoples to the extent to which we work well, to the extent to which we are sincere, to the extent to which we are honest, [*Applause*] to the extent to which we have eradicated demagoguery and lying from politics [*Applause*] and to the extent to which we have eliminated compromise and deceit. [*Applause*]

Because that is precisely what a revolution consists of: bringing about a radical change in society, not only hitting those "upstairs" — the powerful, the exploiters — but effecting a change, hitting them also in their vices, of which compromise, lying, and deceit were among the most characteristic. [*Applause*]

How mistaken — in fact, how stupid — how stupid can they be? The revolution and the leaders of the revolution speak openly — as we did — to the whole world and to close to a million Cubans, saying that our enemies claim that there is discontent — and we say this is true — and that we are facing difficulties — and we say this is true, too. But they are so stupid that they fail to realize the extent of the strength and the consciousness of the revolution. [*Applause*]

Our revolution can challenge the demagogic governments, the lackeys of imperialism in this hemisphere, and the cheap politicians of every ilk who oppress and exploit their peoples to have the courage, just once in their lives, just once in all their history, to tell their people a single truth. [*Applause and shouts of "For sure, Fidel, give the Yankees hell!"*]

When we speak of discontent or inconformity, we speak of discontented persons within the revolution, not against the revolution; to improve the revolution, not to destroy the revolution; to make the revolution stronger, not to liquidate the revolution! [*Applause*] That is the difference, the radical difference that exists between the revolutionary processes and among the discontented within the revolutionary process and the discontented outside the revolutionary processes.

The reactionaries do not understand that revolutions are irreversible, that revolutions march on despite the errors and deficiencies of men. This is because revolutions are superior to men. When the revolution involves the work, the efforts, and the lives of millions of human beings, it is superior to everything; it is invincible! That is why, on one occasion we said that in our revolution we have been promoting and carrying on a revolution that was greater than ourselves. [*Applause*]

Naturally, that is precisely what the fakers, liars, and demagogues try to keep from the peoples: the power, the tremendous power of a revolution.

What better occasion for pointing this out than this anniversary, this tenth anniversary, on which we have been speaking of the growth of this organization — which is but one of the revolution's organizations! There are others. We have such organizations as the Committees for the Defense of the Revolution [*Applause*] — another organization created by the revolution, with 3,222,000 members and 67,200 grass-roots committees. [*Applause*] Many Cubans are members of their workers' organizations, their women's organizations, and their defense committees; in fact, some of them belong to as many as four organizations, since they are also members of the party or the Young Communist League. [*Applause*] They also belong to farmers' organizations. One type of organization to which the revolution gave its full attention during the first few years and which, unfortunately, has not been given all the attention it deserves for the past few years is the farmers' organizations, with a membership of 227,000 farm families — or almost that many, as there are cases of two or three members from a single family.

It is deplorable that we have not given these organizations our full attention and that we have not promoted the development of our workers' organizations to the utmost, for we have 1,895,000 workers in our social productive units — that is, in the productive units that belong to the people: in industry, construction, services, and transportation. One million eight hundred and ninety-five thousand workers!

But we also have our youth organizations, which have developed considerably. The Young Communist League [*Applause*] has done good work in the tasks that have been assigned to it, though it is true that, when its main effort was concentrated on the Youth Column,* it was not able to carry it out and it did not make a similar effort in some other youth sectors. But it has done work of great merit in the Column, which has also been an excellent cadres' school and a fine revolutionary school for the young people. [*Applause*]

We have our student organizations at the various schools, in which, including the adults — as we said on July 26 — the enrollment for the 1969-70 school year runs to 2,289,464, which represents the number of people who are studying in this country. [*Applause*]

Now add the force represented by the FMC; [*Applause*] add that force to the forces represented by the Committees for the Defense of the Revolution [*Applause*] and the farmers', workers', youth, and student organizations — I'm speaking of the mass organizations, though the Young Communist League is partly a militant political organization and partly a mass organization — add up all those forces; add up all those millions, all those well-organized forces; add up all those forces with a correct policy — a policy of education, of organization, and of promoting cadres from the grass roots — add up all those forces as instruments of the revolutionary process, as instruments of our political vanguard, as decisive fighting elements at the disposal of our party. Add up all those forces with a scientific revolutionary doctrine, and you can see that those forces can tackle any task and any difficulty; those forces will emerge victorious from any battle, no matter how difficult — a battle such as that of developing the country [*Applause*] — and those forces will be invincible!

During the past three days — on the twentieth, twenty-first, and twenty-second — the comrades of the party's Political Bureau have been meeting with the party's first secretaries from the six provinces and the Isle of Pines region; the respective organizing secretaries; the national and provincial leaders of the FMC, the Committees for the Defense of the Revolution, and the labor, farmers', and youth movements; and also some other comrades who were asked to participate, considering the tasks they perform, including the comrades who are in charge of political activities in the Revolutionary Armed Forces and the Ministry of the

---

*The Youth Columns are voluntary work brigades organized by the Young Communist League.

Interior. We have been analyzing the experience of all these years, the experience that has been accumulated in every corner of the nation regarding party organization and the mass organizations. We have given this work our individual attention for three consecutive days.

Of course, we cannot devote all our time to analyzing and discussing. We have to choose the days we can devote to this work, in the midst of other very urgent and pressing tasks.

The work sessions ran to thirty-one hours, not counting interruptions. All who participated in the work were of the opinion that it was an excellent experience and that it will yield excellent results. We analyzed problems, failures, and the main difficulties encountered by our party and the other organizations on the various fronts; we analyzed the things that have gone wrong in general, in all respects and aspects; how we are going to remedy these deficiencies and failures; and how we are going to improve the general work of the party and the mass organizations.

How are we going to make use, now and in the future, of the experience we have gained? Of course, we are not yet in a position to solve all our problems. We are making a careful study of every step we are to take. No spectacular solutions will be found for our problems. No. No one should expect miraculous, overnight solutions; no one should dream of solutions in a matter of hours or days. No. We all have to work very hard, not only in our daily tasks but also in the search for increasingly better and more adequate solutions for our problems.

How are we to organize that tremendous force we have been talking about, how lead it and how carry it forward in the face of future tasks to solve the contradictions we pointed out on July 26 that exist between the growth of our young population, that part of the population that is not yet working in production, and the growth of services, such as education, which the country cannot do without — the building of schools, school dining rooms, and day nurseries? How solve the contradiction between the claims of these needs, including those of public health, and those of the defense of the revolution, so vital for this process? Moreover, how achieve the necessary level of production to provide for our most basic needs? How develop the country, starting with what we have to work with?

There are many things the shameless imperialists try to hide — for example, the tremendous efforts they put forth to make our people's battle against underdevelopment that much harder. They try to hide the fact that our country, in order to develop, depends on one basic productive activity: sugar production — an industry which our country can under no circumstances discontinue and which still has a low level of productivity, since the task of raising productivity in that field — especially in the cutting of cane — has turned out to be a difficult one indeed, though the loading of cane has been mechanized almost 100 percent.

But mechanizing the loading of cane does not quite solve the basic problem. What it has done is make it unnecessary for men to work fifteen to sixteen hours a day in the canefields; it has reduced their workday to ten, nine, or eight hours. That is the reality of the matter. The problem is that formerly the sugar harvests were brought in by men who had to work from fourteen to seventeen hours a day. Of course, during those days there was always an army of the unemployed, and the number of students could not even be compared with today's. There was an army of the unemployed in the country and whenever a worker didn't show up for work, couldn't keep up the pace, or fell sick, another was always right there to take his place.

[Minister of Labor] Comrade [Jorge] Risquet explained in his television appearance how we spent 135 million hours in this harvest. This means that 500,000 man-years were spent in the sugar harvest — 500,000 man-years of 260 days; which is the approximate number of eight-hour workdays involved. This was for a sugar and molasses production which was under the one billion peso mark.*

There are countries with natural resources. There are countries with oil, for example. There are countries in Asia and Africa with rivers of oil in their territory, and some in Latin America.

For example, in Venezuela a few thousand men can produce $3 billion worth of foreign exchange a year. The imperialists make huge profits there. But even after the imperialists have taken more than $1 billion, there is still $1.5 billion to $1.6 billion left that has been produced by a few thousand men.

In Chile, 60,000 men produce $1 billion worth of copper a year.

Of course, we have some resources, such as nickel, with which we can produce $1 billion in foreign exchange, using a few thousand men. We have 5,000 workers in the nickel industry. Each worker produces at least $30,000 a year in foreign exchange value. And the value of sugar production is less than $2,000 a year. Nickel, however, requires huge investments. How can we pay for these investments, if not from the sugar industry? Where can our country obtain the necessary resources for its development, if not from the sugar industry? This is why our country must continue to depend on that industry.

Sugar will make it possible for us to diversify and develop our economy. We don't have a developed economy. It is developing or — in many fields — remains to be developed.

Nickel requires not only huge investments, but investments which take time, investments with advanced technology, and installations which are not easily obtained. It isn't easy to obtain the installation for our nickel industry. The Yankee imperialists control the nickel business

*The Cuban peso equals approximately US$1.25.

and many of the technological processes involved in it, and they try to block us from developing our mining resources — especially our nickel.

There is one investment project, though, which is almost completed: the nitrogen fertilizer plant in Cienfuegos. A thousand workers will produce 40 million pesos' worth of fertilizer a year. Of course, we don't import this much fertilizer, but it will produce half a million tons of nitrogen fertilizer. What does this mean? More than 30,000 pesos per man per year. This is development. About 1,000 or 1,100 workers will be employed there. It represents an investment of $40 million and has been put up in record time by our Communist Brigade of Industrial Construction. [*Applause*] They expect to have it completed by the end of the year and have it begin production around April. It's a complicated process, and it will take about two or three months for production to get in full swing.

If we were to import this fertilizer, it would cost us $40 million, what with its actual cost and the cost of transportation. Of course, we will have to transport what is produced at the factory, but we won't have to do so by sea — which, in itself, is a considerable saving. The bulk sugar warehouses are also very important in this regard. For example, the one in Cienfuegos will handle more than two million tons of sugar a year. This means a great saving in labor power — both in the warehouse and on the docks. There is high productivity among the workers there.

The new factories which we will build as our economy develops will be factories with very high productivity, but the resources for all this must come today from an industry in which productivity is not high — in which, in fact, it is low and in which raising it is no easy matter.

The mechanization of the rice-production process is easy. There are rice-harvesting machines, and we harvest all our rice by machine.

Rice is planted, fumigated, and fertilized from airplanes and harvested by machines. Herbicides, especially, are applied from the air, as are some of the fertilizers. The land is also prepared by machines. The development of the great rice areas has been easy. The effort required has been great, but for other reasons — because it was necessary to bulldoze large areas and build huge dams and irrigation systems. We have had to use a great many men and machines in these projects.

Dam construction is also almost completely mechanized. Civil construction is also being mechanized with the use of the prefabricated process. And brigades are being developed. Mechanizing construction is easy. We are making an effort in all fields: on the docks, how to mechanize dock work — in the shipment of sugar, for example.

We are mechanizing eveything we can in agriculture. All possible crops. We are using herbicides, a chemical product. The great majority of the cane this year has been weeded with herbicides. This is a big step forward and a great saving, but we still have to confront and deal with a branch of the economy on which our development depends and in which the problem can't be solved so easily: sugar.

The problem of cutting cane can't be solved with a chemical product, and not enough machines are available. That is, the problem can't be solved so easily. We have some machines and will continue to build more, and we have also purchased some from other countries. We are doing everything possible to solve this problem, because it is vital for the nation for us to do so. But the problem of mechanizing the sugarcane harvest has really turned out to be much more difficult than the other problems we have had to face — such as mechanizing rice production. The weeding of the cane, formerly done all by hand, this year was done almost entirely with herbicides sprayed by means of planes, helicopters, and shoulder packs.

We are still faced with a great difficulty in this key sector — a difficulty which, of course, requires — and receives — the full attention of the revolution, as it is one of our most serious obstacles. We must continue to produce sugar and develop the economy, as well as keep all the other industries in production and develop new ones, and also carry out construction projects and meet all the rest of our people's needs.

But the contradiction isn't easy to solve. When we speak of 500,000 man-years, we have to consider that the harvest doesn't take all year and that the number of men needed is, therefore, greater. It can be the equivalent of the work of 700,000 men working eight hours a day if you reduce the time — the harvest takes six or seven months. This is one of the most serious problems facing our country today.

The resources our people need don't just fall from heaven. They aren't easily obtained. Yes, we have a lot of sun and light. We can build many dams. We will have water in dry years. The dry years and the wet ones will more or less balance each other out, and this will open up great perspectives for our agriculture. We have natural resources, such as nickel. We can produce sugar with natural conditions that are better than those of any other country. But it isn't easy. All this requires great effort. Nothing can be obtained without effort. We must work hard to solve this and many other problems — such as those of education and public health — which cannot be neglected. Defense, too, is a must. And we must do all this without working seventeen, fifteen, or fourteen hours a day, because it is impossible to think that we would maintain such a state of affairs in a revolution. Only the most inhuman living conditions could explain or justify having a man work these hours, for such a long workday is prejudicial to man's life and health.

The revolution has to find other solutions. We can't use these solutions. We have to resort to technology and machines.

But all these things require 100 percent or 200 percent — if it were possible — work efficiency, efficiency in the use of available resources;

they require a 100 percent or 200 percent efficiency in organization and the use of raw materials and any other kind of resources [*Applause*] — of all human energy, as we explained on July 26.

We have to learn how to use human resources sparingly. Man is the most basic, fundamental, and necessary resource derived from the above-mentioned contradictions. This is why our revolution has to learn to use that resource in the best and most efficient manner possible.

When we speak of efficiency, we are referring to the way in which we handle those factors that keep us from making the best possible use of human and material resources.

This is the fundamental struggle facing us in all fields. But to carry it out successfully we must first overcome the weaknesses in the party so it can cope with the situation and meet our needs, thus fulfilling its role as a vanguard. [*Applause*]

We must overcome existing weaknesses in the mass organizations, which have been neglected, and we must develop these and our workers' organizations as much as possible. This won't be easy. Why? Because they aren't like the women's organization or the CDRs, where the activity is carried out in all fields, both horizontally and vertically.

What form are we going to give this organization? This was one of the subjects discussed. How are we going to achieve this? And, most important, we want the comrades at the grass-roots level to participate in the discussions. [*Applause*] The workers at the grass-roots level should participate and give their opinions, and the comrades in leadership positions should also participate, so that we can give the most correct, most effective form to the labor movement.

If we are to solve problems, we must first get more information and opinions and work very hard to give our labor movement the best possible form, so that, in this way, backed by these strong mass organizations and a party which is fulfilling its historic role, we may deal with them successfully.

The objective problems are there, and we can't just wish them away. Where must we wage and win the battle? We can't change the objective conditions: the sun and moon aren't going to move out of their places in the sky for us. We must win the battle within ourselves! Where we can improve, where we can bring about a change in the activity and the quality of the activity is in the subjective factor, in the human factor.

We cannot alter our natural resources by simply wishing them otherwise. But one thing in which we can work and bring about changes — in which we can accomplish much, do a great deal, and make a great contribution — is the quality of our work, the efficiency of our organization, the efficiency in the general effort of the entire people.

It is not a case of the people lacking in will or determination. It has been proved that the mistakes are not found there. It is not a matter of lack of awareness. It has been demonstrated that the mistakes are not found there. [*Applause*]

Sometimes we speak of developing the awareness of our workers, but the fact is that our workers' awareness has developed greatly. And often we must ask ourselves if it wouldn't be more correct to say that it is we who must drink from that fount, from that revolutionary awareness that has developed among our workers! [*Applause*]

At the beginning, the vanguard was a minority; the conscious revolutionaries were a minority. However, as a result of the revolution, as a result of that flame that caught hold in the hearts and minds of our people, as a result of the struggle, the vanguard is no longer a minority. We now have a people in which revolutionary feelings and ideas have taken deep root. We no longer have to look at things from the standpoint that it is a minority that will do the job of developing awareness. No! We must also see it from the standpoint that a minority, charged with specific tasks and functions, must get its awareness from the people. [*Applause*] It is no longer a question of our developing other people ideologically, but of our own ideological development, as well. It is no longer a question of helping the people develop their awareness, but of having the people help us develop ours. [*Applause*]

This is the way to look at things, because this is the way things stand.

This is by no means a question of denying the human condition, the spirit of sacrifice of thousands of unselfish comrades in the political vanguard. No! It is a case of the vanguard's surpassing itself, developing further, learning from its mistakes, and eradicating its weaknesses, looking to its attitude and setting an example in every way! [*Applause*]

Setting an example in every way means being entirely exemplary!

For our revolutionary militants, our cadres, those comrades in posts of responsibility, the greater the responsibility, the greater the obligation; the greater the responsibility, the greater the duty; and the greater the responsibility, the greater the sacrifice. [*Applause*] The greater the responsibility — I repeat — the greater the duty! The greater the responsibility, the greater the sacrifice!

We have succeeded in creating a profound feeling of justice throughout our revolutionary process. We wanted to inculcate these feelings, and they have not only been inculcated but have also developed and gone even deeper. Among the masses there is a strong feeling of equality. Are we to deplore this? No!

There is a political theory, a revolutionary theory that establishes what socialism is, what communism is. Marx himself said that according to the formula of socialism, every man would produce according to his ability and would receive according to the work he had done and that, naturally, some had more ability than others, more energy than others, while others might need less than they. That formula still did not go beyond the narrow confines of bourgeois rights, and only after abundant wealth had poured forth as a result of social work and the narrow confines of bourgeois rights had been overcome could the formula be established that every man produce according to his ability and receive according to his needs — which meant communist society.

It is an unquestionable fact that our people have made great strides forward in revolutionary awareness, in their sense of equality; and it is also an unquestionable fact that we are living in a period of arduous work — one in which, objectively, we must overcome great obstacles; one in which, objectively, we must make sacrifices. And under such circumstances, there is no room for theoretical disquisitions. We must be realists, realists. And the moral principle we should embrace — above all, the revolutionary vanguard, those in posts of responsibility, should be to make even more sacrifices than those we ask of the people. [*Applause*]

And nobody should be surprised if any manifestation of privilege taking should arouse the most profound indignation among the masses. [*Applause*] This is only logical.

These are matters that have to do with the tasks and duties of revolutionaries and of all those in posts of responsibility. These are essential, fundamental matters.

And, to the extent that we assimilate this thoroughly and correctly, we will be establishing the best, the optimal conditions for winning the battles that lie ahead of us, for overcoming the obstacles that lie ahead. [*Applause*]

This revolution is able to count on a magnificent people of which we should be more than proud, more than satisfied. Now we must know how to be worthy of this people. [*Applause*] We must also know how to develop and carry our mass organizations forward to the utmost limits of their infinite possibilities.

This will be one of the duties and one of the basic tasks facing our party, as well as to give the people ever greater participation in the solution of their own problems. The time has come to take qualitative strides forward in the functioning of the process.

We have our own peculiar conditions. We have to seek out our own formulas, basing ourselves, naturally, on historical experience, laying hold of all available historical experiences and applying these dialectically to the solution of our own problems.

Our revolution has demonstrated its quality in many fields; there are others in which it hasn't yet been demonstrated. We have made great advances in our ideological process, but we can say that they haven't all kept pace.

We must progress more in the field of ideological development, in how to bring about a constantly greater participation of the masses in this process and a constantly greater participation of the masses in decision making.

Some of the elementary examples we had pointed out here were how the FMC, working through the school councils or the Militant Mothers for Education movement or other activities, is already working on problems in the schools which are of vital concern to the population.

But we have scores of problems at every level, in the neighborhoods, in the cities, and in the countryside. We must create the institutions which give the masses decision-making power on many of these problems. We must find efficient and intelligent ways to lead them deliberately forward to this development so that it will not be simply a matter of the people having confidence in their political organizations and leaders and their willingness to carry out tasks, but that the revolutionary process be at the same time — as Lenin wished — a great school of government in which millions of people learn to solve problems and carry out the responsibilities of government.

Of course, we can't speak of millions on the same scale, but at least of hundreds of thousands of people participating in these responsibilities and tasks.

We mentioned the 27,730 local units of the FMC and the 67,200 of the CDR, without taking into account all of the country's workers, farmers, and young people. This shows that if we continue to follow a similar policy, encouraging comrades in minor leadership positions to study, promoting cadres and giving them new tasks; if we give our mass organizations ever greater participation in solving problems in the districts and the cities, in the spirit and sense we have explained, arousing the people's energy for the solution of many of these problems, their participation in deciding what problems they can solve, if we give them ever greater participation in the decision-making process, we shall be following the logical and natural course of events in a revolutionary process in which we have unleashed the energy of millions of people. We have released the immense energy of millions of people, despite the fact that we are a small country of only eight million people with organizations of more than a million members, others with two or three million, in such activities as study, in which more than two million people are involved.

What does all this mean? We have been able to unleash in millions of people the energy, interest, and will to move ahead in spite of the fact that we are a small country. Now we must know how to channel that energy, guiding that formidable and extraordinary revolutionary mass movement toward the possibility of ever greater participation in the decisions that affect their lives.

This implies the development of a new society and of genuinely democratic principles — really democratic — replacing the administrative work habits of the first years of the revolution. We must begin to substitute democratic methods for the administrative methods that run the risk of becoming bureaucratic methods.

We don't have the formulas yet. We are expressing aims and opinions; we are indicating the road we intend to travel. We don't have to rush. We can do things well, gather experiences. We must not try to make great and stunning advances over a weak foundation; we must progress in this direction, but over a solid foundation.

Some people ask how this is to be done and others speculate about what forms, what procedures. Some people have little work to do at times and a lot of time to idle away inventing ideas.

We want to find solutions and we will find them! [*Applause*]

In other epochs there were also thousands of strategists on how to make the revolution. It was a difficult problem but its solution was possible. The problem was to find the best formulas, the correct formulas.

The revolution has the tremendous forces of the masses at its disposal and these are conscious forces. The revolution is very powerful, more powerful than ever with those forces. But we must know our weak points, we must know in what direction we must advance and how we must advance. And, as we have said, there are no miraculous or spectacular formulas. [*The crying of a child in the audience is heard.*]

Do you suppose that child is crying because we haven't mentioned the day nurseries? [*Applause*] It wouldn't be surprising, because one of the most critical problems we are facing in connection with the incorporation of women into production is that of the day nurseries and the semiboarding schools — that is, of school dining rooms. Right now, during this vacation period, we are witnessing the contradictions that arise during school vacations in homes where the mothers have taken jobs.

We have also been analyzing those problems, which are just one more proof of how complex the whole thing is. It is not just the nurseries, or the schools, or the workers' dining rooms. It is that when one problem is solved — for example, when the day nurseries are provided, there is the problem of the schools. Then we have the problem of vacation time, and, as a result, we have to organize vacation plans. Thus, it is a whole chain of interlocking needs that can be met only with resources. And that is one of the miracles, as it were, that we have to perform in order to create the conditions so necessary for the incorporation of women into the labor field.

At the moment when our little comrade reminded us of the problem of the day nurseries, we were sketching out some ideas, some principles, some questions, which might be summarized as: How are we going to create and develop the conditions by virtue of which the masses, through their organizations, will have an ever increasing participation in the decisions that must be made in connection with their most vital problems?

It can thus be summarized. And how may we carry that mass movement to its ultimate possibilities? — which we will have to do on sound and solid foundations that have been carefully studied, meditated, and analyzed.

But one thing is clear to us: since the revolution has succeeded in accumulating this enormous amount of force and energy of the people, it is necessary that that energy be channeled toward the field of struggle, toward the field on which we have to win the battle against difficulties.

We think that this anniversary, this example set by the Federation of Cuban Women, affords us a clear idea. As a matter of fact, we should give greater publicity to the data you have given us. The women's federation has published the data in their magazine, but it does not yet have — as none of us have — enough paper to provide copies to meet the demand. We should take advantage of our press to publicize the results of the effort and work and the progress made by this organization and the matters in which it is already taking part. [*Applause*] And this, in our opinion, gives only an idea of the possibilities for the rational development of the mass organizations.

For the immediate future, we must place special emphasis, in the coming months, on the question of the labor movement so as to raise it to the level of the women's federation and the Committees for the Defense of the Revolution. [*Applause*] To boost and give the farmers' organizations all the attention they deserve. [*Applause*] To continue developing and even improving the work of our youth organizations, that is the Young Communist League and the students' organizations. [*Applause*] We have to develop the activities of our young people to the highest level possible, but without relying upon professional cadres. The basic problem presented by our students' organizations is how to develop the grass-roots organizations and even how to hold their congresses without the need to take a young person — since that would be a paradox — from high school and make him a professional militant cadre. That would be a paradox, because it would be in contradiction to the concept of what a school is supposed to be. That is why we must try to find the way in which our students' organizations under the leadership of the UJC — under the leadership of the UJC, which does not mean the identification in that case of the UJC and the organization — all the mass organizations can develop to the maximum, with their very important work activities, including the students' mass organizations.

We have to carry out important work among the Pioneers also.* There is the whole problem of organizing vacations. That is to say, these mass

*The Pioneers is the Cuban children's organization, which organizes recreational, sports, educational, and cultural activities.

organizations have to carry on all kinds of work activities connected with questions vital to the people.

We firmly believe that our possibilities in this connection are extraordinary. And we should embark upon that task as part — only as part — of the work to be done in the coming months.

An enormous amount of work must be done in all aspects of the state's administrative apparatus: in the organizational aspect and, above all, in the political aspect — methods, procedure, and spirit. Furthermore, ladies and gentlemen, the formulas of a revolutionary process can never be administrative formulas. Administrative procedure could reach a given efficiency, but it can never rise above certain levels. Sending a man down from the top to solve a problem involving 15,000 or 20,000 people is not the same thing as the problems of those 15,000 or 20,000 people — problems having to do with their community — being solved by virtue of the decisions of people of that community who are close to the source of those problems! [*Applause*]

No administrative formula, then, can solve problems that are only susceptible to mass solutions. [*Applause*] And these are functionaries who can be replaced at any time of the day or night.

We remember a conversation we had with a group of fishermen in Cienfuegos. They were explaining the problem they had because public transportation lines did not reach their village; the hospital was too far away and they really needed a vehicle there, but not a vehicle for someone to joyride in. And we said to them, "And who could guarantee if we send a vehicle here that the person put in charge of it wouldn't use it for joyriding? Who would that person be? Who are the only ones who could prevent that? You. Only you could prevent that from happening!" [*Applause*] And I suggested to them — at that moment there wasn't even an ambulance, for example, or a passenger car of the kind our rural zones are due to receive for use as taxicabs — "We are going to send you a jeep. But we are going to send it here, to you. Then you'll look for a place to have it serviced. This you can discuss with an agency at the city level, the city administration level. You are to select a man and prepare a set of rules for his daily activities: where he is to park the vehicle, what it is to be used for and under what circumstances; for example, how to carry — in a community such as this there are always three or four children to be taken to the doctor or to the hospital every day. But that vehicle is to be managed by you and it will be your responsibility. You'll see to it that nobody uses it for joyriding." [*Applause*]

It was perfectly clear to us that under any administrative procedure of ownership or control of the vehicle by an administration at city level — involved with the problems of 100,000 people — it would be impossible to guarantee that a perfect, punctual, honest, dependable man would be found who, once at the wheel of that vehicle and with a mission to fulfill, would not be tempted to take it for personal use or for joyriding at one time or another.

This does not mean that this is the way all vehicles should be organized. There are many places where a taxi stand is needed. I don't mean to say that the taxi stand has to be in . . . . I only mentioned this case as an example. I am speaking of the essential idea: that only that group of people could guarantee that that vehicle would be used properly. There could also be a taxi stand belonging to a city organization, but what will happen there unless someone in authority is there to watch over it? What happens when the community is not invested with authority? Say a teacher is needed. It is up to the community to see the problem and take steps to solve the problem; or if someone in a distribution center is guilty of irregularities, the community should act on that. [*Applause*] If anybody, no matter the activity in which he is engaged, commits irregularities, the people should be the authority there, even though the trouble may very well arise in an organization that very well may belong to the city, since the city itself, in turn, can also be an authority organized in the same way. [*Applause*]

Of course there are some things which, because of their nature, cannot be supplied by a small community: the food supply, for example. But how could that unit function without permanent vigilance and channels for the masses to make decisions? And if the authorities appointed by the masses don't do their job well. . . . This is not the much touted "representative democracy"; this is proletarian democracy! Because if it is made up of representatives of the mass organizations, the Committees for the Defense of the Revolution in the area, the women, and the workers, and they all get together and name a man for the job and he doesn't live up to expectations, we say that he can be replaced at once — at any hour of the day or night. [*Applause*]

This energy and strength of the masses must be converted into efficiency. This efficiency cannot be obtained from above: that efficiency can only be obtained from below. [*Applause*] This is an idea which, if developed, can have tremendous possibilities on the regional, city, provincial, and national levels. These are the correct channels for the functioning of proletarian democracy and the guiding of the energy of the masses. We will be training scores of thousands of men in this way, by having them pass through these schools of responsibility.

We are trying to determine how many professional cadres we need. We must do everything possible to reduce the number of professional cadres. Of course there are activities which require a person's full-time attention; some of them have to be carried out by people working full time, and others don't. But if a few thousand cadres work efficiently, they can direct these energies and get the most out of them! It will be the best possible work, the best task to which a citizen of this country can devote his energies.

We repeat, the revolution is now entering a new phase; a much more serious, much more profound phase; one in which our resources of experience are greater than ever before; one in which the revolution will have to tackle ever more complex problems with new methods, with the experiences accumulated through these years, and, above all, with the energy accumulated through these years in the field where we can bring about a change in conditions — that is, in the subjective factor, in the human factor. I repeat: the objective factors are there, but they do not enter into our sphere of activity. We can change those objective factors, yes, but not simply by wishing them otherwise. In other words, some of these factors can be changed; such natural problems as drought, or the climate itself, can be modified by means of dams, and our present low-productivity problems can be remedied by means of new technology, new machines. There are some objective factors that can and should be changed, but only man can effect such changes; only man can alter such conditions — which is why our effort can and should be directed toward man.

The Need for a Democratic Labor Movement

September 2-3, 1970

NOTE: After the victory of the revolution the Central Organization of Cuban Trade Unions (CTC) was reorganized, eliminating its corrupt pro-Batista leadership. From then on the CTC was a firm supporter of the revolution. However, beginning in 1966, the unions began to play less of a role, as many of their functions were taken over in practice by the Vanguard Workers Movement, a group composed of the most dedicated and hard-working individuals. In addition, the unions began to lose their autonomy from the government and the state's economic administration.

As part of the 1970 self-criticism, efforts were made to strengthen the trade unions and restore their autonomous character as the representatives of Cuban workers. A series of meetings were held to discuss this question. On September 2 and 3, a meeting of the CTC of Havana Province was held which Castro attended. It included twelve hours of debate from the floor, at which workers from many different industries stated their opinions, criticisms, and suggestions.

One of the steps Castro proposed at the meeting was to hold trade union elections throughout the country to elect local leaders; previously union leaders had been appointed. These elections were held in November and December.

One of the measures debated at this and subsequent meetings was a proposed antiloafing law. This was designed primarily as an educational measure, something demanded by many workers who resented the relatively large number of absentees who continued to be paid, as well as the layer of able-bodied men who refused to take jobs while still receiving free education and medical care, inexpensive housing, and other benefits of the revolution. Unlike capitalist countries, Cuba had no structural unemployment, and instead faced a serious labor shortage. After debate throughout the country in all of the mass organizations, the law went into effect April 1, 1971.

The following is Castro's speech at the closing of the Havana Province CTC meeting. The text is from Granma Weekly Review, *September 20, 1970.*

Well, comrades if you like, I'll say a few words. [*Applause*]

Comrade [Jorge] Risquet has done a brilliant summing up, giving a rundown of the essential points discussed and of the aims pursued by this meeting.

Throughout the discussions, I have been expressing a few ideas and thoughts, too.

As I was saying a moment ago, with this meeting, we have begun to wage a battle. In order to advance, we have to wage not one but at least a dozen battles, and perhaps even more battles will present themselves along the way. One of the most urgent battles, one that should be given priority, is this one against absenteeism, and it should be followed up by another to prevent any misunderstandings in connection with what Comrade Risquet and I have said here with regard to voluntary work.

Undoubtedly, there has not been an adequate reaction in the face of the difficult situation we are facing — which we described clearly. If, in a critical situation on a battlefield, an army doesn't react by counterattacking and fighting all the harder, then the battle is lost.

Of course, all this took place in the midst of a vacation period following long months of work. This was in July, and we had the carnival, fiestas, and other things like that. Really, it's perfectly logical that we should find this type of phenomenon in August, isn't it? Moreover, we ourselves had said that the workers' vacations should come first and that later we would have to really dig in in earnest. But it could, nevertheless, be said that a reaction worthy of our difficulties and the obstacles we have before us was lacking. There is no doubt about that.

Isn't it true that during these days — due to a combination of circumstances and to the fact that we are none too sure about how we are going to solve these problems — there has been a rise in absenteeism? This is true. Even without the holding of this meeting, absenteeism would go down automatically in September. This is to be expected. It will happen when all the workers who have been on vacation go back to work, when many members of the Lenin Column are back at work and when the people have finally grown tired of abusing absenteeism — if we may put it this way. Therefore, it is to be expected in September.

However, that is not enough. Even winning the battle against absenteeism is not enough. That is only a part of the problem. But, even so, we believe that it is of major importance, since it has to do with the manner in which the workers react in the face of difficulties.

Now then, we are faced with an endless number of problems. Of the problems we are faced with . . . that is, we have objective problems of every type — as we said at the meeting of the Federation of Cuban Women. But the trouble is that those problems become more and more serious to the extent that we are incapable of doing what is required in such a situation. Moreover, we are now faced with many problems of a subjective nature. And these adversely affect production, as well as the workers' attitude toward work and many other things, some of which have already been pointed out here.

We've only mentioned a part of our problems here, and I'm sure dozens — if not hundreds — of comrades still have a lot of things to get off their chests with regard to the different kinds of difficulties encountered in their work centers and everywhere else, but, even so, we feel this subject has been covered quite thoroughly here, with a whole series of things being brought to light which reveal the size of the struggle we will have to engage in if we are to overcome all these difficulties.

The objective conditions in which the trade union leaders and party cadres must work are difficult. If the administrator is lazy, if a man is incompetent, if you are faced with a series of real difficulties — for example, such as those we saw today when we visited the plant whose roof, according to what a comrade said yesterday, has a lot of leaks and is about to fall in.

We made it a point to visit some of the places mentioned in yesterday's meeting. The comrade had stated that men had been there several times and had taken measurements but that nothing more was ever done in four or five years. I asked Comrade [Juan] Almeida to visit the place with me to see if we could find an immediate solution to the problem there. It just so happened it rained while we were on our way to the plant, and after we arrived there it began to rain harder. As a matter of fact, anybody would think that a description of what actually happens there when it rains hard is a little exaggerated. It's really incredible how much water comes pouring in during a cloud burst! It makes you really appreciate the battle that must be waged by a trade union representative or a party cadre at a plant where such things as that have been going on for five years. This plant where so many people work has no workers' dining room — or, rather, it has a dining room, but the food is so bad nobody eats there. And the cafeteria is pretty badly stocked, as well.

It is a fact that even the finished goods get wet there. You can see the finished printed matter getting wet, the things we have acquired with foreign exchange being ruined. The machinery isn't helped any by the moisture, either, and there's a danger of accidents being caused by short circuits in the electrical wiring and things like that.

Then what? This has been going on for five years. It makes you wonder how anyone can speak about saving, economizing on foreign exchange, and making an effort to attain development and promote the economy to 400 workers at a plant where nothing has been done about a leaky roof and merchandise is being ruined as a result.

Undoubtedly, such a situation makes the work of the party and the trade union very difficult indeed.

Obviously, the inverse of this would be for everything to work perfectly — and we would really be supreme idealists if we expected such a thing to happen! It has been a very difficult thing. As a matter of fact, the change that has taken place in the life of the country has been so deep that, in a sense, we are receiving not only the positive but also the negative fruits of the revolution.

This is because the revolution, first of all, creates a tremendous disorder in the whole life of a country, a tremendous change in the mode of production. As a matter of fact, we have gone from virtually a slave mode of production to a free mode of production. That is the essence of the problem. This slavery was not one in which men wore chains on their ankles but rather a subtle — but no less effective — form in which men who had no personal or social wealth either worked or starved, along with their families. Men were forced, under pain of death, to work with punctuality and discipline. The army of the unemployed stood at half a million, and men vied with each other to work at a factory and were proud of obtaining employment at a plant such as the rayon factory in Matanzas, where they were practically poisoned.

And what is the picture today? The conditions created by the revolution have done away with those ominous circumstances. It may be said that work today is voluntary — and I don't mean just the work we do on Sundays when we go and pitch in in agriculture. Under present conditions, work has become practically a voluntary affair for all the citizens in this country.

First of all, this is determined by the fact that many vital problems have been solved. The things the baker brought up: the housing problem has been solved for many; medicines, education, social security — the possibility of everyone's having a secure life. There are no beggars, prostitutes, destitute people, or abandoned orphans in this country. The present generation of young people has not even known the scourge of unemployment. On the other hand, there is a surplus of money over and above the supply of goods to be purchased, making the value of money — the means through which work is remunerated and goods are bought — relative. The goods and services we have available can be bought up to certain limits.

Doubtless, if we had many more goods and services available, these factors would not enter into a situation in which many families have more money than they know what to do with. However, this is not a universal thing, as there are still some cases of workers whose wages are barely enough to support their families.

But there is no doubt that the circumstances in which they are drawn to work are basically factors of a moral order, factors having to do with awareness, a healthy outlook, and a sense of the social and human importance of their work.

Thus, in these circumstances, there has been a tremendous change in work conditions. That is, some people without morals and without a sense of their social duty today take the liberty to scorn their work, remain idle, let the weight of the productive effort fall on the shoulders of others, cheat, and do a million and one other things.

There has been, I repeat, a tremendous change in the mode and relations of production and distribution of social wealth. Moreover — as I said yesterday — with the means of production becoming collective property, the employment of these means of production and human resources in the production and distribution of goods and services creates an administrative problem on a grand scale. I was saying that even the human brain cannot retain many things. No human brain, no group of accountants, can keep track of our stock of merchandise today. Just so, a trip to the moon today would be impossible without computers, because the number of calculations required and the speed at which complex problems must be solved would make this task impossible for the human brain. Neither is it possible, without computers, to keep track of the economy, of inventories, of what is in stock and of what is needed on the tremendous scale demanded by a socialist economy. Even the imperialists, the developed capitalists, had to develop computers, without which they would have been unable to handle their businesses. General Motors would be out of business today were it not for computers. Moreover, if it weren't for computers, that huge Yankee airliner somebody came in on only recently — whose construction calls for millions of parts, parts which must flow smoothly and simultaneously to converge at the factory where thousands of engineers and technicians take part in the mass production of these planes — would not exist.

In comparison with all this, our work is but primitive. We work on an enormous scale, because our problems are the problems of millions and our goods are for millions, but our methods of administration and leadership are still primitive.

Administration on a large scale is a science. And we certainly do not have these kinds of scientists. Therefore, the terrific amount of confusion, mistakes, and snafus that exist in this field are almost understandable. In addition, there are problems of an ideological, political nature. Public administration is still deeply imbued with a petty-bourgeois spirit. We have the problem that there are times when public officials do not look at all like the rest of the workers. It is true that many managers are of working-class origin and have proletarian habits and spirit, but there are others who resemble parachutists floating down from the sky above, absolutely insensitive and lazy, without an iota of proletarian spirit.

There is no doubt that this antiworker spirit, this scorn for the workers, exists among a number of administrators. Such things were revealed in this meeting.

There is also the fact that, as we explained yesterday, problems cannot be solved in a revolutionary society through administrative methods. This is very clear. Even the best administration cannot call forth the control, vigilance, militancy, and mass energy necessary to overcome problems.

We have to wage a battle in every work center; service; and fundamental aspect of our political, economic, and social life, backed by the firm support of the masses — a real battle, in which this meeting is just a first step. The problem of absenteeism we've talked about here is just the first step. Absenteeism is the thing we must tackle with everything we've got right now. But there are other things, like peak organizational efficiency, optimal use of human and material resources, and the great battle for work productivity, which we must wage in the coming months and years, and without which we will never be able to solve our problems.

Along these lines, we haven't limited ourselves to public speeches, but have been analyzing, meeting, and studying all problems, all causes; working, searching, and acting. We have to do more than spend time discussing and analyzing things. A series of concrete measures must be adopted in all fields. We are trying to do this in agriculture, industry, and all other sectors.

We are now under tremendous pressure, having to analyze and mull over the measures that are to be adopted for the advance of the revolution in this stage of its existence and in future years, plus having to do all the concrete work that can't be put off.

These ideas I'm throwing out are a summary of the principal problems we face today. With the elimination of the inhuman factors which forced people to work, the alternative is the development of the greatest possible consciousness among the people and the application of pressure by working society on those who want to live like parasites off the work of others, refusing to fulfill their most elementary social and human duty.

Drawing up the kind of law the workers want against indolence — Comrade Risquet went into this a bit — won't be easy. The different sections will have to be modified and things will have to be added which are more in keeping with the present situation, our new experiences and ideas.

Perhaps the best method would be for a series of surveys to be carried out and the workers polled on their opinions before the law is drawn up in final form. That way, it could be drawn up with a full awareness of the workers' opinions and then be submitted for their consideration. We have to consider the international political aspect, as well, because we can't have people judging the Cuban working class by the bad attitude of a minority of 5 or 10 percent of the people.

I believe that the best thing about the law is that it will spring from the workers. Their opinions should be given wide coverage by the mass media, and they should speak on these problems over television and radio and have their opinions published in the newspapers, explaining their ideas on what to do with the lazy bums and absentees. This way the popular, nonadministrative nature of the law will be clear to all, and the law will express the will of the working people of Cuba. This is very important from the international point of view. Our enemies will surely say, "Look — under capitalism there aren't any laws against indolence. . . ." Of course, capitalism is inhuman, and its blind, ruthless, and criminal laws force people to work and make many of them spend years waiting to find a humble job. Under capitalism, millions of people are kept in ignorance so that they will perform the most brutal tasks, and there is an army of the unemployed held ready as a labor-power reserve.

In a rational and just society, the majority, in defense of its interests, has the right and duty to adopt measures to exert pressure on the tiny minority which refuses to fulfill its social duty after the hateful right of some men to exploit others has been done away with. The capitalists would never enact laws against indolence, because they themselves are the parasites in the society in which they live. The first great blow against indolence was struck when the revolution wiped out capitalism.

Now that we've abolished capitalism, who are the only exploiters that are left? Who are the ones who can exploit us today? Those who try to take privileges. Privileges can be a factor in exploiting the working people. We must always fight with everything we've got against any manifestation of privilege taking.

Leaders must be examples in work and sacrifice. This should be so all the way down the line. [*Applause*]

Take the problem of housing. Early in the revolution there were thousands of empty apartments and houses waiting for people to pay sky-high rent. At that time, the Urban Reform Law provided a remedy for that situation. Many families were then enabled to rent a house, and all of a sudden rent payments ceased to be a source of worry and an instrument of exploitation for millions of people. However, the situation is different today. The population has grown, and house building has not kept pace. There are tremendous tensions in this respect. In such a situation, the administrative official — or, even worse, the political leader — who gets preferential treatment in obtaining a house that becomes available, right before the eyes of thousands of people who don't have a single room and before the eyes of all the people, does a tremendous amount of damage to the authority and prestige of the revolution. Right away, the *gusanos*,* our enemies, the loafers and lumpen elements — all the ene-

---

*Gusano, Spanish for *worm*, is a Cuban term for counterrevolutionaries, especially those who left the country.

mies of work — seize on this as an argument to use against the revolution, trying to demoralize the revolutionaries.

Fortunately, our vanguard has not become demoralized. Our vanguard is made up, basically, of people who have come from the working class. The vast majority of our party members have been selected in workers' assemblies. Those who hold administrative and leadership posts have been selected for party membership taking their revolutionary record and their conduct during the revolutionary process into account. If there are exceptions — if, unfortunately, as has happened, there are cases of privilege taking and even corruption — we have to eradicate them, but completely!

If a cadre or party member has gone sour, he must be replaced; he has to be taken out of the party without loss of time.

Then, that moral factor will not be difficult to obtain. The battle against every manifestation of privilege taking will not be difficult to win. Now then, the other battle is more difficult — the battle against that minority that doesn't have enough consciousness yet, that hasn't been educated properly, that is maladjusted in a society of workers — that battle will prove more difficult.

Those of that minority exploit the rest of us, because even though they don't work they do wear shoes and other clothing, eat food, take in movies and other entertainment, get medicines when they fall sick — and everything is done to save their lives — and receive a free funeral when they die. No doubt about it, they get everything. But every one of the goods and services they receive has to be produced by somebody.

That may be our exploiter today. We have to rebel against these manifestations of exploitation with the same vigor and hatred with which the workers rebelled against imperialist monopolies, the latifundists, bourgeois exploiters, and chiseling merchants, for they are a manifestation of wrongdoing in a collectivist society, and we must put a stop to them. I'm in complete agreement with Comrade Risquet's thesis that this is fundamentally a political matter; that the measures that are taken, besides emanating from the people, should be educational; that 90 percent of the battle should be won by simply discussing and approving the law; that the law be applied against a minority; that we should be well oriented as to how we apply it; and that we know how to distinguish between cases and avoid a mechanical application of the law.

Moreover, gentlemen, I believe that we should keep a file on every worker. Everybody knows everybody else in his work center: those who are liars, those who are honest and good, and those who are dishonest. Everybody knows these things in every work center.

We should do everything possible to avoid simplistic and mechanical solutions in this regard. More than ever, our work should be guided by political principles, taking intelligent measures and distinguishing among cases. Moreover, problems in one work center may be different from those in another. The problems at some places are difficult to solve; there are many places where the workers can't be sure they'll even get a snack. There are workers who, in order to work eight hours, have to spend four commuting — and this under very difficult conditions. And, of course, there are all those administrative and objective factors we see in the factories.

I was saying, if a man sees that the roof in a factory is leaking and things have been getting wet for such a long time, he must have a very deep conviction to believe in the revolution. It wouldn't be hard for him to conclude that this thing is no good, that there is no future for it if five years can go by and a leaky roof in a factory is not repaired. That is the situation there.

Of course, there are many positive things that give encouragement to the people, but these other factors promote discouragement, demoralization, and things like that.

Then again, no two work centers have exactly the same situation. There are many, I repeat, that don't have a dining room, and some where the workers don't even get a snack. There are many places where conditions are much better than in others; we have seen such places. One of the things we have to look into is how we can improve the workers' dining rooms so that in the future every workers' dining room will be like a restaurant, a reasonably nice and pleasant place.

Unfortunately, we don't have all the resources we need, so this can't be accomplished easily.

There are some fields in which the country can make rapid progress. Our fishing fleet is growing, and our high potential for producing milk can and should be taken advantage of. Or breweries can boost the production of malt drinks for the workers' dining rooms. Today we have more resources than ever before for continuing to increase rice production and give a dramatic boost to the production of root and other vegetables. It will be much more difficult — in a short period of time — to increase the production of meat. This is because, notwithstanding the fact that our cattle herds have been upgraded for the production of milk, our pasturelands didn't receive all the attention they should have in the last few years, the birth rate wasn't high enough, and the number of head that had to be slaughtered — because of lack of weight — has been high.

We are now giving the greatest attention to this matter and to the boosting of production of hogs and poultry.

Therefore, relatively soon, we can increase the output of many — if not all — of our important foodstuffs.

We must do our best to try and achieve this, as we are faced with a need to increase the number of children that can be admitted to the day-care centers so their mothers may take jobs; we have to increase the number that can have their meals in the schools' dining rooms, for the same reason; and we have to increase the number that can eat and the quality of the meals in the workers' dining rooms, many of which do not yet have a quota whereby they may be assured of their food supply.

Therefore, we are going to follow a policy aimed at improving the workers' situation — first of all, with regard to food, and then in transportation. We are pushing through a plan in Havana Province's genetics centers aimed at supplying milk to work centers where the work is difficult and protecting the workers' health calls for better nutrition. We have asked the Ministry of Labor to furnish us with a list of the work centers that should have priority for health reasons.

Of course, we can't go by this kind of priority alone. There may be places that, though not on such a priority list because of the type of work involved, have to be considered, since they have absolutely nothing else. If it is possible to furnish at least a snack — some soda crackers with deviled ham and a little milk — even though the work center is not on a priority list on the basis of the kind of work done there, it is right to do so. There are work centers in which, because of the sanitary conditions there, work is not so hard as it is in others, but whereas the latter have something the former don't have anything.

Therefore, we have to try to distribute our products as fairly as possible. I believe that within a year or so we can provide 100,000 workers with an 11-ounce glass of milk a day — that is, if we succeed in finishing those dairies that've already been mentioned here, which the construction workers could finish more rapidly if there were less absenteeism. That is, if the construction brigades raise their productivity; if construction work proceeds at a good clip at the Niña Bonita, Nazareno, Flor de Itabo, Picadura, Niña Sierra, and other dairies. We have the cows, and the equipment for mechanical milking is coming in. Similar projects can be organized in each of the rest of the nation's provinces, since all of them have a large number of dairy heifers with which it would be possible not only to supply milk to the workers' dining rooms but also to increase the amount of milk supplied to the nation's children and the people in general and, moreover, reduce the amount of milk products we are now importing. The problem lies in building the milking facilities and getting them into operation.

There's another formula we are studying. Perhaps the Artemisa Banana Project could arrange for the distribution of bananas to workers' dining rooms. The same thing goes for the Albert Kuntz cracker plant. We could thus continue working out ways to improve the workers' snacks and meals.

We've also decided to organize a few brigades to build dining rooms in places where there aren't any as yet. We could use the dining room at Construimport, or something similar, as our model.

Here, for example, a worker handed me a note which reads as follows: "Comrade Fidel, Unit 209 (previously known as Edimira) in San José de las Lajas invites you and the comrade from the Lincoln Sugar Mill who reported on the difficulties encountered by the dining room there to visit ours, which we made ourselves — even the building blocks — with voluntary work." This proves that things can be accomplished.

We're going to see just how many compressors, how much cork, and how many other raw materials we need to build the refrigerators and cold-storage rooms required. We have to determine what the design should be for 250, 500, 750, and 1000 workers. Within the next few days we should have all that information, and we'll try to get all the necessary materials together.

Another problem we're working on is that of transportation for the factories. Some means of transportation have already been assigned to several of them, and we began with Santiago de Cuba. Why? To help those with the biggest problems, complementing the rest of the urban transportation during the night shifts.

We have a plan . . . the problem is that the 300 medium-sized buses we're building this year are just a drop in the bucket compared to our needs, since, in addition to the great needs posed by rural transportation, we now also have those of the factories. What are we going to do with those buses? We'll turn them into "collective cars" for the workers. They will pick up the workers following a planned route. Those workers who can do so without much trouble will use the regular buses. The factory buses will be for the exclusive use of those workers who have the greatest difficulties in using the regular transportation service. The factory buses can also be used for the workers' vacation trips in the summer, during the hours when they are not being used for taking the workers to and from work. We can coordinate the vacation plans with that in mind.

We also believe, gentlemen, that some things can be distributed at the plants themselves. How should we distribute those refrigerators that are being manufactured in Santa Clara? Some of them will be installed in the apartments we are building for the farmers in the agricultural projects. We're already doing this in every new town. But we will have approximately 15,000 to distribute in 1971. How should we do this? I think we should sell them at the plants, by means of quotas assigned proportionally to work centers, with the workers who are to receive them presenting a card they have received at their work centers when they call at the distribution unit. How can we sell almost half a million pressure cookers? Well, I think we should do this by means of cards assigned at the work centers, too. [*Prolonged applause*]

Then, what will we do? As far as the absentees go, they know they haven't got a chance of getting a refrigerator. Everybody knows they'll never be able to get one, no matter what. [*Applause*]

And, in the same way, when we have enough furniture and other permanent effects produced, we'll distribute them at the factories, too.

The formula somebody suggested with regard to cigarettes resembles this somewhat, but we should go into this question of cigarettes further. That's another matter we'll have to discuss: what to do about cigarettes. I asked the comrades to dig up all the data available on the thousands, the hundreds of thousands of people we would have to use to maintain both the export and the domestic supply, considering the increase in demand.

Therefore, with regard to cigarettes and liquor, we'll have to find a solution on the basis of price fixing. There are some people who don't smoke, but they latch onto a pack of cigarettes and turn right around and trade it to somebody else — sometimes, gentlemen, they even trade it for food! It would be better if the workers would continue paying little for their food and pay a little more for cigarettes. Even the boys are getting into the habit of smoking, because they can get a pack of cigarettes for 20 cents. It's better to invest our energies in supplying the workers' dining rooms with malt drinks, milk, and other foodstuffs than to spend any more energy on an item which has been proved to be extremely harmful.

In short, we believe that, for certain items, such as cigarettes and liquor, we should look for a solution in the realm of price fixing rather than rationing.

When I spoke on July 26, I said that we didn't like a solution based on prices. Why? Ah, because with the existing inequality in wages only some people would be able to buy meat, milk, etc. at high prices. All the people need all the vital products. That is not the case with cigarettes, since the first problem we come across is who smokes and who doesn't, who should be given a quota and who shouldn't. If we ration them, everybody would demand his quota. If we distribute them through the factories, all we would accomplish would be to have the workers smoking more, and we'd be protecting the health of the loafers. We must make use of refrigerators; food; many, many things to improve the standard of living of the workers — but not cigarettes. The question of cigarettes should be settled in another way, by setting prices which will serve to limit consumption and at the same time take up some of the excess currency in circulation. Naturally, these measures should be thoroughly analyzed and discussed with the workers themselves. They have enough intelligence to decide whether or not the country should devote the work of 100,000 or 200,000 more people — which, by the way, we don't have — in addition to other resources to increasing the consumption of a harmful product sold at rock-bottom prices, while at the same time maintaining the same level of exports — which we can't afford to give up, as they are a source of the foreign exchange so necessary for our development. We could also say, "Let's ration cigarettes," and go ahead and ration them. Then we'd have a black market, we'd have the man exchanging his cigarettes for food.

Let's keep this kind of situation in mind, but, just the same, let's discuss and analyze the problem thoroughly.

Getting back to the matter of absentees: in the first place, their right to purchase durable goods is taken away. The time comes when a house in some district needs repairs, and we tell the man, "Just a minute, my friend, you don't deserve it. We are going to give priority to this man, who is a better worker, who does his job right and is always on time. You wait." Necessity isn't enough. When deciding between two people with the same need, we'll give preference to that worker who is a good, conscientious worker in that district. And when the time comes we say to a worker, "Look, you're getting to be a little lazier, a little less conscientious. We are going to deprive you of your quota in this workers' dining room, because you've been showing up for work only two or three times a week." This weapon is a little more drastic. We can go even further and deprive him of his clothing ration card.

With respect to a worker's salary, we have to suspend it if the circumstances so require. His family won't suffer, because they'll get social security. It's better to give the family of a loafer — you understand? — a pension, so they can buy what they need, than to have this loafer appear as the "big shot" who earns a salary and supports his family. [*Applause*] [*Jorge Risquet: "When those elements don't show up, they won't get paid."*]

They don't get paid now, right? But we'll have to look into the vanguard work centers, where we established certain provisions — [*Jorge Risquet: "Yes, but not to include these types."*]

Right. We'll leave them out. There's a whole series of ways in which we can start isolating, cornering, and combating the antisocial elements — and, when necessary, we can apply the most rigorous measures, so as not to have a repetition of the case of the man who nine months ago was given a warning for the seventeenth time and still hasn't showed up for work. It isn't only a case of the harm they do society by their behavior but also the time they make the others lose.

We must be a little more rigorous. Now we can do it, because the majority of our workers are sufficiently conscious. The difficulties, the problems, the complexity of revolutionary work itself, help us to develop an awareness. For one thing can be said, and that is that it is a very difficult — an extremely difficult — process!

Now, another question: the battles for the solution of our economic problems and for production must be waged concretely, not abstractly, plant by plant, whether in graphic arts or in the Téllez factory, where several problems were pointed out. The battle must be waged concretely in the thousands of production centers throughout the country. The administrative agencies must do concrete work, problem by problem. I repeat: problems are solved with concrete measures, not in the abstract.

In our opinion, this meeting has been a great experience; it has yielded a great deal of experience. I wonder what the results would have been if we had held a meeting of the sector in question — for example, that of construction or light industry — with the representatives of the corresponding administration.

Naturally, it's much better when the various sectors are present, since they are interrelated, and often a clearer picture of the problem emerges and the discussion is more fruitful when the various branches are represented at the meeting. Just imagine what it would be like if we had eight or ten of the most important sectors of the economy here, with their respective ministers and deputy ministers, and we held a discussion on the concrete problems faced in each production center. [*Applause*]

The discussion wouldn't be limited to absenteeism or voluntary work or — and we'll have to take this up — the law or what to do about cigarettes.

Having this type of analysis and discussion would be of tremendous interest, because the comrades would be able to go into all the problems, and the minister or deputy minister, the director of an enterprise or the official in foreign trade or any other service who's involved could give whatever information he had, explaining what is and isn't being done and why, what can be done, and what's going to be done.

This would be of tremendous help for improving the state, for having us all become fully aware of our reality.

I tell you, it really hurts me to see one of those factories with a leaky roof. No minister has the right to have the roof of the ministry fixed — or even to have a building to house the ministry! — while the workers' building is threatening to collapse over their heads. This is what I think. This is what I sincerely believe! [*Applause*]

We must see to it that our officials have a clearer, more precise idea, a much more real understanding of just what's going on. We must see to it that ministers visit the work centers, gentlemen. Let them go there, because that is where things are learned. And, to tell the truth, any time I want to find out about some problem I don't go to the ministry; I go to the work center. There is where I learn all about the difficulties and the problems. There is where one learns lessons, where one gains experience, where one catches the spirit of the working people.

We speak of inculcating a proletarian spirit, of creating consciousness. That's a lot of bunk. The way things are today, it is we who must go to the factories, where the workers are, to learn lessons in consciousness from them, not teach them lessons in consciousness. The man who is there in that factory, carrying sacks on his back for eight hours a day at full tilt, or perched up on a scaffold, or hammering away hour after hour, or working with fire and steel, has a greater proletarian consciousness than we, because he is there, immersed in his work, in his struggle, face to face with all the problems and all the realities, overcome by a feeling of helplessness on seeing many problems that nobody bothers to explain to him and about which he can't do anything.

Thus, by going to the factories, we can let the workers in on whatever we know but they don't and pick up whatever information they have that we don't. And, above all, we're there in the midst of necessity, of struggle, seeing a worker with torn pants or boots full of holes. I'm sure that any sensitive individual who witnesses this will immediately be twice as concerned — or three times as concerned — over the problem as he was before. As a starter, he's going to learn about the problem — in case he didn't know about it before.

Then start things going among the workers — we've seen what's happened, with shoes that are falling apart; get in contact with the workers in the shoe industry. Establish contacts with the various factories. Often, these are all dependent on one little old hole-in-the-wall place. Don't go to a consolidated enterprise, go to the factory, and tell them, "Look, according to the plan, your unit is the one that's supposed to make this product for me. When can I have it? When will it be ready?" If the unit is short in labor power — as in the case of the small shop that manufactures the rollers for graphic arts — tell them, "We're sending you three men from our factory to help make the rollers, because we'll have to stop production if we don't get them soon." If it's a case of a small bushing, go to the plant that's supposed to make them. Establish a series of contacts among factories, among workers, always struggling to keep production up. The workers' principal duty is to struggle for production. Why? Because only through production can living conditions be improved. Only through production can there be more footwear, more clothing, more everything.

However, don't be misled into thinking it's easy to solve these problems.

We have more means for solving the problem of shoes. Plastics are going to be a great help to us, and we should be producing some 20 million pairs of plastic shoes next year. This will go a long way toward solving the problem of women's and children's shoes. What with plastic, leather, and other types, we can come close to 40 million pairs. More than four pairs per person. Now the thing is to work on improving quality — especially in leather shoes. To turn out shoes that will not fall apart in a matter of minutes, with soles that stay put, not junk. We must study everything that has a bearing on this problem.

The problem of fabrics is a tougher nut to crack. Even if the labor-power shortage is solved, we still don't have enough installed capacity. Moreover, both the factories and the equipment have put in many years of service, a lot of them are U.S.-built and we don't always have the raw materials at hand. The problem is aggravated by the fact that large amounts of clothing are distributed for certain activities, such as the sugar harvest, that call for a considerable amount of material. Moreover, the population has increased, while we have imported less in the way of textile goods because we ran into problems in maintaining these import levels. And the per capita distribution is very low, gentlemen. It's really shocking how little clothing is being distributed to the population. And this is one of the problems to which we must give special attention.

We have two tremendous problems at this moment: housing and textiles. The government, the country's leadership organizations, those who handle the economy, must do everything under the sun to come up with a means to alleviate the housing problem — which is becoming a supercritical one — and to alleviate the problem of the textile shortage during the next two, three, or four years, while we increase our factories' capacity and finally settle the problem.

In other words, these problems call for special efforts by the nation and an optimal utilization of our means and resources.

Today, when I saw all that hardware lying there in the warehouse of the Ministry of the Sugar Industry (MINAZ), I realized that MINAZ, a sector of our economy, capitalizing on the ten-million-ton harvest, had gone wild and had got in a stock of steel that hasn't even been touched and machinery that hasn't yet been installed. They don't even know what to do with what they've got, while other factories, that would have been improved as a result of a better distribution of the resources that were devoted to the plan for the ten million tons, were neglected.

Now then, the technocrats, the "brains," the "geniuses," and the "superscientists" — all of them knew exactly what should be done in order to produce the ten million tons of sugar. Well, first of all, it was proved that they didn't really know what was what; and in the second place, they exploited the economy, channeling large amounts of resources to that sector. There were many cases of a shortage of steel plates to build a sugar-cane-planting machine while they held onto tens of thousands of tons of steel.

Therefore, the work in connection with planning and distribution has to be much improved over what it has been up to now.

I tell you, these problems are anything but easy to solve. They are difficult and complex. There are some problems which are objective, and we'll have to see how we go about tackling them, while others are completely subjective. It is in connection with these things of a subjective order — the workers' attitude, productivity, organization, administration, leadership, and the leaders' conduct — that we have to attack full force in the immediate future, because this is where we can advance.

I was saying that this meeting was extraordinarily enlightening and that, by all means, we must have many more. It has provided us with experience, leading up to a meeting of another type — not for discussing voluntary work or absenteeism, I repeat, but for taking up the concrete problems in each important work center.

It's a pity that our labor movement isn't more developed, so we could bring the trade union representative from every important factory to this meeting — that is, have the representatives of the trade union, of the Vanguard Workers Movement, and even the party nucleus come here and then, gentlemen, bring the factory managers to the meeting, too, and sit down and analyze all these problems together. [*Applause*]

It has been proved that with a few microphones and a number of comrades to take them from one speaker to the next, everybody can get a chance to speak. Then, if we get a little more light down there in the back, we can see those who are sitting there. And even if we have to hash these problems over for three days straight, look at all the lessons we can gain and all the ideas that will come to light!

What would we accomplish by doing this? We would also be teaching our workers how to solve problems; to submit ideas; to discuss things; to meditate; to have a more complete idea of the interrelationship that exists among all the factories and branches; to have a broader understanding of all problems; and to have the arguments needed for fighting, speaking out, and struggling.

I realize how hard it must be for the comrades in the trade union group and the comrades of the party in that factory where the roof has been leaking for five years and they're still waiting for somebody to show up. I understand their predicament very well. It must be really rough. It calls for a superrevolutionary, a genius, to stay there, wielding a good argument, because things like that are very difficult to understand.

I was saying that there are some people who haven't the slightest idea of how complex a process can be, who can't find any explanations for all these problems and inefficiency and who wind up by losing faith.

The fact that our country has come this far, that our country has successfully put up resistance for eleven years against the world's most powerful imperialist country — the one which could do the most damage to us economically, militarily, and ideologically; a country which had us completely indoctrinated, which had inculcated us with its capitalist, egotistical, thoroughly reactionary policy and its vices, with everything — the fact that our country was capable of holding up against all this demonstrates the strength of the revolution, the power of the revolution. But we have shown a much greater capacity to face the enemy, to lay down our lives, or do anything else that may be necessary, and even to make great sacrifices, than to develop the tremendous energy and initiative of the masses with a view to tackling our problems.

This is a kind of atomic energy, and, once we release it, nothing will be able to stand in its way. Therefore, we must learn how to develop the science of liberating the nuclear power of the masses.

It is up to our party and our mass organizations to develop this technology.

Our comrade the baker was saying that we have a system of social security and rights so generous that they have no equal even in the other communist countries. What a shame it would be if the revolution should have to revert to the old ways; if we should have to begin charging for education, medical attention, housing, children's day-care centers, workers' dining rooms, baseball — No, never!

If, through the work of the masses, we win this battle, we will be able to make great progress. We will make great progress if we establish the greatest possible degree of democratization of the process. No state can be more democratic than a socialist state; no state can or should be more democratic. If a socialist state is not democratic, it will fail. The socialist state is society organized for the solution of the problems of the masses, depending on the consciousness of the individual, not the life-or-death struggle of capitalism.

If we were to use capitalist methods to solve our problems, what kind of a communist man, what kind of a man with a superior mind, culture, and consciousness would we be creating? Impossible! We cannot be socialists with capitalist methods.

If socialism does not spring from the masses, it will fail, because it must work for the masses and it can only solve our problems with the support of the masses. No longer is it the case of the money-making capitalist tending his shop, tending his factory, tending whatever it is, staying there all day long and functioning under the laws of the capitalist economy; now it's a case of the administration of the economy by all the people, the work of all the people.

Without the masses, socialism would lose the battle and become bureaucratic. It would have to adopt capitalist methods and retreat in the field of ideology. No society can be more democratic than socialist society, because without the masses, socialism could not triumph.

Now there are no contradictions in our society; there are no political parties to represent the landlords, bourgeoisie, and bankers; there is only one party, with one ideology, and one society, to the extent that we are able to eliminate all the hangovers from the past. Why, then, not establish the greatest possible participation of that society in the struggle for its life, if — as I firmly believe to be the case — this is the most beautiful thing about a socialist society?

It isn't a case of a group of superintelligent men directing the passive masses for their own good. That is not revolution. That cannot happen in real life, because nobody can solve problems through administrative methods.

Remember that in a collectivist society battles can be won only with the widest possible participation of the masses in the solution of their problems.

Socialism can go forward, and it can overcome the great obstacles with which it is faced — especially in the case of an underdeveloped economy such as ours — only through the widest possible participation of the masses.

We must eliminate administrative methods, because they don't provide real solutions. In the first stage of the revolution, their use was understandable. Then we didn't even have an ideology. What did we have? Terrible ideological confusion: many people influenced by reactionary, capitalist, and egotistical ideas. Today our people have made great progress. Now we must do away with all administrative methods and use mass methods everywhere: from the district right on up to the national level.

We can't do it from one day to the next. It would be absurd for a few of us to get together and start writing a constitution and expect everything to function perfectly, just like magic. We have to move "with all deliberate speed" — but in a relatively short period of time. "All deliberate speed" doesn't mean we'll wait ten years or anything like that. We must start with some of these channels: organizing a district, holding meetings like this one with the main officials from the key production sectors. All these are steps.

One of the most important steps is the establishment of a strong labor movement, so that, together with the Committees for the Defense of the Revolution and the Federation of Cuban Women, we will have a strong labor movement. This is one of the first steps of making things completely democratic. Starting with the workers, starting with the trade unions, and holding absolutely free elections.

Where we find that the workers elect a corrupt trade union leader from the past, this should set off political alarm bells concerning the confusion, backwardness, and bad political work that has been done there. Where we find that they elect an absentee, or somebody who is not a good worker, this should also set alarm bells ringing. Where they elect an agitator or demagogue who takes advantage of a real grievance, it will show that our political work there has left much to be desired.

And I am sure that a work center with a proletarian consciousness will not elect an absentee, liar, political hack, or corrupt trade union leader from the past, because the workers know enough to see through all these people.

We are going to trust our workers and hold trade union elections in all locals — they will now be called locals — in all the factories right away.

[*Applause*] They will be absolutely free, and the workers will choose the candidates. Nobody can buy off the masses: no demagogue can fool the masses.

We must do this in the same way that the exemplary workers are selected. Then the matter must be submitted to an absolutely democratic vote, so that the workers will freely pick their leaders. If they should elect a man who is unworthy of representing the cause and spirit of the proletariat — and I am sure this will happen in only a very few cases — this will give us an idea of the political situation at that work center, and we will know that the center is in bad shape from the political point of view, because there is a lack of awareness and the workers have let themselves be taken in by a liar, a demagogue, a charlatan, or one who is any number of things. This would not weaken the revolution, however; rather, it would serve to keep it alert, vigilant, and militant with respect to the masses.

We will start by making the labor movement completely democratic. If the labor movement isn't democratic, it is good for nothing.

If the worker has really been elected by a majority vote of all his comrades, he will have authority; he won't be a nobody who has been placed there by decree. He will have the moral authority of his election, and when the revolution establishes a line he will go all out to defend and fight for that line. And, if the leader is not true to the spirit of the revolution, the masses can remove him at any time.

We must make it clear that any official can be removed at any time. He can be removed whenever another election is called, so nobody should get the idea that simply because he was elected one day he can spend a year doing just as he damn pleases. In three months or at any other time there can be another meeting or election, and out he goes, and somebody else goes in. But all this must be done through democratic procedures. If the labor movement isn't democratic, then it is good for nothing.

If a socialist society doesn't have the support of the masses, it will fail. And, to have the support of the masses, it must be as democratic as possible and eliminate administrative methods altogether.

If millions of people put their minds to it, we can solve any problem. If we put millions of people to work conscientiously, we can solve any administrative problem. Anybody who is doing things badly, any minister whose work isn't up to par, any regional that is abusing the people . . . none of the problems which were discussed here can last if the masses take a hand in things. Then there'll be sand on the beach, not rocks; the things won't rot; there won't be any waste; the jute bags won't be lying around; and the other things won't be sitting at the docks, abandoned.

None of this will happen once we really get the masses thinking and acting in a conscious manner. [*Applause*]

We are absolutely sure of this, and we think of the great reserve of intelligence to be found in the minds of the people, just waiting to be tapped. There have been many comrades who have spoken here with a magnificent spirit, presenting clear ideas, who have greatly impressed us by the way in which they set forth their problems here. There are scores of thinking minds in our working class.

The ability to think is not the exclusive property of a small leadership group. All the people can think. We must look for all these minds. They won't necessarily all be found among those who occupy certain positions.

Can't a member of the Vanguard Workers Movement come here to present a problem, as has been done now? I think that when we hold a meeting like this, we should bring vanguard workers here as invited guests, in addition to the members of the party and trade union representatives, even though they may not hold any posts in the organizations.

Of course, the most likely thing is that the workers will elect the most talented, the best of their comrades. The most likely thing is that these comrades will already be in the trade union or Vanguard Workers Movement. But there may be cases of skilled and revolutionary workers who hold no official position because, given the task they carry out in the factory, it would not be a very good idea to have them handling a trade union job as well. These cases can occur; there can be workers who are better off free of all these kinds of activity, but still they should be able to come here and discuss important matters.

If we advance along this road, we will win the battle. We believe this is the way we will win the eight, ten, or twelve battles we will have to wage.

The number one contribution of the workers, first — I'm referring to the process of making the process completely democratic — is that of making their own organization completely democratic, establishing a strong and powerful labor movement which, in order to be strong, powerful, and a true labor movement, must be completely democratic in every sense of the word. Don't forget that. A strong and powerful labor movement must be completely democratic. The battles must be waged by ideas and words, not by decree. The demagogues must be confronted with firm ideas and solid arguments. Revolutionaries cannot be timid; they must be trained in the art of debate and must stand by the truth.

Here we have seen comrades who have participated in the debate: some with one argument, and others with another. Leaders, cadres, and party members in general must be trained in the art of debate, in how to defend their point of view, in reasoning and in considering all these problems.

I believe this will prove to be a truly historic meeting. But we're not going to give it that title! Whether or not it is considered to be historic will depend on how well we continue working along the lines which have been outlined here.

All the debate at this meeting will be published, even though I realize you have spoken more freely than you would have if there had been radio microphones or TV cameras in front of you. When we speak over radio or TV, millions of people are listening in, the enemy is listening in, the guy abroad is listening in, and he will have everything you say right there. All that. Although I believe the revolution should never be afraid to say anything, no matter what.

We believe a good job has been done. It is true that the turns were too long and the comrades who spoke at the end were placed under a great pressure of time, hardly getting any chance to speak. This is most unfortunate, because if these comrades had spoken earlier, they might have contributed ideas just like the others. What we will have to do, based on the experience we have gained here, is set up time limits. When there are interruptions, they won't be counted, because sometimes they are necessary in order to ask questions from which worthwhile information may be obtained. I believe this can be done without having to go on till 3:00 in the morning. Perhaps we should take a Sunday and say, "Voluntary work: a meeting at the CTC." [*Laughter and applause*]

We could hold the meeting from 8:00 a.m. to noon, from 2:00 to 7:00, and from 9:00 to midnight. That would make twelve hours. [*Applause*] [*Jorge Risquet: "With an entertainment program."*] Well, at least with piped-in music, or with some of the 150 performers who aren't working coming here to play the guitar. Get the idea? And we could discuss things.

Why do we have a phobia against meetings? Because there have been stupid meetings, mechanical affairs at which everybody says the same old things over and over. But meetings like this . . . look, we've been here for hours and hours and hours, but, believe you me, I prefer this to the best movie. We've really learned something here. We've gotten a good look at what life is really like.

Those of us who are deeply interested in things social and political have really gotten a big bang out of this meeting, as we've discovered, delved into, and learned a lot of new things.

We'd really like to be able to be everywhere at the same time. We'd like to be able to visit all the factories, go around more. We wish we were children's tops — not the yo-yos a worker was talking about here, but tops. [*Laughter*] They're not the same thing. [*Laughter*] [*Shouts from the crowd: "It goes up and down."*]

Well, we can't go around so much, but I will try to visit as many factories as possible. To please the workers? That's not what we're trying to do. We're trying to get a firsthand idea of the problems. In all those places you learn scores of things every day.

And do you know how we can learn how to be efficient and how our ministers can learn how to be efficient functionaries of the people? Do you know how? By going to the factories! [*Shouts from the crowd: "Like Che did."*] [*Applause*]

Che was one of the foremost advocates of moral incentives and of the worth of the workers, voluntary work, contacts among the workers, and democratic processes; he felt all these things deeply. That is why the baker's quoting Che's "There are still a lot of people who are not employing themselves" is so apropos. He was referring to people who worked in a plant but weren't producing. How did Che put it, exactly? [*Baker: " 'Unemployment has come to an end, but there are still a lot of people who are not employing themselves but are still drawing their salaries.' "*]

"A lot of people who are not employing themselves." Yes, that's right. That's nothing but the plain, unvarnished truth.

Che felt and was sensitive to all these problems. He was always trying to set an example of what a worker should be like.

Today, when I was at the factory, I said, "You have to establish contacts." The people there answered, "Yes, CILOS [Committees of Local Industries]." And I asked them, "What do you mean, 'CILOS'?" And they answered, "Che said CILOS had to be established among the factories." This is the same thing we're talking about: establishing contacts among the factories.

I'd like to repeat this: in order to be efficient functionaries of the people, the best thing those who work in administration can do is to go to the factories. That's a sure way of discovering what the realities are, encouraging the workers, and explaining things to them.

While I was at the factory the workers there asked me about a blade for a cutting machine, but what could I tell them? I wished I were from the Maquimport Enterprise, from one of those agencies, or from their own enterprise so I could answer, "Yes, comrades, this type of blade has been ordered; they are coming from such and such a place," or "They aren't coming," or "Only so many have been supplied," or "We're doing such and so about securing them." One thing for sure, it's impossible to do any cutting without blades. That's a fact.

Our ministers must fight for better solutions at the levels where the decisions are made. They must say, "Comrades, I ask you to take this, that, and the other into consideration, because these things are affecting this, that, and the other." This should be done all the time, because a serious problem may arise someday, and if those who direct state affairs are not made aware of it, then what can we do? If, at the time of deciding what resources we must have, we are not aware of certain problems, of things that should have priority, something entailing serious consequences, then we make our plans mechanically and poorly. Why? Because otherwise the various ministers begin asking the moon, and the bill runs into the millions. Then, when you add up all the bills, you cry "Impossible!" And then the trimming process begins. At times, the inexpensive blade so badly needed at the plant goes by the board. Instead of ordering a blade to cut with, in cutting down, you cut it out. That's right. A blade can be cut out before it can do any cutting. [*Laughter*] That's the problem. Then, we find ourselves without a simple blade. But I can't understand how such a place could operate without such a cutting blade. That would be like expecting a textile mill to operate without yarn and shuttles. It just can't be. Or a printing shop without paper.

If the ministers were much better informed and in closer touch with reality, a much more efficient and better balanced plan could be drawn up. Then, all the purchasing efforts would be coordinated and everybody would be better informed about all the problems.

You may think, sometimes, that when we speak about the problems in a factory we really know what we're talking about, right? Not necessarily. The fact is, we have a truly encyclopedic ignorance of the factories' problems. I wish I could be really up on all the problems in the factories, for I'm sure that the more I know about them the more I'll be able to help find some kind of a solution for them. And the same thing goes for all the other comrades: the more they know about the problems, I'm sure the more they can and will do something to solve them. But I don't think anybody will ever do anything about a problem he knows nothing about. That goes without saying.

I've already kept you here much too long, and you must be tired. I hope when you leave here you'll go filled with enthusiasm for work. However, you mustn't think that we've actually solved any problems. Carry that thought with you: we haven't solved any problems here; all we've done is take a short step forward. You should now keep on moving forward, starting from that modest first step, which is no more than a mere beginning. Start working on the most important and urgent things first; begin to meditate, think, and see things clearly — experiences, problems, everything. Start preparing — let's say, for our next meeting — to tackle the concrete problems of production. But concretely, among ourselves here, without any newspaper coverage . . . that is, with newsmen, but without publicity, or with a minimum of publicity.

I'm sure the newsmen here are more interested in what is being discussed than in what they can write about it. I'm positive of that. Yesterday I noticed they were exceedingly interested in the meeting and the topics being discussed.

We'll hold our meeting quietly and do our work. We already have proof that a mass gathering of people can reason. The only thing is, we must work out some method to assure everyone of a chance to speak and say what he has to say and have some debates or discussions within that framework and let everybody express himself with absolute freedom. And, when the time comes to discuss problems, be prepared to present concrete problems. Problems from any and all factories can be discussed here. If in Havana Province we have, say, 67 percent of all the factories — apart from the sugar industry — and we meet here with representatives from those factories, which account for 60 or 70 percent of the nation's production, and we solve the problems of those factories, waging a battle against the concrete problems of each one of them . . .

Comrades, no one, by himself, could wage a successful battle against concrete problems from here. Not even Risquet could do it by himself. Risquet tries to supply the labor power that is requested, and I do something along these lines, too. But if the ministers, deputy ministers, and other comrades are gathered here and we wage a battle against the concrete problems of every work center . . . Ah! Then I feel sure that, within a year, we'll have a radically different situation from the one we're faced with now.

It'll be interesting to see what we can do and how much we can advance in a year, following this policy. And be able to actually measure our progress — as we have in the case of the pressure cookers, of which we are now turning out over 1,000 a day and refrigerators, of which 60 are being produced every day. That's some progress, already. Everybody here applauded when I mentioned the refrigerators, because refrigerators really mean something. This means that 15,000 families will benefit from getting refrigerators for their homes. And 400,000 families will get pressure cookers. Of course, if they can put something in those pressure cookers, so much the better! [*Laughter*]

Well, comrades, that's it for now. We'll see you again before too long.

Patria o muerte!

Venceremos! [*Ovation*]

The Democratization of the
Revolutionary Process
September 28, 1970

NOTE: The Committees for the Defense of the Revolution were formed in September 1960 as an instrument of vigilance against counter-revolutionary activity. Over the years the committees, organized on a block-by-block basis, took on a number of other functions. These included organizing vaccinations and blood donations, maintaining schools and other public buildings, keeping neighborhoods clean, and organizing neighborhood anticrime patrols. In addition, they play an important role in democratic decision making, discussing and voting on legislation proposed by the government.

The following is the major part of Castro's speech to a rally in Havana's Plaza of the Revolution commemorating the founding of the CDRs. He used the opportunity to expand on the themes he had outlined on July 26. The text is from Granma Weekly Review, *October 4, 1970.*

Comrades of the Venceremos Brigade, composed of U.S. young people; [*Applause*] Comrades of the Committees for the Defense of the Revolution: [*Applause*]

First of all, greetings on this tenth anniversary. [*Applause*] It was difficult to imagine on that afternoon, when the idea of the Committees for the Defense of the Revolution came up, that ten years later this organization would have the strength, the vigor, and the record it now has.

This tenth anniversary is being celebrated with the greatest mass rally ever held on a September 28. And it is also being celebrated with the highest combative spirit ever seen in any CDR celebration. [*Applause*]

[CDR National Coordinator] Comrade [Luis González] Marturelos described a whole series of activities carried out by the Committees for the Defense of the Revolution throughout these past years, especially during the last year.

The committees came into being, in the first place, as a mass organization to combat counterrevolution. However, during these years the committees became involved in new activities in new fields. And it can be said that with every year that goes by the scope of the activities in which the committees are engaged increases more and more.

In addition to taking part in activities related to the struggle against the enemy, the organization began to participate in the struggle against illiteracy; the struggle against epidemics; other activities in the area of cooperation with the Ministry of Public Health; and, in fact, a whole series of new activities. Later on there were tasks connected with the recovery of raw materials; activities involving not only the battle for vaccination but also such problems related to preventive medicine as cytological tests, campaigns to educate the people in matters of health, participation in productive work, and mobilizations of various kinds. And I believe that, in making the list of all those activities, the comrades forgot to include in the report they gave me one very important activity in which the comrades of the Committees for the Defense of the Revolution participated: the census on population and housing that was just made in this country. [*Applause*]

Moreover, this is a mass organization which has retained all its strength — which has, in fact, increased its strength during these years — and which has played a decisive role in the battles waged by the revolution through its masses. Some of these battles have been pointed out here.

It is also an organization ever on the alert, ever in combat readiness; an organization whose masses can be mobilized in a matter of hours; an organization that always contributes with its discipline, enthusiasm, and strength whenever the situation calls for it.

The strength of this mass organization can be gauged by the fact that the Committees for the Defense of the Revolution have a membership of 3,222,147, and, if I remember correctly, it has 67,457 grass-roots organizations and more than 600,000 activists. [*Applause*]

It is also worth pointing out that, in the field of education, nearly 250,000 exemplary parents have been selected by the Committees for the Defense of the Revolution. [*Applause*]

Therefore, no matter where this organization brings its weight and strength into play, it makes a tremendous impact.

It can be said that the organization is engaged in territorial work or discharges a function of a territorial character. In other words, it is everywhere.

It has a function that could never be discharged by other organizations. That is why we said that the organization is a complement, first of all, of our political organization; a complement of the workers' organizations, the women's organizations, the youth organizations, and the student organizations. Thus, the Committees for the Defense of the Revolution bring together the revolutionaries of all our people, be they young or old, adults, men or women. This way, the foundation, the basis of our mass movement, is solidly and definitely established.

Therefore, now that the revolution is entering a new, more mature phase, a phase which involves a tremendous battle to overcome the vices that still exist — the old and the new vices, the weaknesses and ineffi-ciences that still exist — our mass organizations will also enter a new phase. [*Applause*] They will enter, among other things, the most impor-tant, decisive phase of the democratization of the revolutionary process. [*Applause*]

Every revolutionary process has had its forms of organization, has had its concrete forms of expression. And thus, too, in the life and experi-ences of our own process, the forms of expression of our revolution gradually appear. Therefore, it is precisely in our mass organizations that the conditions, the foundations for this process exist.

The revolutionary process itself has gradually revealed the inconven-ience of bureaucratic and administrative methods.

In this process, every time mistakes in method have been made, every time mistakes in concept have been made, the negative results have been seen immediately. Every time in our practical work we have strayed from these fundamental concepts and lines — so oft-defined — as to the role of the party and the mass organizations, we have seen the immediate results.

And thus, whenever the party and the administration in some sector or some specific point have begun to become identified, the negative re-sults have been seen immediately. When a mass organization begins to grow weaker, the negative results are seen immediately.

At this moment we are engaged in a great effort to develop our workers' organizations as much as possible. [*Applause*] Why? Because, unfortunately, for the last two years our workers' organizations had taken a back seat — not through the fault of either the workers' organiza-tions or the workers themselves but through our fault, the party's fault, the fault of the country's political leadership.

Was this done consciously? No! It happened somewhat unconsciously, spontaneously; it happened as a result of certain idealisms. And this way, in creating an organization which, we believe, is also important — the organization of the Vanguard Workers Movement — the labor move-ment in general was neglected. And if, in addition to that, there came about certain phenomena, a certain degree of identification between the party and administration, that only served to make the situation even more complicated.

However, ever since the need to strengthen the labor movement was expressed in the last few months — June, July, August, and September — a series of very important steps have been taken. And we have not the slightest doubt that our labor movement will emerge stronger and more democratic than ever before from this situation and these difficulties. [*Applause*] In other words, it will be very strong because it will be very democratic. And an endless number of valuable revolutionary comrades

— that is, an endless number of cadres for the labor movement — will emerge from the working masses.

It is precisely in the labor movement that the revolution has the sector of the working population that can play a decisive role in the processes of production and in the creation of the goods and services needed by our country. Because, if the mass organizations — such as the Committees for the Defense of the Revolution — are located in every block, are everywhere, territorially, the workers' organizations are in every vital point of the productive process; that is, they are in the factories and in every center where the services for the country are in development. It is a fundamental organization with a view to the production of the goods and services the country needs.

The women's organizations, for example, are in the women's sector; they are not organized in line with productive activities — but the workers' organizations are. Hence, any weakening in the labor movement deprives the revolution of its most powerful instrument in the productive process, of its most powerful arms, of its most powerful base in the productive process.

That is why we are now concentrating on the strengthening of the labor movement, and our effort is rewarded by the growing enthusiasm among the working masses in favor of such an effort.

However, this is not only a case of strengthening in the sense of power. We must also give a deep meaning to this strengthening of the mass organizations.

Hence, by supporting ourselves in those mass organizations — the labor movement, women's organizations, youth organizations, student organizations, and farmers' organizations — we have the foundations for the next steps to be taken, which consist of a more direct participation by the masses in decision making and in the solution of problems [*Applause*] and a many-sided participation everywhere, territorially, in those problems directly under their jurisdiction.

This is because whatever goes wrong in any block, work center where a sevice is rendered, distribution center, school, bakery, or any other service center of any kind, has a direct adverse effect on the people who live in that neighborhood and who receive those services.

Any plant that is not operating well adversely affects the economy of every worker in the country.

The one organization that can play a fundamental role in a factory is the workers' organization. Naturally, in this organization we will find young people, women, and members of the Committees for the Defense of the Revolution who, while participating at the block level and as a part of the masses, in the services they are directly interested in, also participate directly in the factory in their concern over and in their struggle to solve the problems that interest them as members of the working class, and as a part of the entire people. [*Applause*]

And there is no doubt about the fact that no problem can be solved through administrative methods — much less in a collectivist society.

What would be the point of struggling for the eradication of classes, the eradication of exploitation of man by man, and the disappearance of these contradictions that constitute the agony of class societies, the divisions in class societies? What good would it do to have united the entire people, eradicated exploitation of man by man, and deprived the exploiters of their instruments of exploitation as long as that tremendous power, those tremendous resources, and those tremendous potentials that a united people implies are not utilized to tackle those tasks of the people and for the people? Who can make up for the efficiency — the infallibility, we might say — of controls by the masses?

Our revolution developed at a time when we were a country with a definitely underdeveloped economy, with primitive methods of production in many ways. A revolution in a developed country would have found great centers of production in every aspect. In a highly developed economy a large number of ramshackle shops and grocery stores and all those small bakeries and miniature drycleaning shops would have disappeared. However, this was the level of our productive forces: thousands of small shops and factories. Every service was rendered in a primitive manner.

Imagine a bakery in some block, a bakery that gives service to every neighbor in that block, and an administrative apparatus controlling that bakery from up above. How does it do the controlling? How can the people fail to take an interest in how that bakery operates? How can the people fail to take an interest in whether the administrator is a good administrator or a bad one? How can the people fail to take an interest in whether there is privilege, negligence, or lack of feeling? How can the people fail to take an interest in the problems of hygiene in that store? How can they fail to take an interest in the problems of production, absenteeism, amount and quality of the product? Of course they can't!

Can anyone imagine a more effective means for controlling that activity than the masses themselves? Can there be such a thing as a method of inspection? No! The man who runs that minicenter of production may turn bad; the man who runs the other service center may turn bad; the man who does the inspection — everybody — may turn bad; but the ones who will never turn bad are those who are affected, the ones who are affected!

Hence, as a result of the development of our productive forces, it is necessary for many of the services in the country to be rendered at the city block level. Nobody can fail to take an interest in how a taxi stand operates. Everybody wants to know what's going on and is interested in everything.

We are trying to find a way how, starting with our mass organizations, to create other organizations in which the workers, as workers; the Committees for the Defense of the Revolution; the women, the young people — in fact, everybody — will be represented, so that they can carry out close supervision of all those activities on a territorial level. This, in addition to supervision, control, and participation in those production centers that already have some development, that have a workers' nucleus. Therefore, nothing will escape supervision and control by the masses.

And our party's role — let this be perfectly understood — our party's role cannot be — nor can it ever be — that of replacing the administration or the mass organizations. Rather, it must direct that phenomenon, direct that process, direct that powerful revolution of the masses.

And it will be necessary to take care of the organizations and take care of the party. Often our party is weakened as a result of the extraction of cadres. We have brought up this problem very often. Why? The party must be protected, because, naturally, it's made of men elected by the masses, excellent comrades, and then they are taken from us and given administrative jobs, and our party begins to be weakened; they are taken away to be converted into administrators and an indentification with the administration begins to be established.

We have said that in a work center the party works with the masses; it has a bearing, through the masses, on the productive processes. But the administration works with machines; it deals with other aspects of production: raw materials, parameters, technology. This does not mean that it should forget the masses, because the masses, the workers, are the fundamental element in production. But, while one centers its attention on the workers, through its party nucleus, party activists, the Vanguard Workers Movement, and the trade union body in the work center . . . the party must seek for the maximum development of the mass organizations, because the party cannot take the place of the masses. If the party turned into the masses, it would cease to be a vanguard, it would cease to be a party, it would cease to be the result of selection. It would be utopian for us to believe that everybody met the requirements for being a member of the party. Not yet. There must come a day when party members will represent a greater proportion of the masses. But the party must be the result of selection; it can neither replace the administration nor can the administration absorb and weaken the party.

Moreover, we believe that just as the trade unions, the Vanguard Workers Movement, and all mass organizations are a source of revolutionary militants, so can the cadres in the mass organizations be an excellent source of cadre material for our party. [*Applause*] And they should gradually strengthen the party with their best people.

It is only on this basis that we can succeed in having a genuine vanguard playing a vanguard, leadership role. This is important, decisive.

Anybody who thinks that taking a cadre out of the trade union and giving him an administrative job is helping production may very well be adversely affecting production; if he thinks that taking a party member and putting him in the administration — and this also means taking cadres out systematically, with no consideration whatsoever for the nucleus, until there comes a time when the party nucleus and the administration become one and the same thing. Anybody who doesn't do his best to avoid doing this harm to the party will be doing serious damage to administration.

They are two different tasks. And it must be said over and over and it must be understood, and it is necessary that the people understand these concepts and take part in the task of supervision.

It must be said that, despite the fact that our party is an organization of selection and the vanguard, who could better supervise our party than the masses, the masses themselves? [*Applause*] And we must say the same thing: it is impossible to control the party's work through inspectors or things like that.

Aside from the fact of active work, aside from the fact that the members themselves carry on an incessant job of supervision and control over the party, the mass organizations must help the party in that task in the face of any deviation, in the face of any sign of corruption, in the face of any sign of privilege. In other words, the masses must take care of the party and see to it that the party sets an example in everything, see to it that the party is in shape to play its role of vanguard. These are fundamental concepts.

A series of meetings are now under way at the work centers, as are plenary meetings. And we have no doubt that the problems which we mentioned on July 26 will be solved. To a certain extent, they are already being solved.

The enemies of the revolution, those who were getting a big kick out of the fact that the revolution was openly and bravely discussing its weak points, almost believed that this was the end of the revolution. Perhaps they didn't imagine that the revolution, in spite of all its objective and subjective difficulties, in spite of all the efforts we still have to make, was about to enter one of its most glorious eras of political self-improvement and strengthening.

Our difficulties will never be greater than the will, spirit, and strength of the people. [*Applause*]

We have no doubt that we are well on the way to solving a number of the problems which we mentioned on July 26. We have no doubt that the results will be seen; they will be seen with figures, regardless of the objective and subjective difficulties which we have — and which we can in no way minimize, because to do so would be to make a serious mistake.

This country has means and resources; a number of resources and means have been obtained. But we must learn how to use these resources in the best, most effective manner possible. We must struggle tirelessly against all that in one way or another conspires against the most effective use of those resources.

In the labor movement the struggle against loafers, absenteeism, and parasitism has reached tremendous proportions. [*Applause and shouts of: "For sure, Fidel, give the lazy bums hell!"*]

Meetings on these problems have been held all over the country, and the workers have expressed themselves in a firm and categorical manner for measures that will eliminate absolutely all these manifestations that conspire against the interests of the people. The law itself still hasn't been discussed in the workers' meetings. The idea is that the law should reflect the sentiment of the workers, and, to a certain extent, we can say that loafing and absenteeism are beating a retreat. We must cut off that retreat, do as the guerrillas do who surround the retreating enemy and wipe him out. We cannot allow a retreat; we must eradicate these manifestations absolutely.

But certain effects have already been noted, certain effects, and the battle has but begun. In large measure, the battle will be won in the discussion of the law itself. Law enforcement will be minimal.

But anyway, in a society, in a collectivist system in which the means of production are the property of the people and their production serves the people, it is indispensable — contrary to capitalist society, in which the owners were the first loafers and there was need for an army of the unemployed as a labor power reserve — in a collectivist society, where man works for society, loafing must be considered a crime, just like robbery.

But why do we punish a thief? Why? Because he is stealing from the people if he goes into a distribution center and makes off with a sack of loot. He is stealing from the people who work and produce. In the same way — or worse— the loafer steals from the people. And he steals more than the thief who one night breaks a window in a distribution center, because the loafer steals from the people every day and at all hours of the day. [*Applause*] The water he drinks and the water with which he takes a bath; the light bulb which gives him light, if he has it; the clothes he wears; the food he eats; the shoes on his feet — all this is stolen, because it takes work to produce all that. The loafer steals from the people every day and at all hours of the day. That is the truth.

A new form of society and production must realize this. And our people are already very much aware of all this.

Of course the problem of the loafer and absentee is just one of the many problems which affect production. They disorganize it; they complicate it; they leave the others with the hardest work, thus irritating the other workers; the production cycle is affected; the whole process is affected. They disorganize, demoralize, and irritate. They irritate, and we must take the necessary measures so that these people will not be able to fit in our society and so that this kind of theft will in no way go unpunished. [*Applause*]

[*Someone shouts something to Commander Fidel Castro from the crowd.*] We have spent twenty-four hours of the last two days in meetings, and now are in another kind of meeting.

[*The members of the Venceremos Brigade display a sign for Commander Fidel Castro.*] Well, I've already seen that. Now take it down, because if you don't those behind you will complain and say they can't see. Those are the comrades of the Venceremos Brigade. [*Applause*]

We were saying that the struggle which began after our remarks on July 26 is being carried out in all fields. We realize that this is not a struggle of a day, a week, or a month. It is a long, ceaseless struggle. But the results in all fields will be seen. Through the workers' meetings a series of mistakes, examples of carelessness and indolence, and many other factors which have held back production are being detected, and a struggle will be waged against all those factors on all fronts.

We must say that we are very optimistic about the struggle which the revolution is carrying out in this new stage. We are sure that just as the revolution has won many battles and resisted the attack of powerful forces and all the pressure of imperialism, we will also win these battles which we must wage among the people against our own weaknesses and mistakes.

We are aware that in a radical process, such as that of the Cuban revolution, these experiences are inevitable, because everything is changed — as we explained at the Federation of Cuban Women meeting.

But the years have not passed in vain. The revolution has grown strong amidst the people: the mass organizations have grown tremendously strong, and those which aren't so strong right now will, undoubtedly, be strong very soon. And we will be able to wage that battle with all the people everywhere and on all levels. [*Applause*]

The Role of the
Communist Party of Cuba

by Raúl Castro

May 4, 1973

NOTE: In the period after 1970, Cuba was able to make progress in many fields. The economy began to move forward and the mass organizations and the unions were strengthened. The Communist Party made progress as well. Its membership grew from 55,000 in 1969 to 153,000 by March 1973, and it strengthened its presence in the workplaces.

The process of institutionalization was also begun. In 1972 the government was restructured with the creation of the Executive Committee of the Council of Ministers. In early 1973 the Communist Party's leadership apparatus was revamped.

The following is from a speech given by Raúl Castro to cadres and functionaries of the CP's Central Committee where he details the party's role in Cuban society. For many years Raúl Castro, a veteran of the Moncada attack, the Granma landing, and the revolutionary war, has been second secretary of the Communist Party and commander of Cuba's armed forces. This excerpt is taken from Selección de discursos acerca del partido *by Fidel Castro and Raúl Castro (Havana: Ediciones de Ciencias Sociales, 1975). The translation for this volume is by the editor.*

This structure of the Central Committee's (CC) apparatus and its mechanisms of functioning approved by the Political Bureau (PB), have been elaborated on the basis of the Marxist-Leninist principles of party organization and the orientation on this question given by Fidel.

The first paragraph of the document approved by the PB, which we've just read, recalls how in May 1970 Fidel raised the necessity of strengthening the administrative apparatus, the mass organizations, *and above all, the party*.

It also refers to Fidel's emphasis on this question in the course of the PB's meeting with the principal leaders of the party, the state, and the mass organizations that took place in August 1970.

And most recently, in a meeting of the PB that lasted eight hours, held

August 30 of last year on the eve of his departure for various countries of Africa and socialist Europe, Fidel raised the need to hold a party congress in the near future, and to study the most appropriate structure to be given to the state and the party.

Shortly after his return, these questions began to be analyzed by the PB in a series of meetings. Following Comrade Fidel's orientation the first thing to be arrived at was the restructuring of the Council of Ministers and the creation of its Executive Committee, something that you all know about. And now we move to determine the structure and operating mechanisms of the CC, so that it will have a functioning organization that will regularize the life of the party and its leadership. This will thus overcome the abnormality that has historically afflicted the party and its leadership of being led almost completely by the Organization Secretariat — something that was really beyond the possibilities of whichever comrade was heading that Secretariat.

This structure now approved by the PB should not be considered as definitive in all its details. It has a certain provisional character until the party congress is held, which will ratify or modify it — although we believe that, fundamentally, the definitive forms that the congress approves will have to be very similar to these.

On the other hand, if we stop to consider the outline that has been elaborated and the document that we've just read — keeping in mind what we've said with respect to the Council of Ministers and its Executive Committee — you will surely have noticed certain gaps regarding the state. Thus, for example, in the department of state and judicial organs, we see a section called "Of the organs of People's Power." This has in mind the future creation of the representative institutions of the state, democratically elected by the masses, whose concrete forms for our country will be a subject for study by the PB in its upcoming meetings.

We believe that for the better understanding of all of these questions — of the party structure approved by the PB and its interrelation with the state and mass institutions — it will be useful to spend some time clarifying the fundamental theoretical concepts on which we base ourselves. Although these seem elementary, they are not always sufficiently mastered or correctly taken into account.

Permit me, therefore, to pass on to an exposition of these *conceptual considerations*.

In a revolution whose objective is the construction of socialism and communism, the establishment of what the classics of Marxism labeled the *dictatorship of the proletariat* becomes necessary and indispensable after political power is taken.

What is meant by *dictatorship* in this case? The political rule that one given social class exercises over all of society. The possession of a power that enables the given class to impose its will and its interests, making these compulsory for all of society, for all the other social classes and groups that exist.

Under the conditions of capitalism there exists the dictatorship of the bourgeoisie in alliance with the rest of the exploiting classes, whatever the forms this takes — more or less fascist, more or less democratic. Since the exploiting classes represent a tiny minority of the population, this will always be a dictatorship of the minority over the majority.

Under the conditions of the construction of socialism and communism, the dictatorship of the proletariat, that is to say, of the *working class* exists.

"The dictatorship of the proletariat," Lenin tells us, "implies and signifies a clear concept of the truth that the proletariat, because of its objective economic position in every capitalist society, *correctly* expresses the interests of the *entire mass* of working and exploited people, all semi-proletarians (i.e., those who live partly by the sale of their labour-power), all small peasants and similar categories."

From this we can see that the dictatorship of the working class is not the dictatorship of the working class alone, isolated from every other social class or group, *but rather the dictatorship of this class in close alliance with the rest of the working and revolutionary masses, principally the peasants*.

That is to say, if the dictatorship of the proletariat signifies that the working class holds the reins of society as a whole, giving it the possibility of imposing its will and its interests on the rest of the social organism in a compulsory way, it nevertheless should be kept in mind that while conserving its hegemonic and leading role, the working class must *exercise its dictatorship in alliance with the other laboring classes. These, as a whole, must have the institutional possibility of participating in the running and governing of society, having the institutional mechanisms that permit them to express their will, and taking an active and constant part in the "dictatorship of the proletariat."*

This is one of the principles we must begin with when the concrete forms of our proletarian dictatorship are established.

On the other hand, it's necessary to keep in mind that the working class as a whole, taken in its entirety, is not in a position to exercise its dictatorship. This is because coming from bourgeois society it brings flaws and vices from the past that make it heterogeneous with respect to its level of consciousness and its social conduct.

Hence, as Lenin said, the dictatorship "can be exercised only by a vanguard that has absorbed the revolutionary energy of the class." Or in other words, the working class can realize its dictatorship and construct the socialist society *only through a political party* that groups its conscious minority.

Lenin insisted on innumerable occasions and with extraordinary emphasis on the need for a political party "steeled and tempered in struggle." And this principle, proven by the diverse experiences of different countries that have undertaken the task of constructing socialism, is codified, in many cases, in these countries' constitutions.

Thus, for example, Article 126 of the constitution of the USSR states that the Communist Party is the leading nucleus of all the organizations of the workers, both social and state.

This is expressed in a similar manner in Article 1 of the Bulgarian constitution, Article 4 of the Czechoslovak constitution, Article 3 of the Romanian constitution, Article 82 of the Mongolian constitution, etc.

This is another fundamental principle to observe at the time when we give form to and institutionalize our proletarian dictatorship: the guiding and leading role of the party within it, completely related to all its activities, both state and social in general.

But the dictatorship of the proletariat is not limited to the important and principal role that the party must play. The party is only the vanguard minority of the most advanced social class, and it is charged with leading and carrying on its shoulders the greatest weight in the construction of socialism. Because of this, to exercise its leading function throughout all of society, the party is supported by the state, the mass organizations, and when necessary, by the direct mobilization of the working masses. *The most ideal and direct instrument to rule society is not a political party, but rather the state*, the apparatus without which the dictatorship and the implementation of the tasks of constructing socialism are not possible.

In addition to the party and the state, the complete system of the proletarian dictatorship includes the mass organizations, which Lenin called "transmission belts" that group one or another sector of society's revolutionary forces. These include the unions, the youth, the women's organization, the peasants' organization, the CDR, students, and Pioneers organizations. In an article written in December 1920 Lenin said: "[The dictatorship] cannot work without a number of 'transmission belts' running from the vanguard to the mass of the advanced class, and from the latter to the mass of the working people."

Thus, the working class taken as a whole cannot directly realize its dictatorship and its mission of constructing socialism. Rather it must do so through the Communist Party, which unites its vanguard minority. But at the same time the party by itself cannot exercise the dictatorship either. It can only realize it through and with the help of the state apparatus and the mass organizations. *The dictatorship of the proletariat is not the dictatorship of the Communist Party*. The party is the *main leading force* within all the mechanisms of the proletarian dictatorship, and it is charged with coordinating, controlling, and channelling the tasks of the state apparatus and the mass organizations toward a single goal.

The state then, is a part of the system of the proletarian dictatorship, its most direct instrument. Different from the party and the mass organizations it has the particular characteristic that its decisions have juridical force and are compulsory for all the citizens of the country. And it has at its disposal a special apparatus of force and coercion to impose its decisions when that becomes necessary.

The party leads and controls through the ways and methods that are appropriate to it, which are different from the ways, methods, and resources the state has at its disposal to exercise its authority.

The directives, resolutions, and provisions of the party do not directly possess that compulsory juridical character *for all the citizens of the country*. They are compulsory only for its members. In addition, the party does not have any apparatus of force or coercion at its disposal to enforce its decisions. *And this is an important difference between the role and methods of the party and the role and methods of the state.*

Someone could claim that, ultimately, the decisions of the state have been previously determined by the party, through a resolution or provision; and that, therefore, when all is said and done, the decisions of the party acquire compulsory juridical force through the state. Consistent with this false reasoning, one could conclude that in the final analysis, the party and the state are one and the same. Or as it is vulgarly put, "the same dog with a different collar."

But this is not so, or at least it doesn't have to be so, if we begin with a correct understanding of the *complementary yet different roles* that the party and the state must play. The party and its institutions must not be identified with the state apparatus and its institutions (in the sense of substituting for them).

The power of the party rests directly in its moral authority; in the influence that it has among the masses; in the clarity with which it expresses their interests and aspirations; in the consciousness that it imbues in them of their revolutionary, economic, and social duties; and finally, in the confidence that the masses put in it. Hence, its actions are based, above all, in convincing — whether it be through actions or through its ideological and political positions.

The power of the state rests directly in its material authority, having at its disposal a special force to make the fulfillment of its decisions compulsory; to subject everyone to its juridical norms. Hence, its action is based, above all, in coercion, in the compulsory nature of the laws, regulations, and orders it issues.

Thus, if the party and the state become mixed up, it first of all harms the effort of convincing the masses politically and ideologically, it harms the work that the party has to carry out and which only the party can conduct; and secondly, it harms the activities of the state, whose functionaries cease to be responsible for its decisions and activities.

The party leads the state, checks on its functioning and the fulfillment by the state of all the directives and plans that have been laid out. The party stimulates, gives an impulse to, and contributes to the best possible work by the entire state apparatus, but in no case may the party substitute for the state.

1. The party leads the state bodies through the elaboration of general directives on the fundamental questions of the country's economic, political, cultural, and social development and on the ways to resolve these questions. The bodies of the *state apparatus must guide themselves and channel their activities through such directives and must not resolve any important question without taking them into account*. These are issued by the highest bodies of the party: the congress, the Central Committee, and the Political Bureau.

2. The party leads the state bodies through the selection and placement of the state apparatus's leading personnel and through educating this personnel for the best fulfillment of their functions.

3. It leads them through controlling (understanding by this checking and observing) the work of the given state bodies through the different departments and levels of the party apparatus, and orienting the corrections of the work that become necessary to make, without meddling in their administrative work and without replacing them in their powers of decision-making.

4. It leads them through the support and help that, through its apparatus and with its methods and resources, it offers the state bodies in the development of their activities.

5. It leads them through the party members, who, wherever they work and whatever position they occupy, are obliged to carry out and apply the party's decisions and *to convince those who are not members* of the correctness of these decisions and the necessity of carrying them out.

6. It leads them through the fact that the main leaders of the party, or at least the greater part of them, are also the main leaders of the state — something that will be necessary and inevitable for a long time to come. Referring to this, Lenin said in one of his interventions at the Tenth Congress of the Bolshevik Party, held in April 1921: ". . . being the ruling party, we had inevitably to merge the party and government leadership — they are merged and will remain so."

This was expressed in a similar sense by Fidel at a meeting in August 1970: "The only place where absolute subordination [of the state to the party] exists is at the highest level, because of necessity it has to exist according to the principle by which the party has the maximum responsibility in the state administration."

And later he added: "There cannot remain the slightest doubt, then, that duality does not exist either on the levels of region, province, or anywhere. That duality is encountered a little higher up for institutional reasons and in order to establish some umbilical cord between the party and the state."

Lenin also emphasized repeatedly the necessary delimitation between the institutions of the party and the state.

In the twelfth point of the resolution of the Eleventh Congress of the Bolshevik Party, which was written by Lenin, referring to the strengthening of the party and its new tasks, it states:

"12. An extremely important task of the times is to establish the correct division of labor between party and soviet institutions and to delineate clearly the rights and duties of the one and the other.

"Already the Eighth Congress of the Communist Party of Russia (1919) in its resolution relating to organizational questions (See "Section C: Relations between the Party and the Soviets"), emphasized: 'In no case must the functions of party collectives be confused with the functions of state bodies such as the soviets. Such a confusion would yield fatal results, particularly in military matters. The party strives to *direct* the work of the soviets, not to replace them.'

"The Eleventh Congress of the Communist Party of Russia ratifies this declaration with special force. Next in turn is the solution of the immense task of restoring the economy, a task that will require many years of untiring work. This task can be resolved only if correct and sound relations are established between party organizations and economic agencies. Just as the party stressed in 1919 that a confusion of functions would yield fatal results in military affairs, so in 1922 the party declares that such a confusion would yield completely fatal results in the economic sphere.

"In no case are party organizations to interfere in the day-to-day, ordinary work of the economic agencies, and they are to refrain in general from administrative orders in the sphere of soviet work.

"Party organizations are to direct the work of the economic agencies, but in no sense are they to attempt to replace them or take over their responsibilities. The absence of a strict delineation of functions and incompetent interference in affairs outside of its jurisdiction, results in an absence of strict and exact responsibility on the part of each person for the work entrusted to him; they increase bureaucratism in the party organs themselves, which in trying to do everything end up doing nothing; they impede serious specialization by administrative officials working in the economy — the study of a question in full detail, the acquisition of truly practical experience — in a word, making more difficult the correct organization of the work."

The party does not occupy its leading position by virtue of a popular election, not even as a product of a vote of the working class, of which it is the organized vanguard. It is not, then, a representative body, through election of the popular will; it is a body of selection.

In one of his interventions in the previously mentioned meeting in August 1970, Fidel said, with complete correctness: "One cannot say that the working class is represented as a class if we're trying to simply have the party represent it. That is to say, that while the party represents the interests of the working class, it cannot be said that it represents the expressed will of the entire class."

The party's leading position is conquered and maintained through struggle. This position is based on being the vanguard of the most advanced social class of society and acting as such: as the most faithful and determined representative of the interests of all the working masses. Its authority is not based on force nor on the possibility of using coercion and violence to impose its will and its directives. Rather it is supported in the confidence and the support that it receives, first of all, *from the class that it represents*, and secondly, from the rest of the working population. *This confidence and support are won through a correct and rational policy, through the party's links with the masses, using as its methods persuasion and convincing, and upheld by the force of its example and the correctness of its policy.*

But starting with these suppositions, we cannot take for granted, as we've already said, that the party represents the will of all the people and consider it to be the supreme organ of power. Because we would then be forgetting *the principles of proletarian democracy that, as we saw earlier, imply the participation of all the members of the working class (and not only its vanguard) and the other laboring classes in the exercise of the proletarian dictatorship, that is to say, in the ruling and governing of society.* This requires the corresponding institutions of power through which the working masses put that right into effect and can express and give value to their will. Already Lenin pointed out to us that "without representative institutions, democracy cannot be conceived of, much less proletarian democracy."

The preoccupation and orientation Fidel expressed in August 1970 has the same meaning, when he said: "The famous democracy of the recall of public officials, which is one of the postulates of Marxism — we will have to see how we are going to arrange to apply it on the national level. But the question, ladies and gentlemen, is how we can begin with some rudiments of democracy, even if they are only rudiments."

According to our understanding, these representative institutions are indispensable — so that the revolutionary people, *considered as a whole*, as the entirety of all the country's working masses, manifest their will and can really participate in the government.

Speech to Thirteenth Congress of the Central Organization of Cuban Trade Unions

November 15, 1973

NOTE: The Thirteenth Congress of the Central Organization of Cuban Trade Unions, held November 11-15, 1973, marked a watershed in the history of the Cuban labor movement. Starting in 1970, the trade unions had been significantly strengthened and began to play a more important role as the workers' representatives. Local leaderships were elected and the unions were reorganized into twenty-three national unions, representing the different branches of production. The Thirteenth Congress marked the completion of this phase.

But the congress was important for another reason as well. It marked an important shift in many of Cuba's economic policies. During the late 1960s the Cuban leadership took what it later termed "idealist" positions, attempting to jump over real economic limitations by sheer revolutionary will. In 1967, for example, charges and payments were eliminated between different units of the state economic sector because these were considered too "capitalist." Likewise, the profitability of different state enterprises was downplayed. In 1968 the connection between wages and work output was severed in an attempt to eliminate material incentives for people to work, in favor of using moral incentives exclusively. From 1967 to 1969, many services began to be provided without charge, including electricity, telephone, and water, in an attempt to achieve communist norms of distribution — to each according to his needs. Resolution 270, passed in October 1968, decreed retirement pensions and sick pay for workers equal to 100 percent of their previous income.

The net effect of these measures in the context of Cuba's material shortages, underdevelopment, and imperialist blockade was the lowering of work productivity, an increase in absenteeism, and a dramatic expansion of the amount of money in circulation without a corresponding increase in the amount of available goods. This last result led to a decrease in the importance of the money people earned, and was thus a disincentive to work.

The Thirteenth Congress dealt with these questions extensively. It called for a return to linking wages to productivity, increasing material incentives (while maintaining the importance of moral incentives), bringing the number of services provided without charge more in line with Cuba's real economic possibilities, and adjusting some prices in order to decrease the amount of money in circulation. One of the proposals passed by the congress was a suggestion to repeal Resolution 270, since it turned out to be a burden the economy could not sustain.

As expected, implementing these measures led to a dramatic increase in work productivity and advances in the Cuban economy.

The following is Castro's speech at the closing of the congress. The text is from Granma Weekly Review, *November 25, 1973.*

Distinguished guests;
Comrades of the party leadership and of the government;
Comrade leaders of the CTC;
Comrade delegates to this congress:

It won't be easy to sum up in a few words all the importance, the richness, the vast significance of this event. It has been said — and rightly — that this, the Thirteenth Congress of our workers, will be a history-making event. And the congress has chiefly reflected the level of political and revolutionary consciousness of our workers.

In this congress — and throughout the process that led up to it — a series of matters of vital importance to our revolution were discussed.

The first thing that stands out is the democratic spirit that prevailed throughout the congress, true to the idea of developing a strong and profoundly democratic trade union movement.

The matters discussed in the theses are closely related to essential questions of our revolution's ideological and political process. However, the decisions made here — even though they reflect, as [CTC leader] Comrade Lázaro Peña pointed out in his report, the opinion of our country's political leadership and of our workers, as well — were not made by virtue of a party decision but were, rather, amply discussed by our workers. No one pushed through any viewpoints; everything was discussed with the workers. Nobody issues measures by decree here — no matter how just and accurate they may be. Fundamental decisions affecting the life of our people must be discussed with the people — and, chiefly, with the workers. [*Applause*]

Some of the points in the theses were really complex. They called for the full understanding of the workers, for broad discussion. Some of them could affect certain workers; others called for sacrifice. But no necessary sacrifice by a revolutionary people, the master of its destiny, is made in the interest of any exploiting class. It is made in the interest of the people.

One of the main points in the theses dealt with the principle "from each according to his ability, to each according to his work." That is an essential question in the construction of socialism, and our socialist, revolutionary workers recognized it as such. And in discussing that principle we have been discussing an essential, key principle of revolutionary ideology, because "that each contribute according to his ability, that each receive according to his work" is a principle, an inexorable law, in the construction of socialism.

When we learn this principle in all its profundity, we go deep into political thinking, into revolutionary thinking, and we learn to distinguish it from another principle, the principle of the communist society, established by Karl Marx: "from each according to his ability, to each according to his needs." This is precisely what differentiates the socialist phase from the communist phase of the revolutionary process.

Quite possibly, all of us find the communist principle more to our liking, more attractive, and more humane. But communism cannot be imposed on human society by decree; it is a goal that must be attained by striving for it, and it can only be the result of a process.

Only a few years ago, the very mention of the word *communism* was unthinkable in our country.

Today, it has become necessary to explain that communism is the final result of the revolutionary social process. And, even though we may be more inclined toward the communist principle, we must first apply the socialist principle if we want to reach communism.

Needless to say, a series of measures and principles of a certain communist character have been put into effect since the triumph of the revolution. There are a number of services that the people are entitled to have, that are provided on the basis of need. For example, public health is a service provided for all our people, for all our workers, regardless of the kind of work they do or their ability. It is a service provided for all our citizens.

Another example: education. Our country is making a tremendous effort to provide education for all our children, regardless of their family's income, regardless of their parents' ability to work.

There are many other services which the revolution provides for the people. But, when it comes to the distribution of income, we can no longer apply the communist principle. We have to apply the socialist principle.

When we said on July 26, during the celebration of the twentieth anniversary, that we should have the courage to correct the idealistic mistakes we had made, that meant that if, in certain cases, we had tried to make more headway than we were prepared for, this called for a reappraisal of the situation. If you try to go farther than you can, you are forced to retreat. Fortunately, in this case, it's a matter not of retreating,

[*Applause*] but of correcting our errors, because we are socialists [*Applause*] and want to be communists! [*Applause and shouts of: "Fidel! Fidel!"*] We will never renounce the communist objective of our revolution and the development of our revolutionary consciousness, but will go on placing altruism, selflessness, and man's spirit of solidarity first of all! [*Applause*] Throughout the years, some wages — for example, for the cutting of cane — have been based on production, and others, on the quality of work done; but paying the same wages for the same work without regard for the efforts required to do it is an egalitarian principle we must correct.

In connection with the principle that each contribute according to his ability and receive according to his work, Marx pointed out that this was a principle that didn't go beyond the narrow framework of bourgeois legality. And he said this was based on the fact that not all men are equal, that not all men have the same energy, that not all men have the same ability.

However, Marx didn't overlook the fact that socialism was beginning to be built on capitalist society, on the ruins of capitalist society. That is why he expressed the following idea — which we recalled on July 26:

"In a higher phase of communist society, after the enslaving subordination of individuals under division of labour, and therewith also the antithesis between mental and physical labour, has vanished; after labour, from a mere means of life, has itself become the prime necessity of life; after the productive forces have also increased with the all-round development of the individual, and all the springs of co-operative wealth flow more abundantly — only then can the narrow horizon of bourgeois right be fully left behind and society inscribe on its banners: from each according to his ability, to each according to his needs!"

There are many examples to show us we are not yet prepared to live in communism — to say nothing of the fact that in order to live in communism, it is necessary to have not only a communist consciousness but also abundant riches as a result of man's work. The development of the productive forces is a must.

It's quite possible that none of us enjoy revealing our own weaknesses and defects in front of such an important audience, broadly representative of the international labor movement. However, if we are to be honest with you and deserving of your recognition, we must, first of all, not hide our mistakes and faults, [*Applause*] but rather have the courage to admit and combat them.

We mentioned a number of these examples when we met with the cigar makers. One day, there were a series of difficulties with the water meters, and the agency in charge of distributing and charging for the water decided to give it away for free.

It looks like a very beautiful, very just decision. Water is a basic necessity. But what happened? The way water is squandered is simply incredible. One of the cities that wastes the most water — when there is water [*Laughter*] and when it runs short of water it's because it squanders it [*Applause*] — is the city of Havana.

It's true that our water distribution networks are quite old and badly in need of repair — a job we expect to carry out as soon as we can, one that is included in the list of work to be done in the coming years — but it is also true that ever since water has been distributed free, people never bother to turn off the faucet.

Ever since water began to be distributed free of charge, practically nobody has bothered to solve the problems of leakage. An awareness of the need to save water simply doesn't exist. Therefore, the communist distribution of water leads to the squandering of water — which shows that we are not yet prepared to distribute water communist-style. [*Applause*]

Let me tell you about the results of an experiment, of a number of studies that were made in the Alamar section of Havana.

We have really conscientious workers, good workers, in Alamar. Still, a test was made, and it was decided to provide a number of families with a certain amount of water — because the fact still remains that a certain amount of water can be given free of charge — and these families were allowed ninety quarts of water a day. Any amount above ninety quarts they'd have to pay for — and at a high price, too. In other buildings, there was no charge for the water, but a record was kept of how much was used, by means of meters. And the result was — I was checking up on the results today, to make sure [*Laughter*] — the result was that the people who didn't pay for water were using four or even five times as much water as those who had to pay for it. Those who had to pay for the excess water they used never went over the limit — not by a single quart. [*Applause*]

We have a plan which includes the building of a plant to manufacture water meters. We're not so interested in how much money we take in; what we are interested in is saving water. It's not a question of bringing in funds from the use of water; it's just that water is an expensive item, calling for numerous installations, the use of electric power, motors, everything. And, since many of the new towns — and the old ones, too — are in need of water, the idea is to install a water meter in every house as soon as we have enough meters. [*Applause*] We have to choose between two measures: either we charge for the water beginning with the first quart, or we provide everybody with a certain basic amount, and anything above that — as was done in Alamar — must be paid for at a high rate, because the idea is, first of all, to charge for the wasting of water. [*Applause*]

Here's another example. This one has to do not with a communist type of distribution but rather with a practically semicommunist type.

We used to have men and women conductors on the buses. And one day, placing our trust in the people's conscience, we decided to do away with the conductors in order to save money. And — we must say this in all justice — even though the immense majority pay their fare, there are some who don't pay, and there are others who just drop any old thing into the slot. And the closer they come to a financial balance, the more people don't pay.

Well, here's a question everybody is invited to discuss. Which of these two would be more useful: 1,000 workers getting paid for working on the buses in the city of Havana, or 1,000 workers working in the textile industry? Anybody will realize that 1,000 workers in a textile plant would produce much more for all our people. And yet, it is quite possible that this society will find it necessary to employ thousands of workers in the nonproductive task of keeping tabs on us, just to make sure that people pay their bus fare.

This is another example that shows — apart from a series of easily understood theoretical arguments — that we are not yet ready for communist distribution.

But we could go on and ask how much fuel we waste; how many raw materials we waste; how much needless use of electricity there is. It is clear that even with campaigns by the mass organizations and appeals to the awareness of the people, we still won't save electricity.

I am discussing the matter because the problem of electricity is a disagreeable one which we must handle, an unpopular problem but one we must solve. [*Applause*] We made a big reduction in the rates the electric company — I don't really remember what it was named — had established. It had a rate to stimulate consumption: the first kilowatts were expensive, but, the more you used, the cheaper it got. We, with our revolutionary inexperience — or we could say our revolutionary shortsightedness — cut the rates of the capitalist electric company in half, all down the line, keeping the rates that promoted consumption.

I described us as shortsighted because we should have thought of the day the electric system would belong not to any capitalist company but to the people. Now the capitalist company belongs to the people, and the people must pay the consequences for any waste of electricity.

We have to spend more and more money in this field all the time. This country is poor in energy resources. It is a long, narrow island and doesn't have any large rivers. It doesn't have any coal; no oil has been discovered yet; and no timber was left in our forests. We must bring fuel from a distance of ten thousand kilometers, across oceans, and invest hundreds of millions of pesos to purchase power plants and transmission systems for electricity. Oil is now three times as expensive on the world market as it was at the time of the triumph of the revolution, while the present rate for electricity is half what it was before the revolution — which encourages consumption.

I am not going into all this detail to prepare you mentally for the government's change in electric rates. I am simply explaining — as we do in every case — why we feel the government should modify the electric rates. Not the basic rates — that is, those paid by people who consume a relatively small amount of electricity — but the rates from certain limits on up. Because we want to make money? No! Cigarettes bring in more money than all the electric systems put together; [*Applause*] alcoholic beverages bring in more money — I know some of those prices aren't popular. [*Applause*] It's because we want to save electricity. If we have an ever-increasing number of electrical items used in the home, where are we going to be if the television set is on all day and the iron is plugged in all the time?

I tell you sincerely that one of the tasks which the government will have to face this coming year is the review of the electric rates. Not to bring in money — I repeat — but to save electricity.

When I talk about saving electricity, it's the centers of production that are primarily responsible for the waste of electricity and especially the administrations. [*Applause*] A lot of electricity is wasted because the administrators are unconcerned about saving electricity.

We feel that one of the indexes for judging the efficiency of any factory or industry should be its use of electricity. This also goes for schools and places that provide services.

Of course, we hope the workers will wage the battle for saving electricity — along with many others — on their job sites. [*Applause*]

One of the important aspects is the distribution of the load. [*Applause*] That is, certain expenditures of electricity should be made in hours when there is little consumption, not when there is a lot, so we can prevent blackouts. I can give you an example: some pumping machines used for irrigation can work twelve, fourteen, sixteen hours. Those machines should be used during the day, not from 7:00 to 10:00 at night. If not, the expenditure is tremendous. Even the industrialized nations with large energy resources have problems during peak consumption hours.

All centers of production or services must distribute the load so everything that has to be done at a certain time of day can be done, putting off everything that isn't absolutely necessary during the peak consumption hours.

Recently, our country was forced to make an extra expenditure of almost $20 million for the purchase of so-called peak-consumption power plants. They will be available to fill the gap until the projects under way in the electrical sector — the plants being built in Havana and Mariel — are completed. The country is carrying out an important program to increase its power output. Power output has increased three times since the victory of the revolution, and the network has been considerably enlarged. But we won't solve anything by enlarging more and more if we keep on using more and more fuel; we must have a policy to promote the saving of electricity and fuel.

The main use of fuel in the country is for generating electric power. Of course, our sugar mills, our cement factories, our industries, our merchant ships, our fishing fleet, our transportation system — everything that moves in this country — functions through the use of fuel. This is why the fuel-saving index of all industries is essential.

The world is facing a growing problem concerning fuel, aside from the fuel shortage brought about by the imperialist aggressions in the Middle East. The future outlook for fuel is uncertain, and the problem will get worse as time goes on. A ton of oil now brings nearly $50 on the world market, and according to the forecasts, it will go up to around $80 or $90 a ton by 1980, and the world will face increasing difficulties with fuel.

This is one more reason for our adopting a policy of saving resources in every respect, but primarily in the use of fuel, which is where the labor movement can be of tremendous help, checking on the use of fuel so as to prevent waste, whether on a farm, in a factory, or anywhere else.

These are the realities which our workers have to face.

The analysis of countless events clearly shows that our society, our people, are not yet ready to live under communism, apart from the fact that we don't have a sufficiently developed economy to make this possible. From a realistic point of view, a very realistic one, we have to implement all formulas corresponding to the socialist stage of our revolution and implement them in every respect, not only in the distribution of goods and services, not only in wages but also in administrative aspects. [*Applause*]

And if we have made mistakes of any kind, we must correct them. [*Applause*]

This workers' congress is just a first step. You have talked a lot and spent a lot of time on the principle of producing more, at higher quality and at lower production costs. This is what the workers have said. And now the administration and the entire economic system of the revolution have to say the same thing. [*Applause*] Produce more, better, and at lower cost, and adopt the measures needed to achieve this!

The labor movement has suggested a series of measures in support of this principle, pointing out the relationship that should exist between wages and the work norms; the relationship between wages and the meeting, surpassing, or falling short of the work norm; the problems related to overtime when a real need for working overtime arises; and the problem of working a double shift, when a worker has to substitute for another worker who didn't show up on the job.

But were these measures and suggestions made in an economist spirit? No! Maybe the most interesting, the most extraordinary, aspect of our workers' behavior, which proves their high level of consciousness, is that there hasn't been even a hint of economism. [*Applause*]

Economism is a vice sown in the ranks of the workers by the bourgeoisie and capitalists. Economism is unworthy of a revolutionary working class which is thinking about the present but which has the still more important duty of thinking about the future; which, while thinking about the present generation, thinks even more about the future generations. [*Applause*]

It wasn't economism but a genuine concern about savings, production, productivity, and work discipline that inspired the suggestions concerning the theses. And, throughout, it was felt that work plans should be met during the normal workday, without overtime.

Are these suggestions, perhaps, opposed to voluntary work? No. The workers understand the educational, revolutionary, communist importance of voluntary work perfectly well and have specified very clearly in their resolutions all those cases in which it is both fair and correct to apply the formulas of voluntary work. Our concern is, rather, to see to it that voluntary work doesn't cause waste, doesn't involve a useless outlay of human and material resources, and that voluntary work doesn't become a means for covering up administrative inefficiency. [*Applause*] Voluntary work should fulfill educational and other goals for the benefit of society, which is its justification and raison d'être.

In propounding its ideas, in clarifying points, and in upholding the banner and principles of voluntary work, our working class has given proof of its high level of consciousness and rendered tribute to the one who set an example as a revolutionary socialist and communist, Commander Ernesto Guevara. [*Applause*]

Voluntary work will go on, and it will do so free of misrepresentations, impurities, and waste!

This is why we say that the absence of an economist spirit has been, to our way of thinking, one of the fundamental aspects of this congress in the implementation of a correct revolutionary principle.

This selfless spirit, this spirit of solidarity and profound concern with the collective interest, the interests of the working class and the people in general, has been shown in other aspects and in other points of the theses, since various points required concrete sacrifices in the economic field.

Such is the case with the repeal of Resolution 270. It wasn't an easy question. It was a delicate one, since half a million workers were already receiving the benefits of Resolution 270. And Resolution 270 had to be repealed!

The workers knew that repealing Resolution 270 would imply sacrifices. What has been their reaction to this proposal? What has been the reaction of those workers who are about to retire? They have shown an exemplary attitude, a truly unselfish attitude.

It's true that this is perhaps one of the most difficult questions, but our workers understand that Resolution 270 had to be repealed because our economy couldn't afford it any longer.

I, personally, bear a lot of responsibility for this resolution. [*Shouts of: "We all do, Fidel!"*] [*Applause*]

I thank you for your solidarity. But, anyway, I'm going to continue elaborating on the idea I had begun.

We started with the idea of awarding a special distinction to those workers having extraordinary merits. [*Applause*] And we wanted to reward not only individual efforts but collective efforts at an important moment for emulation.

From a logical standpoint, this principle was already a faulty one, as was shown later. Workers with enormous individual merits weren't favored by this measure if their work centers didn't meet the collective merit requirement.

This idea, and the ensuing contradiction, show us the dialectical unfolding of the events. It was a good idea, a just idea, in one respect, trying to join two kinds of merits — the individual and the collective — but it changed into an unjust idea when workers having great personal merits were excluded. Then they complained, since, through no fault of their own, they weren't able to get the benefits of the measure, because their work centers didn't have this or that merit, this or that banner.

We were always worried about those workers who had a spotless work record — a record recognized by all the other workers at their work centers — yet, when they got sick and missed work for three days or less, their pay would be docked.

This method was enforced by Law 1100,* since there were many workers — no, we can't say "many"; "many" could mean the majority of the workers — never! There were some workers who used to be sick on Mondays. Also, there were some doctors who used to give excuses for sick leave to their friends. We had thought that the guarantee of an income in the event of illness was the important issue. The purpose of the measure wasn't to allow sick benefits for one or two days of illness, but to provide benefits for workers who had to be away from work for a week, a month, or whatever period of time was necessary. We thought the true essence of social security was to provide a guarantee in the event of long periods of illness, and that's what Law 1100 provided for.

But it always hurt us to think about those exemplary workers who

*Cuba's social security law, passed in 1963.

couldn't get paid when they were out sick for a day, under the assumption that they hadn't really been sick — and they were workers who were well known at their work centers. The same goes for those workers who had reached retirement age after spending their lives doing exemplary work.

Undoubtedly, that idea should have been applied as an exception, not as a rule. And the resolution came out of that idea. We aren't going to blame the Ministry of Labor for that. We are the ones to blame. When the resolution was drawn up, we should have analyzed it carefully to see under what conditions it would work.

We had the duty of seeing to it that it wouldn't turn into a mass measure, but that is just exactly what it did, because of the conditions under which it was applied. It finally became a burden for the economy, forcing on us the bitter necessity of repealing it.

This should teach us, moreover, that any measure of this kind that we adopt must be deeply studied so we can be absolutely certain of its results. [*Applause*]

That's why this was one of the most difficult points of the theses. Nevertheless, over 99 percent of the workers voted to repeal Resolution 270. [*Applause*] The attitude of the overwhelming majority of the workers nearing retirement age was truly impressive, for they approved the thesis to repeal Resolution 270. [*Applause*]

The revolution — as we said at one assembly — can never forget these workers, and it will never forget them.

We had to come to a decision, and there were a lot of different ideas about where to start. Then too, we had to decide whether to make the repeal of Resolution 270 retroactive or not. The party adopted the criterion that it shouldn't be made retroactive, for to do so would constitute a breach of faith and provoke a lack of confidence in the measures taken by the revolution. And it would have been not only ridiculous but inhuman to do that to those workers who had retired under the provisions of the resolution. But then came the situation of those who, out of civic duty and revolutionary spirit, had kept on working, not retiring under the provisions of the resolution when they had a perfect right to do so, or were in the process of doing so, or were about to start the process. It was a never-ending chain. And we had to adopt a criterion, which was that of respecting only the wages of those who had already retired under the provisions of the resolution, because there had to be a cut-off point somewhere.

Law 1100 and possible modifications of it, which are included in the resolutions, were analyzed in the workers' assemblies and the party, and we are in favor of studying Law 1100 and making provisions for having the wages of workers who keep on working after they could retire based on a higher percentage. [*Applause*]

We'll have to study Law 1100 carefully and make some pretty close calculations, with a computer at our fingertips, [*Laughter*] in view of how expensive every measure is and the economic aspect of the matter. And we should submit the modified Law 1100 to discussion by the workers promptly, since this is a problem which should be solved as quickly as possible. [*Applause*]

And there was another sticky matter: the problem of out-of-line, carry-over wages.*

Such wages stemmed from various sources. They weren't, let us say, the result of a hastily drawn-up measure. At first, they arose as the result of a need to establish some discipline in wages, in view of the enormous diversity of wages, the need to establish a scale of some sort, and the wish and aim not to hurt the workers, since many of those wages were the result of earlier struggles by the workers themselves, and the revolution didn't want to adopt any measures that would rebound against the workers.

Later on, they were produced by economic needs, by changes in the productive units, as a result of which workers with different wages were placed together, doing the same work.

This is how out-of-line, carry-over wages came about.

After a while, however, these wages became a kind of vice. New sources of such wages kept popping up, some of them completely illegitimate.

How could this socialist principle be applied if no measures were taken concerning out-of-line, carry-over wages?

Such wages presented a very complex problem because even though the number of workers who now have such wages has diminished, there were new cases of those wages still coming up, and it was, after all, a problem that adversely affected hundreds of thousands of workers.

The criterion was adopted of not taking any radical steps, of not solving the problem in one fell swoop, since many of these wages were perfectly legal, and the workers' confidence in the revolution had to be respected. Therefore, when the time came to face up to that problem, it would have to be handled with great care, with an eye to all legitimately acquired interests. We would have to adopt a progressive policy so as, in the first place, to prevent the establishment of any new wages that were out of line, and, in the second place, to proceed by various means to bring about the gradual but final eradication of such wages.

Logically, with new wage scales and the tying of wages to production by various means, we can go about gradually eliminating these wages.

*Also called "historic wages," this refers to the revolution's policy of not lowering the wage that any worker earned before the revolution — even if this wage was significantly higher than the scale set by the revolutionary government.

We won't do it drastically, and we won't harm the legitimate interests of the workers that the revolution has recognized, but we will work with a will to bring about the gradual eradication of out-of-line, carry-over wages through various ways, including upgrading workers with such wages, and to eliminate all possibilities of new out-of-line wages ever coming into being. [*Applause*]

And of course, every man should be paid in accord with the work he does. And if anybody had a very important job at one time but then had a very modest one, he must give up his important wage and be paid a modest one. [*Applause*] Nobody in this country was born with an important job. [*Laughter and applause*] It isn't a hereditary right. [*Applause*] And we have to apply this principle even if it hurts, even if it involves embarrassing individual situations. We have social security, so nobody will be unprotected in this country. [*Applause*] Any formula is better than that of continuing to give a worker the highest wage he's ever received as long as he keeps working.

This principle should be applied consistently, and everybody now knows that this is the norm, that this is the principle, that this is the law, that this is the will of the workers.

And, logically, every worker's remuneration should be linked to the quality and quantity of the work he does. If he is in a responsible job, an important job, he should be paid more. If later, because he can't handle the work and makes mistakes and can't continue in the job, he shouldn't keep on getting the wages pertaining to it. [*Applause*] This is a basic principle.

Of course, this will take time. You can't force through drastic solutions from one day to the next in such a matter. But we do have to keep on working toward this goal.

Now, let us cite two important examples of the theses to which the workers gave their overwhelming support, even though to do so implied economic sacrifices for many of them.

The assemblies didn't limit themselves to discussing the theses. A lot of other points came up, too. And the congress and the party have taken into consideration the resolutions adopted on the other points. I don't mean to say that the entire process was centered on just certain theses. In the course of the process, other matters that bothered the workers came up, and because a number of workers voiced the same worries in their assemblies, they were taken note of by the labor movement and the party.

Here, for example, we have the matter of revising the wage scale and qualifications, not putting a limit on overtime in certain activities, the accumulation of paid vacations for the agricultural laborer, and wage stabilization in the sugar industry.

There we came across another sticky problem. Wage stabilization in the sugar industry was established one fine day, and a worker representing the trade union at the Cuba Libre Sugar Mill stated here very clearly that 200 workers did all the repair work at the sugar mill under capitalism, while now as a result of this stabilization, there are, I think he said, 702 or 708 workers there. We were too embarrassed to ask him more about it in front of our guests. [*Laughter*]

It's true that we haven't taken part in this congress. We have attended it as guests. People have wondered why we didn't address the sessions, and the reason we didn't is that we didn't come here to talk; we came to hear what you had to say. [*Applause*]

But it struck me that if we asked a lot of sugar mill workers how many workers there were in the mill under capitalism and how many there are now, it could be demonstrated that we use many more men than the capitalists to run the mills less efficiently than the capitalists. [*Applause*]

This doesn't detract from the revolutionary quality of our workers. It isn't their fault. It's our fault, [*Shouts of "Ours, too!"*] because we haven't been able to run the mills at least as efficiently as the capitalists.

It is our fault when a mill gets packed with people. We are undoubtedly to blame for that stabilization, because we heeded those who said there weren't enough men at the mills and that stabilization was a must. So it was carried out, and now we must see what we are going to do about stabilization, in line with the principles of the theses.

Solutions won't be found overnight. None of the solutions we work out can be overnight ones. Everything must be studied carefully. [*Applause*]

Our sugar industry is plagued by a great tragedy. It is a tragedy for the country that its main industry is a cyclical one. Of course, this creates serious problems. The sugar mills work only half a year, and the revolution has sacred duties to the workers, such as finding them all jobs, and jobs that are as stable as possible.

We must see how to go about finding jobs that are as stable as possible for sugar mill workers. We want every mill to become an agroindustrial complex, in which the inactive period is used for repairing not just the mill, but all the machinery, the irrigation system, and all the equipment — in short, the idea is to keep everybody busy. But it is against the interests of the economy for 700 workers to remain in a sugar mill between harvests when 200 workers used to do all the repair work in the past. The comrade said 400 would be enough. He didn't explain why he thought it should be 400, but that is what he said, in all honesty.

If we had more construction materials on hand, when the mill was not operating we could put the surplus workers on construction — we need things of all kinds built everywhere — but, unfortunately, the material isn't available now, so we can't do that.

We feel that your resolution, which calls for studying the matter and trying to find ways to apply the principle at sugar mills, is correct.

Our consciences cannot be at peace as long as we have thousands of underutilized sugar workers at mills by virtue of the stabilization measures.

We don't want measures that will leave any worker unprotected. The revolution will never leave any worker unprotected. It will never abandon a single worker in this country! [*Applause*] But we will search for methods, we will work out methods; we will search for solutions that are just, humane, and economically sound. We must not adopt the easy way out or take shortcuts, for they many damage the country.

Some of those problems are also due to underdevelopment. To the extent that we develop new industries in the sugar mill communities, modernize agriculture, and combine agriculture and industry around the sugar mills, we will have more work possibilities and be better able to solve all these problems.

But, anyway, we must give this matter serious thought.

Cases of disability due to occupational diseases or accidents that were not the fault of the worker were also mentioned. It was proposed that these cases be taken into account when the matter of remuneration comes up, and that a total discount not be carried out with regard to the work they made previously. This is a just concern.

The reestablishment of seniority. Holding down two jobs. The distribution of teachers' time — which is an old problem that has been turning up at all meetings: from production assemblies, to the 1971 congress on culture, to now. Doctors' duty hours. Elimination of wage checks in the mass-media sector — which I believe will now be discussed at the congress of journalists (because they are also workers, and they too have their congresses). The proposal for eliminating the coupons for food and lodging — a proposal which has apparently been very popular here.

Some of these measures were worked out with the best of intentions, and then they became a source of tremendous problems. Many of those matters were not mentioned in the theses, but they were pointed out by the workers and discussed here at the congress. Our party is going to study them carefully, in order to solve those which can be solved now, discussing the problems with the comrades in the labor movement. We can't give a hasty reply to some of these problems, such as the twenty-four-hour duty of doctors, because we must find out what the medical care situation is, what the situation is at every hospital. But we must study the matter and come up with solutions wherever possible. We must also give the green light to the idea of holding down two jobs wherever it will help solve the problems of the economy, production, and services.

For example, it seems quite fair to us that if a retired sugar mill worker goes to work in one of the technological institutes set up there, he should be paid. If we apply Law 1100, and he receives a certain amount of money, and then we give him another job that he can do, he should be paid for doing that work of three or four hours a day. This is quite fair.

As far as the teachers go, there are other problems besides that of the distribution of their time. Teachers have a wage scale which is quite precarious, especially nongraduate teachers. As you know, many of our teachers are not graduates, and they start out earning very low wages. This is a matter we must review and try to solve, because their work is turning out to be very difficult. The successes in the educational field during the last few years are extraordinarily encouraging for the country in every sense of the word. I am sure the workers will agree that we must study the matter to see how we can best aid teachers. [*Applause*]

Regarding some problems, while the process leading up to the congress was under way, the leadership of the party was discussing several matters which you have covered in the resolutions. The leadership of the party adopted certain measures or favorable positions regarding, for example, revision of wage scales, revision of job qualifications, improving payment for work done under abnormal conditions, payment according to yield, and raising the wage scale in work centers where the work is organized and technically normed.

I think you understand this last point very well, but I am going to say a few more things. In a way, the norms trap us, because some norms are very minimal, and some have been adjusted more and others less. This leads to a contradiction, because if it is shown that the norm is low, and it is surpassed, the result could be that the norm is raised.

In the resolutions, you brought up the matter of improving the norms. We must see how we start applying the matter of wages adjusted to norms, and to what norms. As you know, some norms are lower than they should be, and the trade union leaders must honestly consider whether or not the application of these principles might not lead to increasing wages without increasing production. Anyway, we feel that the norms, regardless of their effectiveness, are a fact of life, and regardless of how much you improve them, they will remain with us. When we really work out technical norms, productivity will go up. We feel that at work centers where technical norms have begun to be applied and where, as a result of true technological and scientific norms, productivity increases, a wage scale will be applied which is different from that in effect at work centers with minimum norms. That's the idea. Do you understand? [*Applause and shouts of: "Yes!"*]

The thing is, we want to apply technical norms in a region, in a given industry, due to certain problems. Technical norms are introduced, and a wage scale is set up that is superior to that of a center where technical norms do not exist. That is the reason for the increase in wage scales at places where work is organized and technically normed.

The position of the party is to analyze, together with the leaders of the labor movement, all the matters which you raised in the resolutions and study them carefully in order to solve them as quickly as possible. The leadership of the party has a position on many of these matters.

If you aren't bored, [*Shouts of: "No!"*] it would be interesting — in order to get the most benefit for the revolution out of this congress and the process that led up to it — to point out some of the things which should concern us and give some interesting data.

There is something without which none of the agreements adopted here at the congress could be put into practice. Applying the principle of to each according to his work, paying overtime or for double shifts, and even reviewing wage scales will mean nothing if we don't maintain a financial balance. Even the application of material incentives is useless and ineffective in a situation of tremendous inflation.

We've been able to discuss all these matters in the congress and propose some measures and solutions, because money has started to have some value. When everybody has his pockets bulging with money, none of these things is effective.

Another thing: money is everything under capitalism; money is a life-or-death matter.

We have pointed out our weaknesses and shortcomings. The capitalists and the capitalist system operate through very powerful incentives. In the first place, capitalism has a labor reserve, the army of the unemployed. There is no more effective whip than the fear of losing your job, which means death by starvation under capitalism. [*Applause*]

There's practically a whole line of the unemployed at the door of every factory, trying to get a job. This facilitates capitalist discipline.

Under capitalism, the worker without a job or money dies of starvation, and so do the members of his family. If he or the members of his family get sick, they die if he is unemployed and has no money. His life, health, old-age security, and accident protection, and the education of his children, all depend on his job and the money in his pocket.

That isn't the case in socialism — even though socialism isn't yet communism, even though socialist distribution isn't communist distribution. In a socialist society the problems caused by insecurity, illness, old age, and accidents are eradicated; everybody is guaranteed a job; everybody is guaranteed the best possible medical attention — which is much better than the one the capitalists had for themselves under the capitalist system. We can proudly say that our medical services are much more efficient than those the capitalists had here for themselves and their families. [*Applause*] The revolution has eradicated many illnesses. The infant mortality rate in our country is on a level with that of developed countries — that is, it is minimal. Our medical service is improving and will continue to improve every year, and our polyclinics have already established a house-call service to take care of old people and children who can't be taken to the hospital for attention. [*Applause*]

With socialism, the people, the workers and their families, are guaranteed all these things.

Under capitalism the thing uppermost in a man's mind is survival, health, his children. If he's the head of a family, if one of his loved ones is sick, he's hounded by the thought of not having any money; he's hounded by all the fears on which capitalist labor discipline is founded. In other words, under capitalism, it's the subhuman standard of living that disciplines the workers.

Such motivations don't exist in socialism; in socialism money isn't essential in facing these problems. The important things, the problems that — logically enough — are of vital importance to the workers are solved by the entire society.

That is why the contribution made by the consciousness of the workers, by the political culture of the workers, and by their attitude, becomes an irreplaceable element in socialism, since the workers' motivations are of a different character.

Naturally, in socialism, man becomes fully identified with the means of production, with the country's future, with the country's political process, with the country's political problems. In other words, the worker becomes the master of his country's wealth and the master of his country's destiny.

In socialism, however, moral factors, the factors of consciousness, the factors of culture, are essential. We should never think we are going to solve with money the problems that only consciousness can solve. We must use material incentives intelligently and combine them with moral incentives, [*Applause*] but we must not be deluded into thinking we are going to motivate the man of today, the socialist man, only through material incentives, because material incentives no longer have the validity they have under capitalism, in which everything — even life and death — requires money.

At any rate, an abundance of money, a superabundance of money, has an adverse effect on many people's — not everybody's — attitude toward work. We cannot forget even for a single moment the tens of thousands, the hundreds of thousands of workers, the immense majority of the workers of this country, who are ready and willing — at any time, in every field, and without material incentives of any kind — to make whatever effort is necessary in the sugar harvest, in the defense of the country, in everything. [*Applause*] We can never forget — and some of the workers pointed this out here — the job done by our workers when there were no such things as home appliances, minibrigades, or houses, when there was nothing — which led to their developing the consciousness they have today, of which we are proud. We are proud to have our visitors see this, and, even though we feel embarrassed about our weaknesses, we don't hesitate to admit them. [*Applause*]

A deflationary process, a process of reducing the money in circulation, has been in effect since 1971. In other words, we were millionaires in 1971, and now we are poorer — but still millionaires. Naturally enough, our economy has been growing. It went up 5 percent in 1971, 9 percent in 1972, and 13 percent so far this year — an accumulated total of 30 percent in three years.

Needless to say, one of the sectors to give the greatest boost to the country's economic development was that of construction. [*Applause*] And again, needless to say, we must make it our business to ensure a steady, albeit modest, growth in the future.

In our speech during the celebration of the twentieth anniversary, we mentioned a growth of around 6 percent a year. Six percent is tantamount to doubling all our production in eleven years. It is neither a rhythm to be scoffed at nor a sensational achievement. But one thing we can do is increase this rhythm while doing our planning on the basis of our realities. This is why we say an average growth of 6 percent a year over the next ten years.

Wages have gone up too during this period — or rather, the amount of money spent on wages has increased. There were 2.773 billion pesos paid in wages in 1967; 3.111 billion in 1970; 3.187 billion in 1971; and 3.367 billion in 1972; and it is estimated that 3.690 billion pesos will be paid in wages in 1973.

Even though we are spending more on wages, there is less money in circulation. I'll explain this later on. First, I'd like to add that even with Law 1100 in effect, our expenditures for social security will amount to 547 million pesos, because the number of people receiving social security benefits is larger every year.

The farmers will receive 240 million pesos for agricultural products this year, and payments to private carriers, subsidies to students, etc., will come to 273 million. All told — what with wages, social security, etc. — the people will be receiving 4.750 billion pesos this year.

Wage expenditures have increased by some 900 million pesos since 1967, but in spite of this, the amount of money in the hands of the people has declined, because the people have been spending more than they received during this time. The process started in 1971. In the second half of that year, 150 million pesos were brought in —

Oh! I almost forgot to tell you something I'm sure you want to know — the most money the people ever had in circulation: 3.478 billion pesos. That was the maximum. Now we are poorer.

In the second half of 1971, we brought in 150 million pesos; in 1972, we brought in 680 million; the 1973 estimate is 400 million pesos. In two and a half years, 1.230 billion will have been brought in.

This money came from the people, but it will enrich the people. Although it may seem paradoxical, the more money we have in circulation the poorer we are, for it wasn't the bourgeoisie or the landlords who brought this money in, it was your revolutionary state. [*Applause*]

As you know, this has been accomplished in two ways: by making more goods available to the people and by raising the prices of certain nonessential articles. When I say "nonessential," I don't mean that they aren't popular. [*Laughter*] I simply mean they aren't essential. Not milk, bread, or any other food, but cigarettes and alcoholic beverages. But people were swimming in money, and the effects of the gradual reduction in the amount of money in circulation are already evident.

Is this clear? [*Shouts of: "Yes!"*]

We are very glad to give you this information, because the only way we can advance is by having you, the workers, understand it. We aren't speculators, and we don't like charging high prices for anything. But this sea of money was having an adverse effect on the economy. What would all the agreements of this congress have amounted to in the midst of this sea of money?

We know that if there is more money in circulation than there are goods and services, many people lose interest in money. For one thing, it is no longer needed to solve many of our vital problems, which are now solved by society as a whole. People are no longer worried about their children's future; they don't have to save for a rainy day.

Training a teacher is expensive, very expensive . . . and training a nurse is expensive, very expensive . . . a lot of years have to be devoted to this, starting in elementary and junior high school . . . and a skilled woman . . . we have a tremendous need for teachers. But every time a young man with a good wage married a teacher, he would say to her, "Don't work; there's no need for it." [*Laughter*] And the country would lose the teacher. And the same holds true in the case of the nurse.

When the country loses a woman teacher or nurse it is a sad thing — not only because the money that's been invested in her education has been thrown away, but because it shows that *machismo* and super-he-man ideas still abound. [*Applause*]

What are we going to accomplish with this? Return to the capitalist period, when women lived off their husbands and served as household decorations? [*Shouts of: "No!"*] I am sure that at least Cuban women will never agree to this. [*Shouts of: "No!" and applause*] We mustn't forget that now we have two on the Executive Secretariat of the CTC. [*Applause*]

But all this superabundance of money in circulation was having adverse economic effects: there was a need for workers in many critical sectors — sometimes even in hospitals — and nobody wanted to do the work. There was an abundance of money. This is another example of our lack of readiness for communism. Marx said that work would eventually become the most vital necessity, and not just a way to earn a living. And when our young man got married he kept the teacher at home, showing that work was still not the first — or, as Marx said, [*Laughter*] "the most vital necessity." Not just a way to earn a living.

That was the situation we were faced with: the textile mills had come to a halt; such-and-such a factory had no workers, because those who had started working there quit — 60 out of 100 women quit. There was no stable labor force we could count on. This is a logical result of the superabundance of money. Is this clear? [*Shouts of: "Yes!"*]

Now, the pendulum is swinging the other way. [*Laughter*] A greater demand for jobs has been noted. The time may come when we will have a headache finding jobs for all those who want to work. But what are we going to do? We'll simply have to rack our brains and solve the problem. It will be better than having a factory standing idle because of a lack of workers.

We don't want an army of the unemployed. This is clear. The revolution will never resort to a capitalist method. [*Applause*]

But we must live and meet our material needs; we must advance and overcome underdevelopment and poverty. That is why we must be realistic, understanding all this, knowing what measures are applied, why they are applied, and what is good and bad for the economy; why it is good and why it is bad; how many of us are revolutionaries and the extent of revolutionary awareness; how many of us are communists and the extent of communist awareness; and what we still have to do to become revolutionaries and communists in the finest sense of the word! [*Applause*]

There are 2.248 billion pesos in circulation at present. The amount has gone down. With a bit more of a drop, we'll be within what the experts view as the normal limits of money in circulation. It will be a great thing, a real step forward, to get within the normal limits, for as long as we're outside them, none of the agreements you have adopted — the agreements in the economic field — would have practical effect. They simply wouldn't function.

Thus, this is a very important thing, the financial balance. The amount of money in the hands of the people shouldn't go beyond normal limits, and a balance should be kept between what is paid out in wages and the total goods and services available to the people.

If we start throwing more money into circulation, if we start distributing more through wages than the value of the goods and services we have on hand, we will just be millionaires again — that is, we will have a lot of money in our pockets, but very little to spend it on. It is very important that the balance between the people's total income and the available goods and services be maintained. This is essential. Are you with me? [*Shouts of: "Yes!"*]

Here's a list of what the people spend their money on. Rent, 60 million pesos; movies and theater, 46 million; electricity and gas, 70. These areas don't bring in a lot of money.

There are statistics on how much the people spend on beauty parlors, barbershops, and buses — that is, those of them who pay their bus fare. [*Laughter*]

Now then, next year we expect to bring in a bit more money. It will be very good to be within the limits — if the experts are right about what the limits are.

Now we will look at what we will have to spend next year as the result of wage increases — without affecting prices. Of course, some prices are high: they haven't been changed for a long time. If you want some good news, the comrades in the service sector have suggested a slight drop in the prices of alcoholic beverages. [*Applause*] Some stocks are piling up, and there will be a reduction. If there's a product that can't be exported, the people should have it. That's another principle. Moreover, we must get used to seeing things in the stores. The habit has developed that if there is something, people say, "Why is that there? Why don't they reduce the price?" We must get used to the idea of having things in the store so that what the individual earns means something when he goes to the store! [*Applause*]

But the stock is getting to be too large, and prices will be reduced slightly.

All right: how much will we have to spend next year in more income for the population?

Increase in the work force: 113,500 workers; 177 million pesos. This is every year. When we have more workers the amount will increase.

Drop in absenteeism. There is an optimistic estimate: it represents 37 million pesos more wages. This shows the confidence in the agreements of the workers' congress! [*Applause*]

Changes in jobs: 0.5 million.

Social security, Law 1100: 40 million.

We will be compelled to spend 254 million pesos more in 1974 than in 1973.

Is it clear?

We will have to spend this 254 million anyway, even just employing all those who must be employed and retiring and giving pensions to all those who are eligible. Inevitable expenditures.

Estimates have been made. There are various measures in keeping with the proposals of the workers, which you have approved, some of which have also been approved by the party. These include the elimination of the first two groups in the wage scale, reorganization standards, vacation pay . . . well, there's a mistake in the one about vacation pay. It should read "discount," and I don't see why this should increase spending.

Anyway, the elimination of the first two groups in the scale, which affects agricultural workers, represents 10.5 million pesos.

Increasing wages for technicians — to increase the scale for technicians, working out adequate remuneration for skilled people — represents 67 million.

This is in theory. No decisions have been adopted yet. They are viewed positively, however.

Increasing wages for personnel in charge of directing production: 65 million.

Revision of standards: 7.2 million.

Payment for work done under abnormal conditions: 50 million.

Payment of overtime and double shifts: 55 million.

Linking wages to norms: 44 million.

Technical norming: 2.5 million.

Other: 13.6 million.

This gives us a total of 314.8 million, which is what applying all these things would represent.

It would mean a grand total of 569 million pesos more in wages in 1974.

When we talk about increasing wages for personnel in charge of production, we're talking about such people as brigade leaders and foremen, whose wages must compare favorably with those of tractor drivers and operators of other equipment.

What does all this mean? It means we must be very careful in our application of these agreements, study the production centers, and begin to apply the agreements where all wage increases are accompanied by increases in production that match the wage increases.

Of course, there are fields where wage increases would not be immediately compensated for with production increases that would put more goods in the hands of the people. For example, a power plant that's under construction for two years doesn't represent immediate material income. And there may be an increase in wages in the construction field. These are things which don't immediately lead to more goods for the population.

But anyway, all these measures must be applied gradually and carefully, starting at places where the labor force is the main thing and where a wage increase will immediately lead to making more goods available to the population. Our accounting must be very careful. All this — all these measures and their economic effects — must be discussed with the labor leaders, so these agreements — which can be a tremendous tool in increasing economic efficiency — won't trigger a new inflationary process in which wages, wage income, and expenditures don't correspond to the production of material goods. Above all, we must have a sound financial balance.

If the application of these agreements leads to an upsetting of the financial balance, we won't have accomplished anything.

The labor leaders must know all this, because it is very important.

In spite of everything, there's an increase in material production, but we can't raise wages above material production, because the country has to invest heavily in its development.

This is important.

Sometimes our material production isn't limited by a lack of labor power. If the limiting factor of material production were just the availability of labor power . . . Many industries are already working at peak capacity; they can't up production any more. Other industries are limited by a lack of raw materials — because they're expensive, scarce, or simply not available. That is, some industries can't function at full production capacity for lack of raw materials; others fall down for lack of workers. When the limiting factor is a lack of raw materials, these industries may get them from abroad.

If sugar production increases, its exports also increase, and we have the means for importing raw materials. As exports increase, imports can, as well. It's not easy to resort to imports as a solution. Why? Let me quote some current world market prices to give you an idea. Some say, "There's much more money now; let's import more." This depends, in the first place, on our exports. Some foods have gone up: dried beans from $121.50 per ton in 1969 to $574 per ton in 1974. A ton of corn cost $58.08 on the capitalist market in 1969, but will cost $131.55 in 1974.

Wheat, $71.76 in 1969 and $159.45 in 1974. Rice, $90 a ton in 1970 and $400 a ton in 1974.

Vegetable oil, $228.51 in 1969 and $329.22 in 1974. Powdered milk, $128 in 1969 and $603 in 1974. Vegetable flour, $93.60 in 1969 and $191 in 1974. Fish meal, $129.80 in 1969 and $386.20 in 1974. Phosphorous rock — a raw material — $22 in 1969 and $50 in 1974.

Nitrogenous fertilizers, urea, $80.13 in 1969 and $141 in 1974. Triple superphosphate, $67.57 in 1969 and $120 in 1974. Rayon fabrics, $643.13 per thousand square meters in 1969 and $964.69 in 1974. Woolen fabrics, $871.23 in 1969 and $1,306.70 in 1974. Cotton thread, $227.52 per thousand meters in 1969 and $379.98 in 1974.

Acetate fiber, $1,314 per ton in 1969 and $2,284 in 1974. Nylon fiber, $2,570 in 1969 and $4,155.77 in 1974. Acrylic fiber, $2,360 in 1969 and $4,738 in 1974. Other products follow the same pattern.

What does this mean? There's worldwide inflation; some basic raw materials, such as oil, are getting very expensive. The chemical industry has a lot of weight in the world economy. In general, food is scarce in the world. Many of these products aren't available at any price. Many of these items — flour, fish meal, powdered milk, and especially the raw materials for animal feeds — have gone up tremendously. In spite of this, we've kept up our egg production, and the price of eggs is the same as it was in the past. Milk sells at the same price it always has. Of course, the economy has to meet all these increases in cost.

If we compare the cost of imports with the price of sugar, in accord with the limits of the world market, sugar would be worth 3 cents a pound. It was difficult to reach an agreement at the sugar conference, since the importing countries wanted to establish an unacceptable price ceiling on sugar. We would have had to accept a price ceiling on sugar and then go out and buy all these raw materials and products at these tremendously high prices. That's why we couldn't reach an agreement.

Objectively speaking, the situation is complicated. It's not an easy one. This is why we can't say that through imports we can balance any wage increase. We must take into consideration the objective limitations.

These facts emphasize even more the need for establishing economic efficiency at any cost. They strengthen all the criteria and points of view you've analyzed and the application of the principle of producing more, at higher quality and at a lower cost.

One of the comrades here said that the attitude of the workers throughout their discussions was that of true statesmen. And that is a fact. It is very, very important that the workers take these questions seriously!

In the battle for producing more, at higher quality and at a lower cost, all these things reflect the importance of economic work in general and agricultural work in particular; the importance of the work in the sugarcane projects, the cattle-raising projects, the rice projects. In short, the vast importance that the work done by the agricultural trade union has, in connection not only with savings but also with increasing production.

A series of resolutions relating to the workers' participation in the handling of the economy were adopted by the congress. One of these had to do with the workers' participation in the meetings held by the administrative councils of production units and in those held in the ministries.

The party leadership is in complete accord with that resolution. [*Applause*] But there's more; we decided to invite the representatives of the labor movement to attend the periodic meetings held by the Executive Committee of the Council of Ministers in which the yearly plans are analyzed and decisions are made of vital importance in matters of administration and the economy. [*Applause*]

All these things are but the fulfillment of a long-cherished aspiration of all revolutionaries: to give organized labor the broadest participation in the handling of the economy, as befits a socialist process.

You also adopted another important resolution: to strengthen and maintain the minibrigade movement on the basis of surplus work as the correct method of dealing with and the correct solution for the housing problem.* [*Applause*]

There are more houses being built now than at any time before the revolution and a large number of these are being built by the minibrigades. If we only had more materials, with the kind of work force we could release by applying the resolutions of the workers' congress, you can imagine how many houses, elementary schools, children's day-care centers, and other social installations we could build through surplus work!

At any rate, we shouldn't feel discouraged. Important investments are being made in order to increase the material base for construction work so we will have more steel rods, more cement, more rock, more sand, more material of all kinds. The time will come when we will be able to give a new and even greater boost to construction work by the minibrigades, in order to solve the housing problem. [*Applause*]

It's very important that this movement be kept alive!

You — I mean those of you who haven't been there — will be invited to visit the Alamar section, one of the new communities now under construction. You will be able to verify its functionability, its spaciousness, and see all the facilities that are being created there by the workers for the workers. In fact, the capitalists couldn't even imagine any of their bourgeois residential sections having all the facilities, the beauty, and the spaciousness of this residential section being built by the hands of our workers. [*Applause*]

It is quite possible that the minibrigades from a number of work centers will get so far ahead on the work that they may have their main housing problems solved — which would conspire against the continuity of the minibrigades' work. And that wouldn't be right. It would be fine for them to solve their housing problems, but it wouldn't be right to have this lead to their respective minibrigades being disbanded or becoming discouraged.

As soon as some minibrigades build so many apartment buildings that the situation becomes less pressing for their respective work centers, they should — inspired by a proletarian spirit, by a spirit of solidarity — start building other apartment buildings for other labor sectors: [*Applause*] for teachers, for example, who don't have a powerful labor force for construction, for the simple reason that most of them are women.

*The minibrigade (or microbrigade) system is a program to help ease Cuba's housing shortage by organizing brigades of workers from a particular workplace, relieving them of their normal responsibilities in order to build housing for themselves and others in their workplace. These units have also built schools, nurseries, community buildings, shopping centers, polyclinics, and parks.

And since you say that teachers are overloaded with work, you tell me how they're going to solve their housing problems.

It goes without saying that as soon as we have more productivity in construction work and are able to release more of the labor force, we will also be able to organize state brigades to build houses for such cases, just as we have brigades building houses for technicians — because the least we can do for the technicians who come to work here is give them a place to live.

In the future, what with the prefabrication system and higher productivity, we should not only continue our work with the minibrigades but also have state brigades, to help solve the housing problem, especially for those sectors that are unable to organize their own minibrigades because of the kind of work they do.

This is why it's necessary for the minibrigades to maintain their strength and transfer this strength where it's needed, while keeping in touch with the work centers. We should try at all costs to keep the minibrigade worker in touch with his work center, because it's through the work center that the minibrigade keeps its spirit alive. We have reached certain criteria with regard to their job qualifications. When they're considered construction workers, they can receive the benefits of being minibrigade construction workers, and when they get paid wages below those of a qualified construction worker they can receive higher wages, taking their qualifications into consideration — but without their losing touch with their work centers. If we let the minibrigade worker lose touch with his work center, we destroy the minibrigades.

There's no other way out. When we can have state construction brigades, we'll be able to build more housing. We estimate that for the next ten or twelve years, the minibrigades will be the driving force behind the building of housing and many other social installations, which are also a part of housing facilities. Naturally, the surplus labor force from the sugar mills will be able to contribute greatly in this respect when we have the materials.

We recommend that the labor movement see to it that the minibrigade movement continues.

We've talked about flat-rate contracts for construction workers. Some construction projects have problems not with the availability of workers, but with the availability of materials. In order to establish the system of flat-rate construction contracts, we have to be able to guarantee construction materials.

We mean to experiment with this flat-rate contract system on a few priority construction projects. There are construction projects that have their supply of materials assured. Otherwise, the flat-rate contract system would be of no use. The experiments would be carried out on projects where there's a problem of a labor force but no problem of materials, since they're priority projects.

The construction sector, in agreement with the construction workers' trade union, is going to try out this system.

The distribution of household electrical appliances is another problem we've discussed. We understand that the solutions you've come up with are good ones. Some contradictions have arisen in the process. A worker said it was usually "the good guy," the worker liked by everyone, who got the electrical appliance. But I'm sure this is the exception to the rule, as Comrade Lázaro said.

Now, if a "good guy" can fool the masses, what about the public official? If a public official, instead of the masses, is in charge of distribution, he makes a hundred mistakes for every one the masses made. [*Applause*]

Do you think there's any way of distributing the apartments built by the minibrigades other than through workers' assemblies? [*Shouts of: "No!"*]

Of course, everything in life has its problems, and we understand that these workers' assemblies make additional work for the labor leaders. On the other hand, there's no need for using assemblies to distribute those products that can be freely purchased now. We should be very pleased that there's no need to distribute watches and pressure cookers by means of these assemblies. It will be wonderful when TV sets can be freely bought. Over 100,000 TV sets are being distributed each year. Television sets have been primarily distributed through the work centers, and 250,000 of them have already gone to workers' families.

We don't have a plentiful supply of refrigerators. The number is increasing, but we're going to keep distributing them through work centers.

What will happen if, later on, we set up color TV and the first color sets become available? What if motorcycles have to be distributed some day? What if, after other necessities have been taken care of, the country could make available some thousands of cars? [*Applause*]

What does this mean? That some electrical appliances will be scarce? As they become more plentiful, the situation changes. But we think that as long as these electrical appliances are scarce, the workers should be the first ones to get them. It's a matter of having the workers come first in a nation of workers. Before, electrical appliances were sold to anybody who was willing to stand in a long waiting line in front of a store, and this method caused a lot of irritation. If and when we come up with a method that's better than the one we have now, with the same guideline in mind, we'll adopt it so as to save you all this extra work at the work centers. For the time being, though, don't stop distributing the electrical appliances you're in charge of. Carry on with the work of the assemblies at the trade union locals until we come up with a better way to apply our distribution guideline. [*Applause*]

And don't start thinking about buying cars right away. [*Laughter*]

We're going to import some taxis to replace those old, beat-up ones that make the streets of our cities look so ugly and are so expensive to run. [*Applause*]

We're also going to buy some cars to sell to technicians — we're not talking about a privilege; we're talking about selling cars to those technicians who need them in order to be more productive in their work. Do you agree? [*Shouts of: "Yes!" and applause*] For example, the doctors who make house calls have had an opportunity to buy cars at cost. They pay for the cars in installments and also pay for some of their maintenance and gas. The cars are theirs, and they take very good care of them. Besides, they drive the cars themselves, and the cars are very inexpensive to run.

These things which are luxury items today have to be distributed in accord with their usefulness to the country. You haven't said anything about this, but we're aware of the fact that the labor movement needs some cars. [*Applause and shouts*] Comrade Lázaro and the other labor leaders gave us a very good reason for this. When we asked them how many permanent professional cadres they're going to have — and we're really interested in not having the labor movement overstaffed — they explained that sometimes they need three cadres where one would be enough, because they don't have enough resources to work with. We also discussed the question of the municipal committees. As we understand it, you should employ fewer cadres so as to get the greatest productivity. We can't promise you immediate solutions, but we do assure you that in 1974 we're going to make an effort to provide the labor movement with a basic minimum of cars for its work. [*Applause*] We'll do this with the idea of increasing your productivity as cadres of the workers. [*Applause*]

You have reached agreements about skilled workers. You've even passed a resolution on them here in this congress which will surely be made into a law by the revolutionary government. [*Applause*] Having skilled workers is very important. We estimate that the labor movement must train over 100,000 skilled workers in the coming years, in addition to the skilled workers being graduated from the polytechnic and technological institutes — that is, regular educational channels.

Concerning the training of skilled workers in the coming years, we can say that we can do wonders. Polytechnic and technological institutes are mushrooming all over the country, and every year we're going to place a greater emphasis on schools of this kind.

We're building around 150 new polytechnic institutes and junior high schools every year. This is the equivalent of 150 units for 500 students each. In Oriente Province alone, close to 20 polytechnic institutes have been built in a single year next to the sugar mills! [*Applause*] The Textile Technological Institute has just been opened at Alquitex. In December, a polytechnic institute for 1,000 students will be opened next to the Ariguanabo textile factory. [*Applause*]

The material base for the professional training of our young people has been tremendously increased, and it can also be used by the workers. They can teach their specialties in those schools built next to the factories and get the other teachers in these schools to give them training courses in other things. There are various ways of having the labor movement cooperate with the skilled workers' training programs designed for the young people.

As we said at the beginning of our remarks, this congress is especially significant because it constitutes the first important and decisive step in the search for peak economic efficiency. The search for peak economic efficiency will be one of the revolution's vital tasks in the coming years. [*Applause*] It will be a task for the party, the government, the labor movement, and the youth and mass organizations.

Work is already under way for the 1976-80 economic plan, the revolution's first five-year plan, [*Applause*] whose outlines will be approved at the first congress of our party in 1975. [*Applause*] It will surely be a challenging plan, which will necessitate great efforts on the part of all our people and assure the progress of our country in the next few years.

We expect the labor leaders to help draw up the plan, and all the workers will participate in its analysis and discussion. [*Applause*]

The economic battle is fundamental, and it can be won only with the greatest participation of all our workers.

It will also be necessary to strengthen the authority of the administration. Another of the virtues of this workers' congress was, as Lázaro pointed out, that there was no antiadministration spirit. We trust that there will be close relations based on cooperation and joint work between you — who represent the workers, who, with their hands, create riches — and the administrators — who represent the socialist state [*Applause*] and socialist administration.

We have strengthened the administration's opposite number. [*Applause*] Now we must strengthen the administration. [*Applause*]

Comrades, our party is proud of the results of this congress, of your work and your successes. It has been a tremendous demonstration of political and revolutionary maturity and of the far-reaching nature of the awareness of our working class.

Today you elected the leaders of the CTC. The party had a hand in selecting the candidates, but the party didn't step in and tell you who you had to vote for: the party asked the top leaders of the labor movement what the position of the masses of the workers was, what the position of the intermediate-level trade union leaderships was, and what the position of the national trade union leaders was regarding the candidates to be proposed at this congress. And every single one of the leaders now on the National Committee said, on behalf of the workers, that Comrade Lázaro Peña should be general secretary of the CTC. [*Prolonged applause*]

Comrade Lázaro held an important position in the leadership of the party, but since the revolution feels that a strengthened labor movement is of the greatest importance, the leadership of the party let Comrade Lázaro be candidate and go to work on the labor front.

This election, carried out in a completely democratic manner, reflecting the feelings of the workers — and this is the task of the party, to guarantee the democratic spirit of the process, interpret and back the will of the masses, and guide them in fundamental problems — this election constitutes, in the first place, a tribute to a comrade who has devoted his entire life to the cause of the workers. [*Prolonged applause*] It constitutes a recognition of his position as a teacher of trade union cadres, [*Applause*] because the labor leaders told us that Lázaro had been their teacher and that during the months they worked with him they had learned more about the affairs of the labor movement, dealing with the workers and trade union matters, than they had learned in all the rest of their lives. And it is also a recognition of Comrade Lázaro Peña's great ability in dealing with and leading the workers. [*Applause*]

Comrade Lázaro has also been the heart of this process that led up to the congress, from the work with the theses through the holding of the congress itself. [*Applause*]

Together with Comrade Lázaro Peña, a contingent of young labor leaders has been elected — Agapito [Figueroa] won't get mad because I include him with the young people, and all of us naturally think of him as young because of his enthusiasm. [*Applause*] That contingent of young cadres has great ability, a magnificent attitude, and tremendous prestige in the eyes of the workers, and we are sure they will learn a lot as they work with Comrade Lázaro Peña.

One of the tasks facing Comrade Lázaro Peña will be that of giving this worthy contingent of young cadres, this hope for the Cuban labor movement, his example and spirit.

We're happy about the entire process of the congress and also very happy about the comrades you've chosen. We're pleased with the deeply democratic spirit of this labor movement. In 1970 we were determined to build a vigorous, powerful labor movement, a deeply democratic one, and now we've built the foundations — on solid and indestructible grounds — for this labor movement. [*Applause*]

We're hopeful and enthusiastic about the kind of delegates who've attended this congress and the assurance and self-reliance they've shown in their behavior, their work, and the way they've expressed themselves. We're not the slightest bit afraid of making a mistake when we know that our labor movement and our party have a wonderful source of militant, enthusiastic, honest, and revolutionary cadres. [*Applause*]

Our labor movement never had such great perspectives! Our labor movement was never as solid as it is now!

This means the revolution will be able to count on another force; the party will be able to count on another force in the tasks it has to carry out.

You'll have the duty of continuing along this upward road through your efforts, studies, and preparations, following the great tradition you yourselves have established at this history-making congress.

This congress has also been a great proof of internationalist spirit. With satisfaction, enthusiasm, and firmness, our workers have expressed their solidarity with the causes and struggles of the workers of the whole world. [*Applause*]

Here, before the delegates of almost seventy labor organizations from throughout the world, you have expressed this internationalist spirit, proving your friendship, affection, and solidarity with the workers of the Soviet Union and all the other socialist countries. [*Applause*] You have expressed your unconditional support for the workers of Chile; [*Applause*] the heroic struggle of the Arab peoples; [*Applause*] the beloved people of Vietnam; [*Applause*] the fraternal people of Puerto Rico; [*Applause*] and the fighters who are struggling against neocolonialism, colonialism, and racism in Africa. [*Applause*]

You have expressed your pride for the Cuban workers who are fulfilling their internationalist duty in various countries of the world: [*Applause*] for the medical brigades serving the fraternal people of Syria; [*Applause*] for the construction workers in the Republic of Guinea; [*Applause*] for the doctors, technicians, teachers, and others working in Equatorial Guinea, Algeria, and Yemen. [*Applause*] You've said that brigades of Cuban construction workers should go to Vietnam, [*Applause*] which they'll soon be doing, equipment and all, to make their contribution in the reconstruction of that sister country. [*Applause*]

This internationalist spirit honors all of us. It honors our working class and makes our party feel enthusiastic and encouraged. Without an internationalist spirit, there could never be a communist consciousness. [*Applause*]

Although ours is a small and still poor country, we shouldn't feel the least regret at using some of our resources to help other revolutionary peoples that are even poorer than we are. [*Applause*]

Besides, if there's any one people that has the duty of helping other peoples, it's our people, which has such a close acquaintance with the fruits of proletarian internationalism and received so much help. [*Applause*] The great homeland of Lenin helped Cuba with all available means at decisive moments, and it's only just that we too should help other revolutionary peoples as much as we can. [*Applause*]

This congress has also shown wonderful internationalist spirit from another angle. Delegates of almost seventy labor organizations from other countries are present here. [*Applause*]

With genuine pride, we've seen come before us delegates from the most prestigious and solid labor organizations of the world labor movement. We've had the pleasure of listening to Comrade Pierre Gensous, general secretary of the World Federation of Trade Unions, [*Applause*] and to Comrade Alexander Shelepin, chairman of the Central Council of Soviet Trade Unions and member of the Political Bureau of the Communist Party of the Soviet Union, who brought us the fraternal expressions of solidarity of the Soviet workers. [*Applause*]

We heard the leaders of the labor organizations of other sister socialist countries and of the labor organizations of Africa, Asia, and Latin America, as well as leaders of important world organizations.

We've had the opportunity of listening to warm and profound speeches by representatives of our brother Puerto Rican workers, [*Applause*] the Arab peoples, Vietnam, Korea, and the African workers. [*Applause*] We have among us leaders from the U.S. labor movement. [*Applause*] And representatives of the heroic Chilean workers have been present here. [*Applause*]

Comrade Hortensia Bussi, wife of the late President Allende, [*Applause*] and their daughter Beatriz [*Applause*] were also with us at this congress.

They all had extraordinarily kind, affectionate, encouraging words for us.

As all of them spoke here, we could see for ourselves, as if in an open book, the extent to which our workers and the rest of our people have developed their solidarity with the most just and revolutionary causes all over the world. [*Applause*]

Our country has done and will continue to do its internationalist duty! When we speak of the Cubans who are doing their duty in other countries, we must not forget the comrades of the Revolutionary Armed Forces who, in one way or another, are also doing their duty as technicians in other countries. [*Prolonged applause*]

Special attention has been devoted to Chile in this congress. A forceful appeal to workers all over the world was issued today, calling on them to express their solidarity with the people of Chile and to struggle against the criminal fascist junta. [*Applause*]

We are sure that the labor movement all over the world, and especially the representatives of the workers in European countries who have represented their organizations here in so brilliant and distinguished a manner — we're talking about the workers' representatives from capitalist countries who are present here — [*Applause*] we are sure that they will act on that appeal and view it as their own. [*Applause*]

Thousands of Chileans — and not just Chileans; other Latin Americans, too, who lived in Chile — have been jailed, persecuted, and expelled by the fascist junta. They have been offered hospitality in numerous countries. A large number of them want to come to our country and live here until they can return to a free Chile or to their own homeland once it has been freed.

We have a housing shortage. But to the workers here, we propose that one apartment in every building built by the workers' minibrigades in Havana in the future be offered to a Chilean or other Latin American family. [*Prolonged applause*]

We have around 500 minibrigades in Havana. This means that in less than a year, there will be 500 apartments for those who come from Chile to live in our country. [*Applause*]

We don't have very much, but we will gladly share the little we have with our Latin American brothers who are persecuted in any part of this hemisphere. [*Applause*]

Comrade delegates, all that remains is for me to express to all of you representatives of the labor movement who are gathered here, our infinite gratitude for your presence and to express to all of you, on behalf of our party, our deep recognition of and sincere congratulations for the success of this event.

Long live the Cuban working class! [*Shouts of: "Long live!"*]

Long live the Cuban working class! [*Shouts of: "Long live!"*]

Patria o muerte!

Venceremos! [*Shouts of: "Venceremos!" and ovation*]

The Establishment of People's Power

July 26, 1974

NOTE: By 1974 the process of institutionalization had made big strides. In 1973 the judicial system was restructured, and in 1974 an experimental program was begun in Matanzas Province with the creation of elected institutions of government called organs of People's Power. These were to be a model for the definitive representative institutions later expanded to the entire country.

To highlight the importance of this development, the celebration of Cuba's national holiday, July 26, the anniversary of the 1953 attack on the Moncada garrison, was held in Matanzas. Speaking at this rally Castro spelled out for the whole nation the significance of the Matanzas elections and how People's Power would work. The text is taken from Granma Weekly Review, *August 4, 1974.*

Comrades of the party and government leadership;
Comrade guests;
Comrade heroes and heroines of labor;
Comrade delegates to the organs of People's Power;
People of Matanzas;
Cubans:

The enthusiasm and joy with which the people of Matanzas have welcomed July 26 is truly moving. [*Applause*]

Why was Matanzas chosen as the site for this July 26 celebration? The province did very well this year — the others did, too: Las Villas, [*Applause*] for example, overfulfilled its sugar production plan by 110,000 tons, [*Applause*] contributing more than $40 million worth of sugar — based on its current price on the world market — to the country's economy.

The selection of Matanzas was in no way an underestimation or disregard of the effort put forth by our people in the other provinces. It is simply that the revolution had an old debt to pay to Matanzas, a province which overfulfilled its sugar production plan in 1970 and turned out over a million tons of sugar. [*Applause*]

There's also another reason, a very important one: the fact that the revolution is giving special attention to the revolutionary experiment that is being made in Matanzas with the establishment of People's Power — something which you, the people of Matanzas, have supported with enthusiasm and given your warmest support.

We are all deeply honored by the presence of the delegation from the fraternal people of South Vietnam, [*Applause*] who are represented here by Comrade Nguyen Thi Dinh, deputy commander in chief of the People's Liberation Armed Forces of South Vietnam, and a number of other Vietnamese heroines and patriots.

Our people admire heroism, and we are fully aware of the struggle being waged by the Vietnamese people against our common enemy, Yankee imperialism, which has harassed and attacked us throughout the past years and, at the same time, harassed and criminally attacked the Vietnamese people, 6,000 miles from here.

It is most encouraging and gratifying to see our Heroes and Heroines of Labor, [*Applause*] who, with their outstanding efforts and sacrifices, are contributing to the development of our economy; the magnificent fifty-sixth anniversary of the October revolution and the Evelio Rodríguez Curbelo "millionaire" brigades, which cut 2.5 million cwt. and 2.25 million cwt. of cane, respectively — each of these brigades, with fewer than fifty canecutters, cut as much cane as ten cane harvesters; [*Applause*] and the students from the Karl Liebknecht Junior High School in the Countryside, who, after making a tremendous effort last year, have now won the nationwide emulation among these schools which combine work and study. [*Applause*]

It is especially significant that the delegates to People's Power elected by the people of Matanzas Province are also here. [*Applause*]

Year after year, our people celebrate this date with ever-increasing enthusiasm.

On such days as this we pay special tribute to the men who died at the Moncada. Rather than being forgotten with the passing of the years, their names, their exemplary lives, their unselfishness, and their heroism are remembered by all of us. We see them live again, and we note their presence in the work of the revolution: above all, they remain alive in the consciousness and hearts of all Cubans. [*Applause*]

On days such as this we remember more than just those who died on July 26, 1953; we remember all those who gave their lives for our country.

Every celebration is like a synthesis of our people's glorious history, a history written with great sacrifices and the loss of many valuable lives and much blood.

We must remember that right here in this province, before the rebellions of 1895 and even before 1868, a number of slaves took up arms and rebelled against their oppressors.* This happened in this province of Matanzas, where there were 100,000 slaves in the middle of the nineteenth century and where the slaves formed 46.8 percent of the population in 1868. The largest and most heroic of the slave revolts took place in this province, and the first slave revolt, at the Alcancía sugar mill in March 1843 — a revolt in which the slaves from many other sugar mills joined — took place not too far from here, in the Cárdenas area. [*Applause*] Then, in November of that same year, there was the rebellion of the slaves at the Triumvirate sugar mill, in the jurisdiction of Matanzas, [*Applause*] where a new town has just been built and where one of our country's most beautiful primary schools is located.

In the last century, thousands of slaves all over the region rose up and fought for freedom and justice. Hundreds of them were killed outright; many others were hanged later on; and, what is most impressive, many — a great many — of them committed suicide rather than fall into the hands of their owners and executioners.

That was a glorious page in the history of our country — we mustn't forget that slavery still existed in Cuba up to around 100 years ago — and it can be said that those men were the precursors of our social revolutions. And one day we will erect a monument to the memory of those heroic slaves. [*Applause*]

Also not too far from here, the patriot Juan Gualberto Gómez rose up in arms in 1895, following José Martí's instructions to begin the war of independence.† [*Applause*]

Moreover, the heroic battles of Coliseo and Calimete, during the invasion of the island by the *mambí* forces, were fought near here.‡ [*Applause*]

Antonio Guiteras, Aponte, and several other revolutionaries were killed while fighting against the regime's murderers right here in this province, at the time of the pseudorepublic.§ [*Applause*]

The heroic attack on the Goicuría Garrison, in the days of our revolutionary struggle, took place in the city of Matanzas.‖ [*Applause*]

---

*This refers to Cuba's two wars of independence against Spain. The first one lasted from 1868 to 1878; the second, from 1895 to 1898, at which time U.S. forces occupied Cuba. Slavery was abolished in Cuba in 1886.

†Jose Martí, Cuba's national hero, was the founder of the Cuban Revolutionary Party and led the insurrection that began in 1895. He was killed in combat the same year.

‡*Mambí* is the Cuban term for the fighters in the wars for independence against Spain.

§Guiteras was a leader of the frustrated revolution of 1933. Together with Gen. Carlos Aponte, he was assassinated in 1935.

‖On April 29, 1956, a group of young rebels led an unsuccessful attack on the

Many revolutionaries from Matanzas lost their lives in those years of struggle.

The forces that attacked the Moncada on July 26, 1953, included a large group of young people from Matanzas, [*Applause*] and other young men from Matanzas took part in the *Granma* landing and the initiation of the struggle in the Sierra Maestra. [*Applause*]

And, after the triumph of the revolution, right here on this spot in the early hours of April 17, 1961, the students from the officers' school, following instructions issued by the high command, organized the first of the units that, waging the first battles against the mercenaries that landed at Playa Girón, launched an offensive against the invaders [*Applause*] at the cost of many lives.

This countryside of Matanzas Province was the scene, in the following years, of the formidable struggle against the bands of mercenaries organized by the CIA, which murdered peasants, teachers, workers, and farm administrators and committed acts of sabotage against communications lines and sugarcane plantations in this region.

Thus, the history of this province is full of episodes from the struggle for justice and freedom and against exploitation.

The road hasn't been a short one by any means, and we didn't get this far without a lot of suffering, effort, and sacrifice. In order to celebrate the twenty-first anniversary of the attack on the Moncada, it was first necessary for our people to wage a tremendous battle against the imperialists' acts of aggression and blockade.

At the beginning, our enemies were convinced that the revolution wouldn't be able to hold many July 26 celebrations. Today, they are convinced that it can. And, in this hemisphere, it's the Yankee empire — not the Cuban revolution — that's coming apart at the seams. [*Applause*] The OAS [Organization of American States], the international instrument for aggression against Cuba, is now a corpse in a complete state of decay. [*Applause*] One of the men behind the mercenary invasion of Girón, the present president of the United States, isn't too sure whether or not he can finish his term in office. [*Shouts of "Out with him!"*] Mercenaries trained by the CIA to carry out acts of sabotage, subversion, and aggression against Cuba were later used to spy on and steal documents from the Democratic Party headquarters in the United States. That action, plus the scandal and complications that ensued, prove that the CIA and its mercenaries were much more effective in destroying the presidency of the United States than in overthrowing the Cuban revolution. [*Prolonged applause and shouts of "For sure, Fidel; give the Yankees hell!"*] They took to them a flock of ravens, and now

---

Goicuría Garrison in the city of Matanzas. More than a dozen of the attackers were killed; some of them were murdered after being taken prisoner.

the ravens are tearing out their bowels!

Moreover, the number of Latin American peoples that refuse to obey imperialism is increasing. For example, there are Peru, Argentina, and Panama. [*Applause*] On his recent Latin American tour, the president of Mexico consistently condemned the criminal blockade imposed on our country, [*Applause*] and the free nations of the Caribbean maintain the most fraternal relations with our people.

The fact that the possible nationalization of the country's oil is openly discussed in Venezuela [*Applause*] is a sign of how times have changed, and that sister nation — the birthplace of the liberator Simón Bolívar — is already taking steps to adopt this just and worthy measure.

Several spokesmen of the government of Venezuela have also expressed themselves publicly in favor of normal relations with our country. [*Applause*] For its part, the revolutionary government of Cuba is willing to work in that direction and welcomes that possibility with sincere satisfaction. [*Applause*]

It is expected that, within a few months, several other Latin American governments will reestablish diplomatic and economic relations with our country on the basis of absolute mutual respect and fraternal collaboration. [*Applause*]

Today, the governments of this hemisphere are divided into a minority of lackeys that still blindly follow the dictates of imperialism and a majority of governments that are no longer willing to follow those dictates. [*Applause*] With the majority of governments that are willing to practice an independent foreign policy, our country is willing to collaborate constructively in everything that contributes to the economic integration and defense of the interests of the peoples of Latin America — needless to say, this also includes Canada and the English-speaking countries of the Caribbean. [*Applause*]

The isolation of Cuba is slowly withering away, and the economic blockade of our country can't last much longer. In view of the present conditions of international détente, it is increasingly obvious to all the world that it is an unfair, ridiculous, criminal, and untenable measure.

At any rate, the fact remains that today nobody has any doubts about the reality and irreversibility of the Cuban revolution. The only thing that can possibly happen now is for the revolution to become even stronger — and that's exactly what is going to happen! [*Applause*]

Founded on a tremendous unity and internal political soundness, deeply rooted in the hearts of our people, sustained by scientific revolutionary principles and supported by the firm and indestructible friendship of the Soviet Union [*Prolonged applause*] and the other countries of the revolutionary camp, the Cuban revolution is simply invulnerable.

We are celebrating this anniversary by making progress in every field: education, public health, construction, agriculture, and industry.

In the field of education, the number of students who passed all their tests this year is truly amazing. The quality of our education has improved, and a great many new schools are being built each year.

We can say with deep satisfaction that the Cuban revolution has educated tens of thousands of Cubans for every one who died at the Moncada. [*Applause*] Moreover, education is making such marked progress in Cuba that a million students will be enrolled in intermediate-level courses by 1980. Right now there are more than 300,000 of them. At the time of the triumph of the revolution, there were only 70,000.

In public health, our infant mortality rate is the lowest in Latin America: 27.4 for every 1,000 children born alive. In Brazil, for example, the rate is 140 for every 1,000.

The average life expectancy is now 70, as compared to 54 prior to the triumph of the revolution.

Thus, we can say that tens of thousands of Cuban lives have been saved for every one lost at the Moncada. [*Applause*]

A number of diseases have been completely wiped out, and several others are in the process of eradication.

Construction has increased tremendously in the last few years, and new roads, dams, schools, dairies, hospitals, and other types of construction are appearing all over our country.

A notable improvement has been achieved in agriculture, too. The number of canefields has increased. There's a marked increase in the production of chickens, hogs, milk, and rice. The citrus-fruit plan is developing rapidly throughout the island. Our sugar harvests are increasingly more efficient, and our canecutters' productivity is ever higher. Every year, by employing more machines to cut the cane, we require fewer canecutters. And, as a result, we now have additional labor power for other activities.

Industry has been developing at a good pace. Between 1970 and 1973 the economy registered an overall increase of 26 percent, and this will be maintained in 1974 and 1975.

We're already engaged in drawing up a five-year plan for 1976-80 based on the experience, organization, and know-how we've acquired during the past few years, and we believe we can attain the 6 percent growth rate contemplated for the next ten years, which we mentioned in 1973, without much trouble.

Discussions of the 1975 production plan are now going on, for the first time — this is a novel experience — with the workers of each work center. Moreover, similar discussions will be held on the 1976-80 five-year plan.

Our mass organizations have made great progress since 1970. Today, our party has much greater organization, efficiency, and capacity for leadership.

Thousands of political and administrative cadres are studying, and it can even be said that studying has become a habit among our leadership cadres. The students of the Karl Liebknecht School aren't the only ones studying in Cuba — almost everybody is. [*Applause*]

Moreover, on this July 26 we can speak of the experiment that is being made with the establishment of People's Power in Matanzas Province.

As you all know, it was decided that the experiment be made in this province. When I say "experiment," I don't mean that we're experimenting with whether or not to have People's Power or that our party isn't definitely planning to apply the idea throughout the country. It is an experiment only in the sense that we're testing the methods, mechanisms, regulations, and everything else related to the establishment of People's Power before these things are put into effect on a nationwide scale. In other words, the experiment will help us to perfect the idea — but the idea is to apply these principles throughout the country.

So, the people of Matanzas have had an election — and a very interesting one!

Let me cite a few figures: 71.1 percent of the electors in the meetings to choose chairmen for the assemblies for the nomination of candidates cast their votes. In the assemblies for the nomination of candidates, 72.1 percent participated. A total of 4,712 candidates were nominated in the ordinary circumscriptions, and 1,014 were elected.

Of the 1,014 elected, 46.1 percent are members of the party, 13.1 percent are members of the Young Communist League, and around 41 percent are members of neither. This reflects the broad scope of the nominations and elections and all the people's participation in them.

Some 93.6 percent of the electors voted in the first round, and 91.4 in the second — more than 90 percent on both occasions.

Only 20 percent of those elected have less than a sixth-grade education, and 41 percent of the 1,014 are studying.

The participation of the masses in this election has been really outstanding. It included the mobilizations to elect the chairmen for the assemblies for the nomination of candidates, for the nomination itself, and for the study and discussion of the material; the neighborhood meetings for reading the biographies of the various candidates and to view the educational film on People's Power; the voting in the first and second rounds; the mass rallies in the various municipalities for the presentation of the members of the People's Power municipal assemblies; the mass rallies for the presentation of the members of the regional assemblies; in general, the people's cooperation in such matters as making out applications for identification cards and lists of electors and cleaning and decorating the streets and buildings; and now this mass rally to present the members of the Executive Board of People's Power in Matanzas Province and, needless to say, to celebrate July 26. [*Applause*]

The figures I just gave you were on the election of delegates from each circumscription* and the subsequent election of members of the regional assemblies.

I almost forgot one figure on the elections in the various circumscriptions, and that is that only 3 percent of those elected were women.

A hundred and fifty-one delegates were elected to the regional People's Power. Here, the percentage of women rose to 6.9. The educational level was also higher — only 7.4 percent were below the sixth grade. The number of party and Young Communist League members was also greater: 60.3 percent are party members, and 14.4 percent are members of the Young Communist League. About half of the delegates are studying.

Let us make it clear that when we speak of the number of party members we don't consider it a negative thing for there to be a high percentage of nonmembers in the assemblies. We must never forget that the party is a selective organization, a vanguard. The fact that many people who aren't members of the party were elected isn't a bad thing; it is a good indication of the broad scope and democratic spirit of the elections. Here, too, we must keep in mind that a great many hard-working, dedicated workers who are members of the trade union locals; peasants; and members of the Federation of Cuban Women, the Committees for the Defense of the Revolution, and other mass organizations who aren't members of the party are excellent workers and have more than sufficient merits to deserve the people's trust. [*Applause*]

We must remember that the party is a selective organization, not a mass organization.

The people elected the candidates they wanted, and it turned out that a relatively high percentage of them are party members. This is quite logical, because the party is composed of our most conscious, most advanced workers — although we are sure that there are a great many workers who deserve to be in the party yet are not in it for one reason or another — either because the process of party growth hasn't been put into effect, or what-have-you.

A total of 68 candidates were elected as delegates to the People's Power Provincial Assembly. And in this case, too, the number of women elected was higher: 16 percent. This figure has an added significance which we'll talk about later. Only 7 percent of those elected have less than a sixth-grade education, and 75 percent of the delegates to the Provincial Assembly are members of the party and Young Communist League.

This matter of the number of women elected is very important, and it cannot be denied that the fact that 3 percent of those elected were women

*A circumscription is an electoral district roughly equivalent to a precinct.

is painfully low, especially if one considers that women make up half the population and that women enthusiastically support the revolution. [*Applause*] Women have a high degree of those qualities deemed necessary in a revolutionary, in a leading administrative and political cadre. [*Applause*]

Stated simply, the revolution has not made sufficient progress in this area. And it shows how women still suffer from certain discrimination and inequality, [*Applause*] how we still have residues of cultural backwardness and how we still retain old thinking patterns in the back of our minds.

That is the reality of the situation, and we must recognize it. It is recognized by our party, and the people must recognize it so we can all struggle against such remnants of inequality and injustice. [*Applause*]

This year, the congress of the Federation of Cuban Women will be held, [*Applause*] and this problem of inequality that has hung on is one of the fundamental points of its theses. We should not forget that Lenin said that the proletariat cannot achieve final victory until it has achieved the complete freedom of women. [*Prolonged applause*]

We have here, in the presence of Comrade Nguyen Thi Dinh, deputy commander in chief of the People's Liberation Armed Forces of South Vietnam, an example of women's qualities and of their importance in the struggle for liberation. [*Applause*]

And there you are! The proof is these combative heroines from South Vietnam, on whose chests there is not enough room for all the medals that their heroism has won in battle, in the struggle for the liberation of their country! [*Prolonged applause*]

We have numerous examples in the history of our own country and our own revolution, in the storming of the Moncada itself and in the war in the Sierra Maestra. [*Applause*]

This is said in relation to the self-criticism that we should make. Of course this problem will not be solved overnight. But we must be aware of the need to fight against such holdovers from the past. The entire people, men and women alike, must participate in that struggle. And women must take the lead! [*Applause*]

There are certain theories alleging that women don't like to be led by women. [*Booing and hissing*] But I don't believe that. If there is a speck of truth to it, it will serve to show that a hard struggle must be waged among women themselves; that they must overcome their own prejudices against equality, aside from the struggle that must be waged among the men. [*Applause*] And this should be part of the discussion of the Family Code, which is now being analyzed by all our people.*

*The Family Code was presented for discussion in 1974 to replace the pre-revolutionary laws on marriage, divorce, adoption, and alimony. Its call for wom-

Now let's turn to the things for which we can feel justly proud. The elections that have just taken place in Matanzas have been the finest in the history of our country. [*Applause*] Elections without trickery, without fraud, without demagogy, without dirty politics. No one had to concern himself with the "need" to run, because nomination was not up to the individual; it was up to the collective. There were no campaigns, because the "campaign" here is the record of the life of each candidate nominated by the people as a whole. Each candidate's "campaign" is his life, the record of his conduct and service to the country.

Never before have there been such enthusiastic elections. Never before have more than 90 percent of the voters turned out in an election — not even in the days when votes were cast by "electors" who were dead. And the extraordinary part is that more than 90 percent of the voters turned out not only for the first round, but for the second round as well.

This is the first time in Cuba that we have had elections without rifles and bayonets at the doors of the schools. And this is logical, because they were not rigged, there were no juicy positions at stake. They were elections of a revolutionary people, organized by a revolutionary people. [*Applause*] Even the Pioneers took part in organizing these elections, which were marked by enthusiasm among the masses unprecedented in any other election in the history of our country.

Now, that's the way elections should be!

These elections were very broad. And why were they so broad? At the beginning of the revolution, when the class of the capitalists and the large landholders and their ilk of exploiters still existed, some might have asked if we would hold elections in which anyone could be elected. We could not have permitted it. We conceive of the revolution as the government of revolutionaries, the dictatorship of the proletariat, [*Applause*] which deprives the exploiters of such rights. But now there are no large landholders here, there are no capitalist exploiters, giant industrialists, business moguls, bankers, importers, owners of giant sugar plantations. They no longer exist here because they have left or they no longer have such holdings; they exploit no one. There may be the exceptional case of some who have adapted to the revolution, who have become capable of understanding the revolution, and no one has deprived them of the right to vote. The fact of the matter is that they no longer constitute a problem.

That's why the elections have been so broad, the only restrictions being those which historically deprive of the right to vote those convicted of some crime, or candidates in the rigged elections of November 1958, prior to the triumph of the revolution. Restrictions have been minimal,

en's equality created widespread debate among the population. It was adopted in 1975.

and for that reason — which gives an idea as to the unity and ideological and social progress of the revolution — practically the entire population of Matanzas Province has been able to participate because of this universal suffrage which the people exercised.

We are convinced that this phase of the experiment has been a tremendous success. And for this we can congratulate the party of the province of Matanzas, [*Applause*] the mass organizations throughout the province, and the comrades of the National Commission who participated in organizing the elections. [*Applause*]

These elections have raised many questions and much interest and curiosity abroad. Who ever thought that we would never have elections? Of course we would have elections — revolutionary elections, and infinitely better and more honest than all those bourgeois elections. [*Applause*] And not because the bourgeoisie or international bourgeois opinion demands it — here the demands of international reaction carry no weight. Nor merely to create forms. No! They will be held because they correspond to the principles of revolutionary democracy and Marxism-Leninism! [*Applause*]

Many want to know about the functions and activities of the organs of People's Power in Matanzas. And so we will speak a bit about that, so you will understand the content of the activities of these organs.

They will be responsible for the following activities:

The Ministry of Education: all activities, schools, and related units — except the university — as well as the local, regional, and provincial personnel at different levels of leadership of the ministry. In other words, the administration of all schools except the university will be in the hands of People's Power;

The National Council of Culture: all activities, cultural centers, and related units, as well as all personnel at different levels of leadership;

The Cuban Broadcasting Institute: the two provincial radio stations and all leadership personnel related to the functioning of these units;

The National Institute of Sports, Physical Education, and Recreation (INDER): all activities, sports, and related facilities, and all INDER personnel at the different levels of leadership;

The Cuban Book Institute: all book stores and related facilities, as well as all personnel at the different levels of leadership at the institute, within the province;

The Cuban Institute of Cinema Arts (ICAIC): all movie theaters, mobile movie units, stationary projectors, and related facilities as well as all personnel at the different levels of leadership at ICAIC;

The National Institute of the Tourist Industry (INIT): all restaurants, hotels, and related units — except the tourist complexes at Varadero and the Zapata Swamp — and all leadership personnel at the various levels of INIT at the local, regional, and provincial level;

The Ministry of Domestic Trade (MINCIN): all repair shops dealing in electric appliances, small household goods, electronics equipment, etc., and all related units, and, starting on January 1, 1975, the Office of Consumer Registry, plus the MINCIN administrative personnel necessary for the guidance and administration of such activities;

The Ministry of the Food Industry: three cracker factories, a bakery, and all units related to the same which are administered by the provincial office of the Flour Enterprise, as well as a portion of the personnel which is employed by the aforementioned enterprise and four ice plants, the latter administrated by the provincial office of the Soft Drinks and Liquor Enterprise. This seems like a very small number of bakeries, but the majority are in the hands of local administration already;

The Ministry of Light Industry: a printing shop under the administration of the Graphic Arts Enterprise located in Jagüey Grande;

The Ministry of Transportation: all service and gas stations, etc., engine, body repair, and electric system shops; bus garages and terminals, taxi and Taxi Owners' Association (ANCHAR) garages and stands, as well as all related units administered by the ministry — except rail service and interprovincial passenger and freight transportation of all units related thereto — as well as the majority of the personnel at the various leadership levels of the ministry;

The Ministry of Communications: all the post offices, telegraph offices, and press distribution centers; the Philatelic Commercial Enterprise; and their dependencies (except for the center which distributes the mail) and all the people who work in the mail, telegraph, and press sectors at the different leadership levels of the agency. The activities and the units which have to do with telephone and radio service will remain under the control and administration of the central agency;

The Agency for the Agricultural Development of the Country: the activities and the units now being run by the Provincial Department for the Exploitation of Culverts and Sewers of the Department of Urban Hydrology and all the people who work there in the different levels of the agency;

Of the Agency for the Development of Social and Agricultural Construction: the cabins and other accessory units which were built in Camarioca;

The Ministry of Public Health: all the units and activities which it now directs or administers, including the training of intermediate-level technicians, and all the people who work at the different leadership levels of the ministry. That is, all the hospitals in the province will be in the hands of People's Power;

The Children's Institute: all the day-care centers and other units which aid in the activity it administers and directs, plus all the people who work at the different leadership levels of the agency;

The National Institute of Agrarian Reform: the Department for the Purchasing of Fruits and Vegetables, all the centers and subcenters for purchasing which it now administers and directs, and all the people who work at the different leadership levels of the institute;

Agricultural Transportation: the transportation and support units now used in purchasing fruits and vegetables and the people at the different leadership levels of the agency who are needed to operate, direct, and administer these units;

Agricultural Groupings: a factory which turns out preserves; an aqueduct, its supply center, and six power stations in San Pedro de Mayabón; three grain mills in Máximo Gómez: and an ice plant in Martí;

The National Coordination of Local Administrations: all the units and activities which it now administers and directs and all personnel working at the different leadership levels there; and

The Ministry of Justice: the office of the Urban Reform and the activities carried out there.

In all, the National Coordination of Local Administrations, the agency which now handles all local administration, will hand over to the organs of People's Power the administration of 2,900 production and service units, 265 units pertaining to the Ministry of Public Health; 18 units pertaining to the Book Institute; 84 Ministry of Domestic Trade units (the rest are already in the hands of local administrations), 232 Ministry of Transportation units; 117 Cuban Institute of Cinema Arts units; 145 National Institute for Sports, Physical Education, and Recreation units; 1,115 Ministry of Education units; 41 Children's Institute units; 43 Urban Hydrology units of the Agency for Agricultural Development of the Country; 460 units pertaining to the National Institute of the Tourist Industry; 77 pertaining to the Ministry of Communications; 34 National Council of Culture units; 3 Agricultural Transportation units; 8 pertaining to the Ministry of the Food Industry; 1 pertaining to the Ministry of Light Industry; 42 National Institute of Agriarian Reform units; 2 units pertaining to the Cuban Broadcasting Institute; and 10 pertaining to the Agency for the Development of Social and Agricultural Construction.

A total of 5,597 production and service units throughout the province will be handed over to the organs of People's Power. [*Applause*]

This is the basic criterion: all production and service units that serve the community — that is, the grass roots — must be controlled at the grass-roots level. [*Applause*]

To repeat: all the production and service units that serve a municipality must be under its control; those that serve the region must be controlled by the region; those that serve the province, by the province; and those that serve the nation will remain in the hands of the nation — that is, of the central bodies.

This means that the schools, polyclinics, stores, repair shops, movie theaters, and recreation centers will be controlled by the organs of People's Power in every town.

No longer will a movie theater be administered from Havana without anybody in the town it's in having a say in its management. No longer will a store or school be run from Havana on a centralized basis without anyone in the local community having a say in how things are done.

So this is the principle: it all depends on the service which the unit in question provides — whether it serves the municipality, the region, the province, or the whole country. Sugar mills, mines, the merchant marine, basic industries, banks, the fishing fleet, the railroads, and interprovincial transportation serve the whole country. But local transportation serves the local area. The taxis which operate in a small town or city serve the people there.

I hope you understand the criterion involved. The state is one. The revolutionary state must administer everything, because we have eliminated private owners. The people are the owners, and the people must administer everything now. [*Applause*]

It's impossible to administer all this on a centralized basis; it simply can't be done.

This criterion leads to a great decentralization of administration.

We indicated that the state is one, but the state is organized at different levels, and it administers at different levels.

Of course, this doesn't mean that the people in every community will be able to do whatever they want with the school, hospital, or store or that they will be able to raise or lower prices and wages, change the curriculum at the school or introduce any books they want. No — for, as we indicated, the state is one, and all activities must be normed and resemble each other all over the country.

This doesn't mean that a different thing will be done at each hospital or that one province will start doing things one way and another some other way. No. They will do exactly the same thing: they will provide health care for the population, which is what they are supposed to do, using certain methods, with perfectly normed activities. This will be so because the role to be played by the central agencies with regard to the activities handled by the organs of People's Power will be clearly defined.

Nobody feels that the hospital will be in worse shape. If anything, it may be better off, because sometimes there is a lack of service personnel — they don't have all they need, or there is some shortcoming, some repair work or other things must be done — and the local people can't do anything about it because it isn't under their control. Now local People's Power will be responsible for everything that happens in the hospital and for its operation, for seeing to it that it has enough personnel, and for checking up on what kind of service it gives the people. All those things. The community will be involved in the running of the hospital now.

Up until now, the community received the services which the hospital provided, but wasn't involved in its running or in the running of the poly-clinic, in controlling who took care of the patients, or in straightening things out if they weren't going well or were only so-so. The community couldn't contribute to the running of that service institution with its force.

However, relations have been established between the central state agencies and the organs of People's Power, as follows:

"Regarding norms, procedures, and methods. The central agencies will regulate the general organizational principles governing the internal operation of the units in the field in question. They will determine the methodological principles for norming the activities in the field and set the norms in certain cases. They will set, modify, and channel proposals for setting or modifying prices and rates. They will set the methodologi-cal norms required for complying with their instructions governing the supply of raw and other materials and other things; and, in certain cases, they will set the norms in the field directly. They will establish whatever methodological instructions are required for working out norms to gov-ern the supply of fuel, electricity, and other items in the field. They will establish the necessary methodological instructions for setting norms gov-erning the use of equipment and installations and, in specific cases, set the norms themselves. They will establish specific methodological in-structions or other means for inventory control in the field. They will es-tablish the methodological instructions required for working out a cost-accounting system for the units in their field, in accord with the book-keeping system in effect. They will establish a methodology for check-ing the books in the units of the field, which, once it has been approved, can't be changed without the permission of the agency. They will estab-lish methodological instructions for the evaluation of personnel. They will establish the standards to be met by those holding different leader-ship or specialized positions, in line with the specific positions which exist in the field. They will establish or participate in the establishment of work norms in the field. They will give instructions on carrying out the wage policy in the field. They will supervise and inspect to see to it that regulations issued in keeping with their authority and responsibility are obeyed.

"Regarding technical advice. At the request of the central agencies or organs of People's Power, they will provide technical advice on the new investments that are planned and, once a project has been concluded, evaluate it, checking up on the technological development of the unit in question. They will provide technical advice in all fields in which it is impossible for the province to do so.

"Regarding the training of specialized cadres and the assignment of technical personnel. They will establish the policy on cadre training in the fields under their jurisdiction, enrolling the personnel proposed by the administrative level of People's Power in national or foreign training courses, in keeping with the existing norms and methodology, or those who have been selected by the central agency itself, in the case of skilled technical personnel whose assignment is under their control. They will exercise methodological leadership over the training classes and in the training of personnel in the field units at the provincial level and approve plans to this purpose. The central agencies which have specialized technical personnel remaining centralized for their distribution and national assignment will place these specialists at the disposal of People's Power, which will then be responsible for paying them. All decisions regarding the rotation of these specialists will be in the hands of the central agency, in keeping with national considerations.

"Regarding research and experiments. They will be in charge of norming and determining the methodology to be used in research and experiments in the field, directing the participation of the province in whatever aspects may be required to complement the research and experiments that are being done on a centralized basis and providing advice and backing in those aspects in which this is required for the research and experiments being carried out with the resources of the province, either as a result of its own initiative or under the guidance of a central agency.

"Regarding planning and statistics. They will establish a methodology for processing information through the Statistics Information System. They will require the turning in of information needed in the preparation of national plans and in the standardization of national statistical information. They will work out the technical-economic plans of the fields in question and break down to the provincial level and provide guidance for the work of the administrative sections of the organs of People's Power along these lines. In cases of the allocation of items that are in short supply, the central agencies will retain the authority to move them out of the province, if this is required for the greater good of the economy."

We have just read you some of the general norms which will govern the relations between the central agencies and the organs of People's Power. Don't be discouraged by the technical nature of these norms. It isn't easy to get used to them, and some of us will never get used to them.

But in practice, in exercising the functions that correspond to the organs of People's Power, you will realize the objectives behind all of them. This is why it is so important to study and why the academic level of the individual is so important. However, nobody should be discouraged — even those with less than a sixth-grade education. Of course, it will be their duty to study and raise their educational levels if they aren't already among those who are studying. But, in any case, we are sure that the norms will become clear in practice.

This means that the central agencies won't be cut off completely from these tasks. The Ministry of Public Health will still have a role to play in running the hospitals. And the same general principles that will govern the relationship of the Ministry of Public Health with the hospitals will govern that of the Ministry of Education with the schools.

Now comes the next stage. Each central agency will come to certain agreements with the organs of People's Power to work out their mutual relations. That is, all relations between central agencies and the organs of People's Power will be regulated in accordance with detailed agreements that will be adopted.

These agreements will not become laws, because we mean to consider the results of this experience. We're using agreements now so that when this experiment, or process, is applied throughout the country we can then pass the laws most suitable for guiding these relations.

This is very important, because the organs of People's Power must now learn to administer all their units properly, with full administrative ability, and at the same time fulfill all norms guiding how these central agencies will operate and the activities they will undertake.

You will really have a great responsibility on your hands, a dual responsibility: that of fulfilling these functions and also of doing it as well as possible. From the results of this experiment we will draw conclusions for carrying out this process in the rest of the country.

This doesn't mean that some of the norms and decisions now in effect will be unalterable and that we can't make some future changes based on this experiment. But the fact is that you, as members of People's Power, will administer 5,597 production and service units at the regional, municipal, and provincial levels.

Those of you from other countries who are interested in these matters — and, of course, many of you are genuinely interested in this process — can see the all-encompassing and broad content of the People's Power organization in Matanzas Province and the kind of state we're trying to organize.

What must we do next? What are your responsibilities? You are in charge of administering all these production and service units.

We must also bear in mind some basic principles. First, we must strive for the wise use of all human and material resources. Second, we must adopt the most strict system of accounting. Third, we must achieve the greatest economic efficiency possible. Last, we must avoid bureaucracy.

Let's avoid having the municipalities full of offices and competing for the labor force; [*Applause*] let's avoid from the very start all regionalist tendencies [*Applause*] at whatever level, because the situations of all towns and regions aren't exactly alike. We have rich and poor municipalities, and the country's resources must be fairly distributed in accordance with the circumstances.

We must never forget that our republic is one and indivisible, organized and not anarchistic, socialist and not capitalist. [*Applause*] We have obligations to the community and the entire nation. We must develop our discipline and observe the general norms guiding every activity.

Objectively speaking, you will find many difficulties. We have many needs of all kinds: housing, aqueducts, movie theaters, buildings for primary schools and children's day-care centers. If you make a list, you'll see we have many needs everywhere. We cannot be utopian or idealistic in thinking that suddenly and simply because the organs of People's Power have been established our problems will be solved overnight. Our country has few resources. Our construction materials are particularly scarce.

We know full well how much you're capable of developing, using the strength of the community, if you have all the necessary resources.

Our country is trying right now to produce more cement, reinforcing rods, lumber, and all other kinds of construction materials. We're in the process of buying plants for manufacturing wood out of bagasse by means of a chemical process, wood which can also be used for making furniture. We're in the process of increasing all our material resources. But they're not yet available.

The overall annual cement production in Cuba — about 2 million tons — has already been very much accounted for. In 1976, we'll start producing greater quantities of cement, but even then we'll have to meet specific demands of the nation, which will account for this additional cement. We'll have to wait until 1978 for our country to produce a plentiful supply of cement. At the beginning of 1978, I think we'll already be producing all the cement we need, since two additional plants that are now being set up will be in operation. We'll also have a supply of steel for construction. These plants cannot be set up in one year. It takes at least four years from the time the decision is made, the contracts signed, and the building plans are drawn up to the finishing of the plant.

I'm addressing myself not just to you, but to all the people of Matanzas Province, so you will understand this reality. I don't want you to think that People's Power is going to work miracles and solve all problems immediately.

There's one other thing. You should work with the resources available and those assigned to you. The fact that this experiment will take place here doesn't mean that we will pour all our resources into Matanzas Province. We can't do that. We have to take care of all the country's needs in every province and community.

We're very much aware of what you can do, because we have seen you at work in the minibrigades, where you have shown your work capacity. The work of the minibrigades is limited, since we cannot supply all the needed construction materials.

Our country must now undertake important construction projects for the national economy. We must build new factories, warehouses, dairies, dams, roads, irrigation systems, hospitals, and secondary schools throughout the country, as you know. But, despite the fact that every year we're building 175 schools with room for 500 students each, we're not building enough schools. As I explained previously, according to estimates, secondary school students in Cuba will number one million in 1980. Each year, almost 100,000 new students enroll in secondary schools. We're talking about your children, the children of the workers of this country, who enroll in the junior high, polytechnic, vocational, and military schools after they graduate from sixth grade. They're going to continue their studies, and the revolution cannot just look the other way. We cannot send these young people home. The revolution must educate them! That's why we must give top priority to the building of secondary schools. [*Applause*]

As you all know, all these schools have a work-study program. All the schools being built are, for all practical purposes, work centers within agricultural and industrial plans. We're building polytechnic institutes at the sugar mills to train with the greatest possible efficiency all the personnel who will be in charge of these work centers in the future.

Of course we cannot provide the same materials needed in the construction of secondary schools for the construction of primary schools. I know that old primary schools still exist in many places, sometimes even a thatched-roof cottage has been turned into a school; but we truthfully tell you that we cannot use our material resources in building new primary schools. The old primary schools can still be used. We must have good teachers and all the books and materials necessary. If the school gets to look ugly, we must paint it; if it needs repairs, then we must go ahead with repairs. We must not let the school collapse. We have to utilize the primary schools available. Otherwise, we should lose the mass of young people entering the secondary school level, and our country cannot afford this. We're sure you understand this perfectly. [*Applause*]

The time will come for building new primary schools, as many as we need, just as now we're building secondary schools as never before in the history of Cuba. Just to cite an example, the capacity of the secondary boarding schools we build every year is four times as great as that of all the schools of the same type built in the last fifty years before the revolution. [*Applause*] Let me repeat, the secondary schools being built every year now have four times the capacity as the total capacity that existed before the triumph of the revolution. It's an inpressive figure.

The progress made by our young people and secondary school students is also impressive and we must meet their challenge. That's why we must dedicate all our resources to them right now, and utilize our present primary schools, taking care that they are repaired and kept functioning in the best conditions of maintenance and hygiene. You know full well that we can often change the environment of a place by just adding a few touches. I assure you that the day will come when we'll be able to build as many beautiful primary schools as we need.

We're only building primary schools in the new towns and neighborhoods where otherwise there would be none. But we have assigned no priority and have no resources to build new primary schools in place of the old ones.

We're also aware of the need for many day-care centers in every province. We still have limited possibilities for building day-care centers, yet our economic development requires them so that women can be carrying out many of the activities that now fall to the men. [*Applause*]

We haven't forgotten the children's day-care centers. Right now we have only two construction brigades working on day-care centers, and next year there will be four of these brigades. But we'll have twenty-four construction brigades building children's day-care centers by the beginning of 1976. They won't be able to build all the day-care centers we need, but it's a start.

We also know we need special schools for children with various kinds of handicaps and homes for the aged. It hurts us very much that our country still doesn't have as many special schools as it needs. Construction brigades will also start building these special schools and homes for the aged in 1976.

But we'd like to stress that we won't be able to tackle our housing and other needs with all our strength until 1978.

We have enormous housing needs. So far, we've been building between 25,000 and 30,000 housing units per year. But they're not enough! They're just a third of what we need for a start, but the government is taking all the measures needed for tackling the housing problem with all the strength this will require when the time comes to move ahead.

I'm giving you this explanation because with your new duties and responsibilities as delegates you are going to hear many requests. I'm giving you this explanation to help you and the masses understand our present situation.

Each and every citizen who requests something from you must be given an honest and sincere explanation of the possibilities of having his request fulfilled. We must never deceive anyone.

Moreover, you have the duty of making excellent customer service a habit in all production and service units [*Applause*] — and you will have many service centers under your jurisdiction. This is basic.

Now you will see that every production and service unit in the country belongs not to any one person in particular, but to all the people in general, to each and every one of you. If it functions poorly, you will suffer the consequences. If it functions well, you will reap the benefits. But now, under your management, you will have the opportunity of doing everything you can to make these units function well.

Naturally, the administration of all these units must improve. Why? Because a lot of people would have to fail for these units to function poorly. Up until now, if the Ministry of Public Health or a public health official at the provincial level made a mistake, the polyclinic started functioning poorly. But from now on, if a polyclinic is functioning poorly, it means that the regional, municipal, and provincial administrative agencies; the Ministry of Public Health — which is still responsible for the smooth functioning of these medical centers, though not as an administrative agency — and the regional, municipal, provincial, and national organs of the party have all made mistakes. A whole lot of people must make mistakes before a polyclinic or school will start functioning poorly. [*Applause*]

All of you delegates to People's Power will attend seminars in which all of this will be explained thoroughly and much better than I'm explaining it to you now.

We brought this up now because we think you and all the rest of the people of Matanzas Province and the nation — who have been closely following this process — are interested in it. Later on, you'll receive a detailed explanation of everything that will help you carry out your functions.

I'm stressing the general principles we must keep in mind. We must develop the greatest possible cooperation at all levels; between the municipality and the region, the region and the province, and the province and the central organs.

You can't build socialism without certain norms and methods, without coordination between all levels at all times, without the cooperation of all.

A good example of this cooperation is the chairs you're sitting on. Last night they were being used at the carnival in Havana; today they're here at this celebration in Matanzas; [*Applause*] and tomorrow evening they'll be back in Havana. Now, you really can't get much more out of a chair! [*Laughter*] And if you, the people of Havana, those who ship them, those who handle them, those who set them up, those who store them, and those who repair them are careful with them, they will last a very long time, and we will get the greatest possible use out of them.

Unfortunately, our country doesn't have enough chairs to meet the needs of Havana's carnival, your needs here, and the needs in Las Villas and everywhere else at the same time, so we have to move the chairs around from one place to another. However, this is a good example of the cooperation between two provinces.

And I repeat that you will soon have seminars on all this. Thus, we are sure that you will be well prepared to handle the responsibilities which the revolution and the people are giving you.

Now, we aren't talking just about centralization or decentralization, or of the problems of a municipality as related solely to that municipality, or of any other single unit all the way up to the national level. This experiment implies a step of great practical and theoretical importance for the revolution, and such steps should lead us to the final institutionalization of the socialist state of Cuba.

The revolutionary government is provisional in nature. What does this mean? We had to seize revolutionary power; we had to begin to make the revolution. And, as the only way to do that was by taking the state and establishing a revolutionary government, we seized state power, installed a revolutionary government, and began to carry out the revolution.

But this provisional nature has already lasted fifteen years.

Now we must think of the definitive form the socialist state of Cuba will take. Naturally, it must be built on strictly democratic, truly democratic, bases.

That criterion, applied on the municipal, regional, and provincial levels, will be extended throughout the country and implemented nationally. And, just as we have set up municipal, regional, and provincial power, we will set up the nation's central power — the national government — following this same procedure exactly.

Delegates will be elected by circumscription. They, in turn, will elect the regional delegates, who will elect the provincial delegates, who will elect the delegates to national People's Power. And the provincial executive committee will be set up the same way as will the future national executive — the national government.

All of this will have to be analyzed thoroughly so it will be well done and our institutions won't have to make modifications later on. And all this must be done parallel with the development of the country's constitutional forms, with the final structuring of the country.

You all know that we are entering a period of intense legalization. Revolutions and revolutionaries go through a phase in which they destroy the laws, because those laws were the laws of the oppressors, the exploiters, the rulers. However, those who destroy the old laws have to take care not to fall into the trap of respecting no laws at all. Revolution means destroying the old social order and all the old laws that regulated the life of a society, replacing them with new laws. To put it another way, we must replace our destruction of the old laws with discipline and respect for the new laws. [*Applause*]

Enemies of the old laws and staunch defenders of the new! That is what revolutionaries must be.

Socialist legality is absolutely essential. And the more organized and developed the revolution, the greater the need for the people to know the laws and obey and respect them.

This will permit us, in the course of the revolutionary process, to set ourselves very clear, medium-range goals.

This has already been scheduled for discussion in next year's party congress. [*Applause*]

You are all familiar with the role of the party — which, in accord with the principles of Marxism-Leninism, regulates and guides society and the state. The party doesn't administer the state. The state must be administered by the masses through their organs of People's Power. The party has other functions.

As Marxist-Leninists, we base ourselves on the principle that there is an indispensable need for the party and that it should have the greatest authority and be of top quality. At the same time, there is a need for the state as an instrument of the revolutionaries to carry out the process leading to socialism and communism.

So, we cannot do without either the party or the state.

But the party, as we've already indicated, is a vanguard, a selection which we trust will continue to recruit its members from among the most advanced and revolutionary elements in society. It represents a post at which hard work and sacrifices are the order of the day.

Our party congress will be held in the second half of next year.

We would like to make a request: that when the party congress is held we will be in a position to evaluate the experience and work of People's Power in Matanzas. [*Applause*] The party congress will review all this experience and make a decision on its application all over the country.

Of course, the party is determined to carry this process forward, but your experience will help it to determine just how this should be done and how this method should be applied in the rest of the country.

In view of this, we can set ourselves the goal of applying this process — the exact same process, enriched through this experience — in the rest of the country by 1976, and in the same year, in keeping with these principles, we can establish the definitive forms which the socialist state of Cuba will take. [*Applause*]

Regarding the province of Matanzas, in addition to this process, this experience, we would like to say that the big drawback for its future development is its lack of labor power, its shortage of labor power.

During the last few days there have been a number of reports in the press about the things the revolution has built during these years in the province of Matanzas. There are a lot of these things, but it still doesn't seem like very much to us.

What is the main problem preventing greater development in Matanzas? Labor power. We've even had to bring in workers from other provinces to pitch in on some of the projects here, such as the Southern Highway, the Canímar Dam, and some junior high schools.

But we really liked something we saw in a newspaper which Comrade Rizo said, to the effect that you wanted the men and women of Matanzas to have the greatest productivity in Cuba. [*Applause*] This is really very necessary.

The process of mechanizing the sugarcane harvests is going full speed ahead. This will enable us to use the labor power for other things. If we want factories, we need the labor power to build and operate them. This is why work productivity is so important.

And this is why we say, watch out for bureaucracy; don't use any more people than you really need. This is because any worker who's in a given spot without being needed there is one fewer worker we have to meet another need. We must be very much aware of the need not to underutilize our human resources.

We said that our ability to undertake more construction work is limited by shortages of materials, but this situation will be overcome. The time will come when we will be able to handle many of the things that are facing us now, but we will need labor power. In order to have enough labor power, we must use what we have wisely.

We should have at least one construction brigade organized in the province by 1976 — late 1975 or early 1976 — just for building hospitals, according to the estimated need for hospitals here. At least two should build children's day-care centers, and four, hotels. Does this, perhaps, mean that hotels are more important than hospitals? No. Hospitals are more important than hotels. But then, why four hotel-building brigades? Because you are the possessors of that great Cuban natural resource, Varadero Beach. [*Applause*]

The province now has two important agricultural plans: the Girón Citrus-Fruit Plan and the Matanzas Cattle-Breeding Grouping. Both are important, and I really believe they will contribute to the economic development of the province.

The citrus-fruit plan may be the world's largest. The world's largest citrus-fruit groves are being developed, taking full advantage of the existing natural resources — land that was formerly underutilized and groundwater. This plantation is being worked by student-workers — that is, students from the schools in the countryside. And it is this available labor power which makes it possible for us to go on developing this plan.

The Cattle-Breeding Grouping is being developed with the labor power that was available in the zone, plus resources provided by the province. This shows that there is a possibility of coming up with additional resources for construction work.

There are also the rice plans; the other cattle-breeding plans; the poultry- and hog-raising plans; and needless to say, the vegetable plans and the canefields — all of which should be given our full attention.

But we, the people of Matanzas — and I'm naming myself a resident of Matanzas with this — [*Applause*] must make it our business (with the help of the rest of the country, of course) to develop Varadero, because it's a veritable gold mine. We must do this, first of all, for the enjoyment of the people of Cuba. We must develop Varadero for the benefit of the people of Cuba, [*Applause*] and, in the future, if the circumstances make it necessary — considering, too, that Cubans don't go swimming all year round [*Laughter*] we could also make it a resort for visitors. That is another possibility for our country, another resource for our country. We believe that Varadero is your third most important plan, and we will really start developing it beginning in 1976 — we don't have the resources to do this now. And naturally, we have to start thinking about where we're going to get all the resources we need to put this plan into effect.

You have an impressive construction program. Junior high schools, dairies, and polytechnic institutes are going up right now. The Primary Education Teacher-Training School of Matanzas is under construction. The construction site for the Sports School for Beginners in Matanzas has already been selected, and the groundbreaking operations are under way. This school will free a lot of houses in Varadero which are now occupied by students. Plans have been drawn up for the School for Physical Education instructors. You are also building an excellent stadium which, compared with your population, will be the largest in the country — there are 70,000 people here, and the stadium will seat 25,000. We hope you'll do honor to those who sponsor the stadium and fill it up to full capacity — that is, whenever it's worth doing so. At any rate, I must say you are building a fine stadium.

The streets of Matanzas need repairs, and the city needs a new bridge. I'm talking about just the city now. Generally speaking, you have an interesting, wide-range construction plan, but we don't think it covers all your needs.

Construction work on the first twelve-story building ever to be built in Matanzas will be started pretty soon. With this building, Matanzas will lose some of its small-town appearance. The same goes for Santa Clara, where a number of tall buildings are going to be built. We've got to save on land, because we need it to produce foodstuffs. Therefore, we must begin to build tall buildings.

The construction minibrigades are doing fine, and a number of industrial buildings are going up.

However, this isn't enough, and the people of Matanzas must prepare for even more impetuous development. And the resources needed for this development can be obtained only by rationalizing work, by using our human resources in a rational, efficient fashion, so as to obtain the highest possible productivity.

Now we are saying to Matanzas — this militant, enthusiastic, revolutionary province — what we once said to Oriente: you will have everything you can build and put into operation for your development plans. [*Applause*]

Comrades, I've been talking for quite a while now, and I think it's time for me to sign off. [*Shouts of "No!"*]

Twenty-one years have passed since the attack on the Moncada, on July 26, 1953. Something has been done. We have taken an important step forward; we have created the conditions that we have today; we have created a tremendous political soundness, founded on the efforts, sacrifice, and sweat of our people and defended by the fighters of our Revolutionary Armed Forces. [*Applause*] In sum, we have assured the future. We have a title to the future, and our future will be the one we ourselves are capable of creating.

It is true that in the early years of the revolution our first concern was survival. But in the last few years, the revolution has been concerned not only with surviving but also with making strides forward, building and developing. And the future is entirely in our hands.

Needless to say, there's no such thing as an easy future — not even with a revolution. The road will be hard, and the obstacles always difficult. But we've faced great difficulties in the past — the blockade and the attacks by the United States, for example — and they didn't stop the consolidation and steady advance of the revolution.

We have some objective problems: ours isn't a rich country, and we have to pay our way by means of agriculture, especially sugar — which means hard work. Moreover, our country has had to start from conditions of great poverty and ignorance. But we have a broad road ahead.

One of our main tasks is and will always be that of training the new generations, of giving our young people and Pioneers ever more attention so as to instill in them a solid consciousness, a profound sense of duty to their homeland and humanity. [*Applause*] They must never forget the sacrifices it took to achieve what we now have. [*Applause*]

We must prepare these new generations for the world of the future, which won't be an easy world to live in. The contradictions between the developed capitalist countries and the underdeveloped countries are becoming more acute, as is the crisis of the world capitalist economy. We have a great task ahead; that of integrating ourselves and uniting with our Latin American brothers and sisters. Someday we will be a part of a large Latin American community of nations — after the revolution, of course.

Our people are our most important natural resource, and we must prepare them for the future! [*Applause*]

On summing up everything that our generation has done from 1953 to the present, we feel a certain satisfaction and encouragement, which should stimulate us in working for the future of our young people and humanity.

This is the soundest conclusion we can draw from an inventory of what we've done over the years. We've never before been so fully convinced that our people will march forward successfully and victoriously. Our people are capable of overcoming all obstacles and difficulties. [*Applause*]

Our people are wonderful, and you, the people of Matanzas Province, have shown this with your never-ending enthusiasm, strength, cooperation, and revolutionary spirit. [*Applause*] Your attitude bears out our confidence in the revolution.

Comrades of the party in Matanzas, comrades of the mass organizations and all other men and women of Matanzas, we congratulate you for the outstanding job you have done in the revolutionary task of establishing the organs of People's Power in Matanzas Province, [*Applause*] and we call on you to keep on working and struggling with the same enthusiasm, strength, firmness, and unwavering confidence in the future.

Eternal glory to the heroes who died on July 26 and to all the men and women who have dedicated their lives to our homeland, whether before or after the twenty-sixth! [*Prolonged applause*]

Patria o muerte!

Venceremos! [*Ovation*]

Principles of People's Power

by Raúl Castro

August 22, 1974

NOTE: Following the Matanzas elections, a three-week seminar was held for the more than 1,000 delegates who had been elected. The following is the closing speech to this seminar given by Raúl Castro, where he described in more detail the political significance of the creation of People's Power. The text is from Granma Weekly Review, *September 8, 1974.*

Tonight we bring this seminar to a close. It has covered a period of seventeen days, with thirteen days of intense work on the part of both you and those giving the course. To cope with all the groups, they have not only had to spend eight hours of each working day in the classroom but also long hours preparing their classes.

During this time you have had to study hard in order to fully grasp the subjects given and to pass the exams.

But the effort made was a necessary one. It was essential if you were to be equipped to face up to this, the most important part of the experiment that is being carried out here in Matanzas.

The preparatory stages — first, laying the initial foundations, giving general explanations to the masses, nominating candidates, the elections, and the establishment of the municipal, regional, and provincial assemblies of People's Power — were carried through successfully. Because of this, the people of Matanzas, the party, and the mass organizations in this province, and the National Commission — which has worked through all stages of the process — earned the recognition and congratulations of the party and government leadership, expressed by Comrade Fidel in his speech on July 26.

But the most important and most difficult stage of this experiment starts now. All the preparatory stages are only valid to the extent that they constitute necessary steps in what is to come, which has to do with putting into practice the concrete activities of the organs of People's Power in this province.

The importance of the electoral process — its profoundly democratic

215

nature, the broad and enthusiastic participation of the masses in the nomination of the candidates and then in the election of their representatives — is based on the fact that the representatives will exercise state power, they will guide and direct the administration of economic and cultural affairs, recreation, and services in general in the municipalities, the regions, and the province of Matanzas.

To the extent that those representatives will exercise governmental power, will take part in all state decisions that affect the community, will have authority to support and contribute to the development of all economic and social affairs of the province which are of national importance; to the extent that, through their representatives, the masses are going to participate in a regular and systematic way in the affairs of government and in the discussion and solution of all state problems, the experience gained in Matanzas will be of tremendous importance.

All the work which is to be carried out by the organs of People's Power, the decisive nature of that work, the authority they have, the participation of the masses: all this will become concrete in the new phase that is about to begin and which, a year from now, will give us the results we need for analysis at the first party congress. That is why this is the most important stage of the experiment in Matanzas and we must all be aware of this.

We have reviewed the curriculum which you received, the outlines of the classes given, the bibliography which you studied; we have been given information about the development of the seminars, of your contributions; and there is no doubt that as a whole, we can qualify the seminar as excellent. We are certain that this seminar has achieved what Fidel said on July 26, that it would give you a "detailed explanation of everything that will help you carry out your functions," and that, as a result of the seminar, as Fidel also expected, "you will be well prepared to handle the responsibilities which the revolution and the people are giving you." That is why we congratulate you, the comrades who have organized the seminar, and in particular, those who worked extremely hard with great efficiency and with no loss of quality in giving the seminar.

We are also well aware of what worries you most, the questions you have asked, and the opinions you have expressed on a number of questions. Most of what you asked concerned very basic questions. Your opinions are reasonable and well founded and your worries logical and fair ones.

It was possible to answer some of your questions and clear up some of the doubts. According to the information we have, on each occasion the answers given were clear and precise.

As for the greater part of the opinions, suggestions, and questions put forward, they must be answered and clarified by experience itself in the work you are about to begin. Nevertheless, it seems logical to bear in mind some of the proposals, such as the one made by many of those taking part in the seminar to set up a supply department at every level of People's Power. The proposal to set up a post office and telegraph, transport, and press offices in class A municipalities, specifically in Colón, also seem logical.

However, we must not forget that — as put forward in the material that you studied — that "One of the objectives of the experience in Matanzas of the organs of People's Power is to determine how many administrative departments, and which ones, should be set up at each level if they are to function effectively and with optimum efficiency. That is why the door is being left open for changes as far as the administrative departments go."

You asked many questions that we cannot answer for the time being, or at least for which there is no definitive answer. They are questions which must be answered in the course of experience itself, questions for which you yourselves will have to find the answers. For example, there were questions about the method for distributing housing and building materials among the population and for deciding priorities in housing repairs; there were questions about the internal structure of the administrative departments, the problems of training personnel, control and supervision of cadres which already exist in the different state agencies, problems of the labor force, specific questions concerned with the work of the Urban Reform agencies; there were questions and suggestions as to the advisability of setting up branches of the National Bank in certain municipalities; there were questions as to why on the state farms certain consumer goods were sold only to farmers and not agricultural workers; why radios and television sets are not repaired when the necessary parts are available, and many others. You are the ones who will have to find the answers to these and many other questions; that is what this experiment is for.

What have been worked out are the general principles, fundamental norms, the basic rules for carrying out this experiment. But even many of these norms and rules can, and surely will, be modified as a result of experience.

You, who confront the problems directly and are in daily and direct contact with the people, and who can systematically gather together their opinions and suggestions, are the ones who should meet and analyze each problem, trying to grasp all the different aspects of that problem, the real, concrete possibilites of solving it, proposing solutions, and taking your proposals to the corresponding levels. This is one of your tasks, one of your responsibilities. The delegates must not limit themselves to transmitting the problems and complaints of the masses. Their main responsibility is to study ways of solving those problems, solving them or proposing a way in which they can be solved. This is one of the ways in which the participation of the masses and their delegates in solving and making decisions on state affairs should make itself felt.

In your assemblies you should analyze all the regulations which have been established and all the matters for which tentative norms have been set by the central agencies, and you should discuss those regulations and norms frankly and critically. You should let us know what you feel is correct and what is incorrect, propose changes and modifications on that which you feel should be changed, and regulations for that which you feel should be regulated.

In my concluding remarks I am not going to touch on anything new to you. All the main points about the organs of People's Power that should be explained were explained in Comrade Fidel's speech on July 26; in the speech by Comrade Blas Roca on the setting up of the Provincial Assembly of People's Power; in the law which authorized the carrying out of this experiment in Matanzas Province and which created the National Commission; in the agreements of the Council of Ministers adopted on July 9, which refer to those units and that sphere of activity to be handed over to the organs of People's Power in Matanzas, to the structure of the new administrative apparatus, to banking and financial matters, labor and personnel problems, planning, statistics, and the accounting system — all of which must be taken into consideration in the transfer — and the future functioning of these units when under People's Power; in agreements which deal with relations between the organs of People's Power and the central state agencies, with the present provincial council of the state agencies and the Executive Committee and the changes to which they are subjected, with provisions for a delegate with administrative authority in towns of relative importance and with the very process of transferring units — which should be effected, as planned, during the remaining part of the year, to be concluded by the end of December.

All the documents and study material which you have gone over, and certain questions which were included in the bibliography, should be taken as a basic guide for carrying out the experiment in Matanzas. A book should be published and sent to every delegate, to each member of the executive committees, to heads and other functionaries of the administrative departments, to all the leaders of the party and mass organizations, and to all the leaders of provincial delegations of central agencies. It should serve as a reference book for the delegates on the functioning and powers of the organs of People's Power and on their relationship to other state agencies, the party, and the mass organizations.

The book should contain a subject index which is as detailed as possible so that guidelines may be easily found on all sorts of different questions.

In view of the above, I am only going to stress certain questions which seem to me to be the essential ones, the ones which should have been taken into consideration in the development of that part of the experiment which is to begin now and which, as I already said, is the most important.

You were given a detailed explanation of the dictatorship of the proletariat, and the role of each of its component parts: the party, the state, and the mass and social organizations. Explained to you were the nature of the state, the structure of a proletarian state and its component parts; you studied which of those parts have been present during the past fifteen years of the revolution and those which have not, and you have examined the role that the representative institutions of the state are to play.

In the early years of our revolution the necessary conditions for the setting up of these institutions did not exist, nor was there an urgent or pressing need for them. They weren't decisive in carrying out the tasks which the revolution faced during the early period.

Those first years were marked by a period of rapid change, of deep-rooted revolutionary change.

In those initial years it was necessary to confront continual and increasingly violent imperialist aggression and internal counterrevolutionary activity.

In order to operate in such a situation and face the tasks of the moment, we needed a state apparatus that was both functional and could be quickly mobilized, and which would operate as a dictatorship on behalf of the working people; a state apparatus in which the legislative, executive, and administrative powers were concentrated in one body that was able to make quick decisions.

Our revolutionary government, in which all legislative, executive, and administrative powers were concentrated during the early years, fulfilled those tasks set before it in the initial stage of struggle for survival: it enacted the revolutionary laws, expropriated the imperialists, eliminated the national exploiters, and successfully carried through the political struggle against both internal and external aggression.

At the same time, during those initial years the lack of material resources led to fears about the feasibility of setting up the organs of People's Power when these bodies would not have the necessary resources to cope with certain tasks, including some for which there was great need in the population like housing, maintenance, and repair.

It was feared that limited resources would prevent the organs of People's Power from fulfilling the tasks assigned to them and that the idea of their establishment, which was basically correct, might well be discredited.

In the first years of the revolution we were not equipped to face the task of setting up representative institutions.

At that time, we did not have a strong party, the mass organizations were not sufficiently developed — in short we did not have the organizational tools available to us now.

At the end of the 1960s, when we could possibly have said that the conditions for setting up those representative institutions already existed, we were caught up in the great economic struggle for the giant sugar harvest of 1970. And, as you know and as Comrade Fidel has pointed out on a number of occasions, the concentration of forces in this field led us to neglect other branches of the economy and other work fronts of the revolution.

To all these factors, we should add a certain lack of experience and understanding on the part of many of us regarding the importance of these representative institutions and the role which they are to play.

But, despite the fact that such representative institutions of the state did not exist over all those years, we can safely say that on the whole, the revolutionary government has fulfilled the task with which it was entrusted.

The state was, nonetheless, a provisional state, and it is now necessary for it to assume a definitive form, as Comrade Fidel has stressed.

The institutionalization of our revolution began in 1970 and was accelerated from 1972 onwards, when the conditions ripened and when there was an economic recovery and considerable progress made in giving new life to and strengthening the mass organizations.

In late 1972, the Council of Ministers was restructured and the Executive Committee set up. During 1973, the whole party apparatus, from the Central Committee down to the municipal committee, was restructured, the mechanisms by which they were to function were clearly outlined and their role and responsibilities made clear; at the same time the process of reorganizing the judicial system got under way. In 1973, preparatory work was undertaken for organizing the representative institutions in Matanzas Province in 1974 on an experimental basis. The plan is to extend these institutions to the rest of the country in 1976, after the first party congress.

The setting up of representative institutions of the state constitutes a tremendous step forward in the revolutionary process. With this, our proletarian state is complete; and if at the beginning, during the early years of struggle for survival, they were neither necessary nor vital parts of the state — and indeed, they might well have put a brake on the state which then needed to be quickly mobilized — with the conditions created, they have become an absolute necessity, a fundamental part of the state, through which the participation of the people will become real, will take on a regular, systematic, and institutionalized form.

This doesn't mean that the revolution and its leaders have at any time placed themselves above the people, that the people were forgotten, that we at any point failed to take into account the masses. On the contrary, it was being able to count on the working masses and other sectors of the people that made possible the success of the insurrectional struggle, the overthrow of the dictatorship, the holding of the general strike and the blocking of the plans for a coup.* Only because we had the support of the people, the enthusiastic participation of the masses, was it possible to carry out the profound revolutionary change, to confront imperialist aggressions, the bands of counterrevolutionaries in the Escambray Mountains, Matanzas, and other regions, the invasion at Playa Girón, the situation created during the October Crisis, and the difficulties resulting from the blockade. It has been the people, the masses of our workers, who have been mobilized time and time again, increasingly better organized in the different mass organizations, who have been the decisive factor throughout the development of the revolution.

There is probably no other case in history in which a revolution, the leadership of a revolution, has had such support from the people, such unlimited and unshakable confidence and revolutionary enthusiasm on the part of the masses, such complete unity, as that which our people have given their revolution, its leaders, and especially the beloved and undisputed leader of that revolution, Comrade Fidel Castro.

It isn't a question of our revolutionary state not having been democratic, even when the representative institutions did not exist.

When a state like ours represents the interests of the workers, regardless of its form and structure, it is a much more democratic state than any other kind that has ever existed in history, because the state of the workers, the state that has undertaken the construction of socialism, is, in any form, a majority state of the majority, while all other previous states have been states of exploiting minorities.

The bourgeois-landlord state which existed in Cuba, even in the period before the coup on March 10, 1952† — with its "representative" institutions, the House and the Senate, with its regular elections — was infinitely less democratic than our revolutionary state, because it contributed to the domination of our country by the imperialists, monopolies, and other foreign companies. And it represented their national allies, both Cuban and foreign members of the bourgeoisie and the large landowners. It was an organ of coercion, with its army, police, torturers, gangsters, jails, and courts directed against the interests of the great majority of the people.

---

*After Batista fled Cuba on January 1, 1959, a group of military officers attempted to seize power, trying to prevent the Rebel Army from taking power. In response, Castro issued a call for a national general strike. This was successful and ensured the triumph of the revolution.

†This refers to Fulgencio Batista's coup d'etat against the government of Carlos Prío Socarrás.

The revolutionary state regained control of all our resources which were in the hands of the imperialists and other exploiters and restored them to the people.

The means of production, which were the private property of a few, became the property of all.

Unemployment was eliminated and new work became available for all; illiteracy was eradicated and free education introduced for all; medical care and hospital services were also made free for all; and everyone had the assurance of being cared for in their old age.

The people were organized and given arms and taught how to handle those weapons so they could defend themselves. The masses have participated in the discussion of all the most important aspects of the revolution, the main laws, and now they have started to participate in the discussion of economic plans at the grass-roots level of production and service units.

Our state has been and is an essentially democratic state, a state of the humble, for the humble, and by the humble; a state of and for all the workers. What the creation of representative institutions means, then, is the perfecting of our state, of giving it a complete and definitive structure, of perfecting our democracy.

If socialist representative institutions are an expression of the people's will through the vote; if they represent a means by which the people are not only represented by the state but are, in fact, a part of that state, participating in its decisions in a direct and systematic way; and if the conditions for their creation already exist, then it is essential and imperative that they be set up.

Already in present-day conditions, to paraphrase Lenin, we could say that "without representative institutions democracy cannot be conceived of, much less proletarian democracy."

And here lies the enormous historic importance of the step which is being taken and the extraordinary responsibility and great privilege which you, as members of the first representative socialist institutions to be organized in our country, bear; that of having the opportunity to show through your work the role of these institutions, that of being the protagonists in defining the form that our proletarian state will take in the future.

The representative organs of People's Power come into being after fifteen years of the revolution's development, during which time we have learned from the experience of our successes and failures.

We must make every effort to ensure that these institutions are free from bad habits and practices acquired over the years when these institutions did not exist and when there was an excess of centralization in many areas, when we had inadequate administrative procedures, when there was little understanding of and much confusion about the role and functions of the party, the state agencies, and the mass organizations.

This is something that all of us, we and you, must consider, and especially those comrades, delegates or members of the executive committee of People's Power or functionaries of the new administrative departments, who come from the old administrative apparatus, who worked for years under the old system, and therefore run the risk or at least the possibility of being more heavily imbued with such bad habits or practices.

It is necessary to be aware of the fact that these organs of People's Power, as Fidel said on the occasion of the tenth anniversary of the Federation of Cuban Women, will be "replacing the administrative work habits of the first years of the revolution. We must begin to substitute democratic methods for the administrative methods that run the risk of becoming bureaucratic methods."

The existence and functioning of the organs of People's Power — the representative institutions of our socialist state, the highest organs of state power in the land under our jurisdiction — must stamp out such purely administrative practices and replace all procedures that run the risk of becoming bureaucratic, which, in many cases, in all too many cases, have unfortunately already become bureaucratic procedures.

The organs of People's Power are responsible, at a municipal, regional, and provincial level, for the administration of a number of important affairs that were up to now administered from the center. But the great importance of these organs does not rest in their administrative responsibilities, but in the fact that they are the basic organs of state power and comprise delegations democratically elected by the masses; that they are organs through which the people have the possibility of participating directly in the control and administration of social affairs. The existence of the organs of People's Power should necessarily imply the eradication of bureaucratic centralism, which still prevails in many sectors of our state apparatus, and putting in its place democratic centralism, the fundamental Marxist-Leninist tenet on which the state should function.

You have just studied the basic principles of democratic centralism, but this is one of the points we should like to elaborate on because it is of cardinal importance in the functioning and the very success of People's Power.

Democratic centralism, as applied by the state organs means, in the first place, that the members of these, the highest organs of state power, the representative institutions, are elected from the bottom by the masses. It means that those elected as delegates and members of the executive committees at the different levels must periodically account for their activities, in a regular and systematic way, before those who elected them. And it is one of the most important principles to be taken into consideration in the concrete work of the organs of People's Power and one which must necessarily be transformed from a mere declaration of intent into something which is practical and systematically carried out. At each level of People's Power, the maximum authority does not lie in the hands of those elected, but with those who elect, not individually, but collectively. In this lies the essence of People's Power, that which makes the participation of the masses in state power something real and makes possible the actual carrying out of that power by the delegates.

And in the electoral circumscription maximum authority does not rest with the elected delegate, but with the electorate as a whole. They are the ones who give the mandate to the delegates to represent them in putting forward their problems, complaints, and opinions; they are the ones who can revoke that mandate whenever they feel the elected delegates do not represent their interests. Therefore, it is the delegate who must be accountable for his activities to his electors and not vice-versa. It is the mass of the people who have the highest powers; the power of the delegate is derived from and given to him by the masses.

On the municipal level, maximum authority does not rest with the elected executive committee, but with the municipal assembly that elected it. It is the assembly of delegates that grants the mandate for the executive committee to act on its behalf and carry out the agreements and decisions made in the periods between meetings, and it is the assembly that has the power to modify in toto or in part the membership of the executive committee whenever it deems this necessary. It is therefore the municipal executive committee that is accountable to the municipal assembly, and not the reverse.

Likewise, the president, vice-president, and secretary of the municipal executive committee are elected by this body and ratified by the assembly and consequently, they are accountable to the executive committee and to the assembly, and they must act in accordance with the agreements and decisions of these two bodies of municipal People's Power.

And so the president, vice-president, and secretary of the municipal executive committee are subordinate to the aforementioned executive committee and the municipal assembly; the whole executive committee is subordinate to this assembly and, in turn, the assembly is composed of delegates elected by and subordinate to the mass of electors of their respective circumscriptions — the result being that it is the masses who in practice wield the greatest maximum power and who are, therefore, the real active protagonists of the process, with concrete and institutionalized power through which they can exercise their initiative and their decisions.

If the power structure were the reverse, and the executive committee was subordinate to the president of municipal People's Power; and in turn the assembly was subordinate to the executive committee and its president; and if the masses of electors in each circumscription were answerable to their delegate — then real and primary state power would rest not with the masses, but with the president and the executive committee of municipal People's Power. And each lower rung on the ladder would have less power to take initiative and make decisions, and by the time we reached the base of the ladder, which is the masses, they would have no authority — they would be passive protagonists in the process and mere executors of decisions taken by the higher-ups.

And what we have just explained regarding municipal power takes on even greater importance the more we climb the ladder to higher levels of administration. This is even more so as regards the mechanism that has been adopted according to which the professional members of the executive committee of People's Power at the regional and provincial level are not, in their entirety, delegates elected directly by the masses in the circumscriptions, but rather are elected by the delegates of the masses — those comprising the regional and provincial assemblies.

For that reason it is necessary to have a practical, clear understanding of People's Power at all levels, and to maximize at all levels the exercising of power by the assemblies, the supreme organs of state power at each respective level.

The regional executive committee is elected by the regional assembly to act on its behalf, to carry out the agreements and decisions taken by the committee, and to assume the responsibilities of state leadership in the region in the lapse of time between meetings of the assembly. As a result, the regional executive committee is subordinate to the regional assembly and is accountable to it. The same is true at the provincial level.

In the same way and as we just explained, at the municipal level — given that the president, vice-president, and secretary of the provincial and regional executive committees are subordinate to the respective executive committees — they are also subordinate to the corresponding regional and provincial assemblies, and the delegates that compose them are subordinate to the municipal assemblies that elected them and to the circumscriptions by which they were elected delegates. Once again we see that maximum state power in practice always lies in the hands of the masses. The primary power from which all other power is derived, rests with the masses. Moreover, the masses are ever present in the form of their delegates, directly elected by the masses.

If the hierarchy of decisions and power were inverted in the form that was previously indicated, as we saw, the masses would have no power, and the real centers of power and decision making would, as we ascended the ladder once again, be increasingly out of touch with the masses.

If we really want the masses to participate in state decisions — and that is clearly what all of us want — because this is in keeping with the essence of socialist democracy and the principles of Marxism-Leninism, and because making direct use of all the knowledge and experience accumulated by the masses and their creative initiative makes the work of the leadership apparatus at the same time lighter and much more efficient — if we want the masses to play a real and direct part in the governing of society, we must see to it that the principle of democratic centralism functions in every sense of the word.

Every delegate to the organs of People's Power should meet with the masses in his circumscription once every three months to account for his activity. With meetings of this sort every three months, the first should be held in early December, and throughout the whole experiment there should be four such meetings in all. In between such meetings when the delegates are answerable to all the population living in the circumscription, the delegates should try to hold at least one separate meeting with the people of the area from each Committee for the Defense of the Revolution or from each farm grouping that is part of the circumscriptions. These smaller meetings will enable there to be closer and more direct contact between the delegate and the masses, and will facilitate a more lively dialogue and greater participation of the electorate.

Moreover, each delegate should also set aside a certain period of time each week to meet with the electors of his circumscription on an individual basis to listen to their problems, complaints, and suggestions.

In every collective contact with his electors the delegate should report on the activities and different responsibilities of municipal People's Power; on his personal activity as a delegate, on the way in which the problems which the electors asked him to put before the organs of People's Power have been handled: those which can and those which cannot be solved, or those which can only be solved over a longer period of time, and the reasons for each solution found and each measure taken. Nothing must be left unexplained to the masses.

The delegates must be well informed of the reasons behind the different measures adopted by state agencies, whether they be the organs of People's Power on the municipal, regional, or provincial level or the central state agencies. If the price of something goes up, it must be explained. If the amount of something which is distributed is changed, an explanation must be given to the masses. If a product is delayed more than normal in reaching the people, the causes must be given. If the hours in which a service is given are altered, the people must know the reasons why and, in each case, a convincing explanation must be given. The delegates should never present the masses with absurd explanations or formal reasons to side-step the issue or reasons that convince nobody. At the assemblies to which they belong and in the corresponding executive committees the delegates must demand all the necessary information to give satisfactory explanations to the masses.

In turn, the delegates must gather together all the complaints and suggestions of their electors and present them in the respective assemblies. A complaint, suggestion, or opinion that is put forward and supported by the majority of the electors should be transmitted by the delegate to the organs of People's Power, even if he himself is not in agreement. The delegate doesn't represent himself but the mass of electors who have elected him and his duty is to act in the interests of the opinions expressed and the problems of the masses, not his personal opinions and problems.

We must bear in mind, as Fidel said in his July 26 speech this year, that "each and every citizen who requests something from you must be given an honest and sincere explanation of the possibilities of having his request fulfilled. We must never deceive anyone."

Delegates to the organs of People's Power are accountable not only to their constituency, but also to higher levels of People's Power and of the central state organs, since another basic principle of democratic centralism is that of subordination of the lower to the higher organs. The delegates are accountable to the electors of their circumscription, but also to their municipal assembly and the executive committee. The municipal organs of People's Power are accountable to the regional organs, the regional to the provincial, and the provincial to the central state organs.

The subordination of the lower to the higher organs is determined by the need for adequate uniformity, homogeneity, coordination, and correlation of activities carried out by the state apparatus, regardless of in which municipality, region, or province they take place; and by the necessity to harmonize the particular interests of each municipality with the broader interests of the region, province, and nation.

The regional organs of People's Power respond to and watch over the interests of all the municipalities of a given region. In order to avoid a given municipality adopting decisions or undertaking activities in detriment to the interests of another municipality, the People's Power organs at the municipal level are subordinate to those of the region.

Likewise, the provincial organs of People's Power answer for and watch over the interests of all the municipalities and regions of a given province and, to guarantee that the interests of one municipality or region do not conflict with another, the People's Power organs at the municipal and regional level are subordinate to those at the provincial level and, for the same reasons, these three levels are subordinate to the central state organs.

In this regard, the higher organs have the power to nullify an agreement or decision of the assemblies and executive committees at the lower levels, when these are in contradiction with laws and regulations in force or which affect the broader interests of other communities throughout the country. The agreements adopted by the executive committee of People's Power at a given level can be overruled by the People's Power assembly at this same level to which it is subordinate. It can also be overruled by the executive committee or the assembly of the higher organs of People's Power. Before using the power of annulment, which should be used only under exceptional circumstances, as a last resort, all possible means of reasoning on the part of the higher organs to convince the lower ones that have taken the decision in question must have been exhausted.

We must bear in mind that together with the subordination of lower to higher organs, which guarantees the necessary centralization of norming and methodology, of the planning of resources and all other aspects requiring some degree of centralization, we must ensure and also guarantee the essential autonomy of each level of People's Power in being able to take decisions freely and under its own responsibility in all questions pertaining to its jurisdiction.

The People's Power organization must not simply mean decentralization down to the provincial level, that is to say, decentralization that solely transfers the power and administrative mechanisms until now concentrated in the central apparatus to the provincial organs of People's Power. The establishment of People's Power means decentralization at all levels of the state apparatus; concentration of the absolute majority of the economic and social activities under the lower levels of the state apparatus, that is, the municipalities; decentralization not only of the province with regard to the nation, but of the region with regard to the province, and the municipality with regard to the region; and the future decentralization of the economic units with regard to the state administrative centers.

The lower divisions of People's Power are subordinate to the higher ones, but function autonomously within the legal and normative framework established, and must not be subjected to the constant and limiting supervision of the higher bodies. This mechanism, besides implementing a more efficient, functional process for adopting decisions in accordance with the demands of time and place, also frees the higher organs, and especially the state agencies, from the heavy load of day-to-day administrative tasks, which cannot be correctly carried out in practice and have to be overlooked to a great extent — and which, at the same time, sidetrack these organs from developing their responsibilities and carrying through their tasks in the setting of norms, control, and checking of activities under their jurisdiction.

There are numerous examples that illustrate how an apparently total centralization of even the most insignificant aspects of administration in many cases really means anarchy and decentralization in matters which should be centralized, the violation of the most elementary norms, and the irrational and scattered nature of things that should be homogenous and uniform. We have had examples put forward by you in this seminar.

For example, in many places there is one fare for a journey by taxi or by bus between two given points and another for the return journey, when the distance is the same. Or the price for products and services is the same when they have all the required ingredients and the required quality as when they lack several ingredients and are of poor quality. There are cases of the population not receiving certain services due to shortages of supplies while there is a surplus in other administrative offices in the same locality.

For example, from Coliseo to Limonar, taxis charge five pesos and from Limonar to Coliseo four pesos. From the Matanzas medical center to the bus station in Pueblo Nuevo the fare is 60 cents for three people and from the bus station to the medical center three pesos. On the Jovellanos-Matanzas route, the bus fare is 20 cents from Limonar to Matanzas, but, on return journey from Matanzas to Jovellanos, the fare from Matanzas to Limonar is 65 cents. Ice cream sundaes are the same price when served with all the ingredients as when they simply consist of two scoops of ice cream. Croquette sandwiches, which were formerly served with cheese and ketchup, now cost the same although there is no cheese, no ketchup, and very little croquette. The same being charged by the laundry for starched and unstarched clothes. A pound of bread being sold which only weighs twelve ounces.

The existence and functioning of the organs of People's Power and the correct implementation of the mechanisms which you have studied, will prevent things like this from happening.

Another principle of democratic centralism is that those elected are subject to recall at any moment of their mandate or, as Fidel said: "At any hour of the day or night." In this sense and in line with what has been said on the previous point, we must stress that the power to remove a delegate or a member of the executive committee at a given level of People's Power, never lies in the hands of the superior organs but in the hands of those who elected them. The proposal to do so may come from a superior organ but the decision can only be taken by a vote of those who elected him.

The subordination of the minority to the majority in all the organs of People's Power, which operate on the basis of collective leadership, is another of the basic principles of democratic centralism, which we must always bear in mind during the course of this experiment. The assemblies and the executive committees at the different levels of People's Power are organs of collective leadership, which means that the decisions must always be put to the vote. In the meetings no agreement or decision should ever be assumed or taken for granted; all proposals, amendments, or observations should always be put to the vote. As is clearly pointed out in one of the study materials and at the meetings of the organs of collective leadership of People's Power, all members have equal rights and duties; the chairman and the secretary of the executive committees will be chairman and secretary of the meetings but they will have the same power and responsibilities as any other member and the same obligation to submit all their proposals to the approval of the meeting and subsequently act on the decision of the meeting.

Yet another principle of democratic centralism regarding the organs of People's Power is that the power which the assemblies and the executive committee have at all levels to designate and when necessary, replace, the directors and other main functionaries of the administrative apparatus at a given level cannot be transferred. This is in keeping with established procedure. Thus, for example, the designation and replacement of the provincial directors of the administrative leadership of the provincial People's Power organs will be handled by the provincial assembly, but at the same time, taking into account the opinion of the corresponding central agency; and in the case of public health and education, the selection will be made from a list presented by the corresponding central agency.

These administrative leaderships, their directors, and other functionaries are in charge of the administrative work and the handling of resources and the activities corresponding to each level of People's Power. In carrying out this work the administrative leadership has autonomy in making decisions on a whole series of functional matters, and, in the same way, administrators of production and service units subordinate to the different administrative leaderships should also have certain autonomy in decision making on minor matters concerning the units under their jurisdiction.

This means that it is not the delegates, nor the assembly, nor the executive committee, nor the chairman, deputy chairman, or secretary of the executive committee who directly control these activities which come under the different levels of People's Power, but the administrative leadership and the administration of the corresponding units of production and service. The assembly and the executive committee designate these functionaries to carry out that task, they take decisions and establish the regulations that are to govern the activity of these functionaries and guide, control, supervise, and inspect their works, and when they fail to meet their responsibilities the assembly and the executive committee can remove them.

The delegates are to transmit complaints and opinions of the masses to the assembly and make the proposals which they feel necessary. As members of the assembly they take part in decision making and then, through their contact with the masses of their circumscription and their participation in the working committees of People's Power, they are to check on how administrative leaderships fulfill the agreements and decisions taken by the assembly and the executive committee.

The administrative leaderships are subordinate to the corresponding assembly and executive committee and they are each periodically accountable to these bodies. The directors of the administrative leaderships at all levels must meet frequently and in a systematic way with the members of their respective executive committees. But we warn against the unsound practice of systematically holding meetings of the collective of administrative directors on their own or together with the executive committee, except when it is a case of coordinating some specific task, because in practice, this leads to the bad practice of creating one more decision-making body which would tend to ignore or substitute itself for the powers of the assembly, or at the very least, to act parallel to it.

On filling the posts of directors and functionaries of the different administrative leaderships at each level of People's Power, in the majority of cases, comrades who have been carrying out similar work in the provincial delegations of central state agencies and many of whom are present at this seminar should be the first to be designated. As a rule, designating these comrades would be the most advisable thing to do, especially in the early days, when the organs of People's Power are getting under way, because those comrades have experience in the work, they are familiar with the mechanisms, and can guarantee the indispensable continuity.

Some of these comrades have been in state administration for a long time, some for a shorter period of time, in some cases over a considerably long period of time. And because of this, they necessarily have their weak and their strong points; they are necessarily an integral part of the successes and failures of the administrative apparatus in which they have worked. In cases where mistakes or errors have been noted on the part of certain comrades, we should bear in mind that they have worked under very difficult conditions, in a situation that was unfavorable in many aspects, with administrative habits and procedures and practices which they were not responsible for but with which they were compelled to operate. So while it is correct and not an exercise in apologetics to view any successes and achievements mainly as the fruits of their efforts, it would be unfair to make them necessarily responsible for all the shortcomings and mistakes that are detected in the fields in which they worked.

Only now, with the new situation created as a result of the setting up of People's Power will it be possible to analyze their work, and we are absolutely certain that because of the experience they have and the dedication with which the great majority of them have worked so far, they will be an invaluable pillar of support for the organs of People's Power and will play a decisive role in the success of this experiment. We ask of these comrades their fullest cooperation in this venture.

In many cases, as was explained to you during the course of the seminar, it will become necessary to transfer some of you from one place to another. As you know, most of the units which are to be handed over to People's Power operate at the municipal level, which means that there will be a considerable shift away from the level at which they are administered now to those at which they are to be administered in the future. Of the 5,597 units to be handed over to People's Power, 4,092 were already being administered at the municipal level; but, with the transfer, 4,971 units will be administered by People's Power at the municipal level. This means that almost 900 units will be handed over to the municipality and all are from agencies which did not have municipal delegations. And this, together with the transfer of administrative powers, implies the transfer of the corresponding administrative apparatus and its functionaries. In all cases, the transfer will be effected without affecting income, and the real possibilities of and the problems involved in this transfer will always be taken into account; but the transfer is necessary and for this, we ask the comrades for their full cooperation and understanding.

Another principle of democratic centralism upon which the fulfillment of the principles of collective leadership and the system of accountability depends is the regular and systematic holding of meetings with electors in each circumscription and meetings of the assemblies and executive committees at the different levels.

The final principle of democratic centralism which we wanted to mention is freedom of discussion, criticism, and self-criticism in the organs of People's Power. All members of the different organs of People's Power must exercise the right to express their opinions, sincerely and frankly, on all the matters put to them before a final decision is made; and at the meetings of the organs to which they belong, they must exercise the right to criticize any measure, member, or functionary of the organs of People's Power regardless of his position.

Publicity in the mass media about the well-founded and confirmed criticism of measures adopted by one or another of the organs of People's Power should be viewed as both sound and positive, although this should not necessarily lead to the replacement of the person who is criticized. The people should have detailed information on the work of the organs of People's Power, on their members, and on their strong and weak points. As their name indicates, they are organs of the power of the people, they are institutions of the people, and for that reason the people have the right to be informed about all aspects of their activity and operations. This is also the reason why in one of the study materials, we read, "The meetings of the assemblies will be public unless the executive committee or the assembly itself determines, in exceptional cases, that a certain meeting or part of a meeting should be private."

The organs of People's Power are made up of delegates elected by the people, representatives of the interests and opinions of the people; in their meetings, the people's problems are discussed and they should be discussed in the presence of the people, unless state secrets or national security are involved.

Comrades:

You have also just finished studying the relations that should exist between the party, the mass organizations, and the state agencies, and specifically the organs of People's Power. However, we should like to dwell on a few aspects of this question. In doing so, it would be useful to recall what is put forward in the communiqué of the Central Committee of the party on relations between the Central Committee apparatus and the central state agencies. The communiqué states, textually, "Over the years in which we worked without an adequate party or state structure and without a clear definition of the interrelations and limitations of each, the party and state institutions have, to a certain extent, gone beyond their own limits. They have on a number of occasions and on different matters mutually trespassed on each other's field of responsibility and have mutually substituted for each other in carrying out the powers and duties assigned to them. The logical result was that leaders and functionaries of the two fell into practices that grew stronger and stronger and which today, owing to inertia, tend to remain and create additional difficulties in carrying out the necessary and indispensable task of perfecting the party apparatus, state institutions, and the mass organizations, so that they will all function better, and will thereby lead to a more rapid advance in the historic task of building socialism, the first phase of the communist society. These practices must be uprooted and the ways in which they are manifested resolutely checked. In their place we must develop new practices in accord with the process of defining and strengthening the party, the state, and the mass organizations — a process which is being carried out under the firm guidance of our Political Bureau in keeping with the directives of Comrade Fidel."

The material which you have studied during the last few days, and specifically the communiqué of the Secretariat of the Central Committee, which we have already mentioned, together with the address given by Comrade Blas at the inauguration of the provincial assembly of Matanzas, explain very clearly and in considerable detail the reason behind the leadership role of the party during the phase of the construction of socialism, and the importance of upholding respect for the party in its role of leadership — endorsed and ratified publicly by each and every one of the delegates to People's Power present here. We will not, therefore, dwell more on this matter.

We wish to warn against the possible ways in which hypertrophy of our institutions, bad habits and practices, and general confusion as regards the role of and the relations between the various institutions to which the communiqué of the Secretariat refers, may become manifest. Despite the fact that these have, to a large extent, been eliminated over the past two years, they are still strong enough to make the warning I give to each and every one of you valid: delegates to People's Power, members of the executive committees, heads or possible heads of the administration departments, heads of the mass organizations, and especially you, comrade party leaders. You must always bear in mind that the party is unquestionably the maximum agency of leadership within our society, and that it not only directs other party organizations and their members, but also the state organs and the mass organizations, and therefore, must also direct the organs of People's Power.

But you must bear in mind, and I wish to make special emphasis of this: the methods and channels through which the party should exercise its leadership role. Remember always, in your day-to-day activity, that the party does not administer, that it must never meddle in the daily routine work of the organs of People's Power and its administrative apparatus, and must always refrain from handing down decisions that fall within the responsibility of the organs of People's Power.

You must remember that the party is the highest political and ideological authority in the province, but that the maximum state and administrative authority in the municipalities, the regional districts, and the province of Matanzas does not rest with the party organs, but with the organs of People's Power; and that each level of People's Power is only directly subordinate, as regards state and administrative responsibility, to the higher levels of People's Power, and not to the party. The party must neither replace nor encroach upon the administration and the organs of People's Power, nor violate their powers.

You must also bear in mind that directives, resolutions, and decisions of the party have no legally binding or administrative powers, but are only binding for party organizations and agencies and their membership. And even then, if any member does not carry them out, he may only be sanctioned politically and even expelled from the party. But the party has no coercive apparatus to force its members to follow party discipline.

Regarding non–party members, remember that in order to direct state agencies and the organs of People's Power, the party has only political power, the correctness of the party line, its guidelines, the strength of its example, and the confidence it inspires. And that its only methods can be those which convince and persuade.

At the different provincial levels the party must be well informed of the plans, tasks, responsibilities, and problems of the organs of People's Power. It must give its opinion on important and fundamental questions which come before those organs. It must supervise the fulfillment of the duties assigned to them, if they stick to their functions as established by the higher organs of the party and government. They must help coordinate the activities of People's Power with other state and mass organizations; control and assist the organs of People's Power in selecting and appointing the best personnel for the various administrative posts subordinate to it; contribute to the education and improvement of personnel; establish guidelines and make suggestions relating to the organs of People's Power in order to improve their work and guarantee the fulfillment of their responsibilities; and help achieve through the party apparatus and its membership the most successful evolution of those organs. But the party must do all that without ever infringing on the state's responsibilities and without ever usurping the autonomous decision-making powers of the organs of People's Power.

The party must guide and direct the work of the organs of People's Power within the well-defined framework of the responsibilities of the party and state and of their "complementary but different" roles, the fraternal work relations that should exist between the leading organs of the party and People's Power at each level. The party can and must make suggestions, proposals, recommendations; it must counsel and guide the organs of People's Power, but must never "hand down decisions," never impose decisions, never undertake any manner of reprisal as regards an organ of People's Power or members of such organs who do not agree with or will not carry out something the party has suggested, proposed, recommended, advised, or set down as a guideline.

The party must use as its principal means to guarantee that its guidelines and criteria are put into practice by the organs of People's Power, the work of the party members who are also delegates to those organs or members of executive committees. Party members "wherever they may work or whatever post they hold, are obliged to comply with and carry out the decisions of the party and to convince (and neither force nor oblige) the non–party members of the fairness of those decisions and the need to apply them." If, after exhausting all the methods and resources within their authority and all their relations with other institutions, the leadership of the party at a given level — the municipal level, for example — does not convince the organs of People's Power at that level to follow a recommendation or guideline that it considers important, it must then refer to the next highest level of the party — in this case, the regional — to discuss the matter at the regional level of People's Power. If no agreement is reached at this level either, the regional party leadership — if the matter is of sufficient importance — must refer to the provincial level of the party to discuss the problem at the provincial level of People's Power. In the event — and it seems highly unlikely that this would be the case — that no agreement is reached at this level either, the matter would be taken before the National Constitutional Commission of the organs of People's Power in Matanzas, and in the last resource, if agreement were still not reached, the Political Bureau and the Council of Ministers.

These are the principles on which should be based the relations between members of the People's Power executive committees, the directors, and other functionaries of the administrative departments, on the one hand, and on the other, members of the executive bureaus and heads and other functionaries of the departments of the party committees who are responsible for the same work at different levels of leadership.

It so happens that many members of the executive bureaus and the heads or functionaries of many party committees will have, through the party and all that sphere of activity which the party covers, the responsibility of supervising that which is directed and administered by one or another of the administrative departments of People's Power. And so, for example, at the provincial and regional levels we find in the party committees a department of culture, science, and education and a member of the corresponding executive bureau of the party, supervising through the party, cultural and other activities. We also find at the same level of People's Power a department of culture and a member of the corresponding executive committee of People's Power, directing and administering this activity for the state. And the same is true in other spheres such as commerce, the hotels and restaurants, transportation, etc.

In each and every case, the leaders and officials of the party have the duty and the means of knowing, controlling, and guiding the development of a given activity, and of evaluating and helping the respective party organs which are in charge of that activity. To this effect, the closest and most fraternal relations and coordination of work should prevail between party cadres and the corresponding People's Power cadres.

But in every instance the concrete administrative decisions with regard to the management and use of personnel and material resources for a given task fall within the jurisdiction of People's Power organs, management, their cadres and officials, and not within the jurisdiction of the party's organs, mechanisms, and cadres. The latter can make suggestions or recommendations for the use of particular human or material resources, but without exerting undue pressure to impose a decision, since that decision is not their responsibility. They can and should control the management and use of these resources, warn the People's Power organs about any mismanagement, inform the corresponding party organs about it, and by means of the procedures explained previously, intervene and influence the decision made in a decisive way.

But the party must never take over purely administrative procedures that do not fall within its jurisdiction. Undue interference will make its relations with People's Power organs ineffective. The party must lead organs of People's Power without becoming their guardian. The party must direct organs of People's Power without becoming their godfather.

The leading party organ at a given level and its members can request permission for attending a meeting of the People's Power assembly or executive committee at that level in order to give the party's opinion on a given issue and ask that this opinion be analyzed by the corresponding organ of People's Power. It is always necessary to bear in mind that the People's Power assembly and executive committee meetings are the responsibility of the organs of People's Power and not of the party. These meetings must be presided over by the chairman of the executive committee or a member of the organ of People's Power chosen by those present at the meeting, but must never be presided over by a member of a party organ, who may be attending the meeting as a guest, even though he or she may be the first secretary of the party at that given level.

It is always necessary to respect the essential autonomy of the organs of People's Power in their character as state organs. Otherwise, as expressed in a resolution of the Bolshevik Party put forward by Lenin, "The absence of a strict delineation of functions and interference in affairs outside of its jurisdiction results in an absence of strict and exact responsibility on the part of each person for the work entrusted to him; they increase bureaucratism in the party organs themselves, which in trying to do everything end up doing nothing; they impede serious specialization by administrative officials working in the economy — the study of a question in full detail, the acquisition of truly practical experience — in a word, making more difficult the correct organization of work."

To strengthen and strictly define the role of the party, it is necessary to remove from its jurisdiction all state and administrative tasks which the party has had to take over up until now because the institutions and mechanisms of power had not yet been established. The establishment of organs of People's Power and their correct functioning will enable the party to concentrate on and carry out thoroughly its own responsibilities, playing its leading role within our revolutionary process with greater efficiency.

The functions and responsibilities of the organs of People's Power must also be clearly and well defined in relation to those of the mass organizations, especially those of the Committees for the Defense of the Revolution, which look after people's activities in such a way as to coincide with the responsibilities of organs of People's Power more than with any other organization. Until now, because of the absence of organs of People's Power, the CDRs have had to assume some of the tasks which should and will properly fall within the jurisdiction of the organs of People's Power, as for example is the case of the people's inspectors of retail sales and public transportation.

The mass organizations: CDRs, the National Association of Small Farmers, the Federation of Cuban Women, the Central Organization of Cuban Trade Unions, the trade union locals, and the youth organizations are meant to fulfill a dual function: First, providing suitable leadership so that the revolutionary process can flow in an organized, determined, and decisive fashion, making room for the powerful contribution of initiatives and efforts by various people's sectors in the construction of socialism, and matching their interests with the overall interest of the nation. And secondly, providing leadership which reflects the specific interests and problems of each sector which does not always fall within the scope of activity and work of institutions such as the party and the state agencies, whose fundamental responsibility is the strategic objectives of the revolution and questions of general and common interest to all the people.

We can combine these general interests with the specific and particular interests of each sector with the help of the mass organizations.

With regard to the fulfillment of this dual function, the role of the mass organizations has been masterly synthesized in Lenin's words, calling them "transmission belts" which link the vanguard to the rest of the working masses.

The trade unions, because of the important role they play in the production and service units under the administration of People's Power, must undertake fundamental tasks concerning their relations with the latter, and in other aspects of the economic activity of the municipality, region, or province. Because of the territorial characteristics of the CDRs, ANAP, and the FMC, and their work content, these organizations are meant to play a most important role in supporting certain tasks and responsibilities of People's Power organs.

Finding the most suitable ways of collaboration and coordination between these mass organizations and the People's Power organs is your task. One of the results derived from the People's Power experience in Matanzas Province should be a more concrete and varied definition of these ways and methods.

Comrade delegates, members of the executive committees, and officials of the administrative departments of People's Power:

Before you are tasks of extraordinary historic importance, the results of which will be decisive for the future development of our country.

You are faced with the responsibility of putting the concrete, newly defined forms of our state to the test, because so far these principles are only theory, even though they are of course solid in the sense that they are based on Marxist-Leninist principles which we must simply adjust to our specific conditions.

You are also faced with the responsibility of finding answers to many of the questions in this field for which we haven't even a theoretical solution, so that at the end of the experiment we will have results that will be as complete and far-reaching as possible.

With your work you will have to demonstrate that the actual functioning of the organs of People's Power implies greater efficiency in the work of the state apparatus, and because of this you must wage a resolute struggle against bureaucracy in all its forms, such as endless paper work, passing the buck, needless delays in solving problems, filling offices with unnecessary workers, etc.

We must prevent the organs of People's Power from being needlessly packed with people. Nowhere must there be a single man more than is needed to do an efficient job!

As Fidel indicated on July 26, you must strive for the greatest possible saving of material and human resources, for maximum economic efficiency, and for strict accounting and control.

You must struggle to make possible the fulfillment of the economic plans, technological development in production and services, work discipline, increasing work productivity; and all of that not only in regard to the activities and units which are to be transferred to People's Power, but also in regard to those which are to remain subordinate to the central state agencies from the administrative point of view. And the organs of People's Power must remain closely coordinated with, and there must be mutual aid between them and these units of the central state. Be aware of the problems which they may have and the possibilities which the organs of People's Power may have for helping or giving support to them.

In order to accomplish all this the work commissions for which provisions have been made should be set up quickly, and I should like to suggest to you that before anything else and wherever possible, a work commission should be set up to supervise, to check on — and by this I mean to be informed about and to search for ways of lending a hand — all these activities related to sugar production, both agricultural and industrial — since, as you know, this is our country's main source of income.

I would also like to suggest the setting up of a work commission that would cover the production of root and other vegetables in both the state and the private sector, but with special attention to the latter.

Top priority should be given to the harvesting of root and other vegetables, because this has a great bearing on an adequate supply of food for the population. We know that during the last few years great successes have been achieved in this field in Matanzas. People's Power must maintain and improve upon what has already been accomplished and we are sure this will be so.

You should consider ways and means to solve the problems of services for the population which are poor and, in some cases, practically nonexistent.

We all know how difficult it is to find a carpenter, plumber, electrician, or mason who can do work on a private house, but these are top-priority needs for the population. All the people with these skills in a given area should be located. Ways should be found — duly authorized and controlled ways — for letting them do repair work on the homes of the people in the area during their off hours, the people themselves setting the terms of contract in keeping with norms which it will be necessary to establish, and with the complete guarantee that this will never adversely affect the job they do in the work center.

You must be the zealous guardians of socialist legality, "enemies of the old law and staunch defenders of the new," as Fidel said. You must be on your guard against any violation of the law and see to it that no agreement or resolution of the organs of People's Power contradicts existing laws.

Moreover, the organs of People's Power must not accept or carry out any resolution from the superior levels of People's Power or the central state agencies which violate existing laws.

The organs of People's Power must fulfill and see to it that everyone, and that includes both institutions and people in an area under their jurisdiction, strictly fulfill the law. In order to do so the organs of People's Power should seek the aid of the state prosecutors, whose work must be made more efficient, dynamic, and effective.

As Fidel has said, in all the administrative branches of People's Power and in all the centers of production and services under People's Power, you must instill the habit of treating the people with respect and take all necessary measures to ensure this.

You must obtain more and better results with the same resources.

You must educate your electors, the masses in each circumscription, on the problems we have, on what can and cannot be solved for the time being. You must explain to them that People's Power is not going to produce miracle solutions.

We must avoid creating false illusions among the masses; but it is also your responsibility to ensure that the masses are not let down in what they can and logically do expect from you: you must handle the resources of the people more efficiently and must find ways in which to produce more and better-quality goods and services with the same amount of resources. This is something which is up to you to achieve.

Efficiency, more productivity, better quality, strict control over resources, less bureaucracy, solutions for problems that are in your hands to solve, and proposals for solutions that are outside of your possibilities, but which can be solved at other levels; the correct functioning of the organs of People's Power; ideas as to the concrete forms which are most suitable for the organs of People's Power in our country.

This is what the people of Matanzas and all Cuba — as well as the party, the revolution, and the homeland — expect of you, and we are convinced that, as has been the case in the earlier phase, so in this new phase of the experiment,

Matanzas will also make the grade!

Thank you very much.

A New Type of Election

September 28, 1976

NOTE: Following the Matanzas experiment the process of institutionalization accelerated. A constitution was drafted, discussed in assemblies throughout Cuba, and approved in a national referendum on February 15, 1976, by a vote of 5,473,534 in favor to 54,070 opposed. On July 5 of that year a law promulgating a new political and administrative structure took effect, and two days later an election law was enacted. In August, assemblies were held all across the country to nominate candidates, and on October 10 more than five million Cubans — 95.2 percent of the eligible voters — participated in the first national elections to People's Power.

The following excerpt is from Castro's speech on the anniversary of the founding of the Committees for the Defense of the Revolution where he discussed the character of these elections. It is taken from Granma Weekly Review, *October 10, 1976.*

On these occasions, it is also customary to analyze the work done by the Committees for the Defense of the Revolution in the course of the year. As in all preceding years, we could point out the countless efforts made by the Committees for the Defense of the Revolution in every field with increasing success and efficiency. On this occasion, [CDR National Coordinator] Comrade [Jorge] Lezcano didn't mention any figures in connection with such achievements, since the main topic at this celebration was the efforts made to contribute to the establishment of People's Power and the call for the First Congress of the Committees for the Defense of the Revolution. [*Applause*]

Indeed, in addition to their customary tasks, the CDRs have put a great effort into assisting with the activities that are being carried out in connection with the implementation of the resolutions of the First Congress of the party. A great amount of work was involved in the organization of the referendum to proclaim the socialist constitution of our country. A tremendous effort was also involved in the tasks related to the new political-administrative division and the setting up of People's Power; all the work having to do with the identification cards, registration of voters, and the organization of the whole process; the mobilization of the masses, all the assemblies that must be held. And the Committees for the Defense of the Revolution have participated in all these things!

It's anything but easy work. It may seem easy from afar, but there are many who would wonder how the miracle of organizing such a perfect referendum comes about. How does the miracle of holding tens of thousands of assemblies of different types with such organization and efficiency come about? Of course, there is leadership work done by the party first of all, but there's also the practical work done in the street, throughout the country, by the Committees for the Defense of the Revolution. That's how the miracle comes about! [*Applause*]

The process is going along beautifully. Some of the data are already known: the data on close to 30,000 assemblies that were held to nominate the presidents and secretaries of the assemblies for the nomination of candidates; on the nearly 30,000 assemblies held to nominate candidates, and the names of and information on practically all the 30,000 candidates who were nominated.

Preparations are now being made for the elections on October 10, the date on which the 108th anniversary of the Cry of Yara is commemorated.* [*Applause*] All of us who took part in those assemblies know what tremendous democratic spirit prevailed in them. Comrade Lezcano said that they were the most honest, most democratic elections ever held in this hemisphere, and, in truth, he wasn't exaggerating. All of you know the way in which these assemblies were organized and the way they developed, the way the presidents were elected and the way the candidates were nominated. It wasn't the party or anybody in particular who did the nominating. It was the masses, the people, who did it, taking into account the attitude, the conduct, the past, and the prestige of each citizen.

In order to make our process even more democratic, the number of candidates is not limited to one or two. This is done only in exceptional cases, when the circumscription is very small. Three, four, and even as many as eight candidates are nominated, and in order to be elected to the assembly, a candidate must have 50 percent of the votes plus one. It is not enough for one among five, seven, or eight to get the most votes. He or she must get 50 percent plus one. And, since in a countless number of cases nobody gets 50 percent plus one in the first round, we go to the trouble of holding a second election to choose between the two candidates with the largest number of votes. [*Applause*]

It can be asserted that the number of candidates does not include all the best revolutionaries, because many worthy comrades could not be included in the elections to the municipal assembly on account of their ac-

*The Cry of Yara marked the beginning of the 1868 war for Cuba's independence from Spain.

tivities, of their commitments. But it can be said that the nearly 30,000 candidates who were nominated include many of the best citizens of our country. [*Applause*] And, to tell the truth, it is not at all easy to choose; it is not at all easy to decide who to vote for after analyzing each candidate's record.

There's no politicking of any kind, no personal ambition, no individualism in these elections. It is the people who choose the candidates, not the candidates who choose themselves. Whoever chose himself would never be nominated by the masses. It's the people who decided whom to vote for after having analyzed the candidates' biographies and taking into account the conduct of each citizen. Where, anywhere in the hemisphere, have such conditions ever existed for the elections of representatives of the people's power? [*Applause*]

In the United States they are going to hold a presidential election and, according to the dispatches, estimates are that at least 50 percent of the people will not vote.

Yesterday some journalists asked me what I thought of the elections in the United States. My answer was that if it was true that the majority of the voters in the United States were not interested in the elections, why should we be interested in them? [*Applause*]

In many of the elections that are held in the so-called representative democracies less than 30 percent of the electors vote. Here, in the assemblies to nominate candidates — nomination assemblies, not elections — 76.7 percent of the electors attended and we believe the turnout on election day will be much greater.

Progress has been noted in this process in different areas. For example, following the first assemblies held in Matanzas Province we noted that only 7 percent of the candidates were women, and this time 13.4 percent of the candidates, that is nearly double, are women. [*Applause*]

This means that the effort, the campaign, the struggle for equal rights for women is taking root and gaining ground; 13.4 percent is still not very much, but it is much more than at the start, and in some places it was much more than 13, more than 15, and even as much as 20, especially in urban areas. In rural areas it was generally a bit less. Our peasants still haven't understood these concepts of equal rights for women as well as our urban workers.[*Applause*] And in some provinces it was of course less than others.

On the other hand, a large percentage of the candidates nominated by the masses are members of the party or the Young Communist League (UJC) — 70.4 percent of the total [*Applause*] in spite of the fact that no special effort was made in this regard, because it was pointed out that there might be many citizens who have the merits and the abilities to be representatives in the assemblies even though they are not in the party or the UJC.

But the fact that the masses picked such a high percentage of members of the party and the UJC shows the great prestige which they have in the eyes of the masses. [*Applause*] And it also surely shows that in the ranks of the masses there are many who meet all the requirements to be party members but who are still not in its ranks. [*Applause*] But it is preferable, and it will always be preferable, for our party to be selective and to establish strict standards for entry! It is better to exaggerate in the strict nature of the selective process than to become careless in the selection of members for our party! [*Applause*]

This process also shows that there are citizens who did not have revolutionary merits in the past and, in some cases, they even had shortcomings. But they have made great efforts to improve themselves, as can be seen by the fact that some of the candidates who were nominated have no revolutionary past and some of them even have negative things on their record. However, when it happens that the negative aspect does not appear in the biography and it becomes known, the issue is discussed with the candidate, and he has a choice: he can say: "I resign; I'd rather that didn't appear in the biography," or he can say, "Put it in the biography."

The majority of the people in this situation have decided — and we feel the decision is a correct one — that the matter in question be included in the biography and thus be made known to the masses. [*Applause*] This is really inspiring and human. We feel that any citizen may have made a mistake at a given moment but then he may make great and extraordinary efforts to vindicate himself. [*Applause*]

On October 10, nearly 10,000 delegates will be elected to the municipal assemblies. In late October they will set up the assemblies in their respective municipalities and elect the delegates to the provincial level and the members of the executive committees of the municipal assemblies.

On November 2, those same 10,000 delegates will elect the delegates to the National Assembly of People's Power from their respective municipalities. [*Applause*] On December 2, the day of the twentieth anniversary of the *Granma* landing, the National Assembly of People's Power will be established. [*Applause*] This National Assembly will be the highest organ of state power and it will make the key decisions in state policies, including the power to modify the constitution and make laws. What might be called the provisional period of the revolutionary process comes to an end and our socialist state takes definitive shape.

Nobody claims that what is being done is perfect no matter how much effort we devote to trying to make things turn out in the best possible way. Only life itself will be able to tell us where the shortcomings are and which aspects or details leave something to be desired. But we will always be able to improve the instruments we have established.

This step is of great political and historical importance.

Speech to the National Assembly
of People's Power

December 2, 1976

NOTE: The first meeting of the National Assembly of People's Power, the highest state body in Cuba, took place on December 2, 1976. It marked the completion of an important stage in the institutionalization of the Cuban revolution. At this meeting Castro was elected president of the Council of Ministers and of the Council of State.

The following is Castro's speech to the assembly. The text is from Granma Weekly Review, *December 12, 1976.*

Distinguished guests;
Dear comrades:

With warmth and fraternity we greet the friendly delegations visiting us on the occasion of this meeting and this date. Those who are not afraid to travel to Cuba, those who do not need United States permission to maintain relations with us, [*Applause*] those not ignorant of the un-challengeable right every human collectivity has to build a just future, those who — whether or not they share our revolution's political ideology — know there is no possible alternative to mutual respect, friendship, collaboration, and peace among people, enjoy all our consideration, our hospitality, and our respect.

The highest level of political thought was reached when some men became aware that no people and no man had the right to exploit others, and that the fruits of the efforts and intelligence of each human being should reach all others; that man really had no need to be a wolf, but could be a brother to man. That is the main essence of the premises of socialism. But raised to its highest expression with the ideas of Marx, Engels, and Lenin, socialism also taught us the laws that govern the development of human society and the paths that lead to the final triumph of our species over all forms of slavery, exploitation, discrimination, and injustice among men.

We greet all those who have arrived at these stimulating convictions and we also greet those who, although they do not share these ideas, are honest democrats and progressives, because consistently practiced political honesty is a road that leads man's mind and will to the socialist ideal; for if someone once said that all roads led to Rome, today it can be stated that all roads of progressive thinking lead to socialism. [*Applause*]

At this historic and far-reaching meeting we are witnessing, the revolutionary government's provisional period ends and our socialist state adopts definitive institutional forms. The National Assembly is constituted as the highest state body and assumes the functions assigned it by the constitution. It was a duty and it is at the same time a great triumph for our generation to have reached this goal.

When I speak of our generation, I don't mean only those of us who started the struggle at the Moncada, continued it in the *Granma* and the Sierra Maestra, carried it on during the critical moments of Girón and the hard years of noble, dedicated, and lofty struggle that came afterwards. Here, really, are the fruits of more than one generation's efforts, from those who fought forcefully against Machado* — symbolized today by Juan Marinello, senior president of this assembly [*Applause*] — to our combative and enthusiastic youth — represented as secretaries by the young nineteen-year-old woman worker and woman student [*Applause*] who weren't yet born when the *Granma* landed. And so, on December 4, — in the brilliant military review which bad weather forced us to cancel today — along with the courageous fighters of the Sierra Maestra there will march their sons who are now officers in our glorious Revolutionary Armed Forces, or valiant Camilitos from our military vocational schools.† As the sons of the warriors of '68 fought in the war of '95, so the sons of the fighters of '56 now march with their fathers in 1976. The generation of the grandfathers, fathers, and sons who resolutely confronted imperialism, the tyranny, and social injustice, are gathered in this great assembly. [*Applause*]

Here there are no differences, as there are in the bourgeois world, between military and civilians, whites and Blacks, men and women, young and old, because all of us enjoy equal duties and rights. Nor are there, fortunately, differences between rich and poor, exploiters and exploited, powerful and humble, because the revolution eliminated the political power of the bourgeoisie and the big landowners to forge the workers' state. They are all our deputies: manual or intellectual workers, men and women, old and young, soldiers and civilians, who dedicate their lives to the service of the homeland and the revolution, or study and learn in order to be the heirs of our ideas, our efforts, and our struggles.

In our revolution there are no politicians because we are all political, from the Pioneer to the retired pensioner. Those who work in the party and the state are not those seeking position but those assigned a task by party members and the people. Under socialism positions are not sought,

*Gerardo Machado was the Cuban dictator overthrown in 1933.

†This refers to students at the Camilo Cienfuegos Military School.

citizens do not run for office. Neither wealth, nor social relations, nor family, nor publicity and propaganda — as happens in bourgeois society — determine or can in any way determine a man's role in society. It is merit, exclusively merit — ability, modesty, total commitment to work, to the revolution, and to the cause of the people — that determines the confidence society places in any of its children. One single electoral notice is displayed for the elections: the citizen's biography and work record. And when it comes time to choose, not just a few but many can be given that confidence. Not all the meritorious men and women in our country are present and it is impossible for them to be present in this assembly; but all who are here are men and women of unquestionable merit, worthy representatives of all the people.

These people's representatives receive no pay whatsoever as deputies. Nor do they do their job without control by their fellow citizens. They can be recalled at any time by those who elected them. None of them will be above the law nor above the rest of their compatriots. Their jobs do not bring them privilege but rather duties and responsibilities. Also, under our system, the government and the administration of justice depend directly on the National Assembly. There is division of functions but there is not division of power. Power is one, the power of the working people exercised through the National Assembly and the state bodies depending on it. Our type of state takes into account the experience gathered by other people who have traveled the socialist road, and our own practice. We apply the essential principles of Marxism-Leninism to our concrete conditions, as a truly revolutionary approach requires.

It is not that our revolution acquires a popular character for this reason. Our revolutionary process was profoundly popular from the beginning and was solidly rooted in the masses. The first sovereign action by the people was the revolution itself. Our revolution was not the result of a coup d'etat. We didn't even have an army at the beginning. Our revolution was not imposed by anyone from outside; it was forged in heroic struggle against imperialist domination and the most inflamed and bitter foreign aggressions; our revolution occurred among the people and was conceived and achieved by humble sons and daughters of the people. Thus, our revolution grew from a small seed that has become a huge tree today; it is yesterday's age-old dream transformed into today's beautiful reality, the will of the people that has now become an irreversible piece of history. [*Applause*]

Beyond that, our revolution is not the exclusive product of our ideas; our very ideas are to a great extent the product of world revolutionary thinking. In this hemisphere there are some who level the odd charge against socialism that it is a foreign idea, as if the language we speak didn't once come from abroad, as if bourgeois liberal ideas and all the principles of capitalism weren't historically born in Europe, as if Christianity was the primitive religion of the natives of this continent, as if culture and science weren't universal. The political line of reactionary and ignorant rulers is often reduced to such a diatribe, when faced with masses subjected to cultural and political illiteracy and the most brutal economic exploitation.

Marxism-Leninism is really deeply internationalist and, at the same time, deeply patriotic. The liberation, progress, and peace of the homeland are indissolubly joined, in our view, to the liberation, progress, and peace of all humanity. Anarchy, wars, unequal development, the fabulous resources invested in weapons, and the risks awaiting humanity today, are the natural fruits of capitalism. Only a just distribution of productive forces, technology, science, and living conditions; only an increasingly more rational use of natural resources; only the closest coordination of the efforts of all the peoples of the world — which is to say, only socialism — can save humanity from the frightful dangers that threaten it: exhaustion of limited natural resources, progressive environmental pollution, uncontrolled population growth, devastating famine, and catastrophic war.

Along with its great scientific and technical achievements and the tremendous development of productive forces, capitalism — which came into the world, as Marx said, "dripping from head to foot from every pore, with blood and dirt" — will go down in history as one of the most cruel, predatory, shameful, and deadly dangers in the evolution of human society, because today it represents the most reactionary ideas, the most inconceivable waste of wealth, improvisation, irresponsibility, and weapons more destructive than human genius has ever before conceived. Only the power, resources, and prestige of the Soviet Union, heading the progressive forces of the entire world, with a wise, vigorous, and persevering peace policy, have been able to curb the threats and dangers that capitalism still represents for the world.

That the most absurd things can happen even within the bosom of the socialist family and in countries that were among the first to take that glorious and revolutionary road, when principles are neglected, when ideas are lost, when men become gods, when internationalism is abandoned, is evident in the recent history of China. That country, whose heroic and selfless revolutionary victory after the glorious October revolution, represented one of the greatest and most inspiring hopes for all the peoples of the earth, has been the scene of the most brutal betrayal of the world revolutionary movement. It would be unjust to blame those noble and dedicated people, or the Chinese Communists, who have given so many proofs of their heroic virtues and their revolutionary spirit.

How then can the events that took place there be explained? How can the fact that China's international policy has wound up associated with imperialism's most backward forces all over the world be explained? Its defense of NATO [North Atlantic Treaty Organization], its friendship with [Chilean dictator Agosto] Pinochet, its criminal complicity with South Africa against the MPLA [Popular Movement for the Liberation of Angola], its hatred and its repugnant campaign against the Soviet Union, its cowardly attacks on Cuba — to the extreme of joining with Yankee imperialism's worst spokesmen in presenting Cuba as a threat to the peoples of Latin America, which is like becoming an accomplice in the blockade and infamous policy of imperialist aggression against our homeland.

All that can happen when a corrupt and arrogant clique is able to take over the party, destroy, humiliate, and crush the best members, and impose its will on an entire nation, based on the strength and prestige that emanates from a deep social revolution. I have always believed that the founders of a revolutionary socialist process acquire such authority and prestige among their fellow citizens, such far-reaching power, that the unrestricted use of that authority, that prestige, and that power can lead to serious error and incredible abuses. And so I think and have always thought that whatever the individual merits of any man, any evidence of the cult of the personality must be radically avoided; that no man, whatever aptitudes he may be said to have, will ever be superior to the collective capacity; that group leadership, unlimited respect for the application of criticism and self-criticism, socialist legality, democracy and party and state discipline, and the inviolability of Marxist-Leninist and socialist standards and basic ideas, are the only values which can sustain a truly revolutionary leadership.

Once, precisely on the commemoration of the twentieth anniversary of the attack on the Moncada, I said: men die, the party is immortal. [*Applause*] Today I wish to add: no man can be above the party; no citizen's will must ever prevail over that of millions of his compatriots; no revolutionary is more important than the revolution. The exercise of power must be the constant practice of self-limitation and modesty.

Today there is a new political leadership in China. There has not been enough time yet to judge what is happening there. Incredible things come out about the way a group of adventurers virtually seized leadership of the party. What is not yet clear in the official explanations from China is how that group was arbitrarily able to direct China's policy for many years, and how Mao Tse-tung's widow was able, during Mao Tse-tung's lifetime, within the ranks of a Communist Party and within a socialist state, to commit those crimes. The experience gained from this must inevitably prove useful to the world revolutionary movement.

The developed capitalist world today is sunk in a deep economic crisis. It hurts all the underdeveloped countries, whose traditional markets are affected by a serious depression, and this also jeopardizes our own country to a certain degree. However, there is an exception in the underdeveloped world: the big oil exporters. They are the privileged recipients of a large share of the income from international trade in this area, and all the economically weak nations of the world — which are the great majority — are being ground on a millstone between them and the developed capitalist countries.

The problem is not easy. The capitalist monopolies owned the world's oil sources and set oil prices. Revolutionary opinion insistently denounced the imperialist companies' monopoly prices and enormous annual profits. The just cause of the people's right to own their natural resources, among them oil, was supported by all progressive states in the world. Over a long period, the interests of the oil-producing and other underdeveloped countries were similar. All demanded, with absolute justice, the revalorization of their raw materials and the end of unequal trade with the developed capitalist world. At the same time, a deep crisis was taking place within the industrialized capitalist countries as a basic result of the aggressive, anarchistic, exploitative, and irresponsible nature of imperialism: the war against Vietnam, huge military expenditures, budget deficits, the decay and waste of the consumer societies, and other problems inseparable from capitalist society.

Developed capitalism's well-worn methods for avoiding and postponing the cyclical crises of the system were increasingly ineffective. Inflation became uncontrollable. At the same time, the growing resistance of the working masses to accepting the main burden of the hardships made it more difficult for their governments to apply classical bourgeois formulas. The last war in the Middle East and the subsequent oil embargo by the Arab nations against a sizeable group of industrialized countries that traditionally supported the Israeli aggressor, occurred under these conditions. At this juncture, the price of oil rose sharply, also benefiting the producers that had not joined the embargo. At that point, the OPEC [Organization of Petroleum-Exporting Countries] countries, motivated by strictly economic interests, understanding the power they held by monopolizing the major share of oil commercialized on the world market, and by owning a raw material essential to all nations, set the price four or five times higher than it had been before the embargo, which exacerbated and deepened the world economic crisis still further.

The fact that Algeria, Iraq, and other countries that maintain a progressive international policy were among the oil-producing countries, the sympathies many peoples have for the Arab cause, Yankee imperialism's brutal threats, and other such factors, influenced almost all the underdeveloped countries to make common cause with the oil-producers. Those countries couldn't have acted in a more disinterested and solidary manner since they were unable to bear the enormous economic weight of the exorbitant fuel price for their mere subsistence, let alone any modest development. The very fact that a handful of oil-exporting countries, colonized only a short time before, could impose such a demand without immediately being invaded and occupied by the imperialists, was only possible because of the new world correlation of forces, the bold struggle of all peoples in recent decades, and international solidarity.

That presumed, as an elemental counterpart, that the oil-producing countries would make the cause of the underdeveloped world their cause and would share with it, to a reasonable degree, the new and extensive finances that fell into their hands. That is what the Cuban government proposed publicly at that time. It was essential and at least just to find some solution for supplying those countries with an adequate supply of oil at a reasonable price. This would have been the only sensible and intelligent policy for keeping the peoples of the so-called Third World united in one single front in the common struggle against their historical exploiters. Except for isolated exceptions, nothing like that happened. Some oil-producing countries, particularly the largest producers with the smallest populations, began to accumulate fabulous sums of money and to invest it immediately in real estate stocks and industries in the United States, England, the Federal Republic of Germany, and other European industrialized countries to such a point that, very soon, no one will be able to tell the difference between the interests of those states and the interests of international finance capital, that is, the imperialist monopolies.

This selfish and erroneous attitude is in no way compatible with the exemplary solidarity shown by the underdeveloped countries, and is explicable, among other things, by the widely heterogeneous and diversified beliefs and political systems that exist among the OPEC countries, which practically reached unanimous agreement on one single point only: to raise prices.

Not all the OPEC countries have the same policy: some — like Algeria, Iraq, Libya, Kuwait, Nigeria, and Venezuela — hold progressive positions on many questions and are sincerely concerned by the international economic situation. But it is an undeniable fact that the two biggest oil producers, Iran and Saudi Arabia, where volumes surpass those of all the other OPEC member countries together, waste billions of dollars buying sophisticated weapons in the United States, thereby helping that imperialist country's modernization and sale of surplus and obsolete military equipment, and the maintenance of its war industry, not to mention the employment of thousands of military technicians at incredible salaries stationed in those two countries. The shah of Iran's delusions of grandeur, the fantastic number of weapons that rust in the hands of the inept soldiers of the king of Arabia, and the fabulous luxuries of the reactionary sultans of the Persian Gulf, are paid for with the sweat and hunger of hundreds of millions of men and women, old people and children, in the underdeveloped world. And that is literally so. Because the developed capitalist countries have attached the high price of oil onto all the equipment, fertilizer, food, and manufactured products in general that they export to the underdeveloped countries which, at the same time, have seen their markets drop still further, their export products devalued, while they must also pay almost $100 a ton for the oil they use. The industrialized capitalist countries have still other formulas for dealing with that high price, among them the sale of military equipment, as mentioned before, which becomes useless junk in less time than it takes the oppressed subjects of the Persian shah and the Saudi kings to learn to handle it. It is the repetition, in modern times, of the classical legend of America's European conquerors who bought the Indians' gold with mirrors and colored glass.

No one denies that oil is an exhaustible resource, as are the other minerals that many countries of Africa, Asia, and Latin America also export, and that also deserve to be priced remuneratively; no one denies that oil is a product that has been criminally wasted by the consumer societies and that a policy of conservation and rational use should be applied to it. But why do the underdeveloped countries, with fewer economic and often fewer natural resources as well, have to bear the main, overwhelming, and intolerable burden of the capitalist economic crisis: unapproachable prices for their imports, depression in their markets, and foreign exchange expenditures for oil that are ten times higher than its production costs? What are the short- and middle-range consequences of this situation for the world? How can any campaign be organized against hunger, malnutrition, disease, illiteracy, the lack of drinking water and housing — against poverty, when all is said and done — in a world whose population already stands at four billion inhabitants and in which one out of every three people is undernourished?

Events are demonstrating that the excessive and abusive overvalorization of a raw material in world trade, through the monopolistic and unilateral action of some few who have it, can be effected only at the cost of devaluating all other raw materials and products from which the vast majority of the underdeveloped countries of the world live. That is no way to overcome unequal trade, which is now still more unfavorable for this majority of countries, and it shows no solidarity whatsoever among the exploited countries, but is rather a demonstration of narrow and selfish nationalism. It is not the same to ask from the rich as to rob from the poor.

It is true that among the non-oil-producing underdeveloped countries there are also reactionary governments and unjust social systems, but we defend principled positions.

These burning problems demonstrate the increasingly pressing need for all countries to seek rational means of cooperation, development, distribution of technology and resources. This is exactly what Marx predicted more than 100 years ago, when the planet's population and humanity's difficulties were nothing like today's. No people are willing to die of starvation; and among the underdeveloped nations of the world, the oil-exporting countries are not the only ones who have a right to live.

Recently we discussed Cuba's problems as a result of these factors. Sugar, except for what we supply to the USSR and other socialist countries, is suffering not only from low prices, but from depressed markets. Countries such as Japan, which in recent years purchased as much as a million tons of Cuban sugar, bought only 130,000 tons in 1976, and the same thing has happened in other capitalist markets. This causes problems for us and forces us to apply drastic restrictions in the trade with those markets, because for us, the principle of meeting our international financial obligations comes before the acquisition of new merchandise and industrial plants. The restrictions in the international economy are in no way pleasant. We know that. Improvements will always be accepted with much greater satisfaction. But the strength of a people and of a revolution lies precisely in their ability to understand and face up to difficulties. In spite of everything, we will move ahead in many fields and we will struggle boldly to raise the economy's efficiency, save resources, reduce nonessential expenses, expand exports, and create economic consciousness in every citizen. I said before that we are all political and now I add that we must all be economic as well and I repeat, economic, not "economist," for a mentality of saving and efficiency is not the same as a consumer mentality.

A little while ago it was necessary, for reasons that have been explained, to reduce coffee consumption. This was applied to social consumption and to individual consumption. I must say that the restriction began with the political, mass, and administrative organizations. The quotas for canecutters, night workers, and others were respected as much as possible. I wish to point out that as soon as they learned of these restrictions Comrade Agostinho Neto and other Angolan leaders communicated to our representatives in Angola their readiness to send coffee to Cuba on any basis required. [*Applause*] We were moved by this gesture but to accept it was out of the question. [*Applause*] Fifteen thousand tons of coffee today are worth $40 million and Angola, a country destroyed by war and facing tremendous difficulties, needs that income. We cannot consume in coffee resources that we have helped defend and create with our sweat and our blood. [*Applause*] Neto's gesture was highly internationalist; Cuba's attitude has to be highly internationalist.

Cuba has to produce coffee no matter what the climatic difficulties may be. Moreover, under the new conditions created by the revolution, many peasants tend to emigrate from the coffee-producing mountainous areas where unemployment and hunger drove them in the past. Their children are studying with broad perspectives for becoming technicians and skilled workers. Other hopes are stirred. At the same time, the consumer population is much larger. ANAP must make the greatest efforts to raise the consciousness of peasants in these areas in order to stimulate production. The National Bank must study problems connected with credit and adequate financial resources. The Ministry of Agriculture must consider prices, renewal of plantations, input, and other necessary factors. The policy of establishing junior and senior high schools in the mountains, with their study and work programs, must be continued. In short, special attention will have to be paid to coffee production under the new social conditions. In the name of the entire nation, we urge the eastern provinces, whose representatives are here, to make a special technical and productive effort in coffee cultivation. The same goes for the former provinces of Las Villas, Pinar del Río, and Havana, where there are also coffee plantations on a smaller scale.

The First Congress of the Communist Party of Cuba took place a year ago. Intensive party and state activities have been displayed during the months since then to fulfill its resolutions. The socialist constitution was approved in an exemplary referendum. All the steps leading to the new political-administrative division were taken. The nomination of candidates and election of delegates to the municipal assemblies was carried out brilliantly and enthusiastically and served as the basis for the subsequent steps: election of provincial delegates and deputies to the National Assembly and the establishment of People's Power at the municipal and provincial levels. The new provinces were officially created this past November 7.

At the same time, over months of intensive work, the draft restructuring of the central state body was drawn up according to constitutional principles, the new political-administrative division, the establishment of People's Power, the Economic Management and Planning System which is ready to be applied, and the necessary search for maximum efficiency, uniformity, and minimum cost to the central administration. Although this is terrain over which we still can and must advance in years to come, the functions, structures, and required personnel for all bodies of the state central administration were able to be defined with adequate precision, and written into an important piece of legislation called the Law of Organization of the State Central Administration, passed by the Council of Ministers in one of its last meetings as a legislative power. Under this law, forty-three central organizations were established, thirty-four of which are state committees or ministries whose directors will have the rank of minister and, together with the president of the government and the designated vice-presidents and its secretary, will make up the Council of Ministers. With this structure and the abolition of regions, the administrative personnel in the central administration is considerably reduced under the present plan. The workers who have been made available will be relocated in other service or productive activities. As is logical, they will not be left to their fate, for the government, as it always has, will take whatever measures are necessary for their subsistence and relocation.

At the same time, major administrative decentralization is occurring in state work. The municipalities and provinces now have important functions. The closest coordination among all communities in the country and between them and the central government is more important than ever. Every evidence of local and regional selfishness must be energetically fought, but at the same time it will be the duty of each of the provinces to struggle in a proper, just, and rational way for its development, without ever losing sight of national interests as a whole.

As is evident, profound institutional transformations have taken place in a short time. With the constitution of this National Assembly, the election of the Council of State, its president and vice-presidents, and the designation of the Council of Ministers, this historical process of institutionalization of our revolution is basically concluded.

In the future, the National Assembly will approve the republic's economic plans and budget, among the many and important functions the constitution assigns it. There is no need to fear facing up to the difficulties. And if international economic reality and the limitation of our natural resources force us to make more modest plans, we will do so without hesitation or discouragement, since our motto is and will always be to do the maximum and to do everything for our people. Let's be valiant in performing our duties and let's always behave like true revolutionaries.

Who can deny that this process reaching its culmination today is an advancement we can all be proud of, a settling of accounts with history and with our revolutionary consciences, the happy fulfillment of a sacred duty that emerged at the time of the Moncada, and unequivocable proof of our revolution's loyalty to principles? Now we must all adapt our minds to the changes we have made, work with enthusiasm and confidence under the new conditions, comply strictly with standards, and struggle tirelessly to see that the new institutions function at their best.

Today marks twenty years since the landing of the *Granma*. With the passage of time, the yacht *Granma* seems to all of us to become smaller and the course of 1,500 miles, from Tuxpan to the Coloradas, infinitely longer. Then it seemed to us to be a marvelous vehicle for carrying our eighty-two combatants and the tempestuous sea a beautiful road by which to return happily to the homeland to keep a promise. No one is able to estimate the force and decision that just ideas can generate in the human spirit. Similar deeds took place later in many forms. A victorious army was reconstructed on the basis of seven rifles shouldered by the hungry and exhausted remains of that expedition; with a handful of men, Raúl [Castro] and [Juan] Almeida opened the second and third fronts;

300 fighters defeated an offensive of 10,000 soldiers in the Sierra Maestra; Che [Guevara] and Camilo [Cienfuegos] with 140 and 90 proven veterans, invaded Las Villas in an epic march, fiercely pursued by thousands of enemy soldiers. It is that spirit of the *Granma* that, almost twenty years later, inspired our men who flew 10,000 kilometers across the Atlantic in planes that were over twenty years old, to support our Angolan brothers, [*Applause*] and those who covered the same distance in a voyage of some twenty days in merchant ships carrying three times the personnel they had been calculated to handle in any logistics operation.

Only a few survived the Moncada and the *Granma* and you can count on your fingers the members of our armed forces who participated in those events; but young workers, peasants, and students filled the gaps that death left in our ranks. An entire people enrolled in the cause of the revolution and our force was infinitely multiplied from then on. It was the idea, the conviction of defending a just cause, that created this miracle. A beautiful tradition of heroism was created among Cuban youth that nourished the new combatants with strength, self-confidence, and the spirit of invincible determination. That is why Cuba has been able to resist — lofty, unconquered, and heroic — the assaults of Yankee imperialism.

In recent days the Political Bureau made the decision to designate new names for the ranks of our Revolutionary Armed Forces, to conform with international practice. This was carefully considered over a long period of time. In our lives as revolutionary fighters we were always extremely cautious about rank. Our highest military rank in the Sierra Maestra was major. We really had three ranks: lieutenant, captain, and major. As you know, we began with 82 men, then we were few and later many more. At the end of the war, we had approximately 3,000 men under arms. Those who commanded columns and opened new fronts: Raúl, Almeida, Camilo, Che, and others held the rank of major. Great feats in the military field were accomplished with modest ranks. When the revolution triumphed we maintained our ranks. Our Revolutionary Armed Forces grew tremendously and we maintained our ranks. This became virtually a rule for the revolutionary movements that emerged after the Cuban revolution. Following our tradition, no one held a rank higher than major.

The day arrived when we needed to organize and lead an enormous army with those ranks. At heart, we had a deep hatred of certain high-level military titles. It was logical in those who grew up seeing the abuses, injustices, robberies, and bribery in a mercenary army that oppressed the people and against which we had fought. But it is also true that the victorious revolution had no point of contact in the universal language of military hierarchical terminology.

Beginning with the socialist countries, our ranks were different. We had to direct army regiments, divisions, and corps. We dreamed up the ranks of first captain, first major, etc. Then brigade major, division major, and so on. But we were still unable to make the world understand our military ranks. A deep-rooted modesty prevented us from changing the names of our ranks.

In a country like China, in the crazy years of the so-called Cultural Revolution, they even reached the point of eliminating military ranks. We, on the contrary, reached the conclusion that some day we would be able to eliminate the armies, when socialism becomes a universal system in the world and peace truly reigns among peoples; but that while imperialism exists, the socialist countries needed armies, and while armies existed, military ranks were necessary.

Applying the same principle of eliminating hierarchies to all other institutions, the names of secretary of the party, president of the party, president of the republic, head of state, factory manager, etc., would have to be eliminated.

At the same time, the fact that our country was a state occupied by a mercenary army in imperialism's service during the years of the pseudo-republic, was not reason enough to fail to take into account our heroic *mambí*, who in the wars of independence, 1868 and 1895, used the ranks of colonel and general. Máximo Gómez, Antonio Maceo, and Ignacio Agramonte were generals.* [*Applause*] A few days after he landed at Playitas, José Martí was given the rank of major general of the Liberation Army by Máximo Gómez and received it with deep emotion and pride.

Starting practically from scratch, our revolutionary army confronted and defeated Batista's mercenary army, pulverized the counterrevolutionary groups, wiped out the army organized and trained by the Pentagon and the CIA in less than seventy-two hours at Playa Girón; heroically and unhesitatingly bore the mortal nuclear risk of the October Crisis. It has defended the country against the most powerful imperialism in the world and, on an important internationalist mission, together with its Angolan brothers, destroyed in a few months the imperialist-racist coalition that tried to seize Angola. Our officers have been constantly improving themselves and acquiring skills. At the end of twenty years of its existence, we believe our Revolutionary Armed Forces well deserve to have the appropriate ranks used in all parts of the world to organize and direct the country's defense.

We know our military well, we know what deep ties they have with the people and the cause of socialism, their modesty, their dedication,

---

*Gómez, Maceo, and Agramonte were leaders in the 1868-78 war of independence. Gómez and Maceo also fought in Cuba's second war of independence.

their austerity, their discipline, their patriotism, and their attitude of unconditional respect for our party and our people's state. As Camilo said, they are the people in uniform. Thus, we urge the National Assembly to support and ratify this decision made by our party and our Council of Ministers. [*Prolonged applause*]

A formal act is all we have left: to state that, at this moment, the revolutionary government transfers to the National Assembly the power it has held up to now. Thus, the Council of Ministers invests this assembly with the constitutional and legislative functions it exercised for almost eighteen years, the period of the most radical and deep political and social transformations in our country's life. Let history judge this epoch objectively!

As for me, dear comrades, I am a tireless critic of our own work. We could have done everything better from the Moncada up to today. The light that indicates what could have been the best choice in each case is experience, but unfortunately the youth who start along the hard and difficult road of revolution do not have it. Nevertheless, this helps us learn that we are not wise men and that for each decision, there might perhaps have been a better one.

With extraordinary affection, you attribute great merit to your leaders. I know that no man has exceptional merits and that we can learn great lessons every day from the most humble comrades.

If I were to have the privilege of living my life over again, I would do many things differently from the way I have done them up to now; but at the same time I can assure you that I would fight all my life with the same passion for the same objectives I have fought for up to now. [*Exclamations of "Fidel, Fidel!"*]

Patria o muerte!

Venceremos! [*Ovation*]

Trade Unions in a Workers' State

December 2, 1978

NOTE: The Fourteenth Congress of the Central Organization of Cuban Trade Unions (CTC) was held November 28–December 2, 1978, attended by 2,083 delegates. It marked the continued progress of the Cuban trade union movement in representing the immediate and long-range interests of the Cuban working class. The following excerpts are from Castro's closing speech to that congress, reprinted from Granma Weekly Review, *December 17, 1978.*

Distinguished guests;

Comrades of the leadership of the party and of the government;

Delegates to the fourteenth workers' congress:

It is not easy to give the closing speech of an event that has been so rich in content, in ideas, and in results as this one. I will try to convey some of my thoughts, some of my impressions. Someone said yesterday in a brief conversation that it seemed as though the Thirteenth Congress was only yesterday, and I replied, "Well, it seems to me as though it was this morning." [*Applause*]

That's how fast five years of our workers' and of our people's productive, revolutionary life seem to pass. But what a lot of important events have taken place in these five years since 1973. In the first place, the congress of our party in 1975; then the discussion and approval of the constitution of the republic; the institutionalization; the political-administrative division of the country; the setting up of People's Power; the start made in the establishment of the Economic Management and Planning System; as well as other major efforts that have required the mass organizations to adapt to new circumstances and have required of everyone, especially our workers, an intense activity.

The trade union movement's achievements during these five years were brilliantly analyzed in the main report. The advances really have been impressive. I won't try to repeat them all, but we could give one example: the field of education within the trade union movement, the struggle to reach the sixth grade, a struggle put forward at the Thirteenth Congress, where some doubted that we could achieve a target of one million workers reaching sixth grade between the time of the congress and 1980.

And as the main report said, this target has virtually been reached, which means that the minimum level of education of our workers — the minimum! — will have been brought by 1980 to the sixth grade. And today's sixth grade is not just any old sixth grade; it is not a sixth grade that is easy to reach.

On the basis of this victory, the goal now set for 1985 is the ninth grade. Yes, I know that people are talking about a half-million workers reaching the ninth grade by 1985. This is what you have committed yourselves to. But in reality it is a modest target. [*Laughter*] It's modest, and we think it's fine that you have approved a modest goal; but generally speaking, we must struggle for the ninth grade to be the minimum educational level for our workers by 1985. [*Applause*]

People all over the world talk a lot about how the literacy campaign, the eradication of illiteracy, was a great success for Cuba. However, in our opinion the easiest battle was the battle against illiteracy; it was more spectacular, but at the same time it was shorter. But I think that our revolution deserves more credit for the efforts that have been made since the literacy campaign. And it will be a much greater victory when we can say that our workers have all reached a minimum of the sixth grade, and when we can say that our workers have all reached a minimum of the ninth grade. And as I am an optimist — I was one, I am one, and I think I always will be one [*Applause*] — I go so far as to claim that by the next congress in 1983 we will be close to winning the battle for the ninth grade, and we will be setting ourselves the battle for the twelfth grade by 1990. [*Applause*]

Do you think it's impossible? [*Shouts of "No!"*] Wasn't it more difficult to achieve the educational level our workers now have? [*Shouts of "Yes!"*] Which was achieved at a time when we barely had any classrooms or teachers. Will it be difficult when in just one year, this year, about 28,000 of our citizens graduated as teachers at the various levels?

Just a few years ago 70 percent of our primary school teachers did not have certificates, and by 1980 they all will be certified. And we have tens of thousands of students in teacher-training schools and tens of thousands at universities, and thousands of primary school teachers who are getting ready to study for a primary school diploma at our universities.

The number of schools is going up each year, the number of teachers is increasing, and we have fewer primary school students. That means that our possibilities are increasing, that the situation is improving objectively and subjectively, so that we can give all the desired support to this extraordinary program of educational and technical betterment for our workers. And then we really will be showing the world what a workers' revolution is and what socialism is.

And we could add that of the 145,000 students now at the university, around 50 percent are workers. [*Applause*] As a result, new problems are beginning to emerge, and one of these is the number of workers who have already graduated from the Worker Education Program or senior high school and have not been able to enroll in university courses. Because we are being confronted with a dilemma that arises from the fact that there is a limit to the capacity of our universities and that we have to find room in the regular courses for the enormous numbers of young students who each year graduate from high school or technical school at the intermediate or senior level. This is a problem we have to tackle; we have to find new solutions in order not to stifle this enormous interest and enthusiasm our workers have for studying and which demands, as I said, a search for new solutions, new formulas, so that everyone who wants to take a course at a higher level can do so, one way or another, if not regular courses, then directed study courses.

These problems were spelled out to the party quite forcefully by the comrades of the CTC, to see how solutions could be arrived at for this situation; since for a start we don't consider it correct to block a young person's chances of continuing to study. So, apart from those workers studying at the university in the normal way, we must think about programs so that workers can take directed study courses, take examinations, and get their diplomas. Because if we already have the problem of this enormous demand from more than 20,000 who have graduated from the Worker Education Program and have not been able to get a place at the university, imagine what it is going to be like in 1985 when we have a minimum of the ninth grade, or later when we have a minimum of the senior high school level. Nobody knows how many are going to want to take university courses.

We think that our society should work so that our people are enriched culturally, intellectually, and technically, without restrictions on this process. So that if everyone wants the honor — and I mean honor, because it would be impossible to consider it any other way if this were the general rule — if everyone wants the honor of having a university degree, then everyone should have the chance to get one; without, of course, this implying that if everyone has a university degree, then everyone is going to have a job that corresponds to that degree. But this is a problem that has to be solved by creating facilities for study, and, of course, in the knowledge that having a degree will not automatically guarantee a job that corresponds to that degree.

In other words, a cane-harvester operator, if he or she wants to, can be a mechanical engineer, but someone has to operate the cane harvesters; if that person is a mechanical engineer, so much the better, because I am sure that the productivity and the maintenance will be incomparably better. [*Applause*]

I say this because it is important that we understand that while there was an enormous shortage of university graduates, every university graduate could with that degree immediately get the appropriate professional job. But the day when our society has tens of thousands and hundreds of thousands and perhaps millions with these degrees, then we won't be able to consider university studies as a way to get a job or a professional position. But we must find a solution to this contradiction and instead of saying to part of the workers, "So you want to study? Well, you can't," we must say to them, "So you want to study? Right, we are going to give you every opportunity to study," without this implying, as I said, that when an enormous number of people are getting degrees, everyone will have a job that corresponds to that degree.

I'm sure you all understand perfectly what I'm trying to say. So, are we all agreed? [*Shouts of "Yes!"*] Or are we going to work so that we are all doctors or engineers, dedicated exclusively to medicine and engineering? [*Shouts of "No!"*]

The time will have to come — and it will come — when jobs like that of engineer of any kind, or doctor, teacher, historian, economist, or whatever, will be allocated on the basis of one's university record. Some way will have to be found. [*Applause*] But we are not going to stop this movement, even at the risk of becoming a society of intellectuals. [*Laughter*]

What will a society of intellectuals be like, anyway? Nobody knows. All the same, some will have to face this problem, the problems of the party, of the state, and of the trade union movement in a society of intellectuals. Because we are on the road to becoming a society of intellectuals, but at the same time — and this is what is so good about it — it will be a society of proletarian intellectuals and a society of revolutionary intellectuals. [*Applause*] And for that reason we are not afraid of it.

Now, since we have not yet reached this stage, and since we still need many technicians in many fields, and we need not only technicians with degrees but also intermediate technicians and many skilled workers, let's come back down to earth [*Laughter*] to suggest that we take great care to channel this university study effort toward the basic careers in which there is a greater need at the present time in Cuba, and above all toward the faculties of technology; and of these faculties, in particular, into the faculty of machine construction, which is very important.

We have been making efforts in various areas, and in some fields we have made a great deal of progress, for example in the training of teachers at the various levels; the number of those studying agricultural engineering and agronomy is increasing rapidly; year by year the number of students enrolled in the faculty of economy and in medicine is going up. We must have the same kind of success with students enrolling in the faculties of technology, and we must take constructive, organizational measures to promote these faculties in our country.

The successes of the trade union movement over these years have been reflected in other areas, such as culture, the amateur performers' movement, and in sports. All of the figures point to an enormous growth in these activities. We have been training new trade union cadres; our national school has been operating at full capacity, as have the provincial schools, and training is given not only to our own cadres, but also to lots of cadres from other countries, especially from Latin America.

We have been advancing a lot in terms of experience; we have been advancing a lot in terms of organization. But, what's more — something which in our opinion is essential — we have been advancing in terms of consciousness, and in terms of revolutionary spirit. One example of this spirit is voluntary work, which has been maintained, has been preserved, and has been enriched. Few things have been so impressive as the spectacle of the last Red Sunday, November 5, in honor of this congress.*

Seldom have we seen such an impressive sight as the massive mobilization of our working people to the work centers, to the factories — and with such enthusiasm. All the estimates were exceeded. People were talking of 1.2 million as a target. And there were something like 1.5 million people. And to me it seemed as though there were more than two million, because everybody took part in the mobilization. As a joke I said there were more workers that Sunday than there are during the week. [*Laughter*] Because perhaps the most extraordinary thing was that there was no absenteeism that Sunday, although it was voluntary work. It's impressive how this tradition, this spirit which Che established in our country, [*Prolonged applause*] has been maintained through twenty years of revolution.

Comrade [Roberto] Veiga mentioned almost all the main subjects discussed in the theses and at this congress, and he did not forget to refer to the importance of the innovators movement. We heard a comrade here talk about the innovators movement and what it means. Equally important are the Youth Technical Brigades, what they have been contributing and what they are capable of creating.†

They have been asking for resources and facilities, and it is right that

---

*A national day of voluntary work, also coinciding with the anniversary of the 1917 Bolshevik revolution in Russia.

†The National Association of Inventors and Innovators was created by the CTC in 1976 and had over 33,000 members by 1980. The Youth Technical Brigades were formed by the Young Communist League and are under its direction. They had over 10,000 members in 1980.

they do so; although, of course, you cannot set up a pilot center in every factory. We will have to study which are the centers that have the most facilities and which locality and which region have the most resources and see how we can channel through these centers the facilities they are requesting for their work. He made a distinction between the technician and the innovator, the one who invents; and he said that although the innovators did not necessarily have to be inventors, they could still be of great help.

We think that this movement should receive the utmost attention and support from the administration and the state. [*Applause*]

I would say that the Thirteenth Congress was a much more difficult congress than this one. There were some really ticklish questions at that congress. [*Laughter*] Among other things, there was the question of tying wages to production, which was the central issue at that congress. But we haven't forgotten that there were other questions, like the famous Resolution 270, which turned out to be impracticable. We had to appeal to the revolutionary consciousness of our workers, to their understanding of the problems, in order to adopt some of the measures of the Thirteenth Congress. But the tying of wages to production was the central issue; the formula of socialist distribution which has had such a great effect on our economy.

For the fruits of tying wages to production and applying the principle that corresponds to the phase we are in, that is, distribution according to work, or socialist distribution, are undeniable.

In some lines of work spectacular results have been obtained, as in the case of port workers, where great effort and good organization also played a key role. Just the fact that their productivity has tripled can serve to give us an idea.

A productivity increase exceeding the salary increase has taken place in practically all sectors, with highly positive results for the nation's economy.

And yet it is obvious that we have not benefited as much as we could have from the application of this principle, that we must go on perfecting and strengthening it in practice, while straightening out any aspects or situations mistakenly handled due to the principle not having been correctly applied, and not letting the difficulties discourage us.

A lot has been said here on agriculture, on the question of getting the fields ready for planting, and on a certain lag in applying the above principle, which is attributed to a lack of interest on the part of the management, to the latter's desire to avoid taking the trouble of setting up the needed controls. Some comrades told me that application of such a principle to agriculture entailed an obligation on the part of the management to make a greater effort and exert greater control.

Needless to say, we should not lag in tying wages to production in agriculture, for actually agriculture is one of the fields where we need to make a greater effort for productivity.

To be truthful, there's something that socialism cannot abolish, there's something that the revolution cannot suppress, and that's work. We're all familiar with how things were in the past in our fields: unemployment, on the one hand; on the other, fierce competition among the workers to land jobs which were relatively in abundance during the harvest season and hard to find the rest of the year.

We're all familiar with the situation of the canecutters then, the early hour they had to start work. The ox-cart drivers had to be in the fields by two in the morning to start loading the cane by hand — no cane loaders were around then; we didn't have anything then. Working conditions in the fields forced the agricultural workers to engage for twelve, thirteen, and fourteen hours in rugged, hard work at a fast pace.

All those conditions changed with the revolution: the dead season disappeared, unemployment disappeared, new work opportunities sprang up everywhere — not just in agriculture, mind you. Work was humanized, the workday was reduced considerably — not just from fourteen to eight hours, as it is precisely this eight-hour day we're talking about now. But how can agriculture be developed if you reduce the workday from fourteen to four or five hours of work at a slower pace; if the work done by one man under capitalism takes three men to be completed under socialism? It isn't like that, of course, in all cases, but in some it is.

Of course, technology is a great ally of man. From the moment a cane loader is brought into the picture his strength is multiplied manyfold, his productivity is increased, and then a few thousand men can load all the cane that formerly called for the effort of hundreds of thousands.

Then comes the cane-cutting machine and with it one man can do the work of fifty. What a wonderful thing the cane harvester is! Or take the rice-harvesting machine that substitutes for all that rugged, hard work of harvesting rice manually. Or take the plane that sows rice from the air or sprays the crop.

And so technology is man's great ally; it enables us to humanize work and increase work productivity manyfold. Yet applying technology takes time, and it hasn't been introduced yet in some lines of work although, fortunately, it has been in many.

But even now it's difficult to find in our country someone willing to milk cows by hand; you simply can't find them. All new dairies are equipped with milking equipment. But those old enough to know how cattle were raised under capitalism are aware that a man had to get up very early, round up and tie down thirty zebu cows that are plenty skittish and plenty rebellious [*Laughter*] — one single person to milk thirty cows and get a liter and a half, two liters of milk per cow.

So technology is being progressively introduced, but in agricultural work, since the revolution, technology has been rapidly introduced in our country. Just remember how we first had the cane loaders, then came the cane-conditioning centers, later the cane-cutting machines, as well as other technological advances in agriculture. But work is still needed. You can rely on technology, technology aids work, it multiplies work productivity, humanizes work. These are the characteristics of techno-logical progress, yet it can't eliminate work. It can lessen the intensity; it can reduce the physical effort needed; but we must bear in mind that work can't be done away with. And in both manual work and mechan-ized or agrochemical work we must make the best use of the workday and work with earnestness.

And so it is necessary that the management go to all the trouble re-quired to be in control of the situation and it is necessary that the workers and the trade unions go to all the trouble required to create deeply rooted awareness and to make demands, for we all should make demands on each other.

I can imagine how difficult it must be at present to work as a field manager, because field managers are not class enemies of the workers — they belong to no other class. Under capitalism, yes. The owners be-longed to another class; those in the management, the supervisors, field managers, etc. — I don't even remember what they were called back in those times, foremen, overseers, managers; they all were at the service of the landholders and the owners.

Today the manager or field manager belongs to no other class, is not an enemy of the workers; he came from the ranks of the workers and is friend, relative, neighbor of the people he works with. And so we must all make demands on this man, and demand of him that he make de-mands on all of us. We must ask him and demand of him that he apply controls, that on the job he isn't anybody's friend, buddy, or relative; [*Applause*] that his job is to make demands and apply controls.

We must act firmly and be highly critical of demagogy, irresponsibili-ty, softheartedness, inefficiency — highly critical! [*Applause*] And we must be highly critical of all softhearted managers, highly critical of them. This does not mean in the least that in making demands we mis-takenly confuse duty with despotism, or with lack of camaraderie; by no means!

Yet the capitalist was the master of everything; he went around keep-ing an eye on things. He had a trusted employee, one whose job was to keep an eye out for things. And so, now all managers and administrative cadres are the trusted employees of the working class, of the workers [*Applause*] and, therefore, the masters, the owners — the workers now — must be demanding with the managers administering their wealth.

Demagogy is easy — you all know that — and not for nothing has our working class, our trade union movement, learned so much over these years. Economism is easy — you all know that — and one of the weapons of capitalism to prevent and hold back our revolution is precisely economism.

Economism has caused many a headache to more than one revolutionary process before the workers have had the chance of becoming aware of their role in society and in the revolution, in their revolution. Because inasmuch as the revolution is not their revolution, then it isn't a revolution; and inasmuch as policy is not their policy, then it is not a policy for the workers. And the workers do well to demand as much as can be demanded. But when a revolution is their revolution, when policy is their policy, then the situation is completely different. For they can no longer go against their own interests. The interests of the workers and those of the exploiters are in legitimate contradiction. But, given the identification that comes about under socialism, it would be absurd, impossible, for there to be contradictions between the workers and their interests as workers.

That's why we must be demanding; why we must criticize demagogy, softheartedness; why we must say to managers: You must make demands on me; say: "You must make demands on me because that's your duty. If you make no demands on me then you're not a good manager." [*Applause*] Because the working class, the worker, has no need, absolutely no need, of buddies managing things.

This is another of the important roles the trade union movement has as the management's counterpart.

And this is an interesting topic, very interesting indeed, particularly since we have with us visitors and representatives of the labor movement from many other countries.

I must say here, in the first place, that economism has never been a problem for our revolution, never! [*Applause*]

Ever since the first signs of this being a problem were detected early on, when there were certain mistaken slogans, the way our workers clearly understood the problem was something to be seen; and so we have had no problems of economism in our revolutionary process. And if something were to characterize our labor movement, it is the high political awareness it has.

This is a really interesting topic.

The workers and the trade union movement have two tasks: the first, what their first duty is, the first duty of the workers in the revolution is to build socialism, that's their first duty! [*Applause*] And to do everything that contributes to the building of socialism, because it's their socialism, their society; their wealth belongs to no one else; it's their wealth, the wealth of the nation and of the workers.

And, as has been pointed out here, the labor movement has another role: that of watching over the interests of the workers as workers of a certain branch of the economy, of a certain place of work, and of watching over their rights, over all the prerogatives the socialist state gives it to protect the interests of the workers against any misunderstanding, arbitrary action, injustice. It must be the spokesperson of the interests of the workers as such; of all their problems, as they have been set out here in this congress, as they have been set out in the theses, of all the legitimate, just interests of the workers in all fields and in all senses. It must clarify, set out, demand, and defend the duties and the rights of all the workers.

That's the task of our trade union movement. But, naturally, to those who come from a capitalist country . . . and the capitalists would like to campaign against the trade union movement under socialism and are out to portray it as an appendage of the management. That's what the ideologues and phony propagandists of capitalism are inventing. But we mustn't let that discourage us. And we say that to the labor movement representatives coming from capitalist countries. The thing is that under socialism a miraculous identity and identification comes about between the interests of the workers and the interests of the entire people, who are, of course, a working people. [*Applause*] A fabulous social miracle takes place whereby a people of workers become, for the first time in history, the masters of their labor and the masters of their country's wealth.

That's why there's harmony in socialist society and why we have a labor movement like this.

Why, this labor movement would be a capitalist's ideal, the ideal, mind you. A labor movement talking about production and increasing productivity and improving quality and furthering culture? A labor movement always talking about increasing the wealth of the country? That's what a capitalist would like! But that doesn't even occur to a capitalist because to a capitalist a trade union is the devil reincarnate. [*Laughter and applause*]

Strikes? Who talks about strikes in a revolutionary process, a socialist process? Under capitalism all you hear about is strikes and more strikes at all hours and every day; and there's always something brought to a halt under capitalism. One day TV stations go on strike; another, air-control towers go on strike, and there's one catastrophe after another, there's chaos in the world, because flight controllers are out on strike. Or take the case of New York that went I don't know how many weeks without newspapers, because they were out on strike. Such chaos and disorder are what is most commonplace in capitalist society. And it is logical, logical I repeat, because of the contradiction between workers and capitalists.

One thing that we revolutionary leaders . . . I'm not referring to others, I'm just referring to us, because there are many revolutionary and socialist leaders in the world and I can't say something here alluding to the rest. I can engage in self-criticism, or we can all engage in self-criticism, but we can't apply it to others because then it wouldn't be self-criticism but criticism. [*Laughter*] One thing we are is inefficient, inefficient! Inefficiency lies with us, the managers, the leaders, for we could do things much better and we don't; for we could be much more efficient and we aren't; for we have cooperation in pushing ahead the economy, pushing ahead with work and everything, cooperation that the capitalist never had, and yet, with all these advantages, although we are making progress — nobody is going to deny that we're progressing and progressing a lot — still we could be doing things much better.

We're absolutely convinced that we're working in optimum conditions from a human and social standpoint; from a subjective standpoint; and from the standpoint of the worker, who is the creator of wealth. We may have other problems connected with underdevelopment, the blockade, the shortage of raw materials, and many other things, but, when it comes to the effort and the cooperation that our workers are willing to contribute in connection with any task, that is something no society in the world has ever had before, that no bourgeois leader has ever had before, that no capitalist has ever had before. However, the capitalist is a fiend when it comes to protecting his factory, when it comes to protecting his raw materials and protecting his costs; protecting everything on the basis of an out-and-out contradiction with the interests of the workers. And he defends his interests as a capitalist with the help of the army, the police, the courts, the lawmakers, the press, everybody. Everything is at the service of these interests, but he defends them like a fiend just the same. And he does it efficiently. We cannot deny the fact that when it comes to running a factory, the capitalist is usually efficient.

What should we expect from a socialist manager? We should expect him to be, as a rule, more efficient than the capitalist. And not because he's the owner — because he doesn't own any factories — but because he's in charge of a factory that belongs to the workers, to the people.

If it's a case of a power plant, that plant no longer belongs to K-listo Kilowatt, as the electric power company of the past used to be called; and if it's a telephone exchange, a truck, or a bus, then it doesn't belong to any transnational corporation or transport multinational either; nor is the socialist manager defending any foreign-owned mine, factory, or sugar mill. And it is precisely because the workers know this and are completely aware of it that the minute you walk into a factory you discover the workers' enormous interest in production, their great love for their factory, and their determination to do whatever has to be done.

This means that the workers as such understand these things much more clearly than the managers who come from the working class — and who are of the working class [*Applause*] — in their role as managers. It isn't that I want to criticize managers just for the sake of it, but I understand the realities of the situation.

Of course, we must ask ourselves where our administrative cadres came from. As a rule, they didn't come from the bourgoisie; they chiefly came from the working masses and they didn't have any experience, much technical know-how. We've been developing cadres. It must be said that you cannot generalize about these things, and I'm simply referring to a certain attitude. I'm thinking of the attitude that we must all have toward our work, the attitude that the workers must have when they're working, the attitude of those directly involved in production, and the attitude of those workers who hold administrative posts. I say this because I'm sure that if we were more efficient we would be drawing the greatest benefit from the exceptional subjective factors that favor production in a socialist process.

I believe that we have a magnificent trade union movement, a movement that should be constantly improved and perfected but is, nevertheless, a magnificent movement. I think we can say that our revolutionary process can really feel satisfied with the role being played by our workers and our trade union movement. [*Applause*]

And don't let anybody be deceived into thinking that the trade union movement is an appendage of the administration. Let no one think that. On the contrary, we could say in all justice that it is the socialist administration, the socialist state, that is not an appendage but an instrument of our workers; [*Applause*] that the administration in our own country is an instrument of our workers, of our working class, and of its political and trade union organizations. That's what can be said.

And it's quite difficult — actually impossible — in a capitalist country for the workers to discuss things the way they do in our trade unions and to participate in trade unions like they do here. And this boils down to the fact that in a capitalist society they have no participation of any kind; while here, they participate in everything; in the management of the state, in the party, in everything, because the leader of the Cuban trade union movement attends and takes part in every meeting of the state's highest executive body, the Executive Committee of the Council of Ministers. [*Applause*] And he's there to coordinate, make suggestions, and to constantly remind others what the general and particular interests of the workers are.

We are very happy with the congress and with the presence here of so many representatives of the international trade union movement; the representatives of our brother and sister workers of the socialist countries; representatives of our brother and sister workers of the countries of Latin America, Africa, and the so-called Third World in general, and also developed capitalist countries. We're very happy, very satisfied with the fact that they have had the opportunity to witness what has happened at this congress. [*Applause*]

I would like to point out to them that one of the characteristics of the congress was the broad democratic spirit and the spirit of criticism and self-criticism from the grass-roots level up — ever since the preparations for the event got under way one year ago with absolutely democratic methods.

The delegates spoke here with complete freedom, as long as they liked, on whatever subject they desired; and they have elected their leaders. And, in our opinion, they elected the right ones.

A vote was taken, and some of the most outstanding and valuable leaders of our trade union movement drew a few votes against. I remember that when the votes were being read there was some murmuring and I said to myself, "Very good, very good!" First of all, because the right to vote against is one of a delegate's most sacred rights. [*Applause*] Let's begin by respecting that right and feeling satisfied that we have it. And second, because the job of leading is a difficult, complex, hard job and frequently the opinions of the leaders must clash with other people's opinions. And there may be cases where comrades were told they were wrong and yet for the rest of their lives go on believing they were right and that an act of injustice was committed. This could happen in the case of a promotion — or lack of promotion, or demotion. All these things can happen.

Needless to say, we must ask leaders, demand of them, that they be demanding. We can't have milk-toast leaders; we can't have leaders who avoid contradictions, who sidestep problems; we can't have leaders thinking of the congress, worrying about votes against them. If they've done a conscientious job, if they worked seriously and honestly, they shouldn't be worried about votes against.

It goes without saying that the criterion of the immense majority of our workers is revolutionary, fair — above all, fair — and analytical. And we expect our workers to be demanding, to demand that leaders be demanding and that the work of each leader be evaluated. Because men, being men, can make mistakes; it happens all the time. But the important thing is moral integrity, purity of principles, honesty. And, of course, the role of the leader is not only to lead or demand but also, to a great extent, to understand, help, and teach. And the one thing we must demand of a leader above all is that he be honest, that he never resort to politicking and demagoguery of any kind. To tell the truth. I don't think this kind of leader can exist in our country, because the masses reject and abhor this type, because the masses are allergic to demagoguery and dishonesty. [*Applause*]

We are personally familiar with the work of many of the leaders you have elected. And elections in our country are a complex, rigorous process, mainly because here nobody aspires, nobody can aspire, to a particular post. An individual aspiring to a certain post is something unknown to socialism. In the revolution it's simply inconceivable to imagine some guy running for something, putting up a poster that reads "Vote for Joe Blow" or "Vote for So-and-So." [*Laughter*] There's no such thing in the labor movement or among the delegates. You know very well how the nomination for candidates to People's Power is done. What makes a cadre stand out is the way he goes about his life and work; his concept of the people, the masses, the workers. So far, nobody aspires to anything here.

We must take into account that our trade union movement was dealt a very hard blow, a very hard blow, shortly after the Thirteenth Congress, with the death of Comrade Lázaro Peña. [*Applause*] We all remember the sorrow of our people, and especially our workers, when they learned of that tragedy, of that irreparable loss, and how difficult it was to find a cadre to take the place of Comrade Lázaro Peña.

In those circumstances, which were cause for concern for all of us and for the party leadership, we didn't pinpoint or designate a cadre. We met with the leadership of the trade union movement to discuss the matter freely, and we asked them to study the question at length until they arrived at a practically unanimous decision as to the comrade to propose and elect to take Lázaro Peña's place. And, after thinking over the matter carefully and conscientiously, the leadership of the trade union movement elected Comrade Veiga. [*Applause*]

I think that one of Comrade Veiga's greatest merits is having had to take up such a difficult task — a virtually impossible one for a young cadre of the labor movement — as that of occupying the post formerly held by Comrade Lázaro Peña.

We have seen the way he and the other members of the leadership collective have worked over the years, making a tremendous effort without the authority, the experience, and the universal recognition Comrade Lázaro Peña had. And, in spite of all those difficult, adverse circumstances, they did a marvelous job.

We are well acquainted with them because we are always in contact with them, because they take part in high-level state meetings, and because we've seen how they go about their work; we have seen how they go about things, their concern, their honesty, and how they stand firm. Each time a problem that involves the workers, concerns the workers, affects the workers has been discussed they have responded in keeping with their dual role as leaders of the country; as state leaders, as party leaders, and as the workers' leaders. And their fundamental mission in the leadership of the party — without their ever neglecting the general interests of the revolution — their role has been to keep up to date on every detail, on everything that directly concerns the workers. And we can testify to that.

Therefore, we congratulate the delegates to the congress and the members of the National Council for the election of the members of the Secretariat and the National Committee. [*Prolonged applause*]

The slogan of this congress has been "Let's work for a solution to our basic economic problems!" As Comrade Veiga was saying, the accent of the congress has been on supporting what we consider to be the only reasonable proposal, that we concentrate our ideas and our energies on development and think about development rather than consumption.

This country has serious obstacles to overcome, especially in trade with convertible-currency countries. Exports must be increased in this area and in the socialist sector as well, of course. The country has to increase exports and, as we were saying at the National Assembly, if we have new cement factories, we should not use all the cement ourselves but export some of it; if we have new textile factories, we should not use all the textiles produced but export some; because all these factories also need raw material bought with convertible currency. And we have proposed that we export at least one meter out of three of what we produce in these new factories, to pay for the fibers and raw materials and whatever else we need to buy with convertible currency. Develop an exporter's mentality, because at the moment we only have an importer's mentality.

We had to concentrate more on development than on consumption, we had to realize that this was the real task, the real mission facing us. The most sacred duty of this generation of workers is to devote their efforts essentially to the development of the country. This doesn't mean that things won't improve, that our standard of living won't rise. There's no doubt that we've been making modest yet steady progress in many fields and that we will continue to do so. But what really counts is our awareness, our understanding, and our attitude toward the fact that this generation must concentrate its efforts on development. [*Applause*]

Other generations will live better. But there's no question that this one is living better than the preceding one. [*Applause*] We all would like to have been born in 1995 or in the year 2000, say, and then we could say, "Those who come after us are going to be better off." Yes, they are going to be better off, and we should be happy for them. [*Applause*]

I'm sure that many of our comrades who were born at the beginning of this century, that many of our workers who had to live through all the calamities, oppression, humiliation, abuse, and injustice of capitalism would have wished they had been born today.

Our children today don't suffer from poverty and lack of clothing, they don't have to beg for alms on the streets, they're not neglected by society, they don't have to live under the constant threat of death due to lack of medical care and medicines. In other words, our children are infinitely better off, in every way, than were our children in 1930, or 1940, or in 1950. Much better off.

The present generation is much better off than the past one in regard to social security, medical care, employment, and countless other things. And the state has to invest vast sums in education, public health, defense, and above all, development. These are necessary investments. If we don't invest in development, what could we do instead? Have a little more clothing and stop building factories? That's something we just can't do.

Truthfully speaking, our revolutionary process, in difficult conditions, has been spared a great many sacrifices thanks to international solidarity, the cooperation given by the socialist camp and, above all, the cooperation given by the Soviet Union. [*Applause*] In the face of the economic blockade, of all the difficulties caused by the loss of markets, our economic relations with the Soviet Union — the fact that they buy our sugar, all the sugar we want to sell them; the fact that they pay us prices way above the world market prices; and the fact that they supply us with fuel have meant a great deal to us — all these things have been a great help to our country, have helped our plans for economic and social development. If it hadn't been for this we certainly would have had to have made terrible sacrifices in order to carry through the revolution, in order to maintain our independence. As for defense, you can imagine how much our weapons would have cost if we'd had to buy them in the world market, considering how expensive a tank, a gun, or a plane is.

To the same extent that we've had international solidarity, good relations with the socialist camp, and excellent economic relations with the Soviet Union, we have received the aid that has enabled us today to feel satisfied over the progress we've made and to say that there are no longer any illiterates in our country; that very soon every worker in Cuba will have a sixth-grade education and will go on studying for a higher grade; that we have tens of thousands of workers attending the universities; that there's practically no unemployment here; that there are no beggars and no prostitution; that the calamities that plagued this country in the past no longer exist here; that our infant mortality rate is by far the lowest in Latin America; that we have 1,040,000 students in high schools; [*Applause*] and that we're going through the world economic crisis with success while all we see elsewhere are calamities, unemployment, layoffs, and conflicts of all kinds.

Our five-year plan is coming along quite satisfactorily and we are making progress; our sugar harvests are bigger and more stable every year and we are setting up major industries. We don't deny that we have difficulties, we're not saying that the road we're following is an easy one. We would be lying if we said that. The road to development we are taking is a difficult one. In the world of today it is a difficult road precisely because of the unequal trade between the industrialized capitalist world and the Third World and we're partly dependent on that trade. That's inevitable. However, thanks to socialism in our country, thanks to our relations with the socialist camp and with the Soviet Union, thanks to the efforts made by our workers, our country is making progress and will continue making progress regardless of the difficulties.

We are getting ready not only for the next five-year plan, but also for a twenty-year forecast plan, to know what we will be doing over the next twenty years, just to be able to look ahead twenty years. Under capitalism the most our country could look ahead was twenty days, ten or twenty days. Nobody knew what would happen in twenty days.

So, we will be able to have our path already worked out and we'll be able to get to work all over the country. One of the main virtues of the revolution is that it has been working all over the country; the fruits of the revolution have been carried everywhere: schools of all kinds, technological schools, junior and senior high schools, vocational schools, and sports schools have been built everywhere. The face of the cities in the interior has been transformed and industries have been set up all over the country.

We have delegates from all over the country here, from Pinar del Río, for example. Hasn't that city changed enormously over the last seven or eight years? And from Manzanillo, Holguín, Las Tunas, Villa Clara, Cienfuegos, Guantánamo, Santiago, or wherever. [*Applause*] There have been amazing changes in all of them, especially those which were poorest and most neglected, as shown by the day-care centers, the hospitals, and the university branches; the university branches have been set up in nearly every province.

For the first time there has been a fair distribution of the means of production and social benefits in our country and we will continue working along these lines.

The role of the trade union movement in all this is decisive. Believe me, the revolution could not be conceived of without the trade union movement playing its role. [*Applause*]

What the managers may do doesn't matter; the key thing, the decisive thing, is the workers.

If we want to improve our services and make our education more efficient, continuing the improvement so that this service will be on a par with the best in the world, this will basically depend on the teachers and professors. If we want to continue raising the standards of our public health service and make it as efficient as possible, as we said in the speech to inaugurate this school year, this will basically depend on our doctors and health workers. Without their dedicated effort and backing nothing could be done. If we are going to promote construction, improve transport, improve the ports, or whatever, the key factor is the workers, the creators of the goods and services which the people consume. It is the trade union movement that groups all the workers, which is why it is so important, so decisive, for without the trade union movement the party and the state could not tackle this huge task.

The party's ranks are growing among the working class. In the drive to increase the size of the party stress has been placed on attracting more workers and we expect that the percentage of workers in the party will increase constantly.

The coming years will be marked by effort and hard work. They will continue to be difficult years. They won't be easy years, but there will be constant and steady progress for our people and our revolution.

We don't promise that anything will be easy. It would be demagogic to say the coming years which face this generation are going to be easy ones; they will be years of hard work and difficulties. Let me repeat that we must devote ourselves to development and chiefly for the benefit of future generations. But these generations will also benefit and will have the great spiritual and moral satisfaction that derives from the fulfillment of their historic role. The coming generations will always be grateful and will always appreciate what this revolutionary generation is doing. [*Applause*] Yes, this generation is revolutionary, really revolutionary, a generation with great internationalist awareness. [*Applause*] The real nature of our working class, of our workers today, is shown in their spirit, their role in the revolution, their work and eternal enthusiasm; in the internationalist fighters who fought in Angola and Ethiopia, [*Applause*] the overwhelming majority of which are workers, members of the reserve forces of our glorious Revolutionary Armed Forces; [*Applause*] in the thousands of civilian technicians, construction workers, doctors, health workers, and teachers serving in different parts of the world.

The growing demand for Cuban technicians is a satisfaction and an honor for our country; the fact that many countries call upon us to provide technicians, provide technical cooperation, provide doctors and other experts. Such that the export of technical services and construction aid is becoming another of our country's major economic resources. What do you think of that? Before, there were no doctors to send to a small town like Baracoa but now our doctors are all over the world and our construction workers are in several parts of the world. And the demand is increasing. I must admit, I prefer this resource to that of tourism. Definitely. But we're not going to give up tourism. We need all our resources, we need them all. [*Applause*]

And so, is the country afraid? Afraid of what? A country whose soldiers have proved what they're capable of, whose internationalist workers are proving what they're capable of! [*Applause*]

And this is the best feature of the present stage of the revolution which has moved beyond certain idealist, utopian, unreal stages. Of course, all these earlier stages were motivated by the sincerest revolutionary spirit. We have been overcoming these past mistakes and we've had to establish certain conditions, certain material incentives, certain conceptions as to how distribution should take place under socialism, as to how things should be run under socialism. We have been learning from these past experiences and we have been profiting from them. At the same time our awareness is growing, our revolutionary spirit is growing.

We have been feeding wood to the fire of our revolutionary zeal, as it were. And this has been the case, for instance, with the voluntary work spirit, with the internationalist spirit. In other words, alongside the realist measures — imposed upon us by reality — there have been measures that promote and strengthen our communist consciousness, our revolutionary spirit.

And that should be one index we should always measure ourselves by. And speaking of indexes there's one index that speaks for a revolution, for one congress after another, for the party, and for the workers; and that is that we're more revolutionary every day, [*Applause*] that we're more Marxist-Leninist, [*Applause*] that we're more internationalist, [*Applause*] that we're more communist. [*Prolonged applause*]

Our workers' congress has been held in the midst of important and moving historical dates: on the twenty-second anniversary of the Santiago de Cuba uprising, [*Applause*] on the twentieth anniversary of the battle of Guisa,* [*Applause*] on the eve of the twentieth anniversary of the revolution. [*Applause*] And we're closing this congress on December 2, the twenty-second anniversary of the *Granma* landing. [*Applause*]

On a day like today a group of us made the landing under very difficult, really difficult circumstances, with very serious obstacles ahead and many enemy soldiers facing us; thirsty, hungry, physically exhausted, and with many other problems, we struggled on through the night. Probably none of us at that moment could have imagined that twenty-two years later, at that same hour, we would be present at the closing of this magnificent congress, of this magnificent meeting.

We have come far since then. Together we have marched along the path that began on that December 2, 1956, and has now reached this congress on December 2, 1978. That's why — with all the obstacles, all

---

*On November 30, 1956, forces of the July 26 Movement led by Frank País launched an unsuccessful uprising in Santiago de Cuba, timed to coincide with the scheduled arrival of the *Granma*. The ten-day battle of Guisa, one of the biggest of the revolutionary war, ended on November 29, 1958, with the rebels victorious.

the difficulties, all the victories — we say to you that we were, are, and always will be optimists! [*Applause*]

Patria o muerte!

Venceremos! [*Shouts of "Venceremos!"*] [*Ovation*]

Three Speeches Against Bureaucracy

by Raúl Castro

NOTE: In the summer of 1979, a number of problems began to come to light in various production and service units in Cuba. These included problems with work discipline, absenteeism, and negligent administrators who would avoid problems, trying to cut corners while seeking special privileges. At a meeting of the National Assembly of People's Power on July 4, Fidel Castro criticized a report given by the minister in charge of public transportation in Havana which sidestepped the growing problems with bus service. "We must get to the heart of the issue," he said. "We must put an end to the tendency to shirk problems, to favored treatment for friends, to tolerant attitudes towards indiscipline. All this must stop!"

During the summer and fall this theme was elaborated on in several speeches by Raúl Castro on behalf of the party leadership. In these speeches Raúl Castro indicated the sources of these problems, pointing to a certain layer of demoralized "faint-hearted" functionaries with defeatist attitudes. He put these attitudes in the context of the growing military threats from the U.S. government in the wake of the revolutionary victories in Grenada and Nicaragua, and Cuba's economic problems stemming from the pressures of imperialism.

The following are excerpts from three of these speeches. The first one, given on April 5, 1979, was printed in the August 19 Granma Weekly Review. *The second was given on October 28 to a meeting commemorating revolutionary leader Camilo Cienfuegos on the twentieth anniversary of the disappearance of the airplane he was flying in; it is reprinted from the November 11* Granma Weekly Review. *The third speech was given November 30 in Santiago de Cuba, on the twenty-third anniversary of the uprising in that city led by Frank País. It is reprinted from the December 9, 1979,* Granma Weekly Review.

1. April 5, 1979

Work discipline is the expression of the values that make the working class the most revolutionary class. Without it work collectives turn into a chaotic sum of individuals that, lacking cohesion, are incapable of thinking and performing like detachments of the social force that exercises political power. Working-class discipline, and the political consciousness which is the expression of this discipline, are essential factors in the building of socialism.

This process is in part linked to the weakening of authority and the lack of a demanding attitude as underlined in the resolution of the Eighth Plenum of the Central Committee and denounced by its first secretary, Commander in Chief Fidel Castro [*Applause*] in his recent speeech before the National Assembly. This is a negative, extremely pernicious phenomenon that covers all spheres of our society, and which we must begin to eradicate with the same urgency with which one fights the worst plagues. To do this, the party relies, first of all, on the energy, combativeness, and determination of the workers, who must fight against all signs of indiscipline, against the widespread practice of letting people get away with things, against giving special treatment to friends, against weak management and some tamed trade union leaders, against the workers themselves who come late or skip work, and against all signs of individualism and misuse of social property.

The Political Bureau, taking into account the results of the Eighth Plenum of the Central Committee and the issues raised by Fidel before the National Assembly, adopted a resolution which urges the party's grass-roots organizations to engage in a profound discussion and analysis of these problems. This resolution and the measures that will be subsequently adopted are indicative of the party's desire to use all its influence and all its mobilizing capacity to eradicate these deviations that represent a real risk to our further economic, social, political, and ideological development.

Along with Fidel, we repeat that the order of the day is to be *demanding,* but to be demanding in a calm and mature way and, above all, to settle accounts, regardless of hierarchies, with those who violate work discipline, cover up wrongdoings, behave in an arbitrary fashion, and have a petty-bourgeois concept of criticism and self-criticism. That is, the type of people who agree with the need for criticism and defend it openly at all times, as long as the criticism is of others.

Within the general context of popular support for the statements of the party and Comrade Fidel, there will be those who timidly call for prudence and warn against imaginary excesses. They themselves are not the most calm and cautious people, but the same cowards who are forever doubting the party's ability to act in a firm and thoughtful way.

It is not a question of initiating a campaign. There will be no excesses or improvised measures. The party will not act rashly or with fleeting vigor. But neither will we listen to those voices that try to neutralize this process, a process aimed at putting certain things straight and recuperating some values that have been seriously compromised. The only voice that will be listened to is that of the people, who constantly call for efficient and far-reaching solutions. [*Applause*]

The workers and the entire people are the beneficiaries and owners of the socialist economy, but they are so as a whole and over the totality of goods and services. The distribution of the social wealth takes place directly through wages and indirectly through funds of social consumption. No one has the right to divert any amount of any resources from its original destination, and those who do so act against the general interests of the society, against the working class and, we might add, place themselves outside the bounds of socialist legality.

We could also add that every one of us, at some time, somewhere in Cuba, has come across a "generous" person. In Cuba we have many "generous" people, especially as far as other people's property is concerned, and in particular social property, but stingy enough when it comes to their own belongings.

And the fight against this will not take the form of a transitory campaign, or improvised measures, but measures that have been carefully studied and discussed with the working masses. And we will prepare ourselves for the fight against these vices that I have briefly alluded to, a fight that will last not one year, nor ten years, but decades.

2. October 28, 1979

None who knew Camilo doubt that he would have contributed greatly to advancing the revolution, that he would have worked to make it advance, to consolidate it and defend it, because this was and still is his revolution.

Today, when all our people are doing their utmost to build socialism and wipe out the deformities that have been engendered in our society,

Camilo would be a champion of discipline, an exemplary defender of principles, a front-line fighter for efficiency, and a defender of the revolution's foreign policy. He summed up the nature of that policy even before he had joined the *Granma* expedition, when he said, "All those who fight, no matter where, are our brothers and sisters."

Comrades, it is impossible to conceive of a nationwide tribute to Camilo Cienfuegos on this, the twentieth anniversary of his disappearance, without linking him to our present activities, achievements, and problems.

Such a connection is altogether logical, because what gave meaning to Camilo's life and provided him with the opportunity to materialize his own great desire — a passionate and at the same time well-thought-out desire — to be useful to his class, to serve his people, to protect and do honor to his homeland, was precisely this revolution — the revolution he helped to create and which he was working tirelessly to consolidate, with absolute disregard for personal risk, when we were so abruptly deprived of his exceptional contribution.

This is a solemn occasion on which we pay tribute to a fighter like Camilo and reflect on the fact that his death occurred while he was carrying out a revolutionary mission aimed at putting an end to the consequences of an act of treason nurtured by imperialism and favored by vacillation, opportunism, and cowardice.* And no occasion could be more timely for bringing up the tense and difficult situation our country faces at present.

When we lost Camilo, we were already in confrontation with the imperialist government of the United States, and future developments were clearly outlined. It was the beginning of the Cuban revolution's "original sin," when we decided to put an end to neocolonial domination and develop as a free and independent nation.

Now, twenty years later, it seems as if those who do not resign themselves to respecting or coexisting with that sovereign decision are the dominant ones among our neighbors to the north. This is the elementary conclusion that can be drawn from the provocative and hostile actions of the present Washington administration.

We are all familiar with the artificial problems that were fabricated in high U. S. government circles, to have them coincide with the opening of the Sixth Summit Conference of Nonaligned Countries in Cuba.† Our

---

* Cienfuegos's last mission was to thwart an attempt by Huber Matos, the commander of the Camagüey Rebel forces, to turn those forces against the revolution. Matos was arrested, tried, and sentenced to twenty years' imprisonment.

†With the approach of the September 1979 Nonaligned summit conference in Havana, the U.S. government announced the "discovery" of a "Soviet combat

viewpoints on this were publicly expressed by Comrade Fidel.

Now we can see the results of that adventure: the unfounded and dangerous U.S. military escalation in the Caribbean, the stepped-up U.S. naval presence in the Indian Ocean, the brazen "authorization" for spy flights all over the world, particularly over Cuban air space, in what constitutes a typical act of imperialist arrogance. All this accompanied by a torrent of speeches couched in the poorest electoral rhetoric.

It is no wonder that in Latin America and the Caribbean, government circles included, where today a sense of national dignity prevails and a Latin Americanist and solidary awareness is being developed, people of good sense have spoken to express their disapproval of such measures, which are the product of petty electoral interests and the classic imperialist policy of the carrot and the stick.

After displaying a series of bogeymen whose clothing, curiously enough, was "made in U.S.A.," and having raised a tremendous rumpus with obvious electoral aims, the U.S. administration set up a general headquarters in Key West as command post for its so-called mixed forces, a corps aimed directly at the growing desire for social progress and democracy that exists in the Caribbean and Central America. They legalized and are speeding up the formation of some quick-landing force composed of more than 100,000 soldiers, a project they have been working on for many years now and which is tailor-made for military interventions in the Persian Gulf. The project is now one of the series of measures Carter announced on October 1; they invaded Caribbean waters with a fleet of twenty-five warships, their idea being intimidation. And lastly, they gave one more demonstration of their scorn for the sovereignty of the nations of this hemisphere with the recent landing of marines in the Guantánamo naval base.

To tell the truth, we must confess that after more than two decades of confrontations with successive U.S. administrations, some of which have had the world in suspense, we at least expected our adversaries to be somewhat serious and somewhat responsible in both their declarations and their actions.

However, we must admit that the events we referred to have certainly dimmed our hopes as far as finding the ways of examining the matters in question in a civilized way, based on mutual respect as advocated by the international community.

More recently, the U.S. press disclosed the existence of President Carter's memorandum known as Directive 52, outlining a series of openly anti-Cuban measures and attempting to justify the criminal U.S. blockade on Cuba by means of which the imperialists first tried to starve

---

brigade" in Cuba, referring to military personnel that had been in Cuba for more than seventeen years.

us into surrendering, later to obstruct our development, and, on a long-term basis, to sow discontent among our people.

However, we will continue to be as patient as need be; we will not fall prey to any provocation coming from those whose narrow, petty interests can lead them to endanger world peace.

President Carter's memorandum itself is a clear refutation of his affront and makes it evident that they have no other alternative but to accept the irreversible truth that our country cannot be intimidated, bribed, or bought. [*Applause*]

As communists we are optimistic, and will continue to hope that common sense and realism will one day prevail in the U.S. administration's policy toward Cuba; perhaps for this to happen the magicians behind the throne that U.S. presidents have the habit of hiring will first have to go.

We will not be perturbed in the face of new provocations and threats that serve as the setting for the coming elections in the U.S.A.; we will go on with our combat- and political-training programs, and we will make sure that all the means and measures necessary to guarantee the effective defense of our national territory and the achievements of the revolution are adopted. [*Applause*]

Moreover, as everybody knows, we, the leaders of the party and government, are well acquainted with our internal difficulties; we have detailed information regarding the various problems that exist in the economy and services, and we know of multiple cases of deficiencies of various kinds.

But there's something even more important, which is that we, as well as the people, believe that the time has come to delay no longer in carrying out concrete measures and to be decisive in solving problems that are hampering development, obstructing the normal development of society, and causing well-founded irritation in neighborhoods, work centers, hospitals, schools, everywhere [*Applause*] there has been an outbreak of irresponsibility, disorganization, and a very undemanding attitude toward oneself and others. There can be no putting this off anymore.

And so, considering the general complaints about errors, weaknesses, and deficiencies, we wonder if there can be any specific collectives or any particular managers or political leaders who on hearing such criticism will consider that it is being directed at others and that they are immune to the errors that are being pointed out; if there are any who consider it unnecessary, and even go so far as to refuse to undertake a systematic, in-depth, critical, and self-critical analysis of the job they have been entrusted with.

The interests of our working class and of all our people in general constitute the highest value of our homeland, the very raison d'être of the revolution. [*Applause*] Those who do not respect this principle, in terms of meeting the responsibility that has been assigned to them, must be punished. And if those who are in charge of maintaining discipline are incapable of doing so, then they should step down and make room for more resolute, more capable cadres. [*Applause*]

Some of our most pressing difficulties and problems are well known. First, through the resolution of the Eighth Plenary Meeting of the Central Committee and immediately after, through the speech given by Comrade Fidel in the last session of the National Assembly of People's Power, where he made a critical denunciation of the proliferation of breaches of labor discipline and the undemanding attitude on the part of managers as subjective factors. There are, in addition, other types of difficulties which we can in no way be blamed for — such as the low prices on the international sugar market, as opposed to the higher and higher prices of goods we inevitably have to purchase in the capitalist world.

The Political Bureau of our party adopted a resolution reiterating the basic points contained in the resolution of the Eighth Plenary Meeting and Fidel's statements, giving very concrete guidelines to grass-roots agencies as to the line that was to be followed throughout the country.

As was clearly stated in the Political Bureau resolution, those guidelines are no temporary campaign; they are rather a permanent and systematic style of work which we consider essential, decisive in ensuring that plans for economic and social development are properly carried out.

And as we take a firm stand regarding what is not being done well, so we should also take a firm stand regarding present-day difficulties and objective unknowns. Some of these stem from the world capitalist crisis which inevitably has a bearing on our economy; and there are other climatic and natural phenomena that have recently adversely affected crop yields and have considerably reduced the quantity of cane available for the next sugar harvest, all of which will inevitably be reflected negatively in 1980 and even in 1981.

For our part, we will continue to act calmly, no extremisms, studying the measures we should adopt to tackle and gradually solve these problems that really depend on more effective action on the part of state agencies, the party, the Young Communist League, the labor movement, and other mass organizations.

These measures must be adopted and put into effect in the immediate future. This in itself is a complex task, and it has by necessity to go hand in hand with other priorities.

Only recently Comrade Fidel gave a major speech at the UN,* describing the dismal situation facing most of the countries of the so-called

---

* On October 12, 1979, Fidel Castro addressed the United Nations General Assembly as chairman of the Movement of Nonaligned Countries.

Third World, inhabited by more than 1.5 billion and whose economies are not only stagnant but are tending toward regression. Both reason and moral force were on his side as he spoke on behalf of the children who don't even have a piece of bread to eat; as he asked himself who dared speak to 450 million hungry people and to 900 million people who neither know how to read or write on this planet; and outlined the tragic situation regarding public health in areas that have been the victims of colonialism and are today bearing the brunt of the world capitalist crisis and its nefarious consequences.

Cuba, however, thanks to the socialist character of its economic, political, and social structures, and its fraternal and close relations with the Soviet Union [*Applause*] and the other countries of the socialist community, presents an entirely different picture. Not only is there no poverty and calamity here; the country has also achieved a lot in securing the basic necessities for human existence. And this, we might add, in spite of having to pay the extra daily price of taking a firm stand in the face of a criminal economic blockade that will have been maintained for nineteen years this month.

Difficult situations differentiate those who have their feet firmly on the ground. We are absolutely convinced that, as throughout our history, those who vacillate and are faint of heart will weaken, but our people will grow in the face of adversity and again take on the stature of Camilo. [*Applause*]

More than twenty years ago now, Comrade Fidel arrived in Havana and gave a speech in which he warned, "I believe that this is the decisive moment in our history. The tyranny has been overthrown. Our happiness is immense. And yet, a great deal still remains to be done. Let us not deceive ourselves into believing that from now on everything will be easy; it may well be more difficult."

He added: "The first duty of a revolutionary is to tell the truth. To deceive the people, to delude them with false illusions can only result in the worst consequences, and I believe the people should be warned not to be overoptimistic."

Today we can safely say that Comrade Fidel and the revolutionary leadership he heads have remained true to that principle. We have never had any illusions about the price imperialism would make us pay for opening up an era of genuine independence, sovereignty, progress, and well-being for the masses in the Americas, an era marked by the end of exploitation, discrimination, and oppression. [*Applause*]

We never even insinuated that the challenge would be an easy one; we never hid from the working class, the revolutionary peasantry, and our working people as a whole the fact that there would be severe trials, enormous difficulties and titanic efforts, mass heroism, willingness to sacrifice, firmness, courage, patriotism, and class consciousness required in order to meet the historic need and fulfill our commitment to continue the work of the founders of our country and the pioneers of the revolution, building in Cuba, alongside the most powerful imperialist nation on the face of the earth, the first socialist state in the Western Hemisphere. [*Applause*]

Perhaps this is one of the great truths the enemies of our people have historically ignored, or not taken into account; perhaps this is one of the things that the Pentagon strategists, the State Department planners, and the sinister brains in the CIA have ignored. And this has led them to repeated errors of judgment in their criminal drive to destroy the Cuban revolution, from cutting the sugar quota to the threat of atomic extermination, efforts to assassinate Comrade Fidel, sabotage and attacks of all kinds, the mercenary invasion at Playa Girón, banditry, political encirclement, and economic blockade.

Twenty years later these seeds have borne fruit and are now part of our country's priceless legacy, one of the staunch pillars of the Cuban revolution: the faith, trust, and confidence the mass of our people have in Comrade Fidel, in our party, [*Applause*] and in the future of our socialist homeland.

We will never betray that faith; that trust and confidence will never be called into question! [*Applause*]

However, we would not be telling the truth if we were to say that our bitterest class enemies are the only ones unable to understand the staunch loyalty of the working masses to their revolution.

During our war of liberation, I was able to see how, along with the collective heroism of the fighters of the Rebel Army and the mass of peasants and agricultural workers who supported us, there were isolated cases of vacillations, desertions, and even costly betrayals among people whose conduct until then was such that they had been considered honest fighters against the dictatorship.

At the same time I concluded that these cases did not necessarily come from fearing death, but rather from being overwhelmed by difficulties and losing faith in victory. We noticed that for those who only looked at the surface of things or approached the problem unilaterally, over the months the position of the incipient guerrilla forces got worse and not better and the prospects for a quick and easy victory seemed more and more distant.

It was under these circumstances, when persecution and harassment were stepped up and isolation set in, when the humid forest was our only home and the hard ground our only bed, when we were chilled to the bone by constant rains and weakened by hunger, when the enemy seemed stronger than it really was and some felt we would never be able to overcome our weakness of the moment; it was under such adverse, we might say insurmountable, conditions that the faint of heart began to reveal themselves, lose faith, and renounce their clearly fragile convictions. And since demoralization and cowardice are best endured in the company of others, they tried to seek allies, exaggerating the difficulties, sowing doubt and defeatism. From that moment on we learned to view those who become demoralized as sure-fire deserters; and those who deserted, overwhelmed by the problems which they did not have the spirit of sacrifice, determination, or willpower to cope with, as likely traitors. Having lost all hope for quick and easy victory, they exposed themselves to a risk worse than death, that of living with the stigma of having abandoned the cause of the people. They would live, but inside of them they were dead! [*Applause*]

Over and above the differences, without artificially forcing a comparison and taking into account the fact that we will never again face that sort of situation, I note in the conduct and expression of certain diverse elements of our present-day society signs of that same weakness, of the poverty of spirit and timid psychology of the faint-hearted which flourishes in times of trouble. [*Applause*]

We are no longer a beseiged fortress; we have overcome the political isolation and survived the economic blockade; the solid and growing prestige of our country in the socialist community, in the Movement of Nonaligned Countries, and among the countries of the so-called Third World has been clearly demonstrated; and in general we have the recognition and respect of the international community. And yet, while our people have been the protagonists of the revolution and also been capable of upholding and implementing the principles of internationalism and solidarity, this does not mean we should underestimate these symptoms — much less learn to live with them or limit our reaction to them to one of moral condemnation.

We Cuban revolutionaries, who have rightfully earned for ourselves the fierce hatred of imperialism and world reaction and who are building socialism on the doorstep of the center of world imperialism, cannot indulge in viewing such distortions as inevitable. For this could only lead to inertia and encourage indolence; in short, it is incompatible with the moral standards and principles which have been embraced by the great majority of our people and on whose behalf extraordinary men like Camilo Cienfuegos, Che Guevara, and countless other sons and daughters of our working class gave their lives. [*Applause*]

It would be completely inconsistent on our part to on the one hand call on the people to face up to the severe difficulties and complex problems which lie ahead, to redouble their efforts and consciously take on the sacrifices that are inevitable if we are to develop the nation's economy and promote the well-being of all; and on the other hand to stand idly by in the face of problems of this sort.

We have enough evidence to safely say that some party and state cadres are shying away from coming to grips with those who have made a habit of lacking labor discipline, lacking discipline vis-à-vis society, lacking respect for social property, and lacking respect for socialist norms of conduct. [*Applause*] We know of party members who do not battle against those who have interpreted freedom from exploitation as freedom from work, against those who live like parasites off the backs of others. [*Applause*]

Socialist legality involves drawing up, implementing, enforcing, and obeying the laws of the socialist state, so we must not allow a few turncoats to come up with their subterfuges to use that legality as a cover for violating it with impunity. [*Applause*]

We know that there are those who seek to enjoy the benefits of socialism without contributing anything, or setting things up so as to contribute as little as possible, to the common good.

It comes as no surprise that among those inclined to fall prey to defeatism are those who avoid facing up to problems because they are more concerned about retaining the positions they hold than about the needs of the people they are supposed to serve. [*Applause*]

We are convinced that our society has every right to call to account those who fill the minds of their children with frivolous desires for the superfluous shoddy goods turned out by capitalist consumer societies, [*Applause*] encouraging them to illegally leave the country to become new victims in the paradise of drugs, violence, and moral decadence.

Nor are we unaware of certain gatherings at which the allegedly well-informed, who have no firsthand experience of the misery of capitalism, take on the role of prosecutors and strategists, coming up with instant solutions for every possible problem. It would be better for those wise men to apply their talents in a more adequate and timely manner; but I would like to repeat — as I pointed out on August 5 in Camagüey — that the party has first of all the energy, militancy, and intransigence of the workers who must do battle against all forms of lack of discipline, against the widespread practice of tolerance, buddyism, weak administrations, and certain tame trade union leaderships who must confront workers who are not punctual or frequently absent from work and resolutely battle against all forms of individualism and dishonesty in the administering of social property.

We repeated then what Fidel said, that the order of the day is to be demanding. [*Applause*] But we must be demanding in a calm and mature way and especially settle accounts, regardless of hierarchy, with those who violate labor discipline, tolerate wrongdoing, are arbitrary, and have a petty-bourgeois view of criticism and self-criticism. And we might add that people of this sort accept and defend criticism as long as the criticism is directed at somebody else. [*Applause*]

Allow me to recall, as we pointed out then, in the overall context of the mass support for the views expressed by the party and Comrade Fidel, there are some who timidly advocate prudence and warn against supposed excess. These are not exactly the calmest and most level-headed of people; they are the faint-hearted who doubt the ability of the party to act in a firm and thoughtful manner.

It is not a case of undertaking a campaign; there will be no excesses or improvised measures. The party will not be motivated by temporary zeal or vehemence, but neither will those who try to divert this process be heeded; for this process is aimed at setting things aright and restoring certain values which have been seriously undermined. The only voice that will be heeded is the voice of the people demanding effective, long-term solutions. [*Applause*]

On the other hand, we often notice a certain rigidity in the cadres of our administrative apparatus and in the political and mass organizations. We should ask ourselves if, after twenty years of revolutionary power and in spite of our vast experiences in the affairs of politics and government, after structural improvement with the process of institutionalization, we are still not able to see to it that every worker and peasant, student or soldier, and even every minister or state and party leader, know exactly what their powers, obligations, and tasks are? [*Applause*]

And if we answer the question in the affirmative, then why do many pull back when they face problems and limit themselves to telling those nearest at hand that "things are rough" rather than immediately assuming responsibilities, be they those of a simple worker or those of an official or leader at any level? [*Applause*]

After twenty years of revolution are we going to continue the widespread practice of waiting for somebody to push us to do our duty? Or to be quite clear: How long are we to go on allowing unsolved problems to reach crisis point and then ask Comrade Fidel to take over the situation and pull our chestnuts out of the fire? [*Applause*]

In this simultaneous battle against our shortcomings and against the objective difficulties we face, we have reached this, the twentieth anniversary of the disappearance of Camilo, a sad loss for the revolution.

Today we see many Camilos and Ches, in the centers of production and educational institutions named after them, and we are comforted to see how all our people honor them each year, more and more aware of their historical significance, and with increasing admiration and deeper affection.

In these times in which we are living, our tribute to Camilo Cienfuegos will prove lasting and fruitful if each of us takes to heart what Fidel said following Camilo's death: "All that we ask of our people is that whenever the country faces a difficult situation, they should remember Camilo. . . . [*Applause*] Whenever the people face difficult moments, whenever young people, peasants, workers, students one day believe that the road ahead is long and the path difficult, they should remember what he did, and how he never lost faith even in those difficult times," said Fidel.

We address ourselves to the mass of workers tonight. As Fidel pointed out on one unforgettable occasion, they were the ones who gave rise to our struggles, they are the true protagonists of our revolution.

To the millions or ordinary Cubans who make up our wonderful people, from among whose ranks have come men like Camilo Cienfuegos, we issue on behalf of our party a call to battle: to constantly strengthen our combat readiness in the face of imperialist threats; to overcome our shortcomings and solve the problems which depend on us; to face the difficulties and trials that lie ahead with the spirit of the Moncada, *Granma,* and the Rebel Army, of the fighters in the underground, of those who fought against the counterrevolutionary bandits, at Playa Girón, and on heroic internationalist missions, clearing the way for the socialist future of the country by routing the weak, the cowardly, and the indolent.

3. November 30, 1979

At this moment the most important question is for us to become fully conscious that we are facing serious objective problems caused by the world economic crisis generated by the capitalist system, which has been hit by runaway inflation. It is an undeniable fact that this accounts for daily rises in the cost of the products we must purchase from the capitalist area, while at the same time the price of our sugar has remained very low. All the above, through a process of accumulated effects, has harmed our economy to a greater degree than was the case over the last few years.

In addition, we have faced and are now facing natural difficulties that have reduced even more our leeway. An example of this is the appearance of the blue mould that affected one fourth of our tobacco plantations during the last season and that now is beginning to reappear in some places where planting is going on. Our most recent natural difficulty is the sugarcane smut plague that, together with other negative factors, will substantially affect sugar production levels in the season that just started.

What's more, sugar prices — notwithstanding momentary rises over the last few weeks — are still below average world production costs and do not compensate for the enormous price rises in manufactured goods and, generally, in all the items that we must import, plus freight charges in the capitalist area. All of this has inevitably reduced our financial resources and lessened our country's purchasing power.

Given the existing situation, the freely convertible currency we obtain for our exports and other activities that earn us foreign exchange won't enable us to keep up the pace of development of the last few years, and compel us to redirect our resources and increase the degree of selectivity when making investments in new construction projects. We will try to maintain the levels reached in certain areas of social consumption, but are forced for the time being not to continue increasing these levels at the rate originally planned. In order to maintain such levels we must concentrate our efforts and resources so as to meet as best as possible all the vital necessities of our people in whatever areas are most deficient.

Comrade Fidel has explained that it is only because of the existence of a socialist regime here and our close economic relations with the Soviet Union, that the effects of the present world economic crisis have not led us into economic disaster and bankruptcy, with its sequel of starving people and hundreds of thousands of unemployed.

It is precisely the socialist regime that permits us to unite the efforts of all and overcome the present unfavorable situation that our economy and the world economy are going through.

With this objective in mind, we must make an exhaustive analysis of all our expenditures to cut them down to a minimum, and above all, we must make a careful selection of our purchases from capitalist markets according to the particular economic and social priorities of our social system. We must then use our available resources according to a plan that best responds to our needs.

Thus, resources will be used, first of all, to maintain the population's food supply, making an effort to increase as much as possible the supply of vegetables and tubers; assure an adequate supply of medicines; improve deficient services such as transportation and, with minimal investment, improve repair services of domestic appliances such as televisions. We must substantially increase maintenance and repair of streets, highways, schools and other buildings for social use, and housing, by various means, including selling more construction materials to the population during the coming year.

But this situation should by no means be used as a convenient crutch to lean on to explain all our problems as has been done on more than one occasion where the truly negative consequences of the economic blockade imposed on us by Yankee imperialism as well as by other external or natural factors have been used as pretexts to hide our deficiencies and inefficiencies. Let's not have sugarcane smut be used to hide those difficulties which are the product of subjective factors that are exclusively our responsibility and which we must openly and relentlessly fight against.

To the objective factors we've described we must add the presence of indiscipline, lack of control, irresponsibility, complacency, negligence, and buddyism, which, in addition to aggravating many problems, prevent others from being solved and generate justified irritation on the part of broad sectors of the population, being the principal cause for the notorious lack of efficiency in important areas of our economy. Furthermore, these problems divert the attention of the party and the people and prevent us from fully dedicating ourselves to solving the fundamental problems that slow down and thwart the socioeconomic development of the country.

As the people already know, the party leadership is presently involved in implementing, in the quickest and most efficient way possible, measures aimed at finding true, long-term solutions. In keeping with Comrade Fidel's statements on the need to be more demanding, the Ninth Plenary Meeting of the Central Committee of the party that took place on November 28 dedicated a great deal of time to examining these questions and making decisions — many of them definitive — to deal with them.

When we speak of applying definitive measures, we realize the need to make a detailed analysis of the factors involved and their complex interaction in order to make sure that they will lead to real, concrete, global solutions and not simply promote superficial, transitory campaigns that don't solve anything and create the appearance of making spectacular, demagogic attempts to mitigate the population's irritation, [*Applause*] something which is completely foreign to socialist society and the Marxist-Leninist principles that shape the ideology of real communists.

Our desire to solve these problems as soon as possible should not lead us to improvise, especially since we have learned that no isolated measure, no matter how just or effective it seems, can lead to the true, radical solutions we are aiming for. We must understand above all that the only way to tackle systematically the problems of our economic development and overcome our weaknesses is by dealing with the situation in its entirety and following the laws of the construction of socialism; that no administrative or propaganda measures are capable, in themselves, of automatically eliminating vices that have become habits.

On the other hand, experience has shown that in such circumstances it is necessary to avoid unilateral judgments, avoid excessive zeal, and now, also watch out for those who are too demanding, the demagogic "champions," the petty-bourgeois extremists who tend to crop up in such situations in order to divert the attention from their own faults and weaknesses [*Applause*] and pretend to be demanding when they are really opportunists trying to avoid being called on to account for themselves. With this aim in mind, some people can go as far as perpetrating injustices, using their positions to punish comrades who are perhaps less liable than they themselves. We must demand to the utmost, but we must also watch out for those "superdemanders." We must be firm but just in our demands; we must avoid witch-hunts, which are foreign to our methods, our principles, and the character of our people. [*Applause*]

The comrades in charge of the mass media have an important role to play in this process, for at such a time it is essential to keep the masses well-informed.

I have seen and heard various interpretations of the opinions I gave on behalf of the party leadership on October 28. This is even more unfortunate in light of the fact that in certain cases the interpretations were made by comrades who are supposed to have a certain maturity and have shown themselves on occasion to be capable of making thorough analyses. It is not a question of simplifying the criticism, making it seem that all workers are irresponsible and all administrators and administrative officials are complacent; it is not a question of joking about issues that, rather, should be food for thought.

Sometimes the criticisms are expressed in such a way that one cannot tell whether they are denouncing something that was done, condemning a practice, or simply making fun of those involved. Discipline must be restored at all costs and in all spheres, and to do this we must start at home and start from the top. [*Applause*] It is not exactly the workers who are to be blamed. In the present situation, the revolution will show that the thing which we still haven't rid ourselves of completely in reality — will once and for all become something of the capitalist past.

The fact is that there are many instances of lack of work discipline, unjustified absences from work, deliberate go-slows so as not to surpass the norms, which are already low and poorly applied in practice, so that they won't be changed because they are being more than met. In contrast to capitalism, when people in the countryside worked from sunup to sundown, that is, an exhausting twelve-hour working day and more, there are a good many instances today, especially in agriculture, of people one way or another pulling one trick or another, pulling the wool over their own eyes and harming themselves in the process, and working no more than four or six hours, with the exception of canecutters and possibly a few other kinds of work. We know that in many cases heads of brigades and foremen make a deal with the workers under them to meet the norm in half a day and then go off and work for the other half for some nearby small farmer; or to go slow and meet the norm in seven or eight hours; or do two or three norms in a day and report them over other days, too, days on which they don't go to work, either just to do nothing at all or to do something else that brings in some more money; or to surpass the norm in eight hours but report having worked for ten or twelve hours so as not to have the norm upped.

There are times when the complicity goes even further and brigade chiefs or foremen who have their own work to do and their own norm to meet simulate having done it by reporting a fraudulent norm met by chalking up work done over and above the norm by those working under them. All this is detrimental to production, the costs of the enterprise, and the produce that should be meeting the needs of the people. And all these "tricks of the trade" in agriculture are also to be found in industry, transportation services, repair shops, and many other places where there's rampant buddyism, cases of "you do me a favor and I'll do you one," and pilfering on the side.

But the main ones to blame for all these weaknesses and the lack of work discipline are not the workers but the managers and functionaries of enterprises who, we know, fiddle the statistics, reporting land ready or planted when it's not, production that hasn't been done, using and abusing the prerogatives that go with their post and the resources of their enterprise to solve problems of their own and of their friends. They have no standing when it comes to being demanding of others. [*Applause*]

The weaknesses and negligence are the responsibility of managers and of all of us who have not set up the most adequate work and salary mechanism and have not known how to organize things and create a certain sense of political and work responsibility on the part of the workers. This is something the Executive Committee of the Council of Ministers is at present working on, to come up with a new salary system whereby salaries correspond more effectively with the quantity and quality of work done and the end product of that work; operate more as a means of stimulating increases in output and production, increased efficiency, goods for export, and economizing on resources, all on the basis of a substantial improvement in work organization and norms.

We are working hard to round off economic mechanisms for boosting production, especially agricultural production. We are also working to modify labor legislation within the framework of the economic management system. When fully operational, this should spur on the productive forces which are at present verging on stagnation, idleness, and subutilization as a result of excessively rigid procedures being applied.

Management administers the economic policy outlined by the party and the higher state and governmental bodies. The party needs it to be strong, prestigious, and firm. Nobody wants to berate our functionaries; nobody wants to make them pay for what they haven't done. On the contrary, measures will be introduced to increase their powers and responsibilities. Enterprise heads and managers should have the powers to take action where workers who do not meet their social duty are concerned, because the managers represent the interests of the people and in defense of those interests should have the ways and means of confronting indolent workers who are out to get as much as possible from society while putting as little as possible in. But the party and government leadership cannot tolerate some functionaries losing prestige by not going about their duty. We must not hesitate to call to account all those who prove to be inept, lazy, and weak-spirited; we must demand they be held materially and administratively responsible.

The authority administrators have comes from a job done well, a life given over to work, a work style that is far removed from fraudulent buddyism and warping tolerance, and from living a modest life in keeping with their means.

To be modest means knowing how to relate to one's work collective, being open to criticism, working hard and being demanding of others and oneself, cultivating friendships on a principled basis, being close to the people, and above all living according to the remuneration received for one's contribution to society. [*Applause*]

It isn't a question of petty-bourgeois egalitarianism and demagogy, which would be in contradiction with the functional efficiency of leaders were they not paid in keeping with the responsibility they take upon themselves and the qualifications needed to hold one post or another. All our people understand that functionaries and cadres at a certain level need certain minimum conditions for their work, which in many cases involves the use of a car, say, as an essential work tool. It's a question of not abusing those prerogatives that go with the job and the position, not using them as if they owned what the people have created and paid for with their sweat and toil. [*Applause*] What is under their control and administration is to be used for work and the social good, not for their own or their family's comfort. [*Applause*]

People of Santiago, over a quarter of a century has passed since the attack on the Moncada garrison, and it's twenty-three years since November 30 [1956]; two decades since the people's triumph on January 1. There have been great changes in our country. Nothing is left of the opprobrious regime of exploitation we fought then; Santiago finally knew the peace that comes of liberation. The children were able to study and be happy growing up, and the men and women were able to use their energies in a creative way.

Again the country calls on you, this time not to take up arms, nor shed blood anew, but to surmount the difficulties that come of economic construction, to back party directives, and to move forward under its leadership. [*Applause*]

To the memory immortal of our glorious heroes, in the name of Fidel and the party, we call on the people of the land of the [Antonio] Maceos and on all our people to wage this battle. [*Applause*] It's up to the people of Santiago, their party, and their mass organizations to speak up. It's up to all our people, our party members, and members of the Young Communist League and all mass organizations. Let dignity and decorum, courage and manliness, spirit and revolutionary honesty take the floor. [*Applause*] Let criticism of defects be a constant and be directed at all alike. We are referring to correct criticism, well-founded, healthy, constructive criticsm at the right time and place and formulated in the right way. [*Applause*] We make a clear distinction between criticism formulated by revolutionaries and ill-intentioned, insidious, and slanderous attacks made by the enemy or which play into the hands of the enemy. We must be firm in countering attacks passing for criticism, wherever they are made manifest, as in the high points of the revolution. [*Applause*] Everybody in the country has a place and means for correctly expressing criticism; if they are party or Young Communist League members, in their respective organizations; if they are simple workers, through their union and in production meetings, in the Committees for the Defense of the Revolution, in the Federation of Cuban Women, in the National Association of Small Farmers, and always with a view to strengthening the revolution, not weakening it.

We should not brake the revolutionary criticism of the masses; we should stimulate it. [*Applause*] It is sometimes argued that we should not publicize our defects and our errors because in doing so we are helping the enemy. This idea is completely false. To not be open and frank in facing up to our errors and shortcomings in a courageous, resolute way is what makes us weak and helps our enemies. [*Applause*] The constant fight against our defects and weaknesses is, in fact, a fight against our enemies; and we must always be on the ready. The party, the Young Communist League, the unions, and the other mass organizations bear a large part of the responsibility in this, and we call on them to wage this battle along with our people.

Let us fight with the same energy and firmness of spirit against our defects and the remnants of counterrevolution that hope to raise their ugly heads! [*Applause*] Let us wipe out all our shortcomings and show revolutionary intransigence in putting the detractors and the faint-hearted in their place! [*Applause*] That workers give their all, and that cadres make their lives and work examples of dedication and industry!

No Revolution Can Ignore Its
Links to the Masses

September 27, 1980

NOTE: The antibureaucratic drive Raúl Castro outlined in 1979 set the stage for the events surrounding the exodus of 125,000 Cubans from the port of Mariel in the spring of 1980. The "faint-hearted," "demoralized," and "defeatist" elements Raúl Castro had denounced were a significant layer of those who left.

This was a full-scale political battle inside Cuba. The U.S. government and media presented the Mariel boat-lift as a defeat for the revolution, an indication of its lack of support among the Cuban people. These claims, along with the anger most Cubans felt at those who were abandoning their country and the revolution, led to a series of demonstrations, meetings, and speak-outs throughout Cuba, many of them spontaneous. A common sentiment was "Good riddance" to the escoria *("scum") and a determination to resist whatever attacks the U.S. government might carry out against Cuba.*

The high points of this battle were three giant mass mobilizations. On April 17, one million people marched in Havana; on May 1, 1.5 million assembled at the Plaza of the Revolution for a rally in support of the revolution; and on May 17, five million people — half the country's population — demonstrated in a number of cities. These were the largest mobilizations in the revolution's history. Not only did they demonstrate for the entire world the broad base of popular support for the revolution, but they helped deepen the political awareness of the Cuban people. The Cuban revolution emerged from this whole experience greatly strengthened.

The following are major excerpts from Castro's speech to a rally of over one million people in Havana's Plaza of the Revolution, to mark the twentieth anniversary of the founding of the Committees for the Defense of the Revolution. It was held several months after the Mariel events and the subsequent mobilizations. The text has been taken from Granma Weekly Review, *October 5, 1980.*

Compatriots:
   Actually, it's exactly twenty years tomorrow but the leadership of our party decided we should celebrate today so that the members of the

CDRs and the rest of the people of Havana wouldn't have to give up their day of rest tomorrow. [*Applause*] This is why we're celebrating the twentieth anniversary today, here in the Plaza of the Revolution. And what a celebration! On our way here we witnessed the same scene of completely empty streets that we saw when we staged the Marches of the Fighting People on April 19 and May 17, or when we held the May Day rally. [*Applause*] We had thought that no rally in the plaza would ever be as big as the one held on May Day. [*Applause*] But we can see, in this new demonstration of our people's enthusiasm and of the strength of the Committees for the Defense of the Revolution, that this rally is equal to that held on May Day. [*Applause*]

In the last twenty years, this wonderful, powerful mass organization has accumulated a worthy record of service to our country and the revolution. For many years we met in this plaza, on a different rostrum to celebrate September 28, until the reasonable decision was taken to hold these mass rallies at regular intervals. In every one of those meetings the achievements of the Committees for the Defense of the Revolution and their yearly work were analyzed.

It would be impossible to conceive of the history of our revolution without the CDRs. [*Applause*] In the first place, on account of their defense of the revolution during the most difficult years, when the enemy's hostility was greater, when its plans of aggression, subversion, and sabotage were most actively put into effect. That was, is, and will always be — and I repeat, was, is, and will always be — the first and foremost task and the first duty of the Committees for the Defense of the Revolution, [*Applause*] because the form the struggle takes changes, and, as [CDR National Coordinator] Armando [Acosta] pointed out, we may be faced with difficult times again. This may depend, as he said, on the outcome of the next election in the United States: whether a platform of war or a platform of peace wins out. The prospects for our country, Latin America, and perhaps the entire world of moving in the direction of détente and peace, or to a situation of cold war or even hot war depend on that. However, since nobody can predict the future, we must always be ready to face up to the most difficult situations.

In addition to fulfilling their first, basic duty, the committees have served the country in an exceptional way in many fields: in developing the political and revolutionary awareness of the masses, in the constant mobilization of the people for different tasks, in public health. Who knows how many tens of thousands of lives the committees have helped to save? We must not think that the committees' work is symbolized only by the fact that on a beautiful day like today we have introduced to you from the rostrum a young girl who was born the day the committees were founded. I'm sure that here in the plaza and all over the country there are tens of thousands of young people and others who owe their lives to the work of the committees. [*Applause*] The organization has distinguished itself in the struggle against epidemics and such terrible and painful diseases as polio and tetanus; in the struggle to prevent diseases and to detect them in time; in the matter of blood donations. We could also mention the work of the committees in the field of production: readying the land for mechanized cane cutting, taking part in the sugar harvest and other agricultural projects, weeding canefields, and planting trees.

The committees have helped embellish our cities and gather raw materials for recycling, thus saving our country tens of millions of pesos in foreign exchange. The committees have taken part in organizing every large-scale activity in our country. The committees not only defend the revolution, they also defend the wealth of the people, and this is shown by the fact that night after night, not counting emergency situations, 30,000 men and women who are members of the committees stand guard over our factories, public buildings, and homes. [*Applause*]

Therefore, the organization's services to our country and revolution can be described as extraordinary.

But there's more: the committees contribute to our political defense not only at home, but they also contribute to defending us against attacks from abroad since their work helps to improve the combat readiness of our Revolutionary Armed Forces and to boost their morale. [*Applause*]

However, we should not gauge the merits and importance of the organization solely on the basis of its services. The implications are more important, more far-reaching. The CDRs represent an experiment that other sister nations have begun to put into effect. They also represent an extraordinary political experience; what a revolution really needs to protect itself and to be strong, something that no Marxist-Leninist party can ever ignore, and that is, the closest ties possible with the masses! [*Applause*]

The Committees for the Defense of the Revolution, along with our glorious trade unions, the Federation of Cuban Women, the National Association of Small Farmers, the student organizations, and the Pioneer organization, represent a powerful mechanism and an insuperable instrument to link our party to the masses. [*Applause*] And I dare say that they are unique in the world. [*Applause*] It isn't that many other revolutions and many other parties are not linked to the masses, since all really revolutionary parties have always been characterized by such links. What I mean is that in our country we have the most complete mechanism to link the party with the masses, and the Committees for the Defense of the Revolution are one of the pillars of that mechanism. [*Applause*] Facts show and experience shows that no Marxist-Leninist party can ever neglect its links with the masses. [*Applause*]

This reality in Cuba gives us great confidence in the future of our revolution. And our revolution is no longer a baby. It's not two, five, ten, or fifteen years old. It's already over twenty years old! [*Applause*] And today the CDRs are twenty years old! [*Applause*] Every twenty, fifty, and even one hundred years, the Cuban revolution will recount its history and celebrate its victories! [*Applause*]

It's not true that time dampens enthusiasm. Our own experience has shown that time multiplies the enthusiasm and adds to it revolutionary awareness. [*Applause*]

Several months ago, our enemies deceived themselves as to the power of our revolution. But our people showed their power, to such an extent that they had to be asked to control themselves. [*Applause*] Our people showed their spirit, their awareness, and today the revolution is stronger than ever before. [*Applause*]

With a party closely linked to the people, with a just, honest policy, a revolution is indestructible. [*Applause*] And that is what we, the Cuban revolutionaries of this generation and of future generations, the present leadership of our party and the future generations of leaders must preserve: the close links with the masses, and a just, honest policy. [*Applause*] Our revolutionary generation could have made mistakes and did so, but it always remained loyal to the principle of a just and honest policy! [*Applause*]

These are reflections that have come to mind today.

The Committees for the Defense of the Revolution already have over 5,350,000 members; [*Applause*] there are almost 81,000 CDRs; and, unless my memory fails me, there are almost 10,000 zone committees. However, what's important is the number of members: 5,350,000, that is, practically 80 percent of the adult population. And the only reason for the membership not being larger is that in the past few years the organization has been especially careful in choosing new members. [*Applause*]

This is why, whereas twenty years ago the Committees for the Defense of the Revolution were founded on a relatively small avenue in front of the former Presidential Palace, today, the members of the CDRs practically don't fit in this gigantic plaza. [*Applause*] It's not a question of figures in the millions, but a question of millions of active men and women, a question of the degree of commitment. When I read that the committees had set themselves the goal of bringing over a million people here, I thought it'd be quite a difficult thing to accomplish. And yet today we see more than a million people here! [*Applause*]

You all know that we don't like to exaggerate. And the size of rallies like this one can only be really appreciated from atop the tower or from the air, aboard a plane or a helicopter. Even so, I believe that the photos of this rally will also form part of the documentary evidence of the history of the Committees for the Defense of the Revolution. [*Applause*]

Our country has made a tremendous effort in terms of organization and institutionalization in the last five years. So many things were achieved in such a short period of time! The constitution of our socialist state, approved by over 90 percent of our people; the political-administrative division of the country, which is now a reality, the establishment of the organs of People's Power, which are working with increasing efficiency; the adoption of a series of measures for the progressive implementation of the Economic Management and Planning System; and the increased controls over finance and the economy.

In the next five years especially we will begin to reap the fruits of the decisions taken at the First Congress of the party which have been gradually applied in the last five years. Many industrial centers have been built which are already beginning to produce or will begin to produce in the very near future; other important projects will be completed in the next five-year period. These new factories will increase production and will make available more important products for our economy. For example, the production facilities for cement, steel for use in construction, and textiles, to name only a few, have increased substantially. We have been working on a realistic plan for the next five years, and we hope that with the experience we have accumulated and the measures we have adopted, it will be carried out in full.

While there will be no spectacular leap in our people's living standard, there will be a progressive improvement over the next five-year period. We will, for example, have many more domestic appliances: there will be approximately one million new television sets for the population over the next five years, hundreds of thousands of refrigerators, hundreds of thousands of washing machines, a considerable number of electric fans, tens of thousands of Soviet-made air conditioners. [*Applause*] Over the next five years, 58,000 cars, largely Soviet-made, will be imported into the country; 15,000 will be to replace in part the current cars for hire, around 30,000 will be for sale to the people, and the other part will be assigned to institutions.

Housing construction will increase considerably each year, bearing in mind materials available. Repair work will also continue to have preferential treatment over this next five-year period. And a special effort will be made with regard to growing root and other vegetables, fruit, and other foodstuffs.

Under the current agreements on coordinating plans, we are guaranteed all the fuel we need for our country over the next five years. [*Applause*] We will have enough fuel, although this does not exonerate us from our obligation to economize as much as possible in this direction. Many other raw materials are also assured: a growing amount of sheet metal, chemical products, fertilizer, etc.

We are assured of the number of trucks and public transportation vehicles we need, as well as agricultural machinery and equipment. And I think I can say that, if we keep up the level of efficiency we have reached over the last few months in terms of public transportation in the capital, there will be no more critical problems where that form of transportation is concerned. [*Applause*] Some months ago there were only 19,000 trips a day in all; now there are about 26,000. And if the workers and management of the bus enterprise pull together with us in this, we hope that there will be 29,000 trips a day by the end of the year. [*Applause*] Despite this, however, given that we only have bus transportation, that a city of over two million inhabitants does not have a subway, say, which is what most big cities rely on; the fact that we have to depend on buses alone will always mean a certain strain on public transportation.

The number of doctors today stands at 16,000; at the end of the next five-year period it will be 24,000. [*Applause*] Although our basic educational needs are well on the way to being met, as are our needs for health institutions, we will continue to build more polyclinics, dental clinics, and hospitals; we will continue to build schools, although at a slower pace, given the number of schools we already have. But medical services will continue to improve, as will education and services in general. The internal-order services will improve with the measures we have been taking; our Revolutionary Armed Forces will continue to further their combat readiness; [*Applause*] the Territorial Militia will be set up; [*Applause*] financial and economic controls are to be implemented, and the Economic Management and Planning System is to be fully functioning. It is to be expected, then, that the next five-year period will be one of considerable advances.

We hope that discipline will improve, due not only to recent legal measures but also to the work of the party, the trade unions, and mass organizations, and to the fact that people are better informed and more aware of this problem. We also hope that there will be greater efficiency and a greater sense of responsibility on the part of management as a result of legal measues and the efforts of the party and state to this end. We hope that not a minute will be lost and that people will become more exacting in their work. [*Applause*]

Although there are international problems and dangers, although we must realize that the already grave international situation can become much more critical, we don't have the right to be pessimistic. We must not renounce the right to struggle and do our part for détente and world peace. The world needs peace; [*Applause*] our country needs peace to be able to devote its energies to work.

In the face of the international economic crisis, we have the advantage of our economic relations with the socialist camp, and this year world sugar prices have also risen. We will possibly have another year of good prices, which will help our development and our meeting our economic plans. We mustn't have any illusions as to spending more because the price is up; now while the price is up, we must economize and administer our resources more efficiently than ever. [*Applause*]

This year we have done more weeding than ever before during the revolutionary period — I don't mean the gigantic weeding out of the scum, I mean weeding sugarcane. [*Laughter*] We did more, I repeat, than ever before during the revolutionary period. According to reports we have, the spring planting is also the best of the revolutionary period, to counteract the effects of cane smut; and a great effort has been made for the sugar mills to start on time, to make the most of the harvest. Now that prices have risen, we have no right to waste even a grain of sugar. It is of decisive importance that we do everything to ensure an optimal harvest.

This is the immediate outlook. In this spirit and with this enthusiasm, we approach the Second Congress of our party, [*Applause*] with around 400,000 party members and candidates to membership [*Applause*] and with a strong youth organization. A force of 400,000 revolutionary combatants is extraordinary, especially considering how careful the party has been in ensuring its quality and how careful it has been over recent years in recruiting members working directly in production and services. Four hundred thousand members is a considerable force, especially bearing in mind that there is alongside it a vanguard people, [*Applause*] a people in whose ranks there are millions of men and women like you. [*Applause*] This is what makes our revolution indestructible.

We have everything practically; all we need is that those in positions of responsibility be on top of their work. [*Applause*] We will march forward with you, our unionized workers, our peasants, our women, our students, our children. Which is why, on a day like today, we have even more right to say:

Patria o muerte!

Venceremos! [*Ovation*]

The Ideological Struggle

Excerpt from Report to Second Party Congress

December 17, 1980

NOTE: The Second Congress of the Communist Party of Cuba was held December 17-20, 1980, in Havana. In this section from the main report Castro presents a balance sheet of the Mariel events and the people's response, pointing to their historical significance. It is reprinted from Main Report: Second Congress of the Communist Party of Cuba *(New York: Center for Cuban Studies, 1981).*

At a certain point during this five-year period, it became clear that a number of bad habits were spreading in our country. Perhaps it was felt that the institutionalization of the country, socialist legality, the creation of People's Power, and the progressive implementation of the Economic Management and Planning System would, in themselves, perform miracles and that everything would get much better automatically without the essential, basic efforts of man. What is worse, there were increasing signs that the spirit of austerity was flagging, that a softening-up process was going on in which some people tended to let things slide, pursue privileges, make accommodations, and take other attitudes, while work discipline dropped. Our worst enemies could not have done us more damage. Was our revolution beginning to degenerate on our imperialist enemy's doorstep? Was that an inexorable law for any revolution in power? Under no circumstances could such a thing be permitted. It showed that demands for orderliness should never be neglected in a revolution. So these problems were discussed openly, measures were taken, and the pernicious tendencies began to be surmounted. But that is not enough. We must be constantly on guard and alert in our demands so we can deal firmly with the first signs of petty-bourgeois, accommodating, or undisciplined attitudes and even the slightest evidence of corruption. This should serve as a warning and an example. Our people's unanimous support for the struggle to achieve higher standards and against all signs of softness and accommodation shows how thoroughly our masses have absorbed the moral principles of the revolution and demonstrates that, far from degenerating, our revolutionary process is growing stronger all the time. It has been said that eternal vigilance is the price of liberty. It is also the price of the revolution.

Our people's communist and internationalist consciousness has undoubtedly increased in recent years. When we say this, we are not speaking only — or even mainly — of the important cultural and theoretical advances that have been made. I am primarily referring to specific circumstances in which our people show that consciousness. Throughout the country, attitudes toward work, organization, higher standards, combativity, and revolutionary firmness are all at a much higher level. This is especially evident in our working class and has been brilliantly shown by our intellectual workers as well. Tens of thousands of teachers, doctors, and other professionals and technicians have worked with dedication here and enthusiastically undertaken difficult and honorable missions abroad. Hundreds of thousands of soldiers and reservists in our Revolutionary Armed Forces have expressed their willingness to participate in Cuba's internationalist aid to sister countries that were under attack and millions of our compatriots lead exemplary, genuinely proletarian, austere, collectivist, honest, and disciplined lives.

This, of course, does not mean that we have always done the best possible political and ideological work or that we can cross our arms and say we have won the battle.

It is necessary to understand the special situation in which for over twenty years Cuba has been waging its confrontation with imperialism in the realm of ideas. The existence, just a few miles from our coasts, of the richest, most aggressive capitalist country in the world, a paradise of individualism, gambling, drugs, prostitution, and other alienating vices has forced us to respond courageously to this open and unending challenge.

The United States has always been the sworn enemy of our nation. Ever since the beginning of the nineteenth century, Spanish colonial rule and the powerful *criollos*,* who owned most of the coffee and sugarcane plantations and hundreds of thousands of slaves, fostered a strong annexationist, anti-independence current in our country. Many of those landowners considered the preservation of the slave system through annexation to the United States more important than national independence. They feared that a slave uprising in the struggle for independence would cost them their socioeconomic privileges or that Spain, pressured by England, would emancipate the slaves. This explains why Cuba was the last country in the Americas to obtain its independence from Spain — nearly 100 years later than the other Spanish colonies in the region. Annexationism did not, however, prevent the development of a strong

---

*The local ruling class in Cuba, of Spanish origin.

patriotic movement, which fully demonstrated its strength and desire for freedom in the heroic wars of 1868 and 1895.

Yankee interventionism, the imposition of the Platt Amendment,* the seizure of the country's wealth, and the installation of a neocolonial regime frustrated our people's desires and were a rude blow to our national spirit. In practice, we were annexed to the United States. The Yankee system, ideology, laws, culture, habits, customs, prejudices, and vices became part of our neocolonial, dependent way of life. Our economy became an appendage of U.S. monopoly capital, and Cuba became another piece of Yankee property.

Before 1959, a steady stream of Cubans wanted to leave their underdeveloped country and move to the metropolis, but the United States imposed a number of restrictions to limit to a few thousand this economic migration.

After the victory of the revolution, the United States opened its doors to Cuban war criminals, torturers, embezzlers of public funds, plantation owners, urban real estate magnates, big businessmen, and others of that ilk. At the same time, it went to great lengths to rob us of our engineers, doctors, administrators, and even middle-level technicians and skilled workers. It took advantage of its position as the world's most developed, richest country — with a much higher standard of living and wages than Cuba — to try to bleed us of our skilled personnel and thus destroy the revolutionary process, linking this policy to economic blockade, threats, and aggression of all kinds. The revolution valiantly took up the challenge and permitted everyone who wanted to leave to do so. We were quite ready to create a new homeland and make our socialist revolution with men and women who had freely decided to stay; we also began to develop our schools and universities — in which hundreds of thousands of specialists and skilled workers have since been trained.

Millions of individuals — the vast majority of our people — preferred to live here under economic blockade and the threat of annihilation rather than abandon their homeland. It was our socialist revolution, with its unselfish, heroic struggle, that forged our Cuban patriotic national spirit once and for all. A new generation of doctors, engineers, teachers, and technicians has been trained in the years since the triumph of the revolution, and they have taken their place alongside the many intellectual workers who remained loyal to their homeland. Now we have many more trained, aware, revolutionary workers than we had before, and our technicians are at present serving in more than thirty foreign countries.

---

*An amendment forced into the Cuban constitution by the U.S. government when independence was declared in 1902. It gave the U.S. the right to intervene in Cuban affairs — including militarily — whenever the U.S. government saw fit.

Imperialism, however, has never stopped attacking our Cuban national spirit, constantly putting it to the test. It employs the gross exhibition of wealth, most of which was plundered from the world's underdeveloped peoples; constantly bribes and incites our citizens to desert and betray their country; and takes advantage of the separation of tens of thousands of Cuban families to restrict legal travel to the United States while encouraging, publicizing, and welcoming as heroes anyone who leaves Cuba by such illegal means as hijacking boats, taking hostages, and committing monstrous murders — all to feed its cynical propaganda.

In spite of the tremendous efforts the revolution has made to promote socioeconomic development — especially in education — some social disgrace from the past still remains: a total lack of national feeling on the part of some, combined with the fact that the socioeconomic conditions in our developing country still produce some declassed, antisocial, lumpen elements that are receptive to imperialist enticements and ideas.

For these reasons, a bitter ideological struggle has been waged by our imperialist enemy and the Cuban revolution — a struggle that has been and will continue to be fought not only in the realm of revolutionary and political ideas but also in the sphere of our people's patriotic national feelings. Imperialism refuses to resign itself to a revolutionary, socialist Cuba; a Cuba that has freed itself from the United States forever; a Cuba that has held out and gained prestige in its struggle against the Yankee giant; a Cuba in which patriotic feelings are deeper, more solid, and more lasting then ever.

It is true that our country has a modest way of life, one without luxuries or extravagance, but we are fully convinced of the justice of our ideas, our dignity, and our morale, and perfectly capable of using these qualities to defy all the rottenness of the imperialist consumer society. This time, the imperialists were stopped by our people's courage and could not skim off our specialists and trained personnel. This time they got our scum.

The people's marches — an outpouring in response to the acts of provocation at the Peruvian and Venezuelan embassies, to the Mariel flotilla, and to the Yankee military threats — will go down in history.

Never before have there been such huge mass mobilizations in our homeland. Once again, they underestimated our people's level of consciousness. The revolution and the masses decided, once and for all, to take up the challenge. We remained perfectly calm while the imperialists ground out their version of what happened in the Peruvian embassy. The antisocial individuals themselves — whom the capitalist news agencies started off calling "dissidents" — showed what kind of people they really were, so all our enemy's lies were exposed to ridicule. The people demonstrated that their strength, unity, awareness, fighting spirit, and discipline were unbeatable. Young people won their first revolutionary laurels in the vanguard of this great political and ideological battle. While Cuba made the cleanest sweep in its history, the masses were tempered and tremendously strengthened in the struggle, and their spirit of patriotism and defense of the principles of socialism and proletarian internationalism were deepened. The struggle also boosted production and discipline and helped us find solutions for our own internal weaknesses. The enemy once again learned that our people cannot be challenged with impunity.

We consider the battle that the masses waged last April and May to be one of the most important political, ideological, and moral victories the revolution has won in its entire history.

As we have already noted, it is significant that this struggle had positive repercussions in the national effort to eradicate a series of ideological problems that had been gaining ground in this period.

The people's repudiation of the scum also meant that they repudiated undisciplined behavior, sponging, accommodation, negligence, and other such negative attitudes. The position the people took, coupled with the political, legal, wage, and administrative measures adopted during the past few months, has led to a much greater demand for higher standards and more order in our society. We intend to continue striving to find permanent solutions for these problems.

It is still too early to determine how this policy has affected the Cuban community abroad. Following our people's indignant reaction to what was going on and the repeated acts of provocation at the Venezuelan and Peruvian embassies, their visits were reduced to a minimum. Our policy on this will be determined by the attitude the new U.S. administration takes.

We'll have to see whether or not Mr. Reagan suspends the right of U.S. citizens and residents to travel to Cuba. It is also essential that visits here in the case of individuals of Cuban origin be allowed only to those who have never engaged in any hostile acts against this country, who left Cuba legally, and who are willing to respect the revolution. Drastic measures will be taken against anyone who attempts to engage in any counterrevolutionary activities. Our policy will be based on these considerations, disregarding any profit that accrues to Cuba from such visits.

One of the factors that contributed to a certain degree of laxity in socioeconomic activity was that frequently people were not as critical and self-critical as necessary.

It became evident that this phenomenon was widespread and even affected the party to a certain extent. In some places, the general attitude was formal, conformist, and basically petty-bourgeois in the sense of avoiding problems with everybody — as if the revolution itself were not always trying to straighten out problems involving injustice and poor work. In the administrative sphere, this trend had negative effects on labor discipline, control, and adequate use of resources.

It has been said, with good reason, that our political and ideological work cannot be abstract but must be firmly linked to specific national and international socioeconomic tasks. While we continue to give our party cadres and members and the people in general theoretical training and staunchly defend Marxism-Leninism against all distortion, we must also be especially concerned with the workers' economic education within the framework of the principles and laws of socialism; with the moral training our children and young people receive; and with raising the communist and internationalist consciousness of all our compatriots. We should continue to promote voluntary work, giving it special emphasis as an essential factor in creating a new attitude toward work and society. Generally speaking, the experience of this recent period has reinforced our belief that elements of a moral character should continue to play a major role in our revolution, because they make us invulnerable to bourgeois ideology; strengthen our spirit in the face of the enemy's threats and acts of aggression; and make the people an invincible army, ready to fight for their cause no matter what the cost.

Aware of the importance of this front, our party is waging a determined ideological battle. Since the First Congress, this battle has included systematic work, including plans, special activities, campaigns, exhibits, mass meetings to commemorate important dates in history, and such major events as the Eleventh World Festival of Youth and Students, the Sixth Summit Conference of the Movement of Nonaligned Countries, the sixtieth anniversary of the October revolution, the March of the Fighting People, and the first Soviet-Cuban spaceflight.*

The economic education of workers has been a major topic for the mass media and in all party propaganda, but we still have a long way to go in this direction. Our propaganda should place more emphasis on production problems; present information on the most useful experiences; and, in general, provide a deeper, more consistent view of what is happening.

Mass ideological training, especially the training of children and young people in the principles of socialist patriotism and proletarian internationalism, requires systematic work. Historical events should be used to show these young people that our revolutionary process combines the purest national patriotic traditions with the universal principles of socialism and is part of the world revolutionary movement. The party

*The Eleventh World Festival of Youth and Students was held in Havana July-August 1978. The Sixth Nonaligned Summit Conference was held in Havana September 1979. In September 1980, Arnaldo Tamayo Méndez, a Black Cuban, participated in a space flight together with Soviet cosmonaut Yuri Romanenko.

has encouraged the movement of history activists to contribute to this task.

The principles of internationalism have been set forth broadly and consistently in our work of revolutionary orientation. We have made every effort to ensure that the true image of the Cuban revolution is projected abroad, explaining both our successes, shortcomings, and difficulties and our socioeconomic advances in building socialism. Our people's political understanding is impressive, and they are kept informed about the main aspects of the world situation.

We will continue our efforts to give all our people a scientific concept of nature and society so old prejudices are eradicated while developing new customs and habits that tend to strengthen fraternal relations of solidarity in our socialist society.

In recent years, the party has worked diligently to find ways of keeping its cadres and members more effectively informed on important matters that require their attention, and today we have the valuable contribution of at least 7,000 nonprofessional lecturers. This has helped a great deal, but we are working to guarantee better theoretical training and follow-up courses for them. Through the party's publishing plan, more than 600 political and ideological titles were printed during this period and have been widely distributed and promoted in the libraries set up in our grass-roots organizations. The party's graphic propaganda has improved, but its content and artistic quality could still be better. We have an efficient system for organizing and holding meetings, exhibits, and other political activities. The People's Opinion Teams have continued to ask the people what they think about specific problems. This can be an effective tool for party work and should be further developed.

The party has given priority to improving the quality and political-ideological level of the material that appears in the mass media. In compliance with the thesis of the First Congress on the written press, radio, television, and movies, a number of complementary documents have been adopted, including the resolution of the Political Bureau on attention to the party newspaper and other press organs; norms for circulating and distributing publications; a definition of the structure and staff of newspapers and magazines; a policy on radio and TV programming, and principles and standards for countering propaganda.

The mass media have made major gains in reporting on our socioeconomic development and ideological confrontation with imperialism in this period.

Our written press has continued to grow, and a significant effort has been made to ensure that each province — including the special municipality of the Isle of Youth — has its own newspaper. These papers have a total daily run of over 264,000. New publications for children and young people, for workers and for state and scientific use have appeared. The daily national press run is now up to 930,000, an average of one newspaper for every eight readers. Noteworthy results have been achieved in distributing 1.2 million newspapers daily and more than 5 million magazines and tabloids each month. The technical base of our written press will be modernized as much as possible in the next few years.

Granma, the official organ of our Central Committee, has played an outstanding role in keeping our people informed, guiding them, and helping to raise their level of education and revolutionary consciousness. It has also carried out its responsibility of setting an example for the rest of the mass media in implementing party guidelines.

The magazine *El Militante Comunista* has improved the quality and approach of its articles.

New municipal radio stations have been set up (two are especially directed at students attending schools in the countryside), color TV programming has been increased, and channels 2 and Tele Rebelde have been joined so as to make better use of technical and human resources. Investments in new equipment have resulted in considerable technological improvements in both media, especially radio. With few people, Radio Havana Cuba has maintained the high quality of its political, ideological, and professional programming, broadcasting the truth about Cuba in eight languages and increasing its programming by 27 percent.

Efforts have been made to improve program quality, in compliance with the agreements of the First Congress and the Eighth Plenary Meeting on Programming. Programs for children and young people have been increased, as have informational and cultural programs; sports programs have been broadened and diversified; 60 percent of all TV programming is nationally produced; high quality feature serials have been shown, though sustained efforts must be made to reach greater stability. More films from the socialist countries have been shown on TV; there has been more extensive programming via satellite; and special summer programs were broadcast during this period.

We do not feel fully satisfied, however, with the work done by our mass media. There are still many shortcomings. It is necessary to improve quality both in information and in the analysis and criticism.

Because of their importance in the party's ideological work, we should take special note of the efforts made by the Institute of the History of the Communist Movement and the Cuban Socialist Revolution. In its six years of existence, this institute has laid the basis for its scientific work and done far-reaching historical research which has led to the publication of valuable books and other important works in progress.

Generally speaking, our ideological work has advanced, but we should keep working to overcome the shortcomings that still exist.

Our grass-roots party organizational work should be improved so that every nucleus and every Communist is an active defender of and propagandist for party policy. We must also defy all our ideological work and make the best possible use of the political education system, agit-prop work, the mass media, cultural outlets, sports, recreation, and other avenues of expression.

Ideology is, first of all, consciousness; consciousness is revolutionary militant attitude, dignity, principles, and morale. Ideology is also an effective weapon in opposing misconduct, weaknesses, privileges, immorality. For all revolutionaries the ideological struggle is today in the forefront; it is the first revolutionary trench.

Socialism is a relatively new system in human history, for it has only been in existence for a few decades. Right from the start, it was opposed by imperialist threats, hostility, intervention, and aggression. Fascism made a brutal effort to destroy the first socialist state only twenty-four years after it had been founded. The socialist camp was built on the rubble and ruins that the Nazi hordes left behind them in the most devastated parts of Europe, which were also the continent's least developed areas. It hasn't been easy, and circumstances have hardly been propitious for spreading socialist ideas.

Our enemy has used every means at its disposal to continue fighting socialism. On the military front, it has forced the socialist countries to invest huge sums of money in defense. Politically, it has made every effort to subvert, destabilize, and discredit the socialist countries.

This reality should not be underrated — especially by our country, which is so close to the United States. Only by consistently applying the principles of Marxism-Leninism can we be strong, invulnerable, invincible.

Ours is a state of workers who exercise revolutionary power. The party and its members must always be solidly, closely, and deeply linked to the masses. They must engage in rigorous criticism and self-criticism. They must not deviate from collective leadership, internal democracy, democratic centralism, and the strictest discipline. They must lead a life of austerity and embody the spirit of self-sacrifice, unselfishness, selflessness, honesty, solidarity, and heroism that should characterize every Communist.

Every Communist should be a staunch fighter, convinced of the absolute justice of his cause; he should be studious, hard-working, demanding and deeply committed to his people. The party exists through and for the people. Bureaucratic and petty-bourgeois attitudes are completely alien to its principles. The strongest, closest ties should exist between the party cadres and members and the people, mainly based on the example set by revolutionaries and the confidence inspired by their commitment to the people.

Authoritarianism, demagoguery, a know-it-all attitude, vanity, and irresponsibility are inconceivable in Communists, for they should always have a fraternal and humane attitude toward others and — especially — an internationalist spirit that, while including deep-rooted patriotism, is based on an understanding that their homeland is more important than any individual and that humanity is the most important of all.

If a Communist Party in power commits or tolerates serious errors of principle, those errors will prove very costly to the revolutionary process — as history has shown. Betrayals have done great damage to the world revolutionary movement.

Is socialism in any given country irreversible or not? It is utterly irreversible if the principles are applied. Our people have demonstrated this. We are at Yankee imperialism's doorstep, yet we do not fear its power, do not dream of its wealth, do not accept its ideology, and are not destabilized by its actions.

Have we made mistakes? Of course we have. Have we always been consistent in strictly applying each and every principle, and are we, therefore, unblemished, exemplary Communists who have never done anything wrong — even out of lack of understanding, incompetence, or ignorance? No, but it has always been our policy to be honest, loyal to our principles, and dedicated to the revolutionary Cuban people. The party's close links with the masses make it stronger and guarantee that it will consistently apply the principles that will make it invincible.

In our country, Marxist-Leninist ideas are also profoundly linked to our people's patriotic, heroic traditions. Céspedes,* Agramonte, Gómez, Maceo, and Martí are, for us, inseparable from Marx, Engels, and Lenin. They are linked to our consciences, just as patriotic thinking is linked to internationalism; national liberty to equality and social justice; the history of one country to the history of the world; and our homeland to humanity. The foundations of the country in which we are now building socialism were laid with the sweat, blood, and heroism of our predecessors, and today we are doing what they did when they founded our homeland.

Let us follow the example of those who created our homeland and who opened up a new path for humanity. Let us adhere to these ideas loyally, and no force on earth can separate our party from our people or deter our people from their revolutionary course.

We still have a long way to go and many problems to solve as we build socialism, but history has already shown that our ideas are far superior to and infinitely more humane than those of capitalism. The clock of history never turns back. Capitalism, with its egoism, crime, and vice, will disappear, just as feudalism and slavery did; and, even if one country should take a step backward, humanity never will.

*Carlos Manuel de Céspedes was the central leader of the Cuban independence fighters in the 1868-78 war.

An Interview with
Carlos Rafael Rodríguez
December 1980

NOTE: Carlos Rafael Rodríguez was a long-time leader of the People's Socialist Party before the revolution, and has been a leading figure in the Communist Party of Cuba since its formation. He is currently a member of the party's Political Bureau and is vice-president of the Council of State. In the interview below Rodríguez takes up the question of bureaucracy, the Communist Party, and the relation between the revolutionary leadership and the masses.

The interview was conducted by Marta Harnecker, a Chilean journalist living in Cuba and author of Cuba: Dictatorship or Democracy? *(Westport, Connecticut: Lawrence Hill & Company, 1980). It appeared in* Areíto, *Vol. VII, No. 25. The following excerpts were translated by* Intercontinental Press *and appeared in its July 20, 1981, issue.*

Marta Harnecker: Revolutionary leaderships, due to their multiple tasks in the state apparatus as well as in the party, can fall, and in fact in some countries have fallen, into a state of great detachment from the masses. As a result they have been ignorant of the state of mind of the masses. What mechanisms does the Cuban revolutionary leadership use to maintain its links with the masses?

Has the revolutionary leadership been surprised at any point by concerns of the population that weren't detected in time? Do you think that the new Central Committee of the party, which came out of the second party congress that has just ended and has a significant number of working-class members, indicates an effort to overcome this problem?

Carlos Rafael Rodríguez: Marta, you ask me too many questions at one time. I think we are free from that danger which has brought so many difficulties in other countries.

In my view, the fundamental element preventing the Cuban revolution and its leaders from becoming detached from the masses lies in the personality and the working style of Fidel. I would not be honest if I didn't stress this element as decisive in our work. The great link between the revolutionary leadership and the people is, in the first place, Fidel himself. His continuous contact with the masses, not at the abstract level but in a very concrete manner — on the scene, in the areas of production, education, and research — constitutes a guarantee.

But besides that, I think that the party and the government have taken care to establish permanent links with the totality of the population, so that their problems and judgments reach the high levels of the leadership as rapidly and as accurately as possible.

In this sense, the party is a precious instrument, but I would say that the party still has to improve its political linkages. The rank-and-file party bodies are often absorbed by their responsibilities in productive tasks and their internal functions, and there has been a constant effort by the leadership to ensure that the party — which is the decisive instrument for the communication between the leadership and the masses — engages in much wider political activity, concerns itself with the problems of the working class and workers in general, perceives their concerns, and transmits them to the party leadership, the working class, and the people.

The trade union movement plays a very important role in the process of discussion of concrete labor problems that emerge in a society that's building socialism. We don't think, however, that the unions play the role that they should.

Our unions are much better at transmitting the party's orientations to the working class than they are at gathering from the working class the desires, the criticisms, the suggestions to which the leadership has to be alert. But here, also, we are undoubtedly making progress.

The Federation of Cuban Women, the women's mass organization, and the Young Communist League, the auxiliary political organization to the party, are also precious links of communication between the party and society. But besides all this, the Cuban revolution has created, as we see it, a unique instrument in the process of socialist construction — the Committees for the Defense of the Revolution.

As you know, six million citizens are members of the CDRs: people involved in production and education, as well as housewives and retired persons. We still have a lot to do so that this valid instrument of creativity and opinion generates optimal results. But, without any doubt, the committees constitute now a permanent barometer of the feelings and judgments of our people.

I don't want to exaggerate here the positive aspects of our work in this area because I feel that criticism among us has not yet reached a maturation point. There is sometimes a certain inhibition, an excessive caution in the exercise of criticism, motivated by the desire to prevent irresponsibility or disruption, which would not be, in any way, an adequate way of projecting the feelings and judgments of society.

There is a lot to do in this area, and it is a process of continuous improvement. The decisive factors in terms of the participation of the working class and the people in the transformation of society reside in the raising of the cultural, political, and ideological levels of the masses. Lenin said that socialism is a system in which the simplest cook should know how to handle state problems.

We have organized the state in order to eliminate, as much as possible, all features of bureaucratization and to promote a maximum of participation. People's Power is oriented in that direction.

As you know, the report-back assemblies, the direct forms of nomination of candidates — in sum, all the mechanisms of People's Power — involve a desire and an effort to achieve more complete participation by our people. But the present processes of guiding society are very complex. These are not the times of the Greek *agora*, where the decisions that had to be adopted were few and relatively simple.

The scientific-technical revolution imposes demands that tend to elevate the role of technocrats. Planning, for example, involves a number of technical decisions. If all segments of society were to participate in them, they would need a level of scientific understanding of the economy greater than what our workers have achieved with only a sixth-grade education.

When the revolutionary leadership sets an objective of the working class attaining at least a ninth-grade education, and a secondary education for the party members, it is also thinking about this. A society that achieves adequate cultural and technical levels will reach a more complete and mature form of self-government than a society of illiterate or semiliterate people.

I explain all this to you not because I am convinced that we have reached the desired results in this area. On the contrary. To the extent that criticism is insufficient and superficial — and it still is — and to the extent that transmission channels are not fully utilized, it is possible that certain problems do not strike the leaders' sensitivities with the necessary rapidity.

But I would say that this is not a grave problem, it does not tend to be in our country. There are very few cases in which negative phenomena, which have been rejected by the population nationally, do not reach the leadership, sooner rather than later.

It is obvious that the new composition of the Central Committee of the party, which has incorporated comrades who come directly from the workers', farmers', and women's organizations, is conducive to linking the revolutionary leadership with the people. This has been a constant concern of our party and very personally of Comrade Fidel.

I would not say that we are trying to "overcome" any situation, because, I repeat, the party leadership has always been very attentive to the opinions and feelings of our people. But we are making additional efforts to establish even more direct channels of communication. An example of this is the access that the comrades with important posts in the mass organizations have as alternate members of the Political Bureau.

Harnecker: What mechanism does the Cuban Communist Party have to detect and eliminate bad members? Can the people exercise any kind of control over the party?

Rodríguez: Marta, you could say that the entire life of the party and its organization are aimed at seeing that those whom you call "bad members" are detected in the very course of their party activity and then eliminated from it. The base organizations, the cells, maintain constant collective attention over the political and social life of their members within the workplace.

Criticism of the errors and defects of every member is an organizational principle that the party must carry out. Of course the form in which this criticism is carried out depends on the level of political maturity of the people in the cell and is not the same all over. But the party exerts itself in this aspect of its internal life, and it could be said that the self-purging of the party is a continuous process.

There is a body of sanctions — from private warnings to expulsion from the ranks of the party — that allows the organization to correct the defects of its members and to rid itself of them when experience definitely shows that they do not have the qualities needed to remain in the ranks of the party.

You ask if the people can exercise any type of control over the party. In fact, not only can they exercise it, but they do. As you know, one of the basic ingredients of the education of the party comes through the participation of the workers, in their respective workplaces, in the process of selection.

This doesn't mean that the masses of the workers decide who does or does not enter the party. But it does mean that through consultation with the co-workers of the person who hopes to join our ranks, the party is in a position to know the collectivity's social judgment and assessment of his or her personality and activity. And this is a decisive element.

In cases where the party organization feels that the mass of workers have made an incorrect assessment, it proceeds through the local leadership bodies to discuss with them the criticisms they made of the applicant. This analysis makes it possible to determine the truth from the totality of assessments, which may end up being contradictory.

In the same manner, the member's life is subjected to the population's scrutiny. Our people demand stricter comportment of a party member than for the rest of the workers. Not only in the workplace, where the masses can and do state their opinion on the behavior of party members, but also in the place where they reside. The Committees for the Defense of the Revolution, it must be said, are a valuable auxiliary for detecting any irregularity that might develop in a member's life. They are attentive to it.

The National Control Commission of the Central Committee, headed by Comrade Juan Almeida, and the local commissions not only receive the complaints, criticisms, and denunciations that come from party bodies and members, but they also have the responsibility of investigating any evidence that comes from the general population. More than a few functionaries and members have lost their positions as a result of denunciations from the populace.

But I repeat, this does not mean that organizations outside, even if linked to the party, have the ability to decide the fate of party members. But with their vigilance and their collaboration they do contribute to continuously improving the composition of the ranks of the Cuban CP.

I am sure that here too there is much more to do. Sometimes the masses display a certain inhibition regarding criticism of the member and sometimes there are "defensive" reactions to the criticism. But I am sure that these negative traits are less and less of a factor, while in contrast, the process of constructive and reasonable criticism is increasing.

Harnecker: What measures are being taken in Cuba to attack the seeds of bureaucratic attitudes that can be seen at the state and party level?

Rodríguez: We are all in agreement that bureaucratism is one of the permanent risks of socialism. In places where all the problems of society are in the hands of those who represent that society, and as a result very little occurs outside the sphere of decisions made at the local or national level, the forms of leadership and decision-making become determinant.

Therefore the term "bureaucratism" has many meanings and is used to describe different phenomena. There is the bureaucratic attitude of the leader who is separated from the productive processes and believes that his office is the center of the universe he gets to administer. The lack of contact with reality, with the factory, with the agricultural unit, can therefore lead, and does generally lead, to mistaken bureaucratic decisions.

We also speak of bureaucracy when, in making decisions, the needs and the interests of the population are not taken into account; when the requirements of the citizenry disappear in the endless paper-shuffling, when they get no response to their needs or their questions.

But in the final analysis the essence of bureaucratism is substituting for the role of the masses in the decision-making process, on whatever level those decisions are made, implanting an administrative or political apparatus over the workers and not taking either the workers or their organizations into account. It must be said that the complexity of contemporary political and economic life conspires to transform democracy into bureaucratism. Moreover, the decisions — as I said — acquire an increasingly technical character and the "technocracy" is a close cousin to the bureaucracy.

Lenin was concerned about this from the first moment of the socialist revolution. He fought against the "bureaucratic degeneration" in the revolutionary state. He always fought the "encrustation" of those who lead and was a partisan of airing all the problems before the masses.

You have listened to Fidel, and have listened to his constant criticism of bureaucracy, his concern that the leaders at all levels are linked to the productive process in each one of its stages. This is the policy of our party. These are its constant objectives. I think that the way that we have organized the relationship between the working class and the leaders, the role that we assign to the workers' unions and mass organizations, and our efforts to make sure that the party continually listens to the workers and knows how to assimilate their judgments with sensitivity — all this constitutes ongoing prevention against the never-completely-overcome tendency toward bureaucratic positions.

If I were to tell you that we have attained these objectives, that would be ignoring the realities that are before our eyes. But this is a battle not only of the party and its leaders, but it must be understood as a great people's battle, in which the working class has to play a predominant role.

Defending Cuba's Socialist Revolution

April 16, 1981

NOTE: After the November 1980 election of Ronald Reagan, U.S. threats against Cuba increased even further. Talk about military action and other forms of aggression began to be raised more belligerently. In early 1981, Cuba organized the Territorial Troop Militias, and over a half million men and women were enrolled. Coming on the heels of the big mobilizations of 1980, this step in arming the people was a further demonstration of the identification between the Cuban working class and its revolutionary government.

The following are major excerpts from Castro's speech commemorating the twentieth anniversary of the proclamation of the socialist character of the Cuban revolution on the eve of the Bay of Pigs invasion. It is reprinted from Granma Weekly Review, *April 26, 1981.*

Guests;
Combatants of our glorious Revolutionary Armed Forces;
Combatants of the Territorial Troop Militia:

We commemorate today a very important date, April 16, 1961. On an afternoon like this, sunny and clear, we gathered in a solemn, revolutionary mass ceremony to bury the combatants that had died during the cowardly, criminal, and treacherous air raid launched by surprise against the airports of Ciudad Libertad, San Antonio de los Baños, and Santiago de Cuba. A huge crowd of members of the militia and the people as a whole gathered that afternoon. It was on the eve of the mercenary attack on Playa Girón. It had taken many months to organize everything and all was ready: the mercenary troops, the air raids, the publicity, the propaganda, the cover-up. The whole thing was organized by the U.S. government, the Central Intelligence Agency, and the Pentagon, but that wasn't being admitted publicly.

At that time many lies and myths were exposed, but also the affair taught us a lot. It wasn't like today when after twenty years of revolution our people are much better prepared and better educated politically, with a better understanding of the world's social and political problems. But those outrageous, shameful events taught our people a lot. It was at that time that the socialist nature of our revolution was proclaimed, [*Applause*] and there couldn't have been a better opportunity for it, since another lie was also current: that our people had been deceived, that they had been betrayed by their leaders.

By that time, we could say that the Moncada program had been completed.* [*Applause*] All the laws passed during the first years of the revolution were laws and measures proclaimed in essence in the Moncada program, since it contained the seed, created the conditions for a socialist revolution. [*Applause*] And in our country at that moment there could have been no revolution other than a socialist one, [*Applause*] if any of us were real revolutionaries.

Our enemies said that our struggle against Batista's tyranny had been for another kind of revolution. But at the very moment when we confronted the most powerful enemy, Yankee imperialism; when we resolutely confronted their plans and their forces; on the very eve of battle, when the people prepared once again to struggle, to shed their blood and die, the socialist nature of the revolution was proclaimed.

And no one knew what that struggle would cost, because if the mercenaries had not been defeated immediately, in less than seventy-two hours, thus preventing them from establishing a beachhead, with a solid territory in their hands and with a so-called provisional government which — as the dispatches said — would be immediately recognized by many governments, that struggle could have cost our country hundreds of thousands of lives. And yet our people did not hesitate; they got ready and struggled with all their might, struggled and shed their blood during those heroic days for the socialist revolution of Cuba. [*Applause*] The struggle for the socialist revolution, for the revolution of our people in that historic period, for the only real revolution, had been the struggle, in one way or another, of all those who had died since the last century for the freedom of our country: those who struggled for independence, struggled for a just revolution — which at that time was a revolution of independence that could not yet have been a socialist revolution; those who struggled throughout the period of the pseudorepublic, who struggled at the Moncada, on the *Granma* expedition and in the mountains, those who struggled in the underground; they were all in one way or another struggling for the only just revolution: the socialist revolution. But those who struggled at Girón struggled directly for the socialist revolution.

At that time I said: "What the imperialists cannot forgive is that we are here, what the imperialists cannot forgive us for is the Cuban people's

*This refers to the measures outlined in Castro's famous speech "History Will Absolve Me," which was given at his trial following the 1953 Moncada attack. It became the program of the July 26 Movement.

dignity, their integrity, their bravery, their ideological strength, their spirit of sacrifice, their revolutionary spirit . . . and that we have made a socialist revolution right under their noses, under the nose of the United States itself . . . [*Applause*] and that we are defending that socialist revolution with these guns, and that we are defending that socialist revolution with the same courage shown by our antiaircraft gunners yesterday as they riddled the enemy planes with bullets. And we do not defend that revolution with mercenaries, we defend it with men and women of the people."

"Who has the weapons?" I asked then. "Do the mercenaries have the weapons? Do the millionaires have the weapons? [*Shouts of "No!"*] Because mercenaries and millionaires are the same thing. Do the rich kids have the weapons? [*Shouts of "No!"*] Do the overseers have the weapons? [*Shouts of "No!"*] Who has the weapons? [*Shouts of "The people!"*] Whose hands raise those weapons? [*Shouts of "The people's!"*] Are they the hands of rich kids? [*Shouts of "No!"*] Are they the hands of the exploiters? [*Shouts of "No!"*] Whose hands are these that raise the weapons? [*Shouts of "The people's!" "Fidel, Fidel, Fidel!" "For sure, Fidel, give the Yankees hell!" "Fidel, give them hell, let's make 'em respect us well!" and "The people united will never be defeated!"*] Aren't they workers' hands? [*Shouts of "Yes!"*] Aren't they peasants' hands? [*Shouts of "Yes!"*] Aren't they hands calloused by work? [*Shouts of "Yes!"*] Aren't they hands that create? [*Shouts of "Yes!"*] Aren't they the humble hands of the people? [*Shouts of "Yes!"*] And who are the majority of the people? The millionaires or the workers? [*Shouts of "The workers!"*] The exploiters or the exploited? [*Shouts of "The exploited!"*] The privileged or the poor? [*Shouts of "The poor!"*] Do the poor have the weapons? [*Shouts of "Yes!"*] Are the privileged the minority? [*Shouts of "Yes!"*] Are the poor the majority? [*Shouts of "Yes!"*] Is a revolution in which the poor have the weapons democratic?" [*Shouts of "Yes!"*]

Then I continued: "Comrade workers and peasants: this is the socialist and democratic revolution of the poor, with the poor, and for the poor. And for this revolution of the poor, by the poor, and for the poor we are ready to give our lives. [*Applause*]

"Comrade workers and peasants of the homeland: yesterday's attack was the prelude to mercenary aggression. Yesterday's attack, which took seven heroic lives, was meant to destroy our planes on the ground, and it failed; they only destroyed two planes and the bulk of the enemy planes were damaged or destroyed.

"Here, before the tomb of our dead comrades; here, beside the remains of these heroic young men, sons of workers and sons of the poor, let us reaffirm our determination that, just as these men stood up to the enemy fire, just as they gave their lives, no matter when the mercenaries come, all of us, proud of our revolution, proud to defend this revolution of the poor, by the poor, and for the poor, will not hesitate to defend the revolution against anyone, down to the last drop of blood." [*Applause*]

Thus the socialist nature of our revolution was proclaimed that day. Exactly twenty years have passed and we have the same answers to the same questions; faced with the same threats, the same people have the same determination to struggle and to win.

Twenty years of socialist revolution and socialism have brought many things to our country which no one, not even our fiercest enemies, would dare to deny. Socialism worked the miracle of eradicating illiteracy; that very same year 100,000 youngsters were teaching people throughout the country to read and write. Socialism brought us the battle for the sixth grade, which is now the minimum level of education achieved by all of our workers. Socialism brought us the battle we are now fighting to achieve a ninth grade education for everybody. Socialism has sown schools, technological institutes, universities in our country. Socialism brought us into first place in Latin America in the field of education. No other Latin American country can boast today what Cuba can; [*Applause*] not even the United States can claim that it doesn't have illiterates — there are illiterates and many semiliterates in the United States, and there are many more who have only a second, third, or fourth grade education. As a result, we can say that socialism has put us in first place in the field of education in this hemisphere. [*Applause*]

Socialism worked the miracle of eliminating many diseases and reducing the number of deaths in the first year of life to less than 20 per 1,000, something which no other Latin American country can claim and which puts us on an equal footing with the developed countries of the world. [*Applause*] Socialism has sown hospitals, polyclinics, and health institutes, which through preventive medicine and effective treatment have put our country in first place, not only among the underdeveloped countries of Latin America but among those of the entire world.

Socialism worked the miracle of bringing our country into first place in Latin America in the field of culture. Socialism brought us sports for the people and brought us to the highest levels of achievement so that we are now champions among the peoples of Latin America.

Socialism worked the miracle of eradicating unemployment in our country, putting an end to the layoffs every year at the end of the sugar harvest, and bringing us one of the highest levels of employment in all of Latin America. [*Applause*] Socialism worked the miracle of ending begging in our country, an ill that had existed for many centuries. It worked the miracle of eliminating drugs, prostitution, and gambling. What other country in this hemisphere can say that? Could the United States say that? [*Shouts of "No!"*] A country where crime, drugs, gambling, and prostitution increase year by year? No, it could not say that. And it is socialism that has overcome those things in our country.

Socialism worked the miracle of undertaking the economic and social development which has gone ahead in our country for more than twenty years, under difficult conditions and in the midst of a criminal and brutal economic blockade imposed on us by the United States. Socialism has changed and continues to change the face of our land.

In twenty years, throughout the length and breadth of the island, our cities have changed. Today Holguín, Granma, Camagüey, Santa Clara, Cienfuegos, Pinar del Río, and many other cities in our country are practically unrecognizable. Socialism has dotted our country with factories; it has crisscrossed the island with roads and highways. Socialism has created great hydraulic resources for our agriculture; it transforms our fields and, with the tenacious and self-sacrificing effort of our people, builds a new country.

Socialism has brought a really deep awareness to our people. It has trained hundreds of thousands of technicians at different levels: tens of thousands at the university level, hundreds of thousands of intermediate-level technicians and skilled workers. Suffice it to say, for example, that at present over 15,000 doctors are working in our hospitals and polyclinics, and that five years from now that figure will be well over 20,000, closer to 25,000. Another example: over 200,000 teachers, most of whom graduated under socialism, are now working in our universities, polytechnics, vocational schools, technological institutes, elementary schools, and day-care centers. Our Youth Technical Brigades of inventors have over 140,000 members. Socialism has created a different kind of human being, a new kind of human being in our country.

Socialism opened up our relations with the world and we now occupy, next to the Soviet Union and other countries of the socialist community, a place in the vanguard of the world's progressive peoples, [*Applause*] among the peoples struggling to establish more just societies, more humane societies. Is our socialist society or is it not a thousand times more just, a thousand times more humane than capitalist society? Can anybody deny this? [*Shouts of "No!"*] Socialism brought us that!

And along with justice and awareness it has brought our people tremendous social development. It has brought us the development of enormous forces such as our mass organizations, our workers' organizations, our Committees for the Defense of the Revolution, our peasant organizations, women's organizations, even the Pioneer organization — all of them extraordinary forces that are contributing to the consolidation and further development of our revolution.

Revolutionary awareness under socialism has brought us a vanguard party, a party of organized, disciplined, conscious Communists. The 400,000-plus members of our party and the 400,000-plus members of our Young Communist League are a demonstration of what the ideas of socialism and the ideas of Marxism-Leninism have brought to our country and what they have created here. [*Applause*]

And all this happened, even though we didn't always know how best to avail ourselves of all the advantages and possibilities of socialism. We could say that perhaps our accomplishments might have been greater or higher or fuller if we'd known how best to use all those possibilities and advantages over the past twenty years.

We didn't always act wisely, as we said during the Second Congress, we didn't always make the best decisions. But we were certainly always able, with all the honesty in the world, to detect in time any error, any wrong decision, recognize it, rectify it, and carry on; because even when you travel through the mountains with the help of a compass — and our compass is socialism, our compass is Marxism-Leninism — from time to time there can be some drifting away from the right path — just as ships sailing on the ocean occasionally drift off course a little — but you always keep going ahead in the right direction.

For us, the socialist road was something entirely new, a course that was being embarked on for the first time not only in our country but in the rest of the hemisphere as well. But we can assert, above all else, that we've known how to use our time, that we've been capable of rectifying mistakes and that today our revolution is stronger and more solid than ever before. [*Applause*]

These are not mere words. You, the workers, peasants, students, men and women; you, the fighters, know very well what's being done in our country. The sugar harvest alone is a good example. In spite of the blights — which we fought and overcame — the sugar harvest is being carried out with better organization and greater efficiency than ever before. It's now April 16 and our work in the sugar harvest is practically done. The overall grinding rate stands at 89 percent, a figure that the capitalists never reached — the best they ever did was 85 percent. [*Applause*] And in spite of the fact that our sugar harvest is not based on manual work and animal traction but rather on tractors, trucks, cane harvesters, and other machines — which are much more affected by rain and mud — we surpassed the target of 85 percent which we had set ourselves, and we've reached 89 percent.

We confronted the problem of the tobacco blight, and this year our country has reached an all-time record in tobacco production, [*Applause*] along with an all-time record in the production of vegetables and other produce, and an all-time record in citrus fruit. In fact, we've had record crops in many branches of our agriculture.

Construction work is being carried out with greater organization and efficiency. We are building a number of plants that require thousands of construction workers, for example the nickel complex in Moa, the textile plant in Santiago de Cuba, the spinning mill in Havana, the thermoelectric power plant east of Havana, and our first nuclear-powered electric plant, already under construction in Cienfuegos. In spite of the imperialist blockade and the deep crisis that is now affecting a great part of the world, and thanks to the friendly, fraternal, and generous solidarity of the Soviet Union, the rest of the socialist community and other progressive countries, our country is making steady progress — and that's something that even our worst enemies can't deny. [*Applause*]

We have learned how to manage our economy, our factories, and our agricultural centers; we have learned how to manage our schools, hospitals, and public services with increasing efficiency; but the most important thing is that we will keep on learning more and more. This is because, among other things, socialism means that we are the owners of our factories, our mines, our railroads, our ports, our merchant fleet, our lands, our natural resources. Everything in our country belongs to our workers, our peasants, our students, our men, and our women! [*Prolonged applause*] We own everything we have and we have the right to do our best with what we have.

Speaking of men and women, I often use the term "men," but not as a means to discriminate against women, rather as a generic term encompassing the species, men and women.

When I mentioned the things that socialism made possible I left out another one of our great successes: the end of the cruel discrimination against women and of the cruel racial discrimination that existed in our country, the discrimination on grounds of race or sex. [*Applause*] So we could also ask this question: Has the United States eradicated racial discrimination? [*Shouts of "No!"*] Has the United States eradicated discrimination against women, the exploitation of women, the prostitution of women? [*Shouts of "No!"*] No, a thousand times no! [*Applause*]

These are truths. The facts speak for themselves; they are convincing facts which explain and demonstrate what socialism has meant to our country; hence the importance of the date we're celebrating today.

But is the security of our country any different from what it was in the past? [*Shouts of "No!"*] No, here we are again, getting ready again because again we're being threatened, because new aggressive policies against Cuba are being formulated, because the imperialists are talking about blockades again — and no longer just about economic blockades, but rather about naval, military blockades. Again the imperialists are threatening us, talking about aggression. Hence the similarity between this April 16 and that April 16. This is why we're again having to make a great effort to defend ourselves, to mobilize the people, men and women, all our people, to organize the Territorial Troop Militia and to accelerate the work of fortification and buttressing our defense capacity in every way.

Ah, but there are also differences between this April and that April, quite a few differences. For example, there have been important changes in the world since 1961. The balance of forces between imperialism and socialism has shifted; there have been major changes in the world, and there have also been very important changes in our country. In April 1961, the first tanks, field guns, and antiaircraft guns sent to us by the Soviet Union had arrived only a few weeks before. They were the very first we had and we were just learning how to use them. We had also acquired some weapons in the Western world; they were the first weapons purchased by the revolution, so that the imperialists wouldn't be able to say that we were receiving socialist weapons. And remember too something that happened at that time: the freighter *La Coubre* was blown up in a brutal, savage act that killed some 100 workers and soldiers.

In those days we had those FAL rifles that were raised aloft at the corner of twelfth and twenty-third streets, and we also had the first field guns and tanks, which we were hastily learning how to handle. But we didn't have enough instructors, and it often happened that what our militia members learned in the morning they taught to thousands of others in the afternoon. Thus, in view of the imminent attack, by doing the very best we could given the situation, hundreds of field gun, antiaircraft, and other batteries were organized and hundreds of thousands of militia members throughout the country mobilized in a matter of weeks. There were around 50,000 militia members in the capital alone. And it was like that right across the country. Our army was beginning to learn all about handling modern weapons. And how much time has passed since then, and how far have we come?

Today we have tens of thousands of regular and reserve officers in our Revolutionary Armed Forces; today we have a degree of knowledge, experience, organization, and technical know-how we didn't have then. At that time we didn't have, as we have now, the hundreds of thousands of reservists who have served in our Revolutionary Armed Forces or the tens upon tens of thousands — no, more than that — the tens upon tens of thousands of internationalist fighters who have been through the experience of combat, war, and sacrifice. [*Applause*] At that time we didn't have the possibilities we have now, that have enabled us to mobilize hundreds of thousands of combatants in the Territorial Troop Militia and to train many cadres and chiefs in just a few weeks. [*Applause*] It can be said with certainty that never before was such a large force organized so quickly and efficiently. The record time in which we are organizing and training the Territorial Troop Militia and their cadres is proof of how far we've come in terms of organizational ability and experience.

This means that we're not fooling around; the revolution doesn't fool around. It knows how to do things seriously and it is doing things seriously.

We're not trembling, we're not scared by the imperialists' threats. On the contrary, we turn those threats into a force, and we could say to the imperialists — who made so much use of the slogan "Remember Pearl Harbor" and remember many other things — a few slogans of our own like "Remember Girón," "Remember Girón!" [*Applause*] Girón should have been a lesson to teach them to deal with Cuba in a different way. They thought that when their little planes showed up everybody here was going to be scared out of their wits, but it took only seconds for our militia to respond to the enemy attack by opening fire. That's what our militia artillerymen, whose average age was between fifteen and twenty, did; that's what the militia in Girón and everywhere else did as soon as the enemy appeared. At that time the imperialists were saying they expected our people to stage an uprising, etc. And they had visions of our troops being defeated and scared off. But what happened? They underestimated our people's ability, our people's dignity, courage, and heroism, while their brigades, their planes, and their tanks lasted as long as a lit candle lasts in a rainstorm. [*Applause*]

However, at that time we were prepared to fend off not just one mercenary invasion but rather ten mercenary invasions. And when our tanks reached Girón and set up positions there, face to face with the Yankee warships and aircraft carriers, everybody was very calm and every gun was loaded and ready to fire. In other words, we're not afraid of the imperialists, we're not afraid of their soldiers, we will not hesitate for a single moment to defend our soil, our country, our revolution. We will not hesitate even for a moment, and the imperialists should be well aware of this. They shouldn't forget this experience. If they think they're going to settle the differences between Cuba and the United States through attacks and threats, they're mistaken! If they think they're going to intimidate us, scare us, bring us to our knees by dint of threats and attacks, they're mistaken! This is what we've always told the imperialists and this is what we want to say to them today! [*Applause*]

Our ideas are very clear, our convictions are very deep, our decisions are very resolute: we don't want war, we are not in the habit of provoking conflicts and we don't want to do so, but they should beware of provoking us! They should beware of dragging us into a war, into a conflict! [*Applause*] If they impose a conflict on us, if they impose a war on us, they'll find out what a resolute people are like, what a communist people, a patriotic people, a Marxist-Leninist people, an internationalist people are like. [*Applause*]

This is because socialism made us even more patriotic, because socialism taught us what internationalism means. We're an internationalist people, but at the same time we're a very patriotic people, very much aware of our rights, [*Applause*] very sure of our ideas and of our cause. We have a lot of dignity and are very sure of ourselves.

The imperialists should know that whereas our people were strong in the days of Girón, today they are one hundred times stronger [*Applause*] and better prepared militarily, politically, psychologically.

Now we're again forced to mobilize and prepare ourselves, but this won't make us neglect our revolutionary tasks, our creative work. We will not neglect our factories, our fields, our construction sites, our hospitals, our schools, our public services and this is why we have to make an extra effort. It's true that this takes up a great deal of our time, it's true that it calls for great energy to prepare to defend our country, and it's true that it calls for resources. But our people have the ability of multiplying themselves and, in circumstances such as these, a man becomes two or even three men, a woman becomes two, three, and even one hundred women, and when circumstances so require, what normally takes two hours to do is done in one, and work goes on as long as necessary. We have the resources within us, in our energy, in our will, and this is why we will make this effort to defend our country along with the effort of developing the country and increasing production. That's another thing we'll teach the imperialists so they won't deceive themselves into believing that we're neglecting the development of the country and production while we're organizing and preparing ourselves for defense. We're going to show them that in these difficult circumstances our people rise to the occasion and are capable of handling the two tasks at the same time: strengthening our defense and strengthening our economy! [*Applause*]

In the Territorial Troop Militia there are men of different ages, either because they're very young and haven't done their military service yet or because they're engaged in important production tasks or because they're beyond the age limit to be in the Revolutionary Armed Forces reserves. The women are also of different ages: they are workers, peasants, students. In all, the militia constitutes a formidable force that, along with the regular troops of our Revolutionary Armed Forces, make for an entire people armed and ready to defend themselves.

The imperialists have imposed this effort on us, the same way that they imposed the blockade on us, but our revolution is over twenty-two years old, twenty years have passed since Girón, and here we are, building socialism for more than twenty years, and we'll be here, doing the same for another twenty and the next twenty and as many more as necessary. And if we do things the right way, we'll have an increasingly patriotic, united, and aware people, a people better equipped to cope with any test. Others may be used to trembling before the imperialists' threats, but not our people. Never! [*Applause*]

We should meditate on this date, on this day, and from the bottom of our hearts resolve to make whatever efforts are necessary to fulfill our sacred duties to our country and to socialism.

Circumstances have made this day closely resemble that day exactly twenty years ago. However, happy circumstances have made possible a scene such as this one, to see a people like this, with the same awareness, or better said, with even greater awareness and with the same determination, or even more, than twenty years ago. [*Applause*] Once again we can repeat what we said on April 16, 1961: Let us swear to defend this cause of the poor, by the poor, and for the poor! [*Shouts of "Let us swear!"*] Let us swear to defend our socialist revolution down to the last drop of blood! [*Shouts of "Let us swear!"*]

Patria o muerte!

Venceremos! [*Ovation*]

Revolutionary Consciousness and the Fight Against Corruption

NOTE: One area where Cuba's economic progress since 1970 can be seen most clearly is in regard to rationing. This economic measure for assuring equality had been introduced in 1962 as a form of guaranteeing distribution to everyone of basic necessities. Given the country's poverty along with the previously existing inequality, this meant a big increase in the standard of living for most Cubans. Of course, a form of rationing takes place under capitalism in a different way: a large part of the population cannot afford to buy what is being sold.

As a greater quantity of consumer items became available throughout the 1970s, Cuba was able to gradually reduce the number of items on the ration list. Whereas in 1970 virtually everything was rationed, by 1980 only 30 percent of what a consumer spent in the market went to rationed products. In addition, for many items where rationing still exists, Cuba developed what is called the parallel market: a certain quantity of the product is distributed through the rationing system at a low price; the remaining supply is then sold nonrationed at a much higher price. The result is a wider variety of goods for consumers to choose from.

In the late 1970s and early 1980s, several other measures were taken to help meet consumer demand for certain goods and services. One of these was the institution of free farmers' markets. Although over 70 percent of Cuban land is state-owned and worked by state farms, there are still about 200,000 small farmers who work their own land. While the revolution seeks to gradually collectivize all farming, it has made it a principle that collectivization, as well as the formation of cooperatives, must be a voluntary decision of the farmers, who are guaranteed the use of their land as long as they farm it.

Farmers can now sell their surplus products, over and above what they sold to the state, at the government-organized free markets. In addition to benefiting the small farmers, this procedure makes more products available to consumers.

Besides authorizing the farmers' markets, other measures were taken. A handicrafts market was set up at Havana's Cathedral Square. Also, the newspaper of the consumer institute, Opina, began carrying classified ads for individual transactions of apartments, services, and goods.

In early 1982, a number of instances of corruption and profiteering, based on abuses and loopholes in the new measures, came to light. In the case of the farmers' markets, this involved exorbitant prices being charged for products, and the proliferation of middlemen manipulating the market and making huge profits. There were instances of administrators complicit in stealing supplies to be sold on the black market or on the free market, as well as other instances of administrators cheating the public.

While these and other scandals involved a relatively small number of people, they affected a large number in various ways, and caused annoyance among the population as a whole. If unchecked these instances of corruption could have become more and more generalized and destroyed one of the fundamental tenets of the revolution: its commitment to the equality of distribution of scarce goods. This would have steadily undercut the people's revolutionary consciousness and morale and would have enabled privileges to proliferate among a section of the population, eventually leading to the creation of a privileged social layer distinctly separate from the majority of workers.

At the Fourth Congress of the Young Communist League (UJC), held April 1-4, 1982, a drive against corruption was launched. A number of measures were outlined against the middlemen, corrupt administrators, and the abuses of the free farmers' markets. These were also discussed at the Sixth Congress of the National Association of Small Farmers (ANAP), held May 15-17, 1982. At the ANAP congress, while agreeing with the government's aims, a number of farmers raised concerns and disagreements with the government's proposals on how to eliminate the abuses in the farmers' markets. As a result, the government deferred to the farmers' wishes, saying it would work out alternative proposals along the lines the farmers suggested.

Within several months of these speeches, about 200 people were arrested for their involvement in various types of corruption. At the same time, the government reiterated its commitment to retaining the free farmers' markets and other similar institutions.

The following are excerpts from Castro's speeches to the UJC and ANAP congresses. They are taken from Granma Weekly Review, *April 18, and May 30, 1982.*

1. Excerpt from Speech to UJC Congress
April 4, 1982

We could say that there is one [task] more important than all the others [for the Young Communist League], and that is the organization's work in developing a revolutionary consciousness among our young people. [*Applause*] And that is something vital, absolutely vital, of decisive importance. Nobody can improve on the Young Communist League in this respect because it looks after the young generation practically from preschool age to the time they are of age to join the party. To a great extent, the party will benefit from what the UJC accomplishes. The organization plays a vital, decisive role in developing our young people's attitudes toward study and all their other duties, be it in school, in a military unit, in a factory, in a services unit; as teachers, as doctors, as nurses, or intermediate-level hospital technicians. And it is there, in practice, in the everyday struggle, where a really communist consciousness is developed.

New changes can be seen, and we can now really speak of a new attitude, an attitude that is the fruit of these years of work, of the work of our socialist institutions, of our schools of study and work, of our Pioneer organization, of our revolutionary teachers, of our revolutionary schools, of our mass and young people's organizations, and of the Young Communist League. Yes, it can really be seen.

The organization's concern to develop young people's consciousness is particularly evident in the unflagging interest it has taken in promoting voluntary work. And that, too, is of vital importance. It is of vital importance because the realities of the construction of socialism oblige us to adopt certain formulas and methods that are not communist, but rather socialist — and you are well aware of the difference between socialism and communism. There are two formulas: "to each according to his work." and "to each according to his needs." In socialism, every individual is supposed to contribute according to his capacity, and he receives according to his work. In communism, everyone contributes according to his capacity and receives according to his needs.

There were some idealistic moments when we did want to make shortcuts. We had the chance to see the consequences and we were honest enough to recognize our mistakes and rectify them. There's no question about that. And there's no question either that the communist formula is superior to the socialist. Nor is there any question, either, that the dream of Marx, Engels, and Lenin was the communist society. Marx himself said that in socialism distribution was still within the narrow confines of bourgeois law.

Clearly, if, for example, there are two longshoremen and one of them can carry more sacks than the other, let's say the second one can carry only half as many as the first, the poor fellow will receive half of what the other one received. But it isn't his fault that he's not the kind of man who can carry 200 sacks instead of 100 and, for all we know, his needs may be the same as the other's or maybe even greater. Thus, the socialist kind of distribution is not fair or at least not wholly fair. And we hope that some day the communist society will rectify this injustice.

Linking wages to work norms is naturally a socialist formula. A worker with more ability and more strength — and often the one with strongest determination — can earn more, of course. But there's always an element of imbalance somewhere. Some men have more aptitude for a particular thing, more skill, more strength, more endurance, than others.

We have to resort to material incentives, because it's a strategy inherent in the transition from capitalism to communism; in other words, a need imposed by the socialist stage. I'll never forget how concerned Che was about all these things, his great vocation and dedication and his exemplary attitude in voluntary work. He'd operate a harvester, cut sugarcane, lay bricks, or push a hand truck along the docks, because he practiced what he preached and he was always deeply concerned about these questions.

Nevertheless, we've had to adopt a number of specific measures imposed by necessity, by reality. These measures help in many ways, they develop the economy and the development of the economy makes for greater resources, which, in turn, makes for greater possibilities for the development of society and of society's wealth. If there's no wealth there'll be very few things to distribute. That is a reality, and in rectifying its idealistic mistakes the revolution had the courage to adopt the pertinent measures. But contradictions do arise. And we must guard against socialist formulas eroding communist consciousness; we must prevent socialist formulas from diverting us from our lofty objectives, our communist dreams. We must prevent ideological indolence and misunderstanding of these truths from diverting us from our goal of developing the communist human being. If someone works harder so as to earn more, that's a positive attitude and, in a certain sense, it helps and makes for greater production, but it is not a communist attitude. If one works more because one will receive a material incentive, one may be useful and may help to increase production and wealth and contribute to development, but that is not a communist attitude.

Reality imposes its rules and its formulas on society, and it's up to the party and the UJC to develop consciousness. And I can assure you that being a communist will never depend on there being vast wealth to distribute, wealth so vast that there's enough to spare — and I can't imagine such a thing as wealth to spare in a world where the population is multiplying like guinea pigs and the natural resources are finite. No, no one can expect communist consciousness to be based on abundant wealth.

The way I see it, in the development of the communist society wealth and the material base must grow hand in hand with consciousness, because it can also happen that as wealth increases, consciousness diminishes. It is important for young people to give thought to this matter; I'm sure they've already done so and I'm also sure they have wondered about it — for I myself have thought about this and wondered about it often — and I'm convinced that it is not solely wealth or the development of the material base or anything of the kind that is going to contribute to the development of a communist consciousness. Far from it. There are some countries that are much richer than ours is. I shan't make comparisons of any kind, that wouldn't be correct, but we do know of revolutionary countries where consciousness was overtaken by wealth, and that can lead to counterrevolutions and things like that. But there may be a great deal of consciousness without much wealth.

It's not correct for us to name ourselves, or rather our country, as an example. But I am convinced that in spite of our limited wealth and relatively limited material development, our country has been witness to a vast development of consciousness and that an example of this is found in our people's internationalist spirit. It is very important to understand all these things, because if we don't understand them we become weaker.

An internationalist consciousness means a complete break with chauvinism, it means combating national egoism, because there isn't an iota of Marxism, Leninism, or communism in national egoism.

There have been times when we had to build a road in another country when we were in need of roads in ours, or we built an airport when we ourselves were short of airports. For example, neither Ciego de Avila nor Sancti Spíritus has an airport and yet we have helped to build airports in other countries. Yes, we do make efforts to help other countries and there may be some who wonder why we help others when we are still short of many things. Such an attitude is not a revolutionary attitude but rather one of national egoism.

First of all, internationalism is also a matter of consciousness, and it implies doing without many things in order to help others who are more in need than we are because they are much poorer than we are. Of course, there's merit in a poor country's sharing what it has with others, and we, who are an underdeveloped country, share with others some of what we have. I believe that is a demonstration of internationalist consciousness. And I also believe that when internationalist consciousness and cooperation cease to exist in the world, the future of the world will be really disastrous.

On other occasions I have spoken of situations affecting the underdeveloped world; for example when I spoke at the founding of the Medical Sciences Detachment. Let us think, for instance, of the situation in Ethiopia, a country with 35 million inhabitants and 125 doctors. I believe it had fewer doctors than the Isle of Youth. I don't know the exact number of doctors in that municipality, but I do know that many municipalities in our country have more than 125 doctors. So there were fewer doctors in Ethiopia, a country with 35 million inhabitants, than in some of Cuba's municipalities. If we are incapable of asking our doctors to make an extra effort so we can send ten doctors from a province in Cuba to Ethiopia, or of asking a province to send twenty doctors and another province to send a few others when we know that any province of ours has more, infinitely more doctors than Ethiopia; if we can't ask them to make that extra effort to help us comply with such an elementary duty, then we're really in a bad way.

And yes, we do have needs. Sometimes we do things elsewhere that we could do here, but things that are no longer essential for us. When a relatively small country has built 20,000 kilometers of roads and highways, it's no trouble to us to put aside building an additional 300 kilometers because we're building 200 or 300 kilometers of roads in another country with few or no highways. All these things are relative, and to make some material contribution along with some contributions in terms of expertise does not represent any considerable sacrifice, but does constitute a great example in a world plagued by egoism.

Not all of what our country does abroad takes the form of donations. We donate to the poorer countries, and those which have greater economic resources than we do pay us for our services. Therefore, work done outside our country is also a source of revenue.

A firm internationalist consciousness is something we cannot do without.

At times, for instance, there are all sorts of rumors and comments, such as when a building in the vicinity of the Capitol collapsed, for several reasons. A thorough investigation was carried out and it was found out that several factors, aside from the age of the building, had to do with the tragic collapse; additions to the apartments, done clandestinely, excess weight caused by too much furniture in the upper floors, etc. And there were some who wanted to know how come we exported cement when our buildings were collapsing. Such an analysis couldn't be more simplistic. It also reveals a total lack of understanding of the reasons why our country exports cement, and that is because, unfortunately, it has no other alternative but to export it. It would be wonderful if we could dedicate all the cement we produce to construction work here, but we have to export it because our country must also import many things, everything, beginning with medicines. It has to import raw material in order to produce poultry, hogs, milk, everything. It must import many things and in order to import one must export. It goes without saying that it would be much better for us to dedicate all our cement to construction work. But the problem is that construction doesn't depend on just cement. It calls for steel, lumber, glass, piping, wiring, dozens of other things that must also be bought. And what often hampers construction is not a lack of cement but rather a lack of lumber and other materials that, unfortunately, we cannot purchase abroad because we don't have the resources to pay for them.

In a case like this there are two different attitudes that can be taken. Really, that attitude I mentioned demonstrates not so much a lack of internationalist spirit as simple ignorance. And at other times it's more a lack of internationalist spirit.

Well, since an internationalist spirit is to be defended as a principle, I'm convinced that being an internationalist means giving part of what you have and being willing to give it. You must be willing and prepared to give something up in order to do it. Naturally, we would prefer to have even more doctors than we have now, working in the hospitals, making sure that they have their rest period following guard duty, and so on, but part of our medical force is engaged in internationalist missions. Still, we haven't remained idle; all the time we are training legions of new, good doctors.

I said that the principle of internationalism is to be defended for its own sake. Now, let's take a look at the other side of the coin: what would have become of our revolution and our country without internationalism? [*Applause and shouts of "Being internationalist means settling our debt with humanity!"*] How much have we done for others, compared to what others have done for us in so many fields? Hence, the reason for that watchword, to settle our debt with humanity. Beginning with the arms with which we have defended ourselves: how much do you think they're worth? How much is the economic cooperation that is being given us worth? I don't much like to use this kind of argument because it's not a communist argument. It may be logical, dialectical, but it isn't communist. It does serve, however, to make noninternationalists understand the question a little better; but it's no argument for internationalists. The argument for internationalists goes like this: help others even if nobody helps us. [*Applause*] It's simply a moral duty, a revolutionary duty, a matter of principle, of conscience, even an ideological duty. To contribute to humanity even if humanity has done nothing for us. That's what internationalism means! And we must go on developing this internationalist consciousness which has made great progress in our country. I believe there are many examples of it here.

I said that it wasn't wealth alone that created a communist consciousness. Consciousness must be developed by the party, the Young Communist League, and the revolution itself. And I also said that our modest country had developed a good deal of internationalist consciousness. We're still egoists; we haven't reached the ne plus ultra of internationalist consciousness but there's much more egoism in the rest of the world than in us, for I believe that our internationalist consciousness is continuing to develop. I can give you examples of this. When the call for teachers for Nicaragua was issued I believe that a total of 29,500 teachers answered it, and that was a very difficult job, teaching in the most difficult conditions. And yesterday, when the comrade delegate presented me with an album representing twenty-odd albums filled with the signatures of the 92,000 teachers ready to take the place of Francisco de la Concepción, Pedro Pablo Rivera, Bárbaro Rodríguez, and Aguedo Morales, who were assassinated while carrying on their duty as teachers in Nicaragua, how would you describe that?* [*Applause*] Isn't that a demonstration of internationalist consciousness? Could anyone doubt it? I for one, have no doubt that those 92,000 teachers are willing and ready to fulfill their pledge. And what a wonderful thing it is to be able to say that after twenty-odd years of existence our revolution has 92,000 teachers willing and ready to carry out an internationalist mission in conditions of proven risk! [*Applause*] What a truly extraordinary, admirable, practically incredible thing! And why? Before the revolution, how many teachers were there in Cuba who could offer to go to Nicaragua to teach in the conditions that exist in Nicaragua? Why, we didn't even have enough to send to Güines, which is practically on the outskirts of Havana. We didn't have enough to send to Baracoa, or Guantánamo, or anywhere in the rural areas. We simply didn't have enough teachers. What Latin American country with a population much larger than ours has 92,000 teachers ready to carry out such a mission?

How did this spirit grow? Was it by accident, perhaps? No. It was the revolution that created this spirit, it was the party, it was the Young Communist League. Needless to say, wealth had nothing to do with it. It was the result of political work, of ideological work, of revolutionary work, of example. It wasn't necessary to be richer than the United States to have an internationalist consciousness. A communist consciousness, an internationalist consciousness, must be developed; as someone said here — I believe it was Landy [Luis Orlando Domínguez], paraphrasing Che — internationalism is the highest rung of communist consciousness. Che said "the highest rung of the human species." Landy said "the high-

*Concepción was shot by Somozaist counterrevolutionaries on July 7, 1981; he died two months later. Rivera and Rodríguez were murdered on October 21, 1981. Morales was murdered on December 4, 1981.

est rung of communist consciousness." And this is the truth, because every internationalist is a full-fledged communist. Only a communist can be an internationalist. In fact, we could say that it's impossible to be a communist without being an internationalist. This will give you an idea of how important these questions are in the development of consciousness, of their importance in the development of voluntary work among the youth, that example, that conduct which Che bequeathed us as a priceless treasure. [*Prolonged applause*]

This is the spirit that has prevailed in your voluntary work and especially in your economic initiatives. We urge our young people and our workers in general — but most of all our young workers — to keep this spirit alive.

Mention was made at this congress of the lust for gain, and I think it was an important thing to do. I mean lust for gain on the part of some professionals, and certain highly telling examples were given, like the case of an engineer, an architect, or whatever, trained by the revolution, privately practicing his profession and charging exorbitant fees to workers for drawing up simple plans for home repairs. I myself have seen some of these ads in *Opina* magazine. *Opina* is highly illustrative of many flaws and many irregularities. Just try to advertise certain things and you'll see. Once I happened to be in an office by chance when the phone rang and someone asked about a car supposedly being sold there, I think it was a 1958 Chevrolet. What happened was that the paper had put a wrong number in an advertisement, that of the office I was in, and all sorts of lumpen people began calling in. Well, to tell the truth, even decent people were ringing up the number. I'm not going to deny that. One person asked, "How much?" "Ten thousand pesos." "Why, man, I thought it would be worth $400." Then he said, "No, I can't, there's no way I can." Another was asked, "Have you got the ten thousand pesos?" "Yes, I do, I have them." "You got the ten thousand pesos?" "Yes." "Well! Where do you work?" One of them worked in a spare-parts distributing center, another in a deluxe restaurant. It was very interesting; it wasn't explained where they got the ten thousand pesos from. It was a real mystery.

Well, then, this was simply one anecdote. Another ad in *Opina* — and I'm not criticizing *Opina* — said: "Home plans drawn up." A citizen comes to the city hall and is asked to present a plan for his house repairs. An urbanization office or what have you, asked for a little plan. The man charges 800, 900, 1,000 pesos for drawing up a little plan. For this was exactly what was brought up here, with all the reason in the world. That's robbery being committed by a technician trained by the revolution, who possibly even works in some enterprise or agency here. I think that's a prostitution of the whole concept of self-employment. [*Applause*]

Prostitutions of this sort have occurred in connection with various initiatives, various measures adopted to meet this or that need, or owing to
an effort made to improve services, or to release labor power needed
elsewhere — moves that have immediately been seized upon by poor-
spirited and selfish individuals to devalue the original idea; and many
things have been devalued here, thanks to the collaboration of many
people — because in order for such devaluation to take place many administrators have behaved irresponsibly by conniving, by violating the
rules on certain contracts, tiny groups of workers who, for instance,
earned a few thousand pesos by doing, in their supposedly extra and free
time, what they were supposed to do during their regular work schedule.
It's repugnant to find out about such cases. Earning thousands of pesos
in a few days. Any administrator willing to contract for a group of technicians, a group of qualified workers, anybody, earning thousands of pesos is simply a corruptor of others and is himself corrupted. [*Applause*]

We even had these cases involving party members. What are things
coming to? On the one hand struggling for higher consciousness and on
the other destroying it. And then some would say, "Well, if you go to the
plaza" — and even the small plaza was mentioned, too — "they charge
you fifty pesos for a pair of sandals," [*Laughter*] which is true.

But there's a sort of chain of events here. For if good ideas foster other
good ideas, bad things can foster, on the other hand, other bad things.
It's clear that really any technician here who gets a job from the state,
who has the chance of using his skills properly, should not be entitled to
do such things. That's not a socialist formula for solving the problems.
A socialist formula would be to have People's Power or someone else set
up bureaus, or groups or offices of architects, for example, so that they
can help a worker who needs to repair his home; because now in addition
to paying the cost of materials and paying everything else, he is asked to
produce a small plan — and it's logical that he should need a small plan
so that no clandestine construction can be done that later results in the
building's collapsing. The state should provide a socialist service under
which that architect would earn the same as an architect in Moa or in
Santiago de Cuba, or an architect who is building a school in the countryside or fulfilling an internationalist mission, not ten times more. [*Applause*]

We must search for socialist formulas rather than capitalist formulas
to solve problems, because before we even realize it they corrupt us,
contaminate us, just as Landy said in yesterday's session concerning the
things that contaminate us and contaminate our consciousness. Virtue
must be nourished but vice springs up spontaneously like weeds and
grows by itself. We must bear that in mind. If we do otherwise, while
nourishing virtue we are simultaneously paving the way for vice. We
must use socialist formulas rather than capitalist formulas in all these

matters. That's a reality and we musn't lose sight of it.

I think no one will be granted permission to carry out these activities any more. Let those who graduated before the revolution live according to the way they were trained. They haven't particularly incurred any debt. But the standards for those who graduated under the revolution ought to be different. Our doctors gave up private practice a long, long time ago. And we have a lot of prestigious doctors who could be earning ten thousand pesos in a capitalist country anywhere and yet here they are, earning a modest socialist salary working for our people. These are good examples. [*Applause*] And I think that was in part what Tony [Pérez Herrero] meant when he spoke yesterday on ideological questions, on the need to strengthen our youth so that bourgeois ideology could exert no influence on them.

Because, of course, it goes without saying that under capitalism a prominent person like that earns tons of money. That's why a revolutionary consciousness, a communist consciousness, an internationalist consciousness is so necessary, if one is to work for one's own people for less money, under more modest conditions, under harder conditions. That's the sort of technician, that's the sort of revolutionary, that's the sort of communist we want to train. [*Prolonged applause*]

We don't compete with Yankee imperialism in the matter of money, with the capitalists who have piled up huge wealth exploiting peoples and exploiting workers. They make off with the most talented people everywhere to achieve technological development and technologies of which the underdeveloped countries are deprived. Yes, they have money. But we have something more powerful than money and that is consciousness. [*Applause*] That's why the communist is more powerful than the capitalist, because a communist isn't for sale, a communist has a conscience while a capitalist has money, nothing but money, he has no country. His country is where he can make the most money. Capitalism by nature has no country, it goes where it can earn more. The communist is basically an internationalist, but also a patriot. He fulfills his internationalist duty wherever necessary, and he fulfills his communist duty toward his own people. That is the kind of person we want to form. The young people must undertake this mission, they have an opportunity to form people like that with that kind of consciousness.

This is why what was said about the lust for gain was quite right. And it should not be limited merely to professionals, because another initiative around which speculation and profiteering developed was the farmers' markets, you know? It was a capitalist formula because that is a capitalist formula, one that takes into account the fact that there are still many small private farmers, the fact that there had been some under-the-table dealings, and in order to develop production of some things which the state, the big specialized agricultural firms, do not usually produce, or to put more things onto the market, such as the things that were being sold under the table or used for individual consumption, or to get the farmers to work a little harder, such markets were authorized. Well then, right away a host of middlemen popped up, who didn't produce anything and would buy up and hoard products that in many cases should have been sold to the state for normal distribution. There was one individual who had 50,000 bananas. Imagine, 50,000 bananas stored away, and in the warehouse of a party member. Corrupting our party members, 50,000 bananas from Holguín. How much money would he make selling them at 80 centavos in just a few days? Those are the kind that want to buy everything, even the Karl Marx Theater, [*Laughter*] and if they can't buy the theater then they try to buy the administrator.

So we had a free farmers' market. It was a concession we made, to cope with particular problems. We will have to tackle all this in discussions with the farmers to see what measures can be taken. In one year they earned 200 million pesos and paid only 40,000 in taxes. I think that year's taxes should have been at least 100 million, and since they sell at high prices and earn more than they would by selling to the state, and sometimes things which should have gone to the state end up on the free market, it would be good if that money could go for hospitals, schools, the Pioneers, vacation programs, and things like that. [*Applause*] There are many fine things that can be done with that money they earned, with at least half of it, half for the people, for those same people who are shelling out their money. It should benefit the people in the form of a vacation program, camping, a Pioneer palace; many fine things, I repeat, could be done with that money, much better than making a few people rich and bourgeois, much better than making people corruptors.

We will allow the free market to continue with strict respect for established regulations, but there will have to be significant taxes. It is ironic that this individual can buy eggs at 6 or 7 centavos, well, now it is 9 or 10, for if eggs were not being produced on a large scale by workers on state farms he would be unable to purchase them at such a low price. On its farms the state turns out millions of eggs so everybody can have them. The state also produces almost all the milk the children of this country drink, the milk the families, the ill, and the elderly drink; all the chicken allocated to hospitals, schools, stores, and restaurants is produced by the state. Of course, we haven't got big resources, otherwise we could produce twice the current figure, that's easy, we know by heart how this is done. We also know how many millions of dollars we would have to spend for soya, corn, and other products, products we don't have. Producing food in an efficient manner is easy, we really do it efficiently. We don't have the raw materials, otherwise it would just be a case of building farms, which we know how to do; we are one of the countries which is most efficient in chicken and egg production as a result of the genetic methods and technique developed by the revolution. We can produce chicken and pork very efficiently, we know what is needed; the drawbacks are the raw materials. Food leftovers are used in large quantities to feed pigs. But in spite of all that, the state takes what it produces and distributes the milk, eggs, beef, chicken, or pork to the hospitals, schools, and families.

Here it is not the same as in other socialist countries where the imperialists say small private farmers produce so much of the milk, meat, or eggs; the situation here is very different. Here 100 percent of the milk comes from state farms and it is distributed to the people. Practically all. And it's the same with eggs, chicken, and pork, nearly all the meat which is distributed to the population and produced efficiently. We don't produce more because we haven't the means. At present we can't produce turkeys to be able to distribute turkeys all over the country, a turkey a week, or what have you, who knows how many would be needed?

So what happens is that somebody sells a turkey at the market for 100 pesos. He has modest quantities of things that the state does not produce on a large scale, not for lack of efficiency but because it lacks the means, because everything it has goes into the production of key foodstuffs which are distributed to the people at low prices and in many cases subsidized. Now that individual who's selling the turkey pays the same low price for medicine as everybody else, he pays 25 centavos for a liter of milk and nothing at all for hospital care. He takes a bus for 5 centavos although with the money he has he can take a taxi, and yet he tries to bribe taxi drivers and all, because you can imagine, with all that money. He gets everything at low prices or free and when he sells a worker a chicken he charges 15 pesos, or 80 centavos for bananas because there were no bananas of that kind or a hurricane hit Havana and the bananas were brought in from Cienfuegos or Holguín. Or he sells garlic at a peso a head because we're short of garlic, and things like that.

Of course he doesn't sell eggs for 20 centavos because the state sells all the eggs anybody could want for much less. Who knows how much longer some basic products will have to be rationed; we're trying to do away with rationing as much as possible because rationing is a real nuisance, but we'd be in a fine state if we were to distribute meat on a price basis, because this new bourgeoisie would buy it all up and the worker would go without. If we were to do as is done in some parts of Europe and put meat on the free market at 10 pesos a pound there would be more than enough meat. But such a policy with an essential item would be wrong, and we are seeking socially just distribution. Capitalists solve everything on a price basis, but socialists don't. So when there isn't enough of something there is speculation. Well then, it's right that the free market should be authorized for certain reasons, in pursuit of certain goals.

But I can't conceive of a real Young Communist, not a professional, a Young Communist, selling chicken at 15 pesos or garlic at a peso and bananas at 80 centavos on the free market. Speculating and bringing bananas from hundreds of kilometers away, imagine! I wonder how many people he bribed along the way to get them here and have a warehouse of bananas. No, the free farmers' market is undoubtedly a capitalist method of solving problems.

Well, I hope these problems won't last forever. I hope that this situation will come to an end, with the development of socialist agriculture and of the cooperative farms and the disappearance of this speculative and nonproductive minifundist farming. And if there is going to be a free market, it should be a real free market operating under control and run along different lines, a market in which the real beneficiary will be the people, even though the farmers may also make a little more money from it. I believe that the development of the cooperatives, which is so necessary, will help us to increase production.* And in case of a surplus, even a single leaf of coriander — a spice that is not found in any market — there must be a way to sell that too. And that goes for a turkey too. But it has to be done along different lines. For the time being we'll have to put up with the present situation, and I believe that the best solution is to levy higher taxes to get back a substantial part of the profits, so that when a person buys something he or she can always say, "I'm contributing to the construction of a new school and not just lining the pockets of this crook who's charging too much for his wares."

That's the way things stand. Let's speak frankly. I believe it's much better to speak frankly and let everybody know that we know what's going on and that we don't like it at all. That's the truth. That's no way to develop communists or communist farmers.

There were also many irregularities in connection with the market in Cathedral Square, which was sponsored by the Ministry of Culture. Long before that market started up, when permission was given for freelance activities, privately owned stalls began to appear everywhere and people wanted to set up shop on every corner. A stop was put to this and it was made clear that craftsmen could sell their products, but they had to sell them to the state and the state would take care of retailing them. And that took care of the problem, and just in time too, otherwise the whole city would be full of stalls; because there's always a shortage of something, maybe toothpicks or those clips you hang out your washing with, whatever they're called . . . [*Laughter*]

Unfortunately, there's always a shortage of something. Now then,

---

*In the late 1970s, Cuba started to encourage small farmers to form cooperatives as both a vehicle to increase agricultural production and as a transitional measure to voluntary collectivization in state farms.

how are we going to solve this problem? The capitalist way? I believe that the solution is to be found in local enterprises, in socialist formulas. It doesn't have to be a question of centralization or national planning, but rather of an initiative of local branches of People's Power — for example, opening a factory to make those clothespins or clotheshangers, instead of some character finding out that there are no clotheshangers and deciding to make them himself and sell them in some city corner at a price ten times higher than their real value. That way this character makes ten times what a worker makes; sometimes he even quits his job in a factory or an office and dedicates his time to making clotheshangers. That way doesn't benefit anybody. What we need is a socialist formula, local enterprises to take care of these problems, not capitalist formulas.

Cathedral Square was supposed to be used by real craftsmen, by artists, to exhibit and sell works of art. But it wasn't long before the bourgeois elements, the neobourgeoisie, made their appearance, and the whole trafficking of buying over here and stealing over there, buying leather to make sandals — the famous 50-peso sandals — began. And this gave rise to the development of a neocapitalism. A very interesting experiment, I must say.

Nobody intends to attack the famous square, but it must be run by real artists and real craftsmen. And if they charge too much for their articles, then the state will simply have to levy a high tax on them, too, in order to take in revenue out of the exorbitant prices, because there's no reason for such things to happen.

When a person sells chickens for 15 pesos, even if he did raise them, that person is making more money in several weeks by selling a few chickens than a worker makes in a whole year. Really. And that's just plain robbery. If at least this person would stick to selling chickens to other lumpen elements . . . and that can happen too. A sort of lumpen class grows up, and trade among themselves and charge one another excessive prices. [*Laughter*] But the problem comes when they sell to a worker, maybe a worker who wants to celebrate his daughter's birthday and decides to buy a turkey and pays a very high price for it. Now that worker keeps the transportation system going, he produces textiles, builds housing, schools, and hospitals, grows sugarcane, produces sugar, milk, eggs, and meat for the people. But he earns a modest salary, and meanwhile the lumpen element is making ten times more and putting in much less work than the worker. This can never be reconciled with the concepts of socialism and communism. That's the honest truth.

I'm bringing up these topics here because I believe there's no better place than this congress of the Young Communist League to talk about them. [*Applause*] These things concern us all, because they are capitalist manifestations, bourgeois, antisocialist, anticommunist, and anti-internationalist manifestations, and they promote corruption. But such corruption doesn't develop only in the context of these neocapitalist activities. No! It also develops in the context of purely socialist activities as a result of a lack of control, of weakness, of a lack of strict vigilance. This was revealed in that operation which I believe was called "Operation Crocodile." This had to do with the problem of the queue sharks and the problem with the administrators and employees who allowed themselves to be bribed. There were even tough guys in the queues. But the curious thing is that since we have made great advances in the quality of women, there were tough guys and tough gals, [*Laughter*] both kinds, lining up in the queues; they grabbed the first places for themselves and divided them up among themselves, so any working woman or housewife there who wasn't willing to pick a fight simply couldn't get an electric fan or things like that. Why did this happen? The answer is lack of vigilance and controls. Those people had simply taken over control of things.

This all proves that not all lumpen elements left the country from Mariel. Some of them are still here. I knew this, it's nothing new, but now it's clear that we still have lumpen elements here, it's been proved. [*Applause*] These characters don't work, they just queue up; they really make a living out of robbing the people. They're thieves, unquestionably, no question that they're thieves. They're full-blooded lumpen elements, there's no way there are any Young Communists among them, of course. I was speaking about Young Communists selling a chicken and I said that also amounted to robbery, another type but still a robbery.

These things do happen, and these elements are corrupting people with gifts and things, even with money. And I believe that we must engage in a real battle against these abusive and antisocial activities and that's exactly what the Ministry of Domestic Trade and the National Revolutionary Police are doing. They're really going to go after the profiteering middlemen who made their way into the free farmers' market, [*Laughter*] the queue sharks, the corrupt officials and administrators, and the "businessmen" of all kinds. [*Prolonged applause and shouts of "For sure, Fidel, give the lumpen hell!"*]

Needless to say, I cannot imagine a Young Communist being mixed up in such activities. A law can legalize robbery, as in the case of a turkey being sold for 50 or 80 pesos or whatever it was, or a head of garlic sold for a peso. But no law can condone immoral conduct. And those things are simply immoral, whether or not the law allows them. And a Communist, a Young Communist, simply has to go without some things the law allows him to have, if he wants his conduct to be a moral, revolutionary, communist conduct. We are not yet living in a communist society and neither do all out citizens observe a communist conduct. That is true. But a Communist must observe a communist code of morals and a communist code of conduct.

This is why we are certain that our youth will combat all these vices, that it will combat lack of discipline, lack of responsibility, and every manifestation of corruption wherever it crops up; that they will struggle for quality and results in services; that they will combat fraud and profit-seeking; that they will also combat bad manners and rudeness and will join in the task of educating our youth and all our people in general in this aspect. We know that the UJC will struggle for advanced forms of agricultural production, for the implementation of socialist formulas, for socialist solutions to problems.

It was most encouraging to note in the summary of the main report that whereas 10 percent of our rural population is composed of young people, 20 percent of the members of the cooperative farms are young people. I believe that this battle will be won with the revolutionary spirit of our farmers, who are not to be confused with those lumpen elements, with those middlemen who pop up here and there.

I think the cooperative movement will keep forging ahead, with the help of the UJC and the work of the National Association of Small Farmers.

I've spoken about internationalism and an internationalist consciousness, and I think one of the most impressive moments of the congress was when the topics of defense and internationalism were discussed, more forcefully, more vigorously, than ever before. That gave me a chance to appreciate the work being done by our youth organization toward the development of a communist consciousness, and this was reflected in the efforts made, for example, to organize the Ernesto Che Guevara contingent. [*Applause*] These young people are teaching in Angola and are members of the Student-Teacher Detachment; in the Frank País teachers contingent, also teaching in Angola; and in the Augusto César Sandino contingent, [*Applause*] composed of 2,000 teachers who are working in very difficult and at times dangerous conditions in Nicaragua. And when we speak of internationalism, we also think of the 120,000 or so Cubans in the Revolutionary Armed Forces alone who have carried out internationalist missions, and the more than 150,000 others who have fulfilled internationalist missions in the past few years not only as fighters but as doctors, builders, teachers, and technicians. I consider these figures impressive; I think our revolution and our country have a good record in the field of internationalism. And the work of the UJC has had a great deal to do with the development of this consciousness and this spirit.

The UJC is also to be given credit for being a source of party cadres and members. This is just one more fundamental and decisive task of the organization, and its results are seen in the 92 percent who qualified to enter the process of selection for the party and the 83 percent who went through the process and were selected for membership. I believe that these figures are really encouraging, as encouraging as the increase in the number of members of the UJC who come from the labor and services sectors. Naturally, the requirements for admission to the UJC are different from those of the party, because the UJC also has to work with the students, which is a very important task. It's extremely important to work among the workers, but work among the students cannot be neglected under any circumstances.

We have seen many outstanding examples in this congress. I was deeply moved by the gesture of Comrade René Valdés, a young worker who is being trained in Czechoslovakia and was a delegate to the congress. He donated 1,000 pesos he had won for surpassing the production plan assigned to him. One thousand pesos earned through hard work, and he came here and donated them. With those 1,000 pesos he could have gone to the movies one thousand times. [*Laughter*] And if he keeps away from the free market and Cathedral Square, who knows how many things he could have bought with that kind of money? [*Laughter*] But, instead, he came here and donated it. That is what I call a communist consciousness. [*Prolonged applause*] If he had spent the money he wouldn't have been doing anything at all illegal; it would be absolutely legitimate to spend that money. There would have been nothing immoral; it would have been perfectly honest for him to use that money for his own benefit, because he had earned it with his work by overfulfilling his production plan. No one could deny his right to that money nor the honest way in which he earned it. He didn't obtain it by profiteering or anything like that.

Thinking of this young man's attitude, the attitude of conscious workers, I find it similar to that of the two delegates present here who have already cut more than 1,700 tons of sugarcane in the present harvest, and that of the worker who pledged to turn out so many thousands of meters of cloth as a matter of honor. [*Applause*] Theirs is a communist attitude and these comrades personify Cuba's youth today. I am entirely convinced that all the comrades of the party and of the party leadership who took part in the congress, all of us, are satisfied with what we've heard. I could say, in fact, that we are happy with the results of the congress, happy [*Applause*] because we've had the opportunity to appreciate its quality and how it reflects the quality of our youth.

The skeptic who still has any doubts has had an opportunity to see what our youth is like, during the most recent great battles, the Marches of the Fighting People and in the mobilizations in view of the imperialist threats. In all these events our young people have demonstrated their strength and their fighting spirit.

I believe that the congress has been a faithful reflection of what our youth is like. It has indeed been a magnificent congress, very impressive for its quality, its human atmosphere, its communist and internationalist spirit, [*Applause*] its spirit of brotherhood, its warmth, the purity that has been visible in all aspects; for its sincerity and honesty, for the principled positions and the solid political awareness of all those who spoke here. If I'm not mistaken, more than 170 delegates took the floor. The statements and the correct way in which they were made; the resolutions, which reflected a unanimous spirit, a unanimous consciousness, and a universal education; the speeches, brief yet full of ideas and useful, all interesting and many of them deeply moving; all these things reflected the democratic spirit of this congress, the spontaneous way in which all the delegates spoke and the freedom of expression that prevailed at all times in the presence of numerous delegations of young people from other countries, made us feel very proud.

2. Excerpt from Speech to ANAP Congress
May 17, 1982

We're really pleased that this congress, which is a new lesson, a new test, has been so useful. At a time when many of us were analyzing problems, trying to solve them in all their complexity and coming up with some ideas, some opinions were voiced here in the congress concerning a few complex things. There's no question about it: you corrected those opinions and persuaded us to adopt other, more suitable variants and solutions. What was being expressed here wasn't the wisdom of a tiny group of men but the wisdom of thousands of men, tens of thousands of men who in certain situations are better qualified than any of us to hit on the right idea.

As for the much-debated question of the farm markets, the other comrades and I realized that it involved the farmers' wounded honor — there was a wound, there was a sore — and that their main concern (which was absolutely fair and honest) was that, even if it meant 40 or 50 million pesos coming in from sales in the farm markets, the high tax formula was going to place the farmers in an embarrassing position in the eyes of the people, in the eyes of the workers. It seemed to us that their concern should be borne in mind.

I believe it's a good lesson, when we think we've found good solutions, to mull things over and really consider the feelings and wisdom of the masses. That is true democracy. [*Applause*] That should always be the style of our party and state: not to impose but to persuade or be persuaded — because their role isn't always that of persuading; it's also to allow themselves to be persuaded by the people as many times as necessary, because the greatest wisdom has been, is, and always will lie in the people. [*Prolonged applause*]

As [ANAP President] Pepe [Ramírez] said, inspections and other rigorous measures have been taken not only in the case of the farm markets. A general policy of struggle against greed, immorality, theft, and other manifestations of corruption is being applied. Measures were taken against people who made a profitable business out of selling places in lines, and inspections of all kinds were made: in the dairies and department stores and in the plaza. We will continue to apply this policy systematically. Why? Because there are many violations. Sometimes they're simply administrative violations, but we must combat them, too. The administrative violations lead to and facilitate fraud and theft, and we must be both persistent and tough in the case of theft and all other illegal activities carried out for profit.

We can't allow antisocial, lumpen elements to corrupt our society. [*Applause*] While the corrupted are an insignificant minority we can win any battle. Ah, but if the majority are corrupted, the battle will be very difficult to win. There are cases of corruption in many places. It's sad. There have been cases of dishonesty among judges, lawyers, policemen, ordinary workers, blue-collar workers, intellectuals — everyone. There are cases. Therefore, we have to be relentless against the lumpen elements; the thieves; and those who want to make thousands, tens of thousands, and hundreds of thousands of pesos breaking the law, because they corrupt. Sometimes they begin in subtle ways, like friends lending a little money when you need it, not insisting on being repaid and then lending you more.

We know of cases of good comrades who, little by little, fell into the clutches of these lumpen elements in subtle ways. Sometimes the administrator of a bar may be a lumpen element: if the policy is thirty shots per bottle of rum — I'm just giving a little example; it's always good to give examples when presenting an idea — they stretch it to thirty-five. They're robbing the public. They're pocketing the difference between the thirty shots of rum — it could be Carta Blanca, which you all prefer — and thirty-five shots, pocketing the difference. Or ice cream by the scoop: there should be fifty scoops of ice cream per container. They keep this from the public and shave the scoop, taking out less so there are sixty scoops, and they pocket the difference. This is an example, an example of the procedures some people use. [*Applause*] Or the number of pizzas or the quantity of cheese on the pizzas. When it comes to money . . . There was an administrator, in charge of the Ward Ice Cream Parlor . . . I'm not going to say his name — actually, I don't remember it now — but it's the case, not his name, that's important here. Some days he made 300 or 400 pesos extra, selling ice cream — this guy was selling ice cream like crazy. [*Laughter*] The assistant administrator was also corrupted, and so were several employees. The man had gone and corrupted his assistant and everyone else, with each one getting at least 15 or 20 pesos every day. It was a kind of farm market he had there, buying and selling people.

Well, we don't have capitalists now; the people administer the goods. Every manifestation of corruption of this type is a serious thing, and the people cannot permit it. I believe we should add up our experiences and find what controls are best — but we have to multiply them, increase them, and engage in a relentless struggle, because socialism can't permit this cancer to devour it. There are thousands, tens of thousands of installations to administer. When there is theft, it's the people who are being robbed — nobody but the people. Can you count on a bad character like that, who robs the people, to take up a gun and defend our homeland? That lumpen element is the basis of the counterrevolution and treason.

Sometimes the wrongdoing is rather pervasive because of lack of inspections and controls, and we have to struggle hard against it. We can't allow anybody to steal ice cream from a child or even a shot of liquor from a drunk. Why should they rob a poor drunk? [*Laughter and applause*] A man who spends an afternoon drinking, and spending plenty of money — 'cause rum's expensive here — and, on top of that, he's being robbed.

We have to be inflexible with the thousands of stores and other establishments.

Wrongdoing is pervasive, but we are partly to blame, for we put the church in the hands of the devil — haven't you heard that saying? — through the system that was used to recruit hotel and restaurant workers. I don't want to speak ill of them, for I believe that many of those in charge have low wages that should be looked into. Moreover, there are many good people, many honest workers among them — but there are lumpen elements, too. Why? Because of how they were recruited. We found out about this not too long ago. The Ministry of Labor sent them, but as it wasn't a high-priority job — Moa, this, that, and the other had more priority — the people who were left over went into hotels, restaurants, stores, and services. If a survey were made, it would show that an alarming percentage of them have records of common and even counterrevolutionary crimes. You can't expect good results. We have to completely change our recruiting system. There are honest people, many honest and decent people in all the neighborhoods, everywhere.

Moreover, I'm asking many of those who've retired to come back to work. In these cases, as an exception to the rule, they'll continue to get their full pensions in addition to their wages. [*Applause*] We must find a way to recruit honest people for our hotels, restaurants, services, and stores in general and continue the struggle.

Inspections always reveal quite a number of irregularities. Some of them consist of administrative violations — which should be punished, but not treated in the same way as theft and other crimes for profit. We must be much more severe with those who commit thefts than with those who commit violations in order to profit from them. Administrative violations should be combated, too, though in a different way, because lack of control makes theft possible. We must combat this; not treating it the same way as theft, of course, but we have to have penalties for it. We must teach our workers to do things correctly, to obey the laws and regulations. Often, they think the laws and regulations aren't very important, but they are — disregarding them makes it possible for others to steal.

This isn't a witch-hunt, but we're going to ferret out everyone who commits violations. Sooner or later, we'll smoke them out. We're going to work very patiently, but we're going to find each and every one of them. [*Applause*] We don't make a crusade of it, throwing a lot of people in jail. In fact, some may reconsider their actions and realize that they've done wrong, especially in the case of theft. That wouldn't be a bad idea, because we could give them some consideration if they went and told their superiors, "Look, I did such-and-such a thing." We can be benevolent with them, taking their attitude into consideration, and probably find other jobs for them, studying each case individually. There may be some people — I'm sure there are — who will reconsider and act accordingly. We won't publish their names, and it would pay for them to act that way, because then we wouldn't have to send so many people to jail. But, as far as the others are concerned, they are certainly going to be given the full treatment.

Many of them still have a chance. Whatever measures we take will have to show those who have committed violations the wisdom of turning themselves in and convince them that their crimes won't go unpunished. [*Applause*] We have ways of discovering all these cases of theft; we have ways of finding out, but just taking measures won't prevent these things. You can take a lot of measures, but then you put 3,000 criminals into hotels and restaurants, stores, and other service facilities. Do you expect them to have become saints? Well, they haven't, and they're free to do as they please. They do a lot of harm — especially the ones who set up a kind of mafia. These things happen, and I can give you some more examples — for instance, the distribution of cars. The country distributes thousands of cars every year, but it doesn't put them up for open sale. The state could set up a free market of automobiles at 25,000, 30,000, or maybe 40,000 pesos apiece, but who would buy them? You know who: the lumpen elements, the "businessmen" making 300 pesos a day. Here cars are sold at a much lower price, nearly at cost, and people can buy them on an installment plan. Why do we do this? So the cars will go to technicians, doctors, engineers, vanguard workers, "millionaire" canecutters,* self-sacrificing internationalists, [*Applause*] outstanding teachers, and other blue- and white-collar workers, on the basis of merit. This is how they are assigned.

This year, our country will distribute 10,000 cars. At least two out of every three will be bought by workers connected with production and services: construction workers, sugarcane workers, workers in transportation and in various state agencies. We feel that they are the people who should be given the opportunity to have cars — not the lumpen elements. As you know, motorcycles are also distributed among workers in the sugar mills and factories; many workers have purchased them through this system. The lumpen elements can't do this, but if they have the money, they go shopping for a motorcycle or a car, corrupting, ready to pay as much as 20,000 pesos for a car. They've corrupted vanguard workers and doctors, tempting them to make big money by selling their 4,500-peso cars for 20,000. Which is to say that these things corrupt and change individuals. The people must be relentless against these things, so when they see someone driving one of these new cars they'll know he's a technician, an outstanding worker, and not a bandit.

What need do we have for elements like these who corrupt a worker who, through his merits, has been given an award by society, who has been given the chance to buy a car at a reasonable price? As I said yesterday, those who have sold cars or motorcycles in this way should know that they're going to lose their money, and those who've bought cars or motorcycles in this way will lose them. [*Applause*] There's a clause in the contract that's specifically designed to prevent anyone from speculating with these valuable articles that are sold at low prices. You want to reward a worker; you make it easy for him to buy a car, as he deserves, but you don't intend to give him a gift of 15,000 pesos. There's a clause that says anybody who wants to sell his car should go to the state, to Auto-Import, and sell it there. Then Auto-Import resells the used car at a lower price. This clause has been in the contract ever since these cars and motorcycles began to be sold. Some people have broken the contract, even produced forged papers. We know the little tricks some of them have pulled in these operations. As I said before, the buyer loses the car, [*Laughter*] and the seller loses the money. [*Applause*] I imagine there'll be quite a few people running around tomorrow, arranging and rearranging things, wondering what to do and what's going to happen. [*Laughter*]

There's a contract, and you have to abide by it.

Who does all the buying, and how do we find out who's been doing it?

---

*Members of brigades that have cut over a million *arrobas* of sugar cane — about 25 million pounds.

Who can come up with 15,000 or 20,000 pesos to buy a car? The lumpen elements, the go-betweens who've spent a couple of months in the farm markets, the man who had 50,000 plantains, the man at Ward's who bought eight cars. What do you think of that? [*Laughter*] He had a hobby of buying and selling cars, and he was crazy about the brand new ones. [*Laughter*]

We have to fight against all these things; we have to delve into these problems, because they're related to our workers' attitude, our people's moral principles, the law, respect for the law, and our people's spirit and revolutionary consciousness. This is why we have to wage an all-out war against this greed for profit. Let's hope many of these people straighten up so we don't have to take drastic measures against so many of them. This doesn't mean we're going to stop going after the wrongdoers, but we'll follow a policy that distinguishes between honest people who sometimes act irresponsibly and thieves. Thieves won't have any chance at all in this country. This is a policy that involves all of us, the mass organizations, etc., because we all have to fight this battle. It isn't a matter for the police or Ministry of the Interior alone; it concerns the mass organizations and everybody.

I think the time for the reception's drawing near, and so is the end of my speech. I'd like to say something that I believe expresses the feelings of all who have attended the congress, and that is that we were deeply impressed by what the delegates said here. Your maturity, seriousness, wisdom, honesty, and courage gave us a feeling of security and great confidence in the future.

The day when all our agriculture is organized in cooperatives, with the best farmers — like you who've attended this congress — in charge of them, there won't be many of these pressing problems that we've talked about today: go-betweens, wrongdoers, sharecroppers, wildcat farmers, etc.* What a wonderful outlook our country has with its future in the hands of men and women like you! [*Applause*]

We have made great progress, and we will continue to do so, but it won't be easy. As we stated very clearly in the final session of the Committees for the Defense of the Revolution congress last October, nobody should think that things are going to be easy. We must be prepared to meet difficulties. We have difficulties now, and we'll have even greater ones in the future, even if we do things the right way — and we should do them the right way, even if it calls for our greatest efforts. We have to cope with the objective problems of the international situation, the increasing number of economic measures the imperialists take against us.

---

*"Wildcat farmers" are those that set up unauthorized private farms and are one of the sources of Cuba's black market.

Recently they've even said U.S. tourists can't come to Cuba. There had been some U.S. tourism.* We know about all the measures the imperialists have taken. They combine these measures with hypocritical statements, talking about negotiating positions. What negotiating positions? What proof have they given that they are ready to negotiate and discuss things?

Only a few days ago, the president of the United States said that Cuba would be welcomed in the Western community if it broke its ties with the socialist camp and joined the Western countries. [*Laughter*] I don't know. Sometimes it's very hard to understand their mentality. For all we know, they probably think they're offering us a bargain, doing us a favor by promising us the paradise of that rotten, stinking capitalist society. [*Applause*]

Whatever our defects and errors in these early stages of socialism, how could we conceive all the things you've said here — what the comrade from La Plata, the comrade from Banes, and many other delegates said regarding their pleasure and infinite happiness in having had the privilege of experiencing the revolution and participating in the construction of socialism — without socialism? Regardless of our limitations and defects, our society is infinitely superior to the one that many of you or your parents knew. There's no comparison between that society and the dignified way of life, possibilities, and happiness you've had — not only from a material standpoint, because material things alone don't make for happiness. A sense of justice, dignity, self-respect, respect for others, and love for your fellow men also have a great deal to do with happiness, [*Applause*] as have moral principles; the feeling of being free, equal, and respected and of taking part in the battle for the progress of the world, the world you live in; and working like beavers, shoulder to shoulder with the rest of your people.

We understood that the delegates wanted to say many things when they spoke in this congress. We know what the capitalist hell is like, and we will never return to it. Never! [*Applause*]

Those imperialist leaders show no respect and are insulting, for what the president of the United States said is tantamount to telling a country to commit an act of betrayal, to sell out. Their offer arouses nothing but our utter and complete contempt. [*Applause*]

There are men and governments that have sold out to imperialism, been hired by imperialism, or surrendered to imperialism, but we serve notice on the U.S. government — and it should know, after twenty-three years, that we mean what we say — that our people, our party, and our

---

*On April 19, 1982, the Reagan administration issued what amounted to a travel ban on U.S. citizens visiting Cuba, with the major exception of Cuban-Americans visiting family.

leaders will never hire themselves out, sell out, or surrender! [*Prolonged applause*]

We will confront every difficulty; pressure; and economic, political, or other kinds of attack. We will keep moving ahead. The revolution will go on winning new laurels and scoring new victories. United in a single bloc, our workers, farmers, intellectuals, and students will march forward victoriously, and nothing and nobody can ever stop them.

Long live the solid, indestructible, and lasting alliance between our workers and farmers! [*Shouts of "Long live!"*]

Patria o muerte!

Venceremos! [*Ovation*]

Index

Abortion, 10

Absenteeism, 112, 113, 117-18, 124, 144, 154, 175, 264, 280, 281, 295

Acosta, Armando, 300

Administrative methods, 106-7, 109-10, 116, 117, 130, 131, 141, 223, 231

Administrators, 49-50, 75, 77, 86, 94, 134-35, 142-43, 183, 200, 255, 297; bureaucratic attitudes among, 116, 281, 285, 290, 295-96, 296-97, 311, 320; corruption among, 342, 348, 352-54; methods of, 84, 126, 208; number of, 69, 77-78, 84, 86, 87, 255-56; and People's Power, 222-23, 230-31, 232; selection of, 43, 48-49, 50, 52, 59, 84, 86, 271. *See also* Management

Africa, 16-17, 185

Agramonte, Ignacio, 258, 315

Agrarian reform, 11, 42

Agriculture: need to strengthen, 81-82, 88, 90, 178, 200, 239, 265, 266-67, 292-93; progress in, 16, 78, 101-2, 193, 211-12, 303, 327

Algeria, 73, 185, 251, 252

Alienation, 72, 82

Allende, Beatriz, 186

Alliance of working class and peasantry, 28-29, 31, 148, 358

Almeida, Juan, 114, 256, 257, 320

Angola, 16-17, 254, 257, 277

Anticommunism, 11, 45, 51, 56-57

Antiloafing law, 112, 117-18, 144

Aponte, Carlos, 190

Appliances, 122, 136, 181-82, 199, 293, 303

Argentina, 192

Arming the people, 19-20, 26-27, 31-32, 222, 322, 324

Austerity, 306, 314

Automobiles, 182, 303, 354-55

Batista, Fulgencio, 10, 62, 221, 258, 323

Battle for the Sixth Grade, 260-61, 325. *See also* Education

Bay of Pigs. *See* Playa Girón

Begging, 9, 10, 115, 325

Betancourt, Juan Antonio, 63-64

Black market, 124, 334

Blockade, 11, 16, 18, 154, 213, 221, 250, 275, 284-85, 287, 288, 293, 327, 328, 331. *See also* United States, aggression against Cuba by

Bolivia, 17

Bolshevik Party, 151, 152, 237

Botellas, 78

Bourgeois democracy, 20, 30, 32, 221, 244

Bourgeois revolutions, 72-73

Bulgaria, 149

Bureaucracy: under capitalism, 69, 70-72, 74-75, 80; and Communist Party, 77, 152, 290, 322; danger of, 13, 22, 38, 82-83, 129, 320; methods of, 46-50, 51-52, 56-59, 81-82, 107, 139, 297; mentality within, 68, 71, 76, 83-84, 314; origins of, 22, 68-69, 70-71, 80; in other socialist countries, 22, 79; and People's Power, 204, 223, 240; petty-bourgeois character of, 69, 70, 78, 85; and size of administration, 86-87, 211, 239; after socialist revolution, 74, 75, 79-80, 320-21; as special strata, 12, 22-23, 69-70, 71-72, 75, 76-78, 85, 322; struggle